ARCHBISHOP WILLIAM LAUD

By the same author
Charles I: The Personal Monarch
Royal Childhoods

ARCHBISHOP WILLIAM LAUD

Charles Carlton

Routledge & Kegan Paul
London and New York

First published in 1987 by
Routledge & Kegan Paul Ltd
11 New Fetter Lane, London EC4P 4EE

Published in the USA by
Routledge & Kegan Paul Inc.
in association with Methuen Inc.
29 West 35th Street, New York, NY 10001

Set in 10/12 Sabon
by Input Typesetting Ltd, London
and printed in Great Britain
by Butler & Tanner Ltd
Frome and London

Library of Congress Cataloging in Publication Data

Carlton, Charles 1941-
Archbishop William Laud.

Bibliography: p.
Includes index.
1. Laud, William, 1573–1645. 2. Statesmen—
Great Britain—Biography. 3. Church of England—
Bishops—Biography. 4. Great Britain—History—
Charles I, 1625–1649. 5. Great Britain—Church History
—17th century. I. Title.
DA396.L3C37   1987   283'.092'4   (B)   87–23322

British Library CIP Data also available
ISBN 0–7102–0463–9

H.W.S.
In Memoriam

Contents

Acknowledgments

This, the last part that most authors write and the first that most readers look at, is always a pleasure to draft, not so much because one's labours are drawing to an end as because it is an opportunity to remember and recognise the kindnesses and friendships which have made this the happiest of endeavours.

Research on this book started during the year 1981/2 when I was a visiting fellow at Wolfson College, Cambridge. The hospitality of all members of that college made my stay there both pleasant and productive, while Professor Elton's Tudor seminar, and Dr Cannadine and Dr Morrill's Stuart seminar, have made Cambridge University a most stimulating place for a student of early modern English history.

This book was mainly written during the academic year 1985/6 as a fellow at the National Humanities Center, which, for humanists at least, has truly become 'the Southern part of Heaven'. The staff were kind, helpful, and tolerant; the other fellows were stimulating and supportive. I am especially grateful to James Epstein, Theo Hoppen, Fred Kaplan, Harold Marcus, and Donald Sutherland.

For reading and commenting on drafts I am greatly indebted to Esther Cope and John Morrill. David Griffiths very kindly allowed me to read the manuscript of his essay on Laud's trial, and commented on various parts of the manuscript. I am most grateful to Peter Burke, Ray Camp, G. R. Elton, Anthony Fletcher, Christopher Haigh, Christa Howerton, Brian Levack, Sears McGee, Judith Maltby, Paul Seaver, Kevin Sharpe, and Nicholas Tyacke for their insights into the archbishop's life, and to Charles Mould, Mary Robertson, and Professor Hugh Trevor-Roper for answering my queries.

I would like to thank St John's College, Oxford, and King's College and Trinity College, Cambridge, for allowing me to use their libraries. My own university has been exceedingly generous in providing me with financial assistance. I am obliged to the National Endowment for the

Humanities and the American Philosophical Society for travel grants that enabled me to work in England. Last – and far from least – I would like to thank my wife and daughters for patiently putting up with a middle-aged academic while he was trying to trace the career of another, equally irascible don.

North Carolina State University
September 1986

I

'Where I was bred up'

William Laud was born in Reading, Berkshire, on 7 October 1573, the only son of William Laud, a clothier, and Lucy Webb, widow of John Robinson, another clothier of the same town. Seventy-one years, three months and three days later, on 10 January 1645, after working his way up through the ranks of Oxford University and then the Church of England to become the last great controversial Archbishop of Canterbury, Laud was executed before a huge crowd on Tower Hill. Both events, his birth and his death, are crucial for an understanding of his career and reputation. His humble origins produced a drive to succeed that influenced his career; his death, a martyrdom that he embraced heroically, has exaggerated the importance of his life.

Laud was executed at the height of the English Civil War, when both sides were preparing for what one of their leaders described as the great battle 'of all for all'.[1] His death was almost a spring-cleaning of the Tower of London, where he had languished for nearly four years. A lonely old man from what, in 1645, already seemed like the distant past, Laud was brought out from his cell to be beheaded largely because of the personal spite of his enemies, and to placate the Scots Covenanters.[2] Having failed to persuade the House of Lords to impeach Laud, his foes had parliament pass an Act of Attainder ordering his execution for cumulative treasons. But by now the Civil War had so divided England that the murder of an archbishop caused hardly a ripple.

Fifteen years later, after the Restoration of 1660, Laud became the hero of an Anglican Church as eager to praise him as it was to eschew most of what he had tried to do.[3] During the next century and a half of enlightened rationalism, the archbishop either shrank into merciful obscurity, or, worse still, attracted the notice of historians such as Laurence Echard, who wrote that 'there's nothing as certain in his character as pride, bigotry and invincible obstinacy'.[4] Thomas Babington Macaulay said that for Laud 'we enterain a more unmitigated contempt than for any other

1

character in our history. The fondness with which a portion of the church regards his memory can be compared only to the perversity of affection which sometimes leads a mother to select the monster or the idiot of the family as the object of her special favour.'[5]

Macaulay was, of course, alluding to the Oxford Movement, a group of High Church Anglicans who adopted Laud as their patron saint, whom they usually observed whilst genuflecting in the direction of Rome. Not surprisingly, seen from such a perspective, Laud grew in stature during the nineteenth century. Canon Mozley declared that the archbishop had 'saved the English church', Professor Collins thought that he had 'shaped' it, while Mr Gladstone was convinced that Laud was 'the most tolerant churchman of that day'. Most fulsome in his praises was C. H. Simpkinson, who on the three hundred and fiftieth anniversary of the primate's execution eulogised him as 'the chief advocate of the Working classes, the defender of the poor, the Leader of the Education Movement, and the administrator who endeavoured to exterminate the corruption of the Civil Service'.[6] This portrait of the archbishop as an Anglican superman remained the standard until the Second World War. In 1940 Hugh Trevor-Roper published *Archbishop Laud*, a brilliant biography which blinds nearly as much as it illuminates.[7] It treats Laud unsympathetically as a reactionary politician who tried – with little ability, and even less success – to reverse a process that had been underway since the Reformation and to restore to the church the property it had lost to the rising middle class. Another great Oxford historian, Christopher Hill, elaborated on Trevor-Roper's thesis by arguing that Laud was trying 'to revive the Middle Ages not only in ceremony, but also in economics'.[8]

Since Trevor-Roper's biography there have been remarkably few studies of Laud, particularly compared to the rich harvest of works on early seventeenth-century English history that have appeared since the Second World War. Opinion on the archbishop has varied. L. W. Cowlie called him a liberal. Canon Bourne thought that he was 'the last of the great ecclesiastical statesmen'. In contrast Robert Ashton argued that Laud, more than anyone else, was responsible for the Civil War, while Patrick Collinson denounced him as 'the greatest calamity visited upon the English Church'. Stephen Foster called Laud the 'Caroline Sampson, pulling down the temple on his enemies as well as himself', while J. H. Timmis has described him as 'Charles's evil genius'.[9]

To some extent the consensus on the archbishop has broken down because there is no longer a generally accepted interpretation about his period, and, in particular, about the origins of the English Civil War. Thus a fresh look at Laud in the context of recent scholarship may shed enough light to sketch a new portrait of him – perhaps of a less significant, although far more human man.[10]

Laud agreed with his contemporaries that the foundation of his character lay, as it does with most of us, in his earliest years. ' 'Tis true, I am a man of ordinary but very honest birth; and the memory of my parents savours men very well to this day, in the town of Reading where I was born', was his answer, in 1641, to Lord Saye and Sele's aristocratic sneers about his humble roots. Now an old man, held prisoner in the Tower, Laud went on to defend himself: 'Nor was I so meanly born as perhaps my Lord would insinuate; for my father had borne all the offices in the town, save the mayoralty.'[11] Although his father was not as important as the archbishop claimed – the only municipal office he ever actually filled was the insignificant post of constable, and that only briefly – in his parting shot he neither exaggerated, nor failed to turn the tables on his aristocratic prosecutor: 'I have done honour to my birth, which every man hath not done, that hath had an honorable descent.'[12]

Laud came from merchant stock. His father was a prosperous clothier who had moved the eight miles from Wokingham to Reading, presumably to be an apprentice.[13] Laud senior owned several looms of his own, as well as being an entrepreneur who farmed out work to many spinners and weavers in the cottage industry, gaining, his son boasted, 'a good Esteem and reputation amongst his neighbours to the very last'.[14] Laud was especially proud of the fact that his father was both a successful businessman and a generous benefactor who kept his workers in employment in bad times as well as good. William Laud senior was well enough thought of in St Lawrence's parish to be elected a churchwarden, and prosperous enough to leave a large house on Broad Street, as well as goods and cash worth £1,200.[15] As the archbishop told his friend, and first biographer, Peter Heylyn, 'though he had not the good fortune to be born a Gentleman Yet he thanked God he had been born of honest parents, who lived in a plentiful condition, employed many poor people in their way, and left a good report behind them.'[16]

Very little is known about Laud's relations with his father, who died on 11 April 1594 – 'when I was yet young' noted his son in the prayers that he composed to commemorate this sad anniversary.[17] That he wrote such devotions, and asked God to fill the void, would suggest that he felt the bereavement very deeply. Although he did not lose his father at an especially early age by sixteenth-century standards, Laud believed that he had been deprived of a pillar of authority long before he was old enough to live without such support. Half a century later, during the Prayer Book Rebellion, his father's memory returned as a great comfort. 'I dreamed that my father (who died 46 years since)', Laud wrote in his diary for 24 January 1640, 'came to me, and to my thinking he was well and as cheerful as ever I saw him. He asked me, what I did here: And after some speech, I asked him, how long he would stay with me. He answered, he would stay till he had me away with him. I am not much moved with dreams; yet I thought fit to remember this.'[18]

Laud's father was his mother's second husband, Lucy Webb being the daughter of John Webb, also a clothier from Wokingham. So she almost certainly knew her second husband when they were both children. By staying in Berkshire, perhaps to marry young, she did not do as well as her brother and sisters who went to London. After serving an apprenticeship to a London haberdasher, her brother William Webb married the daughter of Sir Christopher Draper, Lord Mayor for 1566–7. Through this connection Webb became the alderman and sheriff in 1581, and Lord Mayor and a knight a decade later. One of Lucy's sisters, Anne, married Sir Wolstan Dixie, Lord Mayor for 1585–6, while another became the wife of Sir Henry Billingsley, Lord Mayor for 1596–7. Lucy's children by her first husband, John Robinson, a Reading clothier, did nearly as well: Amy married Dr Robert Cottesford, Prebendary of Hoxton; Bridget married Dr Edmund Layfield, Vicar of Bromley; while William became a Doctor of Divinity, Prebend of St David's, and Archdeacon of Nottingham.[19] Since Laud left generous bequests to his half-brothers and -sisters, and to their families, and stayed with them, being buried in All Hallows Barking by the Tower, where his nephew was vicar, it seems reasonable to assume that they treated the child of their mother's second marriage kindly. In addition it seems probable that they approved of her remarrying, the older children at least realising that another husband was the best way in which a widow could restore her fortunes.[20] Lucy's second union was a happy one, free from the ghosts that so often haunt the remarried. She encouraged William's academic bent, taking pleasure in the ecclesiastical achievements of her two sons, both called William. She died on 24 November 1600, and was buried beside her second husband in St Lawrence's churchyard. Laud remembered his mother with obvious affection. He wrote in his diary for 5 January 1627, 'I dreamed that my mother, long since dead, stood by my bed, and drawing aside the clothes a little, looked pleasantly upon me; and that I was glad to see her with so merry an aspect. She then showed to me a certain old man, long since deceased, whom, when alive, I both knew and loved.'[21]

It was almost as if the middle-aged Laud was trying to return to the secure world of his childhood spent in the large house, worth some £30 a year, on the north side of Broad Street. He grew up in a provincial town, forty miles west of London, with about 5,000 inhabitants. Reading was a fairly prosperous place. Before the Reformation it had paid about £450 worth of taxes, making it the tenth highest assessed provincial town in England.[22] Although the dissolution of Reading Abbey hurt the town's economy, by 1560 it had recovered sufficiently for the corporation to take over financial responsibility for the grammar school. Production in the wool trade went up and down, and during the latter part of the century Reading suffered so severe a recession that part of the city hospital had to be turned into a poor house.[23] Laud was thus born in a town with a reasonable economic base and a commitment to the education of its children.[24]

He was a sickly infant and nearly died on several occasions (even as an adult he was very small, and his health remained precarious). He learned to read and write English, and possibly some Latin, at a local dame school, before entering Reading Grammar School. It was an ancient foundation dating back to 1139, and if typical would have had some forty or fifty boys, divided into six forms, the first three taught by an usher, the second three by a master. Both drilled their pupils in Latin to prepare them for the universities. Next to nothing is known about Laud's school days, though he remembered the excitement over Sir Peter Wentworth's imprisonment in the Tower (almost certainly referring to the troublesome MP's 1587 incarceration). Laud came from a family with a firm commitment to education and hard work. He was an ambitious, diligent pupil, and he attended school and university at a time when English education was expanding dramatically. This growth was due to a new concern on the part of urban parents to safeguard their children's futures, as well as to the development of new pedagogical theories by writers such as John Colet, Sir Thomas Elyot and Richard Mulcaster, which came out of the Reformation.[25]

More important than new curricula or social attitudes, Reading Grammar School gave Laud a link with St John's College, Oxford. It had been a Reading boy, Sir Thomas White, who founded St John's in 1555. In doing so White remembered his roots by endowing two scholarships at St John's for pupils from Reading Grammar School.[26] The connections between the school and the college worked both ways. In 1569 John Smith, a Reading boy and sometime fellow of St John's, became the grammar school's headmaster. Smith was probably the author of several books, including *The Doctrine of Prayer in General* (1595), although the exact number of his publications cannot be given due to the ubiquity of his name. Thomas Bradock, fellow of Christ's College, Cambridge, succeeded Smith as headmaster, and supervised the last year of Laud's schooling. He may have influenced his pupil's faith, since Bradock later translated Bishop Jewel's *An Apologie or answer in defence of the Church of England*. Although Laud remembered Smith as 'an ill schoolmaster', he retained a lifelong affection for his old school. As Archbishop of Canterbury, he took great pains to improve the quality of the teaching there, and to strengthen its links with St John's. In the late sixteenth century such bonds between schools and colleges were very common; three-quarters of the boys entering St John's College, Cambridge, for instance, came from tied schools.[27]

Laud entered Oxford as a commoner in 1589 at the comparatively early age of sixteen, being in the youngest third of his year.[28] On 30 June 1590, on the nomination of the mayor, the college awarded him one of the scholarships Sir Thomas White had reserved for Reading boys.[29] It was said that a Mrs Buningham paid for his first year's studies, which is surprising since Laud's father was a prosperous businessman. Laud became a fellow of St John's in 1593, a Bachelor of Arts a year later, and a Master of Arts in July 1598. At about this time he made the logical decision for any educated, ambitious young man of the period who did not want to become a lawyer or doctor, and entered the church, being admitted a deacon on 4 January 1600, and being ordained on the following 5 April. Since Laud was seriously ill on at least three occasions as a young man, he could have interpreted his survival as divine approval of the choice of his career.[30] Years later he remarked, 'I was the tenth, and paid to the Church.'[31]

His university career flourished. On 9 May 1601 he became a senior fellow of St John's, entitled to vote in college elections. The following year he was appointed to one of the two divinity fellowships which Dr John Cave's will had established at £2. 10s. a year. Laud also held the main college lecturership in divinity, taking his Bachelor of Divinity degree in July 1602 with a thesis on the efficacy of infant baptism and the need for bishops. Four years later Laud capped his formal education by becoming a Doctor of Divinity.[32]

As an undergraduate and graduate Laud studied the usual subjects 'with great diligence', gaining a reputation as 'a very forward, confident and zealous person'.[33] He won few friends as a student, and not much of a following as a teacher. But reserve and youthful gravitas may be valued in a proctor, to which position Laud was elected in May 1603 – 'so soon as by statute I was capable of it', he boasted in later years.[34] His fellow proctor, Christopher Dale of Merton College, was an unpopular man whom the undergraduates hissed at convocation. Laud too had his problems with the rowdier elements. When he tried to move a drunken student who was lying on a public bench, he received the reply, 'Thou little morsel of Justice, prithee let me alone and be at rest.'[35] Laud seems to have taken it in good part, for there is no record of the young man being punished. (Later the archbishop was to hand out harsh punishments to those who insulted authority.)

At Oxford Laud made some lasting friends, among them Humphrey May, the son of the Master of the Merchant Taylors' Company, who entered St John's a year after Laud and introduced him to his family.[36] Laud held the college divinity lecturership which Humphrey's mother endowed; Humphrey's sisters Joan and Elizabeth were also generous donors to the college. In his will Laud left 'Mr Thomas May, my ancient friend, my ring with an emerald, in which only my arms are cut'.[37] James Whitelocke, another Merchant Taylors' lad, who entered Oxford a year before Laud, became college steward in 1601. Years later, his radical son, Bulstrode Whitelocke, refused to take part in the prosecution of his father's friend and former teacher, declaring that 'it was not fit for me to appear in it against one to whom I had been beholden for my education'.[38] Surprisingly Laud, the gownsman *par excellence*, got to know William Chillingworth, citizen and later Mayor of Oxford, well enough to be invited to serve as godfather to his son and namesake. Perhaps their families shared some common mercantile bond, Oxford and Reading being only twenty miles apart.

Laud spent thirty-two years of his life at Oxford, describing St John's as the place 'where I was bred up'. More than anything else Oxford shaped him. He recognised what he owed to the university, never ceasing to try and repay that debt. The most lasting reforms he made were as Chancellor of Oxford University. Today his most enduring physical monument is the great quadrangle at St John's. As an old man Laud listed twenty-three 'THINGS WHICH I HAVE PROJECTED TO DO, IF GOD BLESS ME IN THEM'. Eight involved Oxford.[39]

For a young man of humble origins and great ambition Oxford was both an opportunity and a trap. It provided him with a ladder of upward social mobility that more often than not ended in a dead end. Most such men, after working hard, passing examinations, winning fellowships and the support of their seniors, did not achieve the power and influence which they believed was their due. Overqualified, they became the alienated intellectuals of the seventeenth century.[40] Paradoxically, the few successful intellectuals, such as Laud, felt equally ill at ease, for they had won power in a world where lands and birth counted far more than brains and learning.

The system which educated Laud valued – as do most – knowledge far more than brilliance. His training had been a long hard grind in the classics, prizing the translation of other men's ideas far more than critical thought or originality. To excel in such a system required a certain kind of mind: pedantic, precise, knowledgeable, and an almost encyclopaedic memory to compensate for the lack of bibliographies, indices and finding aids that scholars enjoy today. There was a remoteness to Laud's learning, a scholasticism so archaic that at times it seemed to lose touch with reality. There was a cleverness too – a relish for plays on words that may be forgiven in the undergraduate but become tiresome in middle age. His education taught Laud how to find the correct classical, biblical or patristic text rather than the truth. His was an education in which the footnotes counted as much as the text, if not more. Correct citations and precise details were valued more than the right conclusions. His education taught him to worry about the small things: if they were right then the whole would automatically be correct. His training taught him to look for general principles. Learning became a game of erudition, with truth on the side of the biggest battalions of citations, that somehow grew into an Armageddon between the forces of right and wrong. Since it does not usually matter too much who wins an academic debate, its protagonists often pursue victory with a rare ferocity.

Oxford shaped Laud institutionally as well as intellectually. He was a college man who in his later years seemed almost to treat the realm as if it were a particularly refractory group of fellows and undergraduates in dire need of the Visitor's intervention. Laud first went to Oxford when the university's discipline was being tightened. The aristocracy and the gentry who had just started sending their sons to university wanted to make sure that the boys came to no harm. So by 1570 nearly every Oxford college had instituted a system of tutors, who in addition to supervising undergraduates' education were responsible for their finances and morals, trying to keep them out of debt, taverns and brothels. To exclude such temptations colleges built high walls about themselves, with gatehouses whose massive gates were locked at night.

While Laud embraced this concept of *in loco parentis*, he found the duality of Oxford hard to accept. By the time he went up to the university, Oxford had ceased to be mainly a seminary for priests and a training academy for a few skilled professions such as medicine, becoming in addition a finishing school for the sons of the elite. Between the old and new clientele – between the players and the gentlemen, so to speak – tensions were inevitable. While the training of the players – by now the minority of undergraduates – might be a university's chief intellectual function, the education of the gentlemen gave it the power, prestige and wealth that the senior members, who were in effect the successful players, relished. They needed such reassurance, for dons were not quite gentlemen. Having as students been those best able to play the game, they were all too often the people least able to do so once they ventured outside the university's walls into 'the real world' where the gentlemen set the rules.

As a young student and college fellow Laud was content enough to accept the discipline of the community in which he lived. After his mother's death in 1600, and his election as a senior fellow, in many ways St John's became his family.[41] It was a closed community of bachelors who fought over the most trivial matters. The smaller the bone the fiercer the fight. Feuds festered for years. Such an approach to politics, which Laud carried with him when he left the university, was alien to the outside world.

In this wider world of court intrigue, parliamentary factions, cabals, relatives and retainers, Laud was at a distinct disadvantage. He had no wife and did not get on well with women, which later put him at a disadvantage with Charles's queen. He had no woman to turn to for advice, or to help salve the wounds of the political struggle. Instead he let them canker and cause an immoderate desire for revenge that produced enemies. Perhaps if Laud had had a wife he would have avoided that terrible self-certainty which his friend Clarendon noted:

> He was a man of great courage and resolution, and being most assured within himself, that he proposed no end in all his actions and designs but that what was pious and just. . . . He never studied the easiest way to those ends. . . . He did court persons too little; nor cared to make his designs and purposes appear as candid as they were.[42]

A wife and children might have helped Laud understand the essentially dynastic nature of seventeenth-century politics. In early modern England nearly all politicians gained and exercised power through a network of family connections; they used their power primarily to help relatives. For this reason the elite English families remained remarkably stable for generations, rarely having, for instance, to sell their country houses.[43] Thus what to Laud might seem inexcusable nepotism was to most Englishmen perfectly proper loyalty to kith and kin.

As a fellow of a college Laud could not marry and have children. Taking a wife would have meant immediate resignation, and exile to some parochial backwater. In any case it seems that Laud's sexuality was not such as to prompt him to throw away his career for feminine delights. In his diary, a remarkably frank document, he never once expressed the slightest physical interest in a woman, being instead troubled with a sense of intense guilt, the cause of which remains unclear.

Religious doubts due in part to having been a fellow of St John's exacerbated Laud's guilt. It is hard today when we view the college from St Giles', or walk through its gardens, among the most splendid in England, to think of St John's as a new college for the sons of new men. Founded in Mary Tudor's reign, it retained a Catholic flavour that survived the Elizabethan settlement, having a distinctly urban student body, some 45 per cent of its undergraduates coming from towns.[44] It served the aspirations of the new mercantile middle classes. St John's grew slowly, not reaching its full complement of fifty fellows until 1583. It took advantage of the general increase in the number of university students that peaked in 1589, the year that Laud went up to Oxford, and then had to deal with dwindling enrolments. As always in a buyer's market, dons had to change their standards. If parents wanted tutors to discipline their sons, the man best able to do so would attract the most students, and so augment his small college stipend. If he were able to win the favour of influential parents he might reap rewards beyond mere gratitude – a private tutorship to some aristocratic scion with an all-expenses paid Grand Tour of Europe, or, better still, a comfortable billet as chaplain to some great noble household.

Laud achieved such favour on 3 September 1603, when Charles Blount, Lord Mountjoy, made him his chaplain. The obscure Oxford don could not have hoped for a better connection. Blount was the hero of the hour, having just completed the conquest of Ireland by defeating a Spanish expeditionary force and accepting the surrender of the Earls of Tyrconnel and Tyrone. In July 1603 he returned home in triumph to be elevated Earl of Devonshire. Only one thing marred his happiness. As a young man Blount had fallen in love with Penelope Devereux, sister of his political ally, and Queen Elizabeth's favourite, the Earl of Essex. As attractive and headstrong as her brother, Penelope came to know Sir Philip Sidney intimately enough to be the Stella of his sonnets. But in 1580, at the age of nineteen, she was forced to marry Lord Rich, a coarse and brutal fellow whom she soon forsook for Sidney's bed. In 1586, a couple of years after Sidney died, she entered Mountjoy's, having by this time borne her husband seven children. Rich eventually lost patience with his wife (who was as highly sexed as she was fertile) and obtained a divorce of *mens et thoro* from the Court of High Commission. If anything this seemed to confirm Penelope and Mountjoy's irregular union. They had three children, living happily together as husband and wife; they were accepted as such everywhere, even at court. But acceptance in the eyes of men was not enough. On 26 December Laud formally married them in their country house at Wanstead, Essex. Immediately doubts arose as to the legality of Laud's action. Mountjoy defended the wedding by pointing out how badly Lord Rich had treated Penelope, and arguing that his marriage to her was contrary neither to scripture nor to common law.[45] Then in the middle of the scandal Mountjoy died, on 3 April 1606, leaving his domestic chaplain's reputation in ruins.

Laud now realised that he had made a terrible mistake, perhaps a fatal one, for James I, the ultimate source of all future preferment, was mortally offended. Years later Laud explained to Peter Heylyn that he had agreed to perform the ceremony because Mountjoy had 'dealt so powerfully with him'.[46] But in his heart of hearts he recognised the hollowness of the excuse that he, a young priest only a few months in the service of a national hero, had been bullied into carrying out a wrongful marriage. In a private response he wrote to Mountjoy's apologia, he admitted that marriage was indissoluble, and that while canon law might permit divorce for adultery, it never allowed remarriage, not even for the innocent party.[47] Nowhere did Laud mention the excuse, advanced by Heylyn, that the marriage between Penelope and Rich had been invalid all the time because she had previously betrothed herself to Mountjoy.[48]

Laud could never completely escape the stigma of the Mountjoy marriage, about which he had nightmares. For the rest of his life he kept its anniversary, St Stephen's Day, as one of prayer and fasting. He composed a special prayer for 26 December in which he confessed, 'I am become a reproach to thy Holy name by serving my ambition and the sins of others.' Having paid the price for going against his conscience Laud was determined never to do so again, no matter what the cost. 'Neither let this marriage prove a Divorcing of my soul from thy grace and favour,' he continued (unable even in this moment of repentance to resist a clever academic allusion), 'for much more happy would I have been, if being mindful of this day I had suffered Martyrdom, as did St Stephen, the first of Martyrs.'[49] St Peter, or St Paul, might have been more appropriate comparisons, for like the man who denied his master twice, or who persecuted His followers before seeing the light on the road to Damascus, a deep-rooted need to atone for guilt became a mainspring of Laud's life. Thus he ended his anniversary prayer by admitting how low he had fallen: 'Be merciful, O Lord, unto me, harken unto the Prayers of thy humble and dejected Servant, and raise me up again.'

Prayer alone would not rescue Laud's career. He returned to those means which had helped start it – to hard work, and the patronage of like-minded friends.

Next to nothing is known about Laud's early religious beliefs. Possibly his family were Calvinists, like many merchants at that time. According to a not very reliable Oxford tradition, on coming to the university Laud reacted to the many elaborately carved effigies of Christ by observing sardonically, 'Is not this the Carpenter's son?' At Oxford he came into contact with Arminianism, but as he approached thirty his views were not yet so firmly set, or else not well enough known, to prevent him from becoming chaplain to Lord Mountjoy, whom the 1604 parliament considered a Puritan, whose will had a distinctly Puritan preamble, and to whom George Wiley, a minister later suspended for Nonconformity, dedicated his *Doctrine for the Sabbath* (1604). Perhaps Laud's ambition conquered his theological scruples, for the same year as he accepted Mountjoy's chaplaincy he had his first public quarrel with the Calvinist Vice-Chancellor of Oxford, George Abbot, a dangerous man to cross, who a few months earlier had imprisoned 140 undergraduates for refusing to stand in his presence.[50] It could well be that Laud's theological views hung in the balance, possibly with a leaning towards Arminianism, until the catastrophe of the Mountjoy marriage turned this into a lifelong commitment.[51]

Arminianism is a difficult doctrine to define. It was named after the Dutch Protestant theologian Jacobus Arminius, who was born in 1560 and studied at Leiden, Marburg, Geneva, Basel and Padua before being appointed, amid much controversy, to a post at the University of Leiden in 1603. Arminius tried to reconcile the ideas of the Supralapsarians with those of the Infralapsarians, and came up with a subtle but effective reply to the Calvinist doctrine of predestination, emphasising the importance of free will. The Remonstrance that his followers sent to the States General of Holland and West Friesland in 1610, the year after his death, summed up Arminius's teachings: election to salvation was conditional, atonement universal, men were unable to achieve anything good without the Holy Spirit, and Grace was sufficient for victory over sin, although once gained it could still be lost.[52]

Laud very emphatically agreed with Arminius's rejection of predestination, Calvin's dogma that the Almighty had preordained whether an individual was saved or damned even before his birth, because it fundamentally altered the relationship between God and man. 'My very soul abominates this doctrine,' wrote Laud, 'for it makes God, the God of all mercies, to be the most fierce and unreasonable tyrant in the whole world.'[53]

On the other hand Laud rejected many of Arminius's ideas, such as his emphasis on toleration, which were to make his teachings most appealing to later divines like John Wesley. 'I Pray God', wrote Laud, 'that point of Arminianism, *libertas prophetandi* [the right to proclaim different opinions] do no more mischief in short time than is expressible by me.'[54]

If Laud was not, on balance, an Arminian in the Dutch meaning of that word, was he in the English? In a sense the question is both self-fulfilling and moot: Arminianism has often been defined in terms of English history in association with Laud. That he was an Arminian was a charge he was reluctant to answer, and one that, when pressed, he denied.[55] When in December 1630 Samuel Brooke, Master of Trinity College, Cambridge, asked Laud if he would kindly read the draft of the monograph attacking predestination on which he had been working since 1615, the bishop replied, 'Fifteen years' study cannot but beat out something . . . and if God give me leisure, and the tract be not too long, I shall be glad to read it,' before concluding that 'something about these controversies is unmasterable in this life. Neither can I think any expression can be so happy as to settle these differences.'[56] Years later, as an old man on trial for his life, Laud declared, 'I have nothing to do to defend Arminianism,' adding, 'I do heartily wish these differences were not pursued with such heat and vigour.'[57] Because he believed that debate over questions such as the criteria for salvation produced far too much heat in return for hardly any light, Laud preferred to confine his theology to political matters. As we shall see in Chapter III, his published theology emphasised the relations of the individual to the state, and those of the various branches of Christianity to one another, as opposed to those between man and God.

Since even one of the leading English Arminians, refused to define Arminianism, it is not surprising that the doctrine created nearly as much confusion among contemporaries as it has with later historians and theologians. According to one contemporary jest someone interested in learning about the Arminians' beliefs asked, 'What do the Arminians hold?' Back came the answer 'All the best deaneries and bishoprics.' Indeed, Arminianism should perhaps be viewed, not as a coherent theology, but as a political faction of like-minded men determined to use it to shape their careers as much as their nation's religion. Sometimes the dividing line between the Protestant factions became blurred: Laud encouraged Bishop Hall, a Calvinist, to write a defence of *jure divino* episcopacy, while Hall dismissed the whole debate over Arminianism as 'busy and bootless babbles'.[58] The vagueness of its definition gave Arminianism, like its antithesis Puritanism, a political potency that today we can see in similarly vaguely defined terms such as 'socialism', 'liberalism', 'communism' or 'conservatism'. It is just because intellectuals find it hard, if not impossible, to agree on precise definitions for such words that politicians are able to use them to describe their friends, so widening the boundaries for political alliances, and to castigate their opponents in order to play on people's fears. The ill-defined nature of Arminianism allowed it to grow out of the universities to become at the end of James I's reign – and even more so during Charles I's – the dominant faction within the Church of England.[59]

For Laud, as an ambitious academic, Arminianism was less a matter of dominance than a means for survival, that enabled him to make friends – powerful ones – at a time when he desperately needed them to rescue his career. At the universities Arminianism appealed to the young Turks, the junior dons, who, despising their seniors, cared almost as much for the future of their careers as they did for that of their souls. During Elizabeth's reign the Church of England had moved firmly towards Calvinism, until by Whitgift's archbishopric it had become the dominant orthodoxy. For instance most Anglican bibles were bound with a Calvinist catechism. Towards the end of the century, after the defeat of the Armada and the conquest of Ireland, the threat of Catholicism from abroad declined. Consequently the need for a rabid anti-Papist ideology lessened. Ironically it was a Spanish refugee, Antonio Corro, who first laid the foundations for Arminianism at Oxford. He lectured there from 1578 until he was expelled for his teachings in 1586. During the 1590s, Peter Baro, a refugee from France who was appointed Lady Margaret Professor of Divinity at Cambridge, criticised predestination there.[60] After Baro's disciple William Barret, Chaplain of Gonville, openly attacked predestination in a university sermon, the Calvinist establishment passed the Lambeth articles which declared that 'God for eternity hath predestined some to life and has reprobated some to death'.

Official pronouncements about the intentions of the Almighty, coupled with the Mountjoy disaster, made Laud less rather than more cautious. On 21 October 1606 he preached a sermon at St Mary's Church, Oxford, defending bowing at the name of Jesus, a practice that Dr Henry Airay, Provost of Queen's College and the new vice-chancellor of the university, had recently criticised. To protect himself from censure the junior lecturer of divinity appealed to Sir William Paddy, a physician and patron of St John's. Paddy called upon the Earl of Dorset, who was Lord Treasurer of England as well as Chancellor of Oxford University, persuading him to write twice to Airay stating that Laud was in fact 'a very excellent learned man' whose sermon had been approved 'by two or three learned men about the court'.[61] There may be more to this incident than meets the eye. While it certainly saved Laud from the humiliation of a public recantation, its main purpose may have been to bolster Airay's position. His election as vice-chancellor earlier that year had been the first victory of the university's Arminians. What better way of overcoming the reservations of the dominant Calvinists than by having him attacked by a notorious young radical? Be that as it may, for Laud the lesson was clear: no matter what games dons might play, or what squabbles they might indulge in, no matter how erudite might be the books they wrote or the sermons they preached, ultimate survival depended on having friends at court.[62]

The Airay incident confirmed Laud's membership in the small but growing group of Oxford Arminians. In the following year Sir Thomas Cave presented him with the living of Stamford, Lincolnshire, and in 1608, through the intervention of John Buckeridge, Laud's tutor and President of St John's, Bishop Neile of Rochester adopted him as his protégé. He made Laud one of his chaplains and gave him the living of North Kilworth, Leicestershire – which Laud promptly exchanged for West Tilbury, Essex, to be closer to his patron.[63] The following year Neile arranged for Laud to preach before the king at Theobalds, where he failed to make a good impression. Through the Bishop of Rochester's influence Laud obtained the reversion to a prebendary at Westminster Abbey, which meant that when the office next became vacant through retirement or death, he would succeed to it.[64] In late May 1610 Neile obtained the living of Cuckstone in Kent for his follower.[65] Having saved Laud's Oxford career, Neile's patronage then seemed to end it. Laud publicly embraced Arminianism following the catastrophe of the Mountjoy marriage – after all, Mountjoy was a Puritan, and if Laud could not blame the sinners he could at least blame their sin. For a young man in disgrace Arminianism provided a group of friends ready to challenge authority and further his career. If they did set him up (as seems possible in the Airay case), they rewarded him afterwards. He became a member of a faction of radical yong dons, intent on dominating not just the university, but the nation and church as a whole.

Any such an outcome was, of course, far from Laud's mind in late 1610 when he realised that his university career had reached a dead end

and he must leave Oxford to become vicar of Cuckstone in Kent. A quarter
of a century later he recalled, 'I know what it is to send a young deserving
man from his friends and hopes here into those parts.'[66] It took him nearly
five months before he could bring himself to resign his fellowship at St
John's, the college that had been his home for twenty-one years. Then he
waited another five weeks before setting out for Kent. When he got to
Cuckstone he promptly fell ill, surely from emotional strain. As the winter
of 1610 set in it seemed as if the brilliant springtime of his life had turned
to premature autumn. In this provincial backwater it seemed that he would
be forced to spend the rest of his days performing pastoral duties for which
he had not been trained and for which he had no inclination, deprived of
stimulating discussions about books, ideas, or even college politics.

II

'I made all quiet in the college'

When Laud heard that the Archbishop of Canterbury, Richard Bancroft, had died on 2 November 1610, and that the king had appointed his old adversary George Abbot primate of England, he must have felt that his nadir was complete. Immediately on arriving to take up the living at Cuckstone, having reluctantly resigned his Oxford fellowship, Laud fell ill of 'the Kentish Ague'. His sickness lasted for nearly six months, during which he came to London where the medical care was better than in a small country village. Laud had hoped that the king would choose Bishop Lancelot Andrewes of Ely to succeed Bancroft. Andrewes was a good friend of Laud's former tutor John Buckeridge, President of St John's, with whom Laud eventually edited a collection of Andrewes's sermons. The death of Abbot's main advocate at court, Lord Dunbar, on 30 January 1611, further encouraged Andrewes's friends. But King James dashed their hopes four weeks later when he let it be known that he had selected Abbot 'as being an able man, and recommended by the late Earl of Dunbar, whose memory is dear to me'. It was a bitter blow for Laud. In April 1611 he called the new archbishop 'the original cause of all my troubles'.[1] And yet, as was so often the case, the moment Laud's fortune touched bottom it started to rise up again with a marvellous speed.

The vacancy at Canterbury was not unexpected, for Bancroft had died after prolonged agony from bladder stones. Long before James formally appointed Abbot to Canterbury the jockeying began, being set in motion by Abbot's nomination to the bishopric of London on 24 December 1609. A year later James translated Neile from Rochester to the resultant vacancy at Lichfield, and on 29 December appointed Buckeridge to the opening at Rochester.

A month earlier five senior fellows of St John's, William Juxon, Theophilus Tuer, Edmund Jackson, Richard Tillesley and Thomas Downer, met for dinner at the Golden Cross inn on Oxford's Cornmarket to discuss the choice of the next president of the College. After the table was cleared the five signed a pact (which was soon afterwards burnt) that if three of them agreed on a candidate the other two would support him for president. Straight away they settled on Laud, and started to campaign for his election, apparently without letting him know their plans. News of the cabal soon leaked out. During the Christmas vacation, convinced that Andrewes would beat him to Canterbury, Abbot told his patron Lord Chancellor Ellesmere, who was also Chancellor of Oxford University, that Laud was 'at the least a Papist in heart and cordially addicted to Popery'. Neile countered by telling the king that Laud was an able man against whom Abbot had an old and utterly unwarranted grudge. James, who always professed the desire to lead a don's life while despising donnish politics, agreed to let the election run its course.[2]

There was another candidate for the presidency of St John's. John Rawlinson had entered the college in 1591 from the Merchant Taylors' School. His career was far more distinguished than Laud's. He had a reputation as 'a fluent and florid preacher', having delivered four of the prestigious St Paul's Cross sermons outside the London cathedral. These he published in addition to four devotional works. Rawlinson had held livings in Taplow, Buckinghamshire, and Asheldham, Essex, and was currently Principal of St Edmund's Hall, as well as being chaplain to both the king and Baron Ellesmere, which explains why the Lord Chancellor tried to intervene on his behalf.

While Laud had neither Rawlinson's scholarship nor his reputation, he had equally powerful allies at court, and friends where it most counted – among the electors of St John's.

As vice-president of the college a physician, Richard Andrewes, was responsible for conducting the election. He ruled that the undergraduate fellows were not entitled to vote. Even though the college statutes gave them this right they had not exercised it since the 1570s. Four of the undergraduate fellows who supported Rawlinson, William Harris, Christopher Reeley, William Rippin and Adam Langley, petitioned Ellesmere protesting against this ruling. Though Laud later claimed that he was in London incapacitated with the ague, he was well – and worried – enough to draft a petition to Henry Howard, the Earl of Northampton and Lord Privy Seal, in which he argued that the disenfranchised fellows who supported him were really graduates entitled to vote. He asked Northampton, who was also Chancellor of Cambridge University, to request the king to appoint a committee consisting of himself, Ellesmere and Bishop Bilson of Winchester to decide if junior fellows were allowed to vote. Rawlinson reacted to this ploy by preventing three pro-Laud undergraduate fellows from taking their degrees until after the election, which prompted Martin Okin, Nicholas Cliff and William Juxon to protest to Ellesmere.[3]

This flurry of petitions notwithstanding, the election was held on 10

May, and Laud won by twelve votes to eleven. The contest was particularly close and bitter. After a long interview Bishop Neile pressured John Towse into switching sides and voting for Laud. Just before the result was announced Dr Richard Baylie, one of Rawlinson's main supporters, rushed up, grabbed the tally and tore up the papers. Afterwards the losers alleged that Laud's faction had blackmailed one fellow into voting for their man by threatening to reveal that he had committed 'a foul crime that deserved more than expulsion', and had forced the father of another Rawlinson supporter to remove his son from the university until the election was over. Not surprisingly the vanquished appealed to the college visitor, Thomas Bilson, Bishop of Winchester.

The college statutes appointed the Bishop of Winchester as visitor to adjudicate in just such disputes. But Thomas Bilson was far from being an independent party in what, in some respects, was a preview of the struggle between Arminians and Calvinists that emerged on the national stage half a generation later. Three of Laud's supporters, Christopher Wren, William Juxon and Thomas Tucker, went on to become prominent Arminians. Rawlinson was a Calvinist with many like-minded friends at the university, such as John English, a fellow who voted against Laud. Bilson was a moderate Calvinist, as was Arthur Lake, Dean of Worcester, whom he asked to help investigate the ruckus. After Juxon, Tuer, Jackson, Tillesley and Downer all admitted to having signed the agreement at the Golden Cross inn, Bilson wrote to the king that illegal means had been used in Laud's election. Six weeks later, on 30 July, Juxon, Jackson and Tuer petitioned James to disqualify Bilson as visitor on the grounds that he had exceeded the powers granted him by the college statutes by ordering fellows to appear before him 'under pain of expulsion'. With magnificent under-statement they concluded that 'the government of the said college is not a little interrupted'.[4]

In all this turmoil Laud was no passive spectator. He told the Bishop of Winchester that the fellows Rawlinson claimed had been driven out of Oxford during the election in truth 'went away of themselves'.[5] He made copious notes on the election, its procedures and the fellows' oaths of office. He drafted an earlier version of the petition that Juxon, Jackson and Tuer sent to the king on 30 July.[6] The same day Laud wrote another petition to the king on his own behalf, although he must have had second thoughts, because he never actually sent it.[7]

Perhaps Laud sensed that the tide was turning in his favour. On 5 August, the same day that Bilson wrote to the king justifying his powers as visitor, James commanded all the interested parties to appear before him at Tichborne, Hampshire, on the 29th. For James, who relished the epithet 'Britain's Solomon', the thought of playing the don, the challenge of settling a college election without cutting the fellowship in half, was intriguing. In practice it proved rather tedious. For three hours both sides droned on with their bitter charges of petty deceits. Exasperated, James finally threw up his hands, declaring, 'No election of any college is such as we could wish.' This one was worse than most, being replete with malice, mayhem and faction. Indeed, an honest election was, the king lamented, 'a matter to be hoped for in this usage'. A second contest would only compound the mess. Thus James reluctantly let Laud's election stand, while making some face-saving gestures about clarifying the college statutes in future.[8]

Once again Laud had been rescued in the nick of time. He admitted as much by celebrating 29 August as the day when 'His Majesty King James heard my cause about the election to the presidency of St. John's College' as a special anniversary on which the king 'with great justice delivered me out of the hands of my powerful enemies'.[9]

Bishop Bilson was equally aware of the significance of Laud's victory. With ill-concealed irritation he wrote to the fellows of St John's informing them of the king's decision.[10] A month later Neile persuaded James to make Laud a royal chaplain. It was a hollow honour. Even though Laud spent much time hanging around the court he was a marked man, constantly blocked by Archbishop Abbot. So for most of the next decade Laud had to exercise his talents as President of St John's College, Oxford.

To the victors went the spoils of college office. Laud rewarded all five of the fellows who had signed the compact at the Golden Cross inn. He made Juxon vice-president, Tuer bursar, and had Buckeridge appoint Jackson his chaplain. Downey became vicar of Kirtlington, and rector of Radnage, Buckinghamshire, while Tillesley married one of Laud's nieces, and was made Archdeacon and Prebend of Rochester. On the other hand Richard Baylie, the impetuous young man who tore up the election tally, was expelled from his fellowship. He appealed to Bishop Bilson, who reinstated him. Eventually Laud and Baylie became firm friends. Laud used his influence to have Baylie appointed proctor in 1615, and 'trusted him with all his weighty business'.[11] He married Laud's niece Elizabeth Robinson, and in 1633 succeeded Juxon as college president. Those fellows who were 'not easily to be gained by favours' Laud harried out of the college. In all he handled his takeover of the presidency with skill. After rewarding his friends, and attacking the obdurate, he took a remarkably deferential attitude to the rest of his colleagues. For instance in a letter he wrote in late 1611 to Sir David Williams, a King's Bench judge, Laud was adamant that he must consult the fellowship, 'whose consent I must have in all such business of the college', over a dispute concerning fishing and fowling rights on the river Windrush in Oxfordshire.[12]

As the head of a university college Laud had surprisingly little to do with learning, scholarship or education. After he became famous and powerful few students recalled their old teacher with affection, even though there were obvious advantages in publicly doing so. With his obsession for order Laud appointed six o'clock as the hour for dinner, which before had been held at any convenient time.[13] He served as one of the selectors for college fellowships, being insufficiently swayed by considerations of friendship to vote one to Juxon's nephew in 1618. Only once was Laud recorded as having used his influence to help a graduate student. On 20 September 1613, he and several other fellows, including Juxon, Jackson and Tuer, wrote to the Warden and Assistants of the Carpenters' Company on behalf of William Sherbourne, whose £4 a year exhibition they had not renewed for a third year. 'The youth is of a great hope, and I would not have him disheartened,' pleaded Laud. It worked. The Carpenters continued Sherbourne's fellowship for another seven years, and eventually he became Canon of Hereford.[14]

Laud's published scholarship was scanty enough. He penned a rather humdrum Latin poem in *Justa Oxoniensium* (1612) mourning the sudden death of James I's eldest son, Prince Henry, and the following year wrote an equally tedious, although shorter, Latin poem about the Thames merging with the Rhine to celebrate the wedding between James's daughter Elizabeth and Frederick, the Elector Palatine. Laud's scholarly following was equally thin. As President of St John's only one book, Alexander Ross's *Liber Quartus* (1612), was dedicated to him. At Oxford the wits preferred to portray him as 'a little morsel', satirising him as a member of a mock foundation for fools and innocents, known as Gotham College. The jest must have stung Laud, for years later, when he had access to the state papers, he carefully annotated the satire to try and answer its jibes.[15]

As President of St John's Laud spent much of his time improving the college's finances. On 11 November 1611 St John's had cash in hand of £258. 7s. 10d., and capital valued at £93. 6s. 6d. Ten years later, when Laud left the presidency, the college cash had increased by £127, and he had managed to attract £1,436. 13s. in donations.[16] He bought Bagley Wood as a source of college firewood, built a new kitchen and four more rooms for the fellows, repaired the original college buildings, which had been a medieval monastery, and put battlements around the old quadrangle. During his presidency the college built up a respectable library, to which he gave several manuscripts.[17] He arranged for a fellow to be paid an additional £3 a year to act as librarian. The achievement which gave Laud the most pleasure was the beautification of the chapel, for which he personally contributed £44 out of the total cost of £1,436. 13s. Using Sir William Paddy's bequest, Laud installed a new organ loft in 1619, painted the ceiling, and placed stained glass telling the story of St John in the east window. Two years later he replaced the stonework over this window, and refurnished the communion table with crimson and purple velvet. He commissioned Orlando Gibbons and Michael East to compose anthems for the chapel, and had a register listing all donations to the college drawn up.[18] Long before he became Archbishop of Canterbury Laud's emphasis on the altar and the beauty of holiness in worship was obvious. He was careful to let large benefactors know how well he was spending their money. In October 1616 he wrote about the progress of building and repairs to Sir William Herrick, an old friend of St John's, whose mother-in-law, Lady Mary May, had founded the divinity lectureship which Laud had once held.[19]

Laud worked to improve the college's finances. For instance, one of his first economies as president was to abolish the custom of giving each fellow a £10 gratuity on resigning office to help him make the transition to outside life. He sold off some three hundred duplicate volumes from the library. In 1619 he insisted that the city of Oxford carry out Sir Thomas White's bequest by ensuring that the £100 he left to be used as venture capital by some merchant be given to a Mr Cokram and a Mr Newson, both clothiers, and thus possibly connected to Laud's father. Even though the Merchant Taylors' Company were the college's most generous benefactors, giving St John's the bulk of the £439. 6s. 6d. it received in 1616, Laud refused to surrender the advowson of Crick, Northamptonshire, which the company had presented to the college to supplement the income of the senior fellow who had attended its school.[20]

On the whole, however, Laud's decade at St John's was a time of growth. While enrolments at the university as a whole fell, the college expanded to become intimately involved with national affairs for half a century. 'I made all quiet in the College,' Laud declared when he looked back on his presidency, 'I governed that college in peace, with not so much as a show of faction, all my time, which was near upon eleven years.'[21] His boast was indeed correct. As a college president he set the pattern for his future career by maintaining internal order, albeit with a heavy hand, while provoking those outside.

For example on Shrove Tuesday, 21 February 1615, Laud preached at Oxford vigorously attacking Puritans, whom he likened to Presbyterians as being no better than Papists. The following Easter afternoon, Dr Robert Abbot, the Archbishop of Canterbury's elder brother, and another old enemy who had prospered enough to become Master of Balliol, Vice-Chancellor, and Regius Professor of Divinity, replied with a sermon at St Mary's. Since Laud missed this violent rejoinder his friends urged him to return the following Sunday, 16 April, when according to custom the homily was repeated. 'I was fain to sit patiently and hear myself abused about an hour,' Laud lamented to Neile. 'That man under pretence of Truth and preaching against the Puritans, strikes at the heart and roots of Faith and Religion now established among us ... to seduce the young students.' He went on to suggest that Abbot and his cronies were really closet Catholics, who 'do beat a little about the Bush, and that softly too, for fear of troubling or disquieting the Birds that are in it'. Although Laud claimed that Abbot's attack had not upset him personally, the fact that two decades later he took the trouble to annotate the state papers dealing with the episode suggests that the scars were still raw.

Once more Laud's career hung in the balance. 'I would have taken no notice of it,' he told Neile, 'but that the whole University apply it to me, and my own friends tell me I shall sink my credit if I answer not.'[22] Summoned to London, Laud was convinced that he had lost his fight with the university's vice-chancellor, the archbishop's brother, and that it might be years, if ever, before he was allowed to return to Oxford. But on 10 June James – who had just heard John Howson, Prebend of Christ Church, debate at great length in the most violent fashion with Abbot, and was sick and tired of academic squabbles – sided with the President of St John's, whom he allowed back to the university, announcing that 'Dr Laud shall have peace & be no more troubled in this matter.'[23] Archbishop Abbot had to acknowledge his brother's error, for which he 'asked pardon'. Perhaps Neile, whom the king had just appointed Bishop of Lincoln, once again moved decisively behind the scenes. Certainly James had lost confidence in his Calvinist archbishop, who opposed his scheme to let Frances, Countess of Essex, divorce her husband the earl so she could marry the royal favourite Sir Robert Carr. In addition, James hated Puritans as much as Laud did. They were the 'very pests of the commonwealth', the king told his son. 'I protest before the great God that ye shall never find any Highland or Border thieves greater in ingratitude and more lies and vile perjuries than with these fanatic spirits.'[24]

The sermon that Laud preached to the court at Woodstock a year later on 27 August 1616, in which he used Miriam's leprosy to castigate 'detraction from princes' government', was well received.[25] It may have prompted the king to make him Dean of Gloucester the following 21 November. The promotion delighted Laud, who over the last half-decade had with growing desperation haunted the court in search of preferment. He interpreted the appointment as an indication that 'he was not so contemptible in the Eyes of the king as it was generally imagined'.[26] James's understanding might not have been so generous, for he told the new dean that Gloucester Cathedral was in 'no good office', and 'that there was scarce ever a Church in England so ill governed and so much out of order'. Thus, Laud continued in his letter to Miles Smith, the Bishop of Gloucester, His Majesty 'withal required me in general to reform and set in order what there I find amiss'.[27]

Bishop Smith was part of the problem. The son of a butcher, Smith had gone to Oxford, taking his Doctor of Divinity degree in 1594. He became chaplain of Christ Church. A distinguished orientalist, he was one of the translators of the King James Bible, being responsible, with Bishop Bilson, for the final revisions of the Old Testament, for which he wrote the preface. As a reward James made him Bishop of Gloucester in 1616. It is conceivable that Smith's friendship with Bilson had already brought him into conflict with Laud long before he became Dean of Gloucester, for three years earlier, on 9 April 1614 Laud noted in his diary, 'My great misfortune by MS began.'[28] Certainly the two men had little in common: Smith was a mild-mannered scholar rather than an ambitious university politician. It was said that he used 'instruction and rebuke to the contrary minded', teaching them with 'sweet and soft words' — all very different from the style of the President of St John's.[29]

As a Puritan who disliked ceremonial, Smith sympathised with the leading citizens of Gloucester, which was a hotbed of religious radicalism. As the decline in the wool trade hurt its economy, two-thirds of the city's parishes became too poor to support resident vicars, and had to be served by badly paid, ill-educated curates. To remedy the lack of godly preaching the corporation appointed William Groves, a local Puritan, to give a weekly sermon at St Michael's Church, and afterwards paid Thomas Prior and then John Workman, two Calvinists, to preach there twice a week.[30]

Laud knew nothing — and cared even less — about the religious sensitivities of Gloucester's citizens. After being installed as dean by proxy on 20 December, he rode to Gloucester, where he attended his first chapter meeting on 25 January 1617. Laud immediately had the chapter pass two acts, one for the repair of the cathedral's fabric, and the other moving the altar from the middle of the building to the east end.[31] He may well have told the chapter to improve their record keeping by opening an act book. He cannot have remained in the city, for it is unlikely that John White, Bishop Smith's chaplain, would have dared write to the chancellor of the Gloucester diocese complaining about their new dean's high-handed actions and accusing him of popery had the ferocious little man still been around. One thing was certain: as far as the corporation and chapter were concerned Laud could not boast 'I made all quiet there.' The chapter was badly divided. On 21 February two prebendaries, Henry Aisgill and Elias Wrench, wrote to their dean that a copy of John White's letter had been prominently posted on the pulpit at St Michael's Church, the source of so many Puritan sermons. They begged Laud to have the Court of High Commission examine the libel, whilst reminding him to make sure that none of the investigators 'favour the schismatical faction of the Puritans'.[32] Two days later Thomas Prior, the sub-dean, who had been flirting with both sides, reported to his superior that he had expelled a pair of choristers, Vernon and Farley, apparently for having a part in this libel, and asked for Laud's advice. Attacks against their dean were not the only assault on the great chain of being to trouble Gloucester, for Prior concluded his letter by reporting that a child with two heads and four legs had just been born in the city.[33]

Prior's equivocations failed to placate Laud, who heard that his sub-dean was in fact scheming against his reforms. Laud wrote immediately to Bishop Smith, his theoretical superior, demanding that he stop these libels, about which he must tell the king. Four days later Laud sought Neile's help: if his enemies continued to attack him could Neile please let the king know what an excellent job he was doing in Gloucester?[34] Apparently Laud was afraid that the chapter might mutiny during the summer when he was away in Scotland with the king.

Laud need not have worried. His opponents in Gloucester recognised his selection to accompany James north as a clear sign of royal favour. Thomas Prior made an abject surrender. Miles Smith was so upset that it was said that he never again set foot in his cathedral. Faced by Alderman John Jones's threat to haul them before a High Commission, the corporation caved in. For Laud it was a most satisfactory episode. As he told Heylyn, 'the Rabble . . . began to be more sensible of the errors that they had committed, the fury of their first hurt being abated, and Reason beginning by degree (as is ordinary in such cases) to take place of Passion'.[35]

The Gloucester incident was the first time that Laud had exercised power outside Oxford University. It confirmed his view that if you treated troublemakers, like fractious dons, firmly, they would soon calm down, see the error of their ways and conform.

The fact that he learned the wrong lesson, but learned it well, never seemed to bother Laud, and during his visit to Scotland he behaved equally insensitively. The king and his party left London in March, and, after a pleasantly slow progress enlivened by hunts, receptions and banquets, crossed the border on 13 May. Three days later they entered Edinburgh. During the three months he spent in Scotland Laud managed to alienate a goodly proportion of its Presbyterian inhabitants. This was not a particularly difficult achievement, for the Scots have always been a prickly people, and in 1617 they were convinced that the king had returned to the land of his birth to force them to accept an alien form of worship. The English craftsman who installed a new organ in the Chapel Royal at Holyrood Palace complained that he would have been better treated by Turks. Thus it was almost inevitable that a priest as tactless as Laud would upset the Scots, particularly after he insisted on wearing a surplice at the funeral of one of the king's guards. This might explain why James, who had sense enough to shelve any plans to introduce Anglican worship north of the border, let Laud go home early.[36]

Back in England, university and court business kept Laud so busy that the king wrote to the Gloucester chapter in October that they were to postpone their annual November meeting to a time convenient for their dean.[37] Over the next four years, Laud visited Gloucester about every six months, usually in February or March, and again in October or November. He tried to raise money for a new organ, the old 'being in great decay and in short time likely to be of no use'. He reinstituted the practice of cathedral prayers at five each morning. Several of the chapter found getting up so early such a strain that they had to designate a junior choirboy to rise first to prepare the service and then wake them. The dean ordered that the cathedral archives be catalogued, and had the floor of the dining room in his house replaced because of dry rot. He dealt with disciplinary matters, admonishing Richard White, a clerk, for frequenting taverns. Another clerk, Rowland Smyth, proved even more intractable. After reprimanding him for beating up a tailor, and again for being drunk in the cathedral, Laud dismissed Smyth for attacking the city mace bearer with a knife.[38]

By the time of Smyth's expulsion, Laud must have felt that his own career was equally out in the cold. Neile had done what he could to warm it. In August 1617, for instance, he inducted his protégé into the living of Ibstock in Leicestershire.[39] The following month, soon after Laud's return from Gloucester, a major fire broke out at St John's. It must have upset the president greatly: for the rest of his life he kept 26 September as a special day of atonement, as terrible an anniversary as his mother's and father's deaths, or the Mountjoy marriage.[40]

Laud continued to hang around the court in the hope of some ecclesiastical crumb. On the way back to Oxford from one such abortive mission 'I fell suddenly dead for a time at Wickam, in my return from London, April 2, 1619'. The cause of the attack is not known. He fainted whilst riding past an inn, very nearly died, and was only nursed back to health with great difficulty.[41]

The following year, as Laud's health mended, so too did his professional fortunes. On 22 January 1621 he was installed as a prebend of Westminster Abbey. Bishop Neile had obtained the right of appointment, known as the reversion, for Laud a decade earlier, so he had had to wait a long time 'in expectation of it'.[42] Once gained, the prebendary provided a useful base in the capital. With it came a house, possession of which Laud tried to obtain from the sitting tenant, Ellis Wynn, at the first chapter meeting which he attended on 4 May. Since Wynn turned out to be an obdurate fellow, Laud had to wait five years before taking possession. In the long run this inconvenience was an advantage, for it meant that Laud could still stay with his old mentor, Bishop Neile, at Durham House, and thus cement their friendship. As a prebend of Westminster Abbey, Laud started to perform several public duties. He certified that Sir Francis Steward, Walter Steward, William Carr and James Maxwell, all suspected recusants, had in fact taken communion regularly.[43] In May he attended his first convocation, helping vote the king three subsidies, a far more generous tax than that given by parliament.

The following month James was equally bountiful. Laud recorded in his diary, 'The King's gracious speech to me on 3 June 1621, concerning my long service. He was pleased to say he had given me nothing but Gloucester, which he knew as a shell without kernel.' Since the news of James's intention further to reward Laud immediately became public, no one could fail to realise that the sermon he preached before the court sixteen days later was of especial importance. He chose as his text Psalm 122:6–7, 'Pray for the peace of Jerusalem; let them prosper that love thee.' Laud excelled himself. Using the rhetorical style of his hero Lancelot Andrewes, the greatest preacher of the day, he argued that 'The Church can have no being but in the commonwealth . . . and the Commonwealth can have no blessed and happy being but by the church.' Laud went on to say that 'Peace is one of the greatest Temporal blessings that a State or Church can receive.' Harmony at home: peace abroad – the king could not have asked for more. A true believer in the divine right of kings, who was much troubled by Abbot, his far too independently minded Archbishop of Canterbury, James relished Laud's argument that church and state were interdependent, and he immediately ordered the sermon printed. After three decades of academic life it was the don's first book. The king also welcomed Laud's defence of his pacific foreign policy. An instinctively pacific man – some said a cowardly one – he was trying to resist intense pressure from his current favourite, Buckingham, and his son Charles, to join the Thirty Years War.[44]

Laud knew only too well what the king thought of him. According to John Hacket, the contemporary historian, who made up for his lack of reliability by a nice turn of phrase, when Buckingham first suggested giving Laud a bishopric James dredged up the Mountjoy marriage, asking, 'Shall I make a man a prelate, one of the angels of my church, who hath a fragrant crime to him?' The king's opposition to Laud was not based solely on that youthful indiscretion; indeed, James, who was remarkably indiscreet throughout his own life, rarely held such peccadilloes against any man. What worried him most about Laud was that quality which had first brought him to his attention. According to Hacket, James explained that 'the plain truth is that I keep Laud back from all place of rule and authority because I feel he hath a restless spirit, and cannot see when matters are well, but loves to toss and change, and to bring things to the pitch of reformation'.[45]

Such men are often useful, but they are seldom loved – particularly at court. And yet in the intense, petty, hothouse world of college and church politics, men such as this may form friendships, win patrons, and adopt protégés, that will both last and shape their lives far better than any alliance made in high society.

John Buckeridge, Laud's tutor and first mentor, introduced him to Richard Neile, the bishop who did most to further the young don's career. Neile arranged for his protégé to preach at court, obtained livings and then exchanged them for him, made him one of his chaplains, and shielded him from the consequences of the Mountjoy marriage. Perhaps the most lasting effect Neile had on Laud's career was to make him a member of a group of like-minded clerics. They included men such as Augustine Lindsell, Bishop of Hereford; Thomas Jackson, President of Corpus Christi, Oxford, and Dean of Peterborough; John Cosin, Bishop of Lichfield; Dr Benjamin Lang, Master of Queens' College, Cambridge, and Dean of Rochester; William Juxon of St John's; Robert Newell, Prebend of Westminster; Gabriel Clarke, Archdeacon of Durham; Eleazer Duncan, Prebend of Durham; Richard Montagu, Bishop of Chichester; and William Robinson, Laud's elder half-brother, whom Neile made Archdeacon of Nottingham.[46] During the 1620s and 1630s these men formed the nucleus of a movement that was to dominate the higher reaches of the Church of England. They may be defined in ideological terms as Arminians, not so much because they accepted the teachings of Arminius as because they were united in their opposition to the Calvinistic doctrine of predestination, which prompted one of their enemies to describe them as 'a schismatical crew of upstart reformers'.[47] But they were united by far more than an intellectual consensus. They were friends, who on their visits to London stayed at Neile's episcopal palace, thus becoming known as the Durham House group. They shared a common university background, usually coming from merchant stock, which set them apart from England's secular elite, who came from long-established landed families. They helped promote and protect each other. As Laud's Oxford sermons attacking Abbot and his Calvinist friends showed, they came together as angry, ambitious young men rebelling against the old guard. So we should not be surprised that on gaining power they treated their opponents in the younger generation with far less tolerance than their elders had shown them: ex-poachers usually make the most ferocious gamekeepers. Rarely, however, are they allowed free run of the big house. And this was the Durham House group's main problem. While under the first two Stuarts they became more influential in the Church of England than the Calvinists had ever been in Elizabeth's reign, they never enjoyed quite the same power in government. In part this was due to their personalities. Except for William Juxon, they were noted for their lack of charm. But more significant, as their influence in the church grew, the nature of royal government changed. Royal favourites who monopolised power replaced the old system in which political factions competed to influence the sovereign. Since the basis for the favourite's influence was the king's court – and sometimes his bed – bishops would have been at an obvious disadvantage had they tried to operate within such a context. The best they could do was to play the pimp by dangling a new favourite before the king, as Abbot tried to do with Buckingham.

Laud first realised the limits of the Durham House group's influence in the years just before 1620, when he started to look for a new patron. He found one in Bishop John Williams.

Williams was born in 1582 of a proud Welsh family which like all Cymric clans had pretensions to lineage. Educated at Ruthin Grammar School, he entered St John's College, Cambridge, in 1598. At heart Williams was a Welshman on the make. Like Laud he was an outsider. Indeed, Clarendon's description of Williams as 'a man of a very imperious and fiery temper . . . of great pride and vanity' could apply to them both.[48] A childhood accident may have made Williams even more single-minded than Laud. When he was seven he jumped from a wall to the beach at Conway sure that his long cloak would act as a parachute and cushion his fall. Instead he fell on a sharp stone, which as his first biographer coyly put it 'caused him an infirmity fitter to be understood than described'.[49] So Williams's libidinal drives may have found an outlet in his career, in which, unlike Laud, he never tied himself to any one clerical faction. His faith was as shallow as it was broad. Whilst a young fellow of St John's, Cambridge, he offended the undergraduates by defending the teaching and practices of the established church, and irritated the dons by attending William Perkins's Puritan sermons. As Williams grew older and his touch more delicate, he managed to reap rewards from both sides. Seeing him as the coming man whose excellent sermons greatly impressed the king, all sought his favour. Lord Chancellor Ellesmere (Laud's opponent) made Williams his chaplain in 1610, while four years later Neile (Laud's patron) appointed him rector of Walgrave, Northamptonshire.

While continuing to collect preferments with an ostentation that Laud found abhorrent, in 1620 Williams managed to further his career greatly by persuading the Catholic heiress Lady Katherine Manners to become an Anglican. Because James refused to let Buckingham marry the richest heiress in the land while she remained a Papist, the royal favourite was so grateful that he asked Williams to officiate at their wedding in May 1620, and the following July had him appointed Dean of Westminster. Buckingham soon came to appreciate the Welshman's shrewd advice, particularly when he overlaid a dearth of scruples with the patina of piety.[50]

In Williams, James recognised a man of sound political judgment and utter – albeit temporary – loyalty to the person best able to further his career. He welcomed the Welshman's sturdy defence of the prerogative of monarchy by divine right, which he considered a more than adequate compensation for a lack of legal knowledge. So in July 1621 he made him

Lord Keeper, replacing the recently impeached Francis Bacon. But just in case Williams was tempted to accept bribes as had his predecessor, James made the appointment without tenure, but with the lucrative bishopric of Durham.[51]

Williams's elevation to the Lord Keepership prompted a muted but profound change in his relations with Buckingham, who had been pushing Lionel Cranfield, and then Sir James Ley, for the post. It is unlikely that Laud was Buckingham's client at this time.[52] Even though they had known each other since at least 1616, when Laud preached at court criticising 'detractions on priestly government', his later sermons bitterly attacking war show that he had no sympathy for the favourite's bellicose foreign policy.[53]

Williams's motives for having Laud made Bishop of St David's are hard to explain. The two men shared neither friends, friendship nor mutual beliefs. If they had anything in common it was that prickly pride, springing from their humble roots, which eventually made them such bitter enemies. Perhaps Williams saw Laud as the hub of a party that would protect him as he ventured into secular politics, or else as a bridge to the growing Arminian faction within the church. On the other hand Williams may have wanted to demonstrate that he could reward his followers in spite of the king's opposition. 'Take him to you, but on my soul you will regret it,' the king is said to have warned Williams when he eventually agreed to the promotion.[54]

Williams shared much of James's ambivalence. On 9 June 1621, six days after James promised Laud some reward, John Chamberlain, the well-informed London letter writer, reported that Laud would succeed Williams as Dean of Westminster. But Williams opposed the move. Wanting to remain in Westminster, close to the court, he had declined the more distant but far better paid deanery of Salisbury a year earlier. So Williams could well have persuaded James to send Laud to St David's, a bishopric with far more prestige than pay, to demonstrate his own influence with the king whilst removing a potential rival from the centre of power.

Once more Laud's ambitions were filled only to be dashed. To his diary he confessed his bitter disappointment: 'The General expectation in Court was I should have been made Dean of Westminster and not Bishop of St. David's.' He could not even take advantage of the consolation prize that Williams had arranged for him: 'The king gave me leave to hold the Presidentship of St. John Baptist's college, in Oxon, in my *commendam*, with the Bishopric of St. David's. But by reason of the strictness of that statute, which I will not violate, nor my oath to it, under any colour, I am resolved before my consecration to leave it.'[55]

Thus on 17 November 1621 Laud resigned the presidency of St John's. The next day the Bishops of London, Worcester, Chichester, Ely, Llandaff and Oxford consecrated Laud Bishop of St David's. Not even the absence of Archbishop Abbot (debarred at Laud's insistence for having accidentally killed a gamekeeper a few months earlier) could have done much to assuage his disappointment.[56] After wandering for so long in the wilderness, Laud found that his promised land was to be in the wastes of West Wales.

III

'Pastors, labourers, and watchmen'

Tens of thousands of Englishmen celebrated 17 November 1621 as a day of thanksgiving, as well as one of regret. On that date sixty-three years earlier, in 1558, the Catholic Queen Mary had died, and was succeeded by Queen Elizabeth I 'of blessed memory'. Very soon after her death in 1603, and the accession of James I, Englishmen started marking this anniversary by ringing bells and hearing laudatory sermons. Thus they praised the old queen and, by implication, criticised the new king, as well as his Scots ways, friends and government. In sum Englishmen looked back with nostalgia and forward with apprehension.

For Laud 17 November marked a very different occasion. Yet the transition he began that day would – in retrospect, at least – confirm many of his fellow countrymen's worst fears that England was in danger of changing from a true Protestant state to a false new order that stank of Rome. On the 17th Laud resigned his presidency of St John's, on the 18th he was consecrated Bishop of St David's, and on the 19th he took his seat in the House of Lords, where he received his first taste of the practical political problems that faced a Jacobean bishop. Within the space of three days Laud had to adjust to a new political world that was very different from the one he had known and mastered as head of an Oxford college. In doing so he understandably retained many of the attitudes of a don. For instance, as a new member of the House of Lords he quickly concluded that those opposing the royal prerogative did so in bad faith, under pretence of religion, and that bishops such as himself who sat in the upper house were to blame for permitting such seditious cant.[1]

As a bishop Laud's responsibilities and powers extended far beyond the Palace of Westminster. He was a prince of James I's church, an institution that some have seen as a sink of corruption relieved only by mediocrity, and others as the high point of early modern Anglicanism. Bishops were, however, in an acutely ambiguous position in late sixteenth- and early seventeenth-century England, particularly when they tried to expand

31

powers based on a clerical corporation into a world where hereditary wealth and dynastic interests predominated. While displaying a blithe ignorance of the long-term ambiguity of his station, Laud knew only too well how badly he needed a powerful patron to further his episcopal career. Over the next four years he switched his loyalty from Williams to the Duke of Buckingham, the powerful royal favourite, whose star was on the ascendant. The links by which he allied himself with Buckingham were essentially academic and theological. Buckingham originally needed Laud to stop his mother from becoming a Catholic, a conversion that would hurt him politically far more than it would personally. To dissuade her Laud used all his pedagogical skills, crystallising his three decades of thought and reading at the university into a comprehensive ideology that became both a springboard to the world of action and a straitjacket once he entered that realm.

These will be the three themes of this chapter: the new bishop's roles as a prelate charged with governing a diocese of the established church, as a client who needed a powerful patron to further his career, and as a theologian who worked out an ideology which would serve him, for better and ill, after he achieved power. In his first years on the episcopal bench, then, Laud both accepted and went beyond John Jewel's classic definition of bishops' duties. They should, wrote the Elizabethan Bishop of Salisbury, be 'pastors, labourers, and watchmen'.[2]

Bishops – like all churchmen in positions of authority – are in an anomalous position. They are expected to be not of this world, and also very much part of it. The twenty-five bishops of the Church of England, and the archbishops of Canterbury and York, were men of considerable worldly power. Each diocese was subdivided into deaneries, and then parishes, of which the Church of England had some nine thousand. Dioceses had developed haphazardly, differing greatly in size and wealth. For instance the bishops of Ely or Winchester had incomes ten times greater than that enjoyed by their brethren at St Asaph's or St David's.

A bishop's activities varied nearly as widely. Some had endowments to administer, while others preferred to preach extensively. All had to confirm the young; a few might bury the dead. Bishops licensed ministers, lecturers, schoolmasters, and even surgeons and midwives. They held courts which heard tithe, matrimonial and probate cases, and also enforced sexual morality, being able to fine and excommunicate the guilty. Bishops sat on the High Commission, the church's supreme court, where they could punish with fines, mutilation and imprisonment, and were active voting members of the House of Lords. Periodically they would visit the parishes in their diocese to inspect them, and assess the performance of vicars, rectors, curates, schoolmasters and churchwardens, in order to encourage the worthy and rebuke the delinquent. Such visitations could be intimidating, with curious outsiders prying into local affairs using long lists of potentially embarrassing questions known as visitation articles. Naturally men as powerful as bishops made their fair share of enemies. How could those who claimed to be pastors, labourers and watchmen, and yet frequently acted as policemen and place-men, fail to do otherwise?

Medieval clergy had acknowledged this dilemma by going through the charade of refusing promotion thrice before being prevailed upon to accept it. For late sixteenth- and early seventeenth-century English bishops this anomaly was particularly acute and could no longer be wished away by a hollow game. Between the Reformation and the Civil War they had great difficulty defining their proper role. They could no longer play the lordly medieval prelate: Wolsey's fall proved that. On the other hand Englishmen of the time took religion too seriously to allow their bishops to degenerate into the worldly yet harmless prelates of the eighteenth century who were often more concerned with trimming and with swilling port than with serving principles or exercising temporal power for spiritual goals. Elizabethan and Jacobean bishops could not have been the superintendents that Luther envisaged, nor could their training and the size of their dioceses permit them to become the *primus inter pares* of the clergy that Calvin advocated. Their role was ambiguous.

Ambiguity was not necessarily a disadvantage; indeed, theologically, it has often been one of the Anglican Church's strengths. But social ambiguity can be an embarrassment. Bishops were exceptions to the rule in early modern English society. While they were, of course, members of the hierarchical order that James summed up in the adage 'No Bishops, No kings', they gained their status within that order in a very atypical fashion. Most Englishmen who exercised authority, from the king to the gentry, did so because their fathers had done so. The great chain of being was forged on the anvil of birth. Bishops, on the other hand, owed their appointment largely to ability. While influence, even toadying, was necessary to be appointed to, and promoted within, the episcopal bench, intelligence and hard work were vital to win the university degrees, which usually included a doctorate of divinity, that were the qualifications for preferment. Thus it is no accident that most bishops came from the only other significant group in which ability was a major credential for social advancement. Bishops Buckeridge, Juxon and Wren had all been pupils at the Merchant Taylors' School in London, Bishop Potter's father was a merchant from Kendal, Bishop Cosin's one from Norwich, Laud's had been a Reading clothier, while Archbishop Harsnett was the son of a Colchester butcher. The vast majority of bishops came from the lower and middle orders, not from very wealthy merchant families. Like the latter, bishops excited the envy of old-established rural families, but unlike prosperous merchants they frequently had no familial networks to further their careers. True, at the universities they made friends who might be able to help them, but they also tended to make nearly as many enemies who did as much, if not more, to stand in their way. For instance, while Laud might have a Neile, he also had an Abbot. Bishops lacked the landed elite's great personal wealth to buy clients, or votes, having few retainers or tenants to support them. Because they often moved from diocese to diocese, they could never hope to create the sort of networks of influence, or power bases, that aristocrats or gentry, some of whose families had lived in the same county for centuries, enjoyed.

Jacobean bishops were men of a new order. Their careers, based on examinations and university degrees, and shaped by college contacts and corporate mentors and factions, were the closest the seventeenth century came to those of a modern executive, civil servant or professional. And like many new men they profited from the system that they controlled. For instance, of the first generation of Elizabeth's bishops 5 per cent died rich, 45 per cent poor. Of the first generation of James's bishops the figures were almost reversed: 5 per cent died poor and 32 per cent died rich.[3] While the average Jacobean gentleman neither knew nor could appreciate such statistics, he was only too aware that in his grandfather's day prelates invariably travelled on horseback whereas now they progressed by carriage in great style and comfort – and at great expense. He was also convinced that it was the gentry, men such as himself, who paid for such new-fangled luxuries, because most bishops were trying to augment their incomes at the expense of his own.

These then were some of the challenges that Laud had to face as he sought a powerful patron and friends at court. After arranging for William Juxon, the man who had done so much to bring about his own election a decade earlier, to succeed him as President of St John's, the Bishop of St David's turned his attention to becoming a political prelate. James invited him to preach at court in February and May 1622. The king – who on leaving the Bodleian Library at Oxford was once heard to remark that if he had not been a monarch he would have liked to be a don – may have enjoyed Laud's ponderous scholarship. It contained a strange mixture of cleverness and pedantic erudition that both reinforced the savant's high opinion of his own intelligence, and convinced the insecure person of the stupidity of most of his fellow creatures. Certainly the sermon that Laud preached at the state opening of parliament on 24 March 1622 impressed the king greatly. Under intense pressure from his son, favourite and subjects to join the Protestant side in the Thirty Years War, and thus help restore his daughter Elizabeth and son-in-law Frederick to the German Palatinate from which Catholic troops had expelled them three years earlier, James found Laud's exposition of Psalm 21: 6–7 most comfortable:

For Thou hast set him as blessings for ever: thou hast made him glad with the joy of thy countenance. Because the King trusteth in the Lord: and in the mercy of the most High he shall not miscarry.

Ever since King David's day, Laud argued, God had especially blessed monarchs who trusted in Him, and gave their people the bounty of peace.[4] Laud's first recorded venture into diplomatic affairs, his presence at the reception at the Parliament House on 14 April for Count Schwartzenburge, the imperial ambassador, could well have been an attempt to demonstrate his belief (and the king's) that Frederick and Elizabeth could best regain their lands peacefully through the intervention of the Holy Roman Emperor.

During his first few months as a bishop, Laud was far more interested in old feuds at home than in new wars abroad.

On 21 July 1621, whilst out hunting with his friend Lord Zouche at Bramshill Park, Archbishop Abbot accidentally shot and killed a game-keeper with his crossbow. Even though everyone agreed that it was entirely the dead man's fault, Abbot was desolate. He gave the widow an annual pension of £20 – on the strength of which she promptly remarried – and retired to his birthplace, Guildford, talking of giving all his property to charity. Abbot's enemies were far more interested in the future of his office. Prompted by the primate's independence, his moderate Calvinism, and opposition to joining the Thirty Years War, as well as the usual jockeying for place and endemic feuding, they tried to strip the archbishop of his office. Three days after the accident Lord Keeper Williams advised the king that according to common law a primate guilty of manslaughter must be suspended and his estate forfeited to the crown. In October James appointed a commission that included Williams, Laud, Andrewes and Buckeridge to look into the matter. Largely due to Andrewes's influence they recommended against taking any action.[5] Publicly Andrewes argued that if an Archbishop of Canterbury could be deprived of office for an accident then no bishop was safe. Privately he was afraid that Williams might step into the vacancy that would be created by hounding Abbot out of office. Laud, the most junior member of this commission of prelates and jurists, played little part in its deliberations, and may have gone along with Andrewes's arguments partly because he had a high opinion of episcopal office, and because he was beginning to realise that his new mentor, Williams, might become a much more dangerous threat than Abbot.

By a stroke of luck Oxford University provided the new Bishop of St David's with his first opportunity to make a name for himself with the government in London. On 14 April 1622, John Knight of Broadgates Hall preached a sermon at Oxford in which he argued in favour of killing tyrannical monarchs. James was outraged. The doctrine of tyrannicide terrified the king, who, having survived several attempts on his life, wore a padded waistcoat to protect him from an assassin's stiletto. He ordered Knight to be arrested, and his sermons to be seized and publicly burnt by the common hangman, and that students should stop arguing over the heretical doctrines of both the Jesuits and the Puritans.[6] In Oxford, London and Cambridge booksellers' shops were raided for works that advocated tyrannicide, and these were also consigned to the flames. 'May they commit murder with impunity?' demanded the king.[7] Since Laud had been the first to inform him of this 'treasonable sermon' and knew Oxford better than any bishop at court, James naturally called upon him to help draft the Directions to the Church which he sent to Archbishop Abbot on 4 August. Laud's influence was apparent in the covering letter the king sent to the prelate. 'At this present time divers young students do broach many times, unprofitable, unsound, seditious and dangerous doctrines to the scandal of the church and the disquiet of the present government,' wrote James. The bishop's hand is equally obvious in the accompanying Directions: all sermons must be based on the 1562 Articles of Religion or the official Book of Homilies, children must be taught the catechism, priests should neither engage in doctrinal disputes nor make 'indecent, railing speeches against either Papists or Puritans'. They must instead teach obedience to the crown and the established church. Order, obedience, conformity and hierarchy, all enforced on orders from above, were the hallmarks of the 1622 Directions.[8] Not only did they permit Laud to put his mark upon the church in a fashion permitted to few junior bishops in their first year in office, but they set the Church of England's agenda for the next two decades.

The Doctrines also marked the growing rift between Laud and Williams. The latter resented Laud's growing influence, and thought him far too intolerant. 'Show indulgence to the young ones, if they run into Error before they come to be settled,' urged the Lord Keeper about Knight, who had only just taken orders, for 'every apprentice is allowed to mar some work'.[9]

The first open breach between Laud and Williams involved the living at Crick, Northamptonshire, which Sir William Craven had given to St John's in 1613 to be held by the senior fellow of the college. Whilst president Laud had appropriated it for his own benefit – an offence which in later, more prosperous years he found intolerable in others – and was upset when Williams, in his capacity as Lord Keeper, ordered the college to surrender the rectory or 'show cause in a short and summary hearing'.[10]

As Laud moved away from Williams he entered the orbit of the king's favourite and the most powerful subject in the land – George Villiers, Marquis of Buckingham. Villiers came from a family of minor Leicester gentry. As the second son of a second marriage he had little inheritance beyond his good looks and ready charm. His mother sent him to France as an adolescent to acquire courtly manners and polish, and they were a great help when he returned to England. It is said that he first met James when the king was inspecting the kennels at Apethorpe House, Northamptonshire – an appropriate venue for a favourite who was to sign himself 'Your Majesty's most humble slave and dog'.[11] Soon afterwards the two became intimate at Farnham, Surrey.[12] Villiers's rise in the king's favour was so spectacular that one contemporary bitterly observed, 'No man danced, no man runs or jumps better, indeed he jumped higher than any other Englishman did in so short a time from private gentleman to dukedom.'[13] James made him his Master of the Horse and a viscount in 1616, Master of the Wardrobe and an earl in 1617, a marquis a year later, and a duke in 1623. Nothing seemed too much for the royal favourite. 'Christ had his John, and I my George,' James told the privy council with an honesty that was as refreshing as it was blasphemous.[14]

For an ambitious man Laud was surprisingly slow in attaching himself to Buckingham. Even though the king had publicly compared the favourite to the apostle Jesus most loved as early as October 1617, apparently Laud made no overtures to him. To a man with all the bishop's latent fears, Buckingham's blatant homosexuality might have been particularly disturbing. Youthful charm and academic gravitas rarely have much in common. Moreover, until Laud broke with Williams, he and Buckingham were in different political camps, the latter, for instance, having campaigned against Williams's appointment as Lord Keeper.[15] Two events brought them together. The first was the Declaration of August 1622, which Laud helped draft at the king's command. Since Buckingham was acting as the king's chief minister, naturally he worked closely with one of the architects of royal religious policies.[16] Secondly, by 1622 Buckingham was far more concerned about the state of his mother's religious future than that of his nation. After her third marriage, to Sir Thomas Compton, Mary Villiers came under the influence of Catholic missionaries, and was on the verge of converting to Rome. The prospect horrified Williams, who warned Buckingham of the political dangers of such a step. So on April 23, the king sent for Laud and told him to instruct Mary Villiers in the truth of the Anglican faith and the errors of Rome by debating with the Jesuit Father John Fisher. On May 10 Laud travelled to Greenwich in a carriage, in which he returned closeted with Buckingham. Nine days later Laud sent him a set of papers defining the differences between the doctrines of the Church of England and those of Rome. On May 23 he had his first interview with Mary Villiers, and the following day started the debate with Father Fisher before Buckingham and his mother. 'I had much speech with her after,' Laud wrote in his diary, which suggests that the king wanted him to have far more than the last word.[17] If his arguments had little effect on Mary Villiers, they moved her son greatly. 'My Lord Marquis

Buckingham was pleased to enter upon a near respect to me,' Laud noted on 9 June. 'The particulars are not for paper.' Two days later he confided to his diary, 'I became Confessor to my Lord Buckingham.'[18] On 16 June Laud gave him Holy Communion at Greenwich. Almost immediately, however, another, equally important pastoral obligation interrupted their growing intimacy, for a fortnight later (and seven and a half months after being consecrated as Bishop of St David's) Laud finally had to leave London for the land of his episcopal obligations.

Wales was a remote place of exile, its valleys having kept a cold welcome for the ambitions of many an English churchman. Laud crossed the border on 5 July, arriving at Brecon on the 9th to preach at the college. A fortnight later he reached St David's, where he gave several more sermons. At their first meeting he reproached the Dean and Chapter for letting the cathedral fall into a deplorable condition, and ordered the clerk to keep safely all the chapter's decrees, leases and correspondence. After dismissing the local schoolmaster as 'insufficient', Laud moved on to Carmarthen, forty-six miles to the east, where the bishop had his palace.[19] He furnished the house, donating communion plate worth £158. 8s. 4d. to the new chapel which he built for the incumbent's use. He sent his chancellor and commissioners to inspect the parishes. They visited Tenby on 16 and 17 July, and Haverfordwest on the 19th and 20th. He issued them with a set of 113 questions, based on Archbishop Abbot's 1616 articles, with variations he personally wrote in: Had the parish a bible? a prayer book? a font? 'a decent and convenient communion table'? 'a comely pulpit'? 'a fair communion cup'? 'a register book in parchment'? and so on.[20] Whether or not all these questions had any effect is hard to say, for the bishop's register has been lost. But Laud was in St David's for only six weeks, far too short a period for any of the seed he had scattered to take root and flourish. He left Carmarthen on 15 August and hurried home to England, where the Lord had, he believed, a far more important harvest for him to reap.

On 1 September Laud held his second major disputation with the Jesuit Father Fisher at Windsor, debating with him before the king and Prince Charles, as well as Buckingham, his wife and mother. Laud was well prepared for the confrontation, having borrowed books on the Reformation and the dissolution of the monasteries from Sir Robert Cotton's library, a resource widely used by seventeenth-century disputants.[21] Cotton owed Laud a favour, for Laud had allowed him the unique privilege of borrowing a manuscript from the library of St John's.[22] Obviously Laud acquitted himself well during this debate, for even though Mary Villiers eventually went over to Rome, the king thought his arguments a strong enough defence of the established church to merit publication.

James, who loved public debates — as king he invariably won them —

worked closely with Laud in setting the agenda for the conference with Fisher. The king gave him nine questions to ask the Jesuit, and they had three long discussions about Catholic theology at Christmas 1622, and another extended one the following February. Like the Hampton Court Conference of 1604, when James tried to reconcile Puritans and Presbyterians to the established church, the Fisher debate was the sort of discussion that the king relished. In addition it did much to lessen James's long-standing distrust of Laud, while bringing the bishop far closer to the Duke of Buckingham.

Together with Laud's two earliest published sermons, the first preached on the king's birthday in 1621, and the second on the anniversary of his accession a year later, *A Relation of the Conference between W. Laud and Mr Fisher, the Jesuite* forms the core of his theology, and provides an invaluable insight into his thought, particularly at the start of his political career. As he was trying to use his position as a bishop to exercise a wider power, he was forced to pause in order to crystallise his ideas.

Laud, of course, only published at the king's command. His publications were all official statements, the work of an ambitious middle-aged churchman striving to win the king's favour by preaching or debating to order. Laud's printed works could well be a biased sample of his overall religous thinking, for they do not include the many hundreds of conventional sermons that he delivered at weddings, burials, christenings, in college chapels, at cathedral services, or to his friends and servants at their private devotions. For instance, his published pronouncements lack the homely turn of phrase and the devotional intensity found in his private papers.

In spite of the limited and probably distorted nature of his printed work, Laud was a theologian of no mean worth. Even Sir Edward Dering, a critic, had to concede that 'His book against the Jesuit will be his lasting epitaph'.[23] Laud's learning was extensive; his arguments were rigorous and exhaustive – sometimes, indeed, exhausting. Other pedants, led by the king, applauded, for Laud managed to popularise with his text, as he overwhelmed with his references. He was not an original thinker, but drew largely from the works of others, such as Bishops Andrewes, Montagu, Bilson and Bancroft. For example, he took his arguments against the Council of Trent straight from Bishop John Jewel's *Apologia pro Ecclesia Anglicana*. He was a traditional Anglican, who managed to encapsulate mainstream thinking while moving it decidedly to the right.

This process is evident in the four influences that helped shape Laud's theology.[24] The first two were traditional. Laud frequently referred to the early Christian Fathers, and particularly to St Thomas Aquinas, borrowing many of their concepts and expressions. The second two were reactive. Calvinism influenced Laud because he spent so much of his time opposing it. Arminianism did so to a lesser extent, since he may be described as an Arminian more because of his rejection of predestination than because of his acceptance of the teachings of Jacobus Arminius. For this reason he demanded that the accusation by Theophilus Buckworth, Bishop of Drummore, that 'I had set up men to maintain Arminianism', should be punished as a 'contempt of falsehood and vanity'.[25]

Laud's published theology focused largely on the relations between the Church of England and other groups – the Catholic Church, the crown, Puritans, and the people. This is not surprising, since the main objective of Laud's conference with Fisher was not to convert Mary Villiers to Christianity, but to keep her within one particular church. Thus Laud's theology has little to do with faith, or even an individual's relations to his or her Maker. He ignored these subjects not just because they were inappropriate for an official theological statement, but because he considered them far too personal to discuss in public. Even in his private devotions Laud was reserved. He could not consciously admit the depth of his passion for God. Only in his dreams was he ever able to do so completely. On 30 January 1624 he wrote in his diary, 'Sunday night. My dream of my Blessed Lord and Saviour, Jesus Christ. One of the most comfortable passages that ever I had in my life.'[26]

His dry, restrained, even pedantic style was, of course, well suited to a public debate on the merits of the established church. To argue that all Catholics were wicked and condemned to eternal hellfire would carry little conviction with his sophisticated courtly audience. Thus Laud had to approach the split between Rome and Canterbury more in sorrow than in anger. He called the Reformation 'this miserable rent in the Church of Christ – which I think no true Christian can look upon but with a bleeding heart'.[27] On the other hand, the Church of England was not to blame for this unhappy schism: 'He makes the separation that gives the first just cause of it, not he that makes an actual separation upon a just cause proceeding.'[28] Such sentiments were bound to please the king, who always had a strong leaning towards Protestant ecumenicalism.[29]

Once he accepted – reluctantly – the divisions within Christianity, Laud had to answer the question of how they might be rendered legitimate, since mending them through reunification was obviously impossible. 'The Roman Church and the Church of England'. Laud asserted, 'are but two distinct members of that Catholic Church which is spread all over the face of the Earth', and which the Nicene Creed called the 'one Holy Catholic Church'.[30] It consisted of several churches, including the Greek Orthodox Church, which all shared the fundamental teachings that the Nicene Creed laid down – in God, in Christ as His son and their saviour, in baptism, the Eucharist and the Bible.[31] 'Scripture is the ground of our belief', concluded Laud.[32]

The Church of Rome, he wrote, was 'a true church', not *the* true church.[33] It was only one branch of a universal Catholic church; although its members, like those of all Christian churches who accepted certain basic beliefs, could be saved, it remained nonetheless a church in grievous error. Thus Laud opened his conference with Fisher by attacking the Roman doctrine of infallibility, which he argued was based on a completely false reading of the early fathers. The Papists were also wrong to worship images, such as the Blessed Virgin Mary and the saints, and to teach that the Mass transubstantiated the bread and wine literally into the body and blood of Christ. The essential cause of all these mistakes, Laud maintained, was the doctrine of papal infallibility. Rather than allowing one man, with a dubious connection to St Peter – and far more dubious predecessors – to rule as the Roman Church's supreme authority, that power should lie with a general council of bishops. Indeed, to let general councils have final authority would, Laud believed, hold out the best chance for eventual reunification.

Laud felt far more comfortable protecting his right flank than his left. At one level his theology was broadly based, and has much to say to modern Christians concerned with ecumenicalism. 'Thus I said, and thus I still say; for though the foundation be one and same in all, yet a "latitude" there is, and a large one too, when you consider not the foundation common to all, but things necessary to any particular man's salvation.'[34] So he could accept a faith as distinct as the Greek Orthodox Church as part of the universal church, and later did much to encourage studies in its theology. On the other hand there is no doubt that he found those faiths that were closer theologically to his own far harder to stomach, largely because they were also geographically nearer, and thus a much more immediate threat than the bearded priests and icons of the Levant. Hardly any Englishmen would take issue with Laud's assertion of the necessity of infant baptism, for in the 1620s Baptists, who believed in the total immersion of adults, were few and far between.[35] But when he told Mary Villiers that Catholics could go to heaven if they led a good life, Laud upset not only the rabid Puritans who were convinced that all Papists were damned, but also the majority of staunchly Protestant Englishmen who believed in the Calvinist doctrine of predestination.

He disliked those who stood to his theological left much more than those to his right, because they lacked discipline and order rather than than for their beliefs. Roman Catholics accepted a single, well-established dogma, an ecclesiastical hierarchy, and were not continually squabbling over doctrine or authority. If they disagreed with Laud, they rarely fought him or one another in public.

In contrast the bishop openly spurned the limited role that Calvin assigned to rationality in proving belief. 'Give even natural reason desire to come in, and make some proof,' urged Laud.[36] For instance, while he believed that scripture was fundamental, he also feared that it could be fractious. Most folk, he maintained, were 'too giddy', or 'too heady and shallow', to interpret scripture for themselves. Letting them do so would result in 'so many faiths and fancies, or no Christian Faith at all. From which evils, sweet Jesus, deliver us!'[37] Laud was also sure that the Church of England was the faith closest to that of the earliest Christians. 'Truth usually lies between two extremes,' he concluded as an old man in the Tower, 'and is beaten by both (as is the poor Church of England) as, at this day, by the papist and the separatists.'[38] Thus whilst Roman Catholics attached too little weight to scripture, and the Puritans too much, the Church of England had got the balance just right.[39]

Nowhere did the Church of England hold the middle ground more correctly than in its teaching about bishops. Although he liked the orderliness of the Catholic ranks of bishops, archbishops, cardinals and pope, he was ill at ease with their almost military chain of command. As a student he had accepted the Aristotelian idea of the universe as an organism in which the parts were interdependent and related in a hierarchical order. As a prelate he urged that bishops were an order separate and superior to the priesthood. They were a semi-aristocracy, who enjoyed rights inherent to their offices rather than ones bestowed upon them through royal appointment. On the other hand he found Calvin's teaching on bishops patently distasteful:

> Only this I will say, and abide by it, that the calling of bishop *jure divino*, by divine right, though not all adjunct to their calling. And this I say in direst opposition of the Church of Rome, as to the Puritan humour. And I say further, that from the apostles' time, in all ages, in all places, the Church of Christ is governed by bishops, and lay elders never heard of till Calvin's new fangled device at Geneva.

Laud in fact exaggerated when he asserted that bishops had ruled *jure divino*, spiritually at least, ever since the earliest days of the church. This was a fairly recent claim that emerged after the Reformation, becoming widely accepted in James's reign by many bishops, and in Charles's by most.[40] But during the latter reign it was a doctrine that drove a serious wedge within the Church of England between the bench of bishops and the rank and file who thought of themselves as Protestants plain and simple, and yet somehow chosen by the Almighty. As one commentator has pithily observed, 'In place of the Elect Nation Laud offered the Elect Church.'[41]

As the religious crisis worsened, the doctrine that bishops ruled by divine right complicated the relations between the Church of England and its supreme head, the king, who also ruled *jure divino*. Even though in theory the authority of bishops was spiritual and that of the king temporal, in practice the line between the two spheres was so blurred that it fostered a tension that was sometimes hidden, frequently ignored, but always there. If both king and bishops ruled by divine right what happened if they disagreed? The Almighty could not possibly take both sides at the same time. If the king was, as parliament (a secular, not ecclesiastical body) had enacted, head of the church, with the ultimate right to define doctrine and to appoint bishops, how then could bishops claim to be a separate order with powers that came from their office rather than from the man who gave them that office?

Laud tried to sidestep this dilemma in three theoretical ways, none of which he found ultimately, to his intense personal anguish, worked in practice. First, while denying that the monarch had any spiritual power, he accepted that he had power over spirituals, being able, for instance, to make laws regulating, and even suspending, the rights of bishops to exercise their spiritual authority within his dominions. 'For though our Office be from God and Christ immediately, yet we may not exercise that power,' Laud explained, 'but by and under the power of the king given us so to do.'[42] While in good times this was an intellectually satisfying argument, and thus was widely accepted, in bad ones its consequences could be particularly painful. It justified Abbot's suspension (of which Laud approved), as well as his own arrest and imprisonment (which he found especially hurtful).

Secondly by asserting that the coronation made the monarch 'an ecclesiastical person', Laud tried to co-opt the crown into the church.[43] But the coronation service – like the marriage service – was more a statement of pious hopes and good intentions than a personal metamorphosis. Afterwards kings – like newly-wed men and women (and even newly consecrated priests or bishops) – remained much the same fallible sort of folk that they had been before.

The bishop tried to wriggle out of this dilemma by using Richard Hooker's assertion that church and state should be as one and support each other – rather like husband and wife. This is like saying that the way to avoid divorce is to love each other. If church and state were in agreement, the fact that both were divinely appointed institutions did not cause conflict. But what would happen if the two fell out? Laud – like James – blurred his answer. 'The king is God's immediate lieutenant upon earth,' he preached, echoing the king's famous axiom, 'and therefore one and the same action is God's by ordinance and the king's by execution. And the power which resides in the King is not any assuming to himself, nor any gift from the people, but God's.'[44] Even though in the next world kings must render account to God for their stewardship in this world, they were obliged to

do so neither to their people nor – Laud was forced to admit – to their
bishops.

While Laud had an exalted opinion of prelates and princes, he demonstrated little faith in ordinary folk. 'None but God can "rule the raging of
the sea and the madness of the people," ' he maintained.[45] To avoid such
storms, he laid great stress on obtaining national unity, on peace abroad
as well as at home. 'Nor is he a Christian that would not unity, might he
have it with truth,' the bishop told Father Fisher.[46] 'The Church can have
no being but in the Commonwealth,' he preached in 1621, 'and the
Commonwealth can have no blessed and happy being but by the Church.'[47]
For the whole of his life Laud adhered to these public declarations,
repeating them in private letters to friends. 'I am heartily sorry and have
been since I was of any understanding of matters of religion to hear of
sides in the Church,' he told Sir Kenelm Digby in 1636.[48]

When Laud wrote to Digby in 1636 he was at the height of his power
– Archbishop of Canterbury and the king's minister and trusted religious
adviser. But when he debated with Father Fisher he was a very junior
bishop from a remote diocese. In writing his account of the conference,
Laud was able to define the theoretical bases for his actions before he
moved into a position of power where he could take political action. Rarely
does a statesman have such an opportunity. Writing ideas down forces one
to crystallise them, to tame the concepts that have been running wild in
one's mind. At least twice and at great length Laud argued with Fisher that
Divinity is a science based on fundamental principles.[49] Like all intellectuals
he wanted to get back to basics. By defining his terms he eschewed that
pragmatic fudging that so often allows statesmen to find consensus and
thus make the system work. However, putting ideas into print also tends
to fossilise them in the author's mind. Giving them form and order freezes
them within the confines of the printed page, making them hard to recon-
sider, particularly for someone who found the act of writing itself a painful
chore best not repeated. For example, in his confession Laud compared the
church to a beehive, in constant danger of being raided. Thus the king,
priests and bishops must unite to protect the church from those who would
steal its revenues, 'or else the bees shall make honey for others, and shall
have none left for their own necessary sustenance, and thus all is lost'.
Once in power Laud worked assiduously to protect the hive. In doing so
he was guided by two principles he advanced to Fisher. First, that while
the king could not abrogate laws, he could set aside their penalties, and,
secondly, that the bishops formed an aristocracy who had ruled the church
since its earliest days.[50]

The conference with Fisher, and its publication, were a poor preparation for Laud's political career in another important way. By trying to
prevent Mary Villiers from converting to Rome, he was protecting his right

flank, as it were. Thus he worked hard to find common ground with Roman Catholicism, admitting, for instance that Catholics could be saved and that they belonged to the universal church. In doing so he challenged a basic English shibboleth of English Protestantism, encapsulated in these lines by the poet Richard Crashaw:

> In sum, no longer shall our people hope
> To be a protestant is but to hate the pope.[51]

But in fact the main religious challenge to Laud came from the left, from that ill-defined group of Protestants whom he called Puritans.[52] One of their leading lights, Simonds D'Ewes, described Laud, after hearing him preach, as 'somewhat popish'.[53] In his public pronouncements the bishop failed to emphasise the points he had in common with the other members of the Church of England, such as believing in the use of the state to revive the church. Instead he stressed those items, such as the liturgy and ritual, which divided Anglicans. In doing so Laud unintentionally secularised much of the religious debate for the next two decades, during which hardly a whiff of heresy troubled the Church of England. Instead of disputes over dogma, it was rent with squabbles about symbolic matters as the prayer book, the placing of the altar, church ales or recreation on the sabbath. Because these disputes about the external trappings of religion developed into quarrels about discipline, they turned minor issues that during Elizabeth's reign had been ignored as irrelevant into fundamentals that brooked no compromise. In sum, by the time he entered the world of politics Laud had built his main theological armament. The problem was that his main intellectual weapons pointed in the wrong direction, and the consequences were catastrophic.

In comparison with the Protestants to his left, Laud saw himself as an orthodox moderate who stood firmly in the centre of a tradition which went directly back to Christ and the apostles.[54] Compared to his actual policies, his theology was remarkably tolerant, particularly towards those who stood on his religious right, which prompted others, invariably those on his left, to interpret the discrepancy as rank hypocrisy, particularly when they felt the sting of his tongue or the lash of his punishments. In truth, however, many of the most controversial elements of his theology came from recent developments at the universities. He never realised – or at least admitted – that Oxford was not England, and that Arminianism was actually an innovative reaction to the Calvinist orthodoxy that dominated the late Elizabethan church. His contradictions were, it must be admitted, consistent. For a man who disliked disruption, Laud was eager to disrupt. For someone who prized the unity of the individual with his king, God and fellow creatures, he pursued remarkably disruptive policies. For someone whose early career had on several occasions been rescued by secular intervention, he was particularly determined to maintain the integrity of the church. For a man whose university career had been fuelled by controversy, Laud had a strange distaste for public disputes. The publication of the conference with Fisher neatly illustrated the contradictions between his ideas and his actions. When James ordered the conference printed it first appeared in 1624 as an appendix to Francis White's *A Replie to the Jesuit Fisher's answere*, under the pseudonym 'R. B.', perhaps to divert attention to Richard Baylie, Laud's chaplain, for as he confessed to his diary, 'I am no controvertist'.[55] In practice, however, Laud's own summation of his theology was very different from the policies he pursued in trying to further his career.

Nowhere was this more true than at court. He preached at Westminster in October 1622, and January 1623, and at Whitehall the following March.[56] He continued to grow in favour with Buckingham. 'My Lord Buckingham and I in the inner chamber at York House,' he noted in his diary for 11 January 1623.[57] The next year James appointed both men to a committee to hear complaints about abuses of power.[58] While this committee, which the king had originally promised parliament two years earlier, never amounted to much, because it duplicated the courts of Star Chamber and Requests too closely, Laud and Buckingham continued to work well together. As the favourite's power grew to extend beyond the court and secular politics, he needed someone to advise him on church affairs. For this reason, as Edward Hyde, the contemporary historian, explained, Buckingham 'transplanted Laud out of his cold barren diocese of St. David's into a warm climate'.[59]

The occasion for this transition was a voyage to an equally sunny place. The journey of Prince Charles and Buckingham to Spain in 1623 was one of the most extraordinary incidents in the history of British diplomacy. After spending the summer in Madrid trying to court the King of Spain's sister, the pair returned to England in October to be welcomed by what Laud described as 'the greatest expressions of joy by all sorts of people that I ever saw'.[60]

Buckingham's decision to accompany Charles to Spain created a profound power vacuum in England; it set the established political order in turmoil. 'O most merciful God and gracious Father, the Prince had put himself to a great adventure,' Laud prayed; 'I humbly beseech thee to make a way clear before him: give thine Angels charge over him, be with him Thyself.'[61] The Spanish trip also marked the final breach between Williams and Buckingham. Initially the favourite resented the Lord Keeper's warnings about the political perils of leaving the realm in order to conduct a dubious, and unpopular mission: 'The Prince is in a great danger to suffer exceedingly in the Hearts and Affections of the people here at home, and your Lordship sure enough to share in the Obloquies.'[62] After he split with

Buckingham during the summer of 1623 over the conduct of negotiations in Madrid, Charles turned to the Lord Keeper to try and help him win support in England for the concessions he was making in Spain. So once the negotiations collapsed, and Buckingham and Charles were reconciled on the way back to England, Williams was left holding a baby whose paternity neither the favourite nor the heir to the throne was prepared to acknowledge. Buckingham had even more cause to destroy a dangerous rival, while Charles was as eager as ever to have someone else to blame for his own failures.

Years later Laud claimed to have acted as Buckingham's agent at court during his absence, and to have tried to thwart attempts by Williams, and Lionel Cranfield, the Earl of Middlesex and Lord Treasurer, to displace the duke in the king's favour. In fact Laud exaggerated his influence and loyalty. Of the forty batches of mail the royal party sent from Madrid to London only four contained letters for him.[63] Not until the return of Buckingham and Charles from Madrid, and the ensuing political struggle they had with the king, did Laud finally break with Williams to join Buckingham.

The Spanish trip altered the shape of English politics. Coming as it did on top of the outbreak of the Thirty Years War, it inflamed the fears of many Puritans. As they pressed the king to take action, James recoiled, veering to the right.[64] The journey to Madrid also confirmed the duke's hold over the prince, and set them both at odds with the ageing king. Originally Laud had supported James's pacific foreign policy, preaching before him at court in 1621 on the blessing of peace. But three days before Charles and Buckingham arrived back in England he quarrelled bitterly with Williams, 'whom I found had done me some very ill offices. And he was very jealous of Lord Buckingham's favour.'[65] Three weeks later Laud told the favourite of their row, which had so disturbed him that on the night of 14 December 'I did dream that the Lord Keeper was dead . . . his lower lip was infinitely swelled and fallen, and he rotten already. This dream did trouble me.'[66] Laud, who disliked confrontation while constantly seeking it, remained especially agitated and depressed. He recorded in his diary for 25 January 1622:

> It was Sunday. I was alone, and languishing with I know not what sadness. I was much concerned at the envy and undeserved hatred borne to me by the Lord Keeper. I took unto my hands the Greek Testament. That I might read the portion of this day. I lighted upon the xiii chapter to the Hebrews, wherein that of David, Psalm lvi, occurred to me thus grieving and fearing. 'The Lord is my helper: I will not fear what man can do unto me.' I thought an

example was set to me; and who is not safe under that shield?
Protect me, O Lord, my God.[67]

As Laud broke with Williams, and as Buckingham's hold over Charles
became well-nigh complete, the bishop moved into the prince's inner circle.
Now he felt he could do so because he approved of Charles's religious
views. Soon after returning from Spain, where he had served as Charles's
chaplain, Matthew Wren had a private conversation with Bishops Laud,
Andrewes and Neile, who were very concerned about the prince's religious
leanings. Wren reassured them that they had nothing to worry about:
Charles firmly supported Arminianism.[68]

Therefore by 1624 Laud was literally and figuratively close enough to
Charles to be able to stand behind his chair at dinner, and hear his conversation about the choice of a career. One thing he could never be was a
lawyer. ' "I cannot," saith he, "defend a bad, nor yield in a good cause," '
Laud noted. As the bishop added the pious hope 'May you ever hold this
resolution, and succeed (Most Serene Prince) in matters of greater moment,'
he little thought that a quarter-century but two days later Charles would
give his life defending the best cause that the two of them had ever known.[69]

But in early 1624 Laud's cause was far from sure. On 14 January, a
fortnight before the dinner, Williams defeated Buckingham in the privy
council by nine votes to three on a motion recommending war with Spain.
The duke was so angry that he strode up and down the chamber 'as a hen
that hath lost her brood'. He determined to use the parliament that he had
persuaded the king to call for 12 February 1624 to push James into war,
and to punish his own enemies.[70] As soon as it met, parliament was only
too happy to oblige by impeaching Lord Treasurer Cranfield. Taking heed
of the received wisdom that 'the Lord Treasurer cannot go without his
Keeper', Williams realised that his only hope of avoiding Cranfield's fate
was to endorse Charles and Buckingham's plans for a war. He tried to win
the pair's favour by revealing the Spanish ambassador's plot (which he had
discovered through one of the diplomat's mistresses) to turn the king against
the duke. All these machinations angered parliament greatly, adding to the
popular clamour for war with Papist Spain.

Laud's part in the 1624 parliament was curiously muted. He joined in
the anti-Spanish hysteria by calling for the disarming of English Catholics,
and the blocking of Milford Haven, the harbour in his diocese, against any
armada.[71] In the House of Lords he also supported the third reading of a
bill confirming Buckingham's title to York House, traditionally the London
residence of the Archbishop of York.

In other respects Laud was more solicitous of the church's economic
interests. In order to pay for a Spanish war, Convocation, the church's
parliament, assessed from itself four subsidies valued at four shillings in

the pound. Laud thought that this gigantic levy would cripple the poorer clergy, many of whom, he asserted, paid more taxes than the richest gentlemen in their counties. So he asked Buckingham to relieve the clergy of this excessive burden. When he told Neile and Williams of this request, they agreed that 'it was the best office that was done for the church this seven years'. Abbot's reaction was very different. He told Laud that he had no business meddling in matters that did not concern a junior bishop, and publicly declared that 'he had given the church a blow that he could never make whole again'. Once more Laud clashed openly and bitterly with his old enemy. But this time he was the up-and-coming prelate. He told Abbot that while he was sorry to have offended him, the poorest priests could not possibly pay three, let alone four, subsidies at one time. With his conscience clear and his enemies in rout, Laud concluded, 'so may God bless me his subject labouring under the pressure of them, who always wish me ill.' As a result of his stand, many in the church wished Laud well. Richard Montagu, Archdeacon of Hereford, wrote to his friend John Cosin, 'I hope to see him one day when he will both do and say for the church.'[72]

During this disagreement over clerical taxation Abbot had made the serious mistake of threatening to inform Buckingham of Laud's insubordination. Once the duke realised what the Bishop of St David's had done, argued the archbishop, he would never let him into his presence again. But Abbot miscalculated. He did not understand that Laud defended the minor clergy because he was now confident of the duke's support. Early in May Laud went to visit Buckingham, who was ill of a fever, having called constantly from his sickbed for his confessor.[73] On the 15th of that month in the House of Lords Laud defended his incapacitated mentor's conduct of the negotiations in Madrid, by maintaining that he had never done, nor could ever do, anything to hurt the Church of England.[74] The most convincing sign of their growing friendship came in June when Laud confided to Buckingham 'of my hard hap in my business with Lord Charles Devon', the scars of the Mountjoy marriage being still raw.[75] After spending the summer visiting the parishes of Crick, Northamptonshire, and Ibstock, Leicestershire, of which he was an absentee minister, Laud returned to London to help Buckingham. When the duke asked if he could dissolve the Charterhouse to use the charitable foundation's money to raise ten thousand troops Laud answered, 'It may be lawful for a state, in point of necessity, for public defence, to dissolve a society.'[76] After a two-week bout of fever Laud claimed his reward. Whilst flattering Buckingham by saying – quite incorrectly – that he had only become a bishop through 'your Grace's sole procurement', and warning that Abbot would do his utmost to frustrate him, Laud asked the duke to have him appointed to High Commission.[77] The duke readily obliged the friend with whom he loved talking about a host of arcane subjects ranging from witchcraft to astrology: the king made him a member of the court on 23 January 1625.

By now the king's health was rapidly declining. When he heard that his old crony the Marquis of Hamilton had died on 2 March 1625, James fell ill. After the royal doctors assured him that there was nothing seriously wrong, he recovered, only to relapse a few days later. He summoned his son and favourite for a final blessing, Bishop Williams gave him the last rites and the next day, 27 March, he died. Many were glad that the old, pathetic, worn-out monarch had gone, making way for a young man full of promise. At Cambridge, for instance, one observer tactfully noted that 'the joy of the people devoured their mourning'.[78]

But Laud's regret was quite genuine. He was preaching the Mid-Lent Sunday afternoon sermon at Whitehall to many members of the court, when he saw a look of anguish spread across the faces of the congregation. Realising the king must have passed away, he stopped the sermon in order, he claimed, to be better able to comfort the bereaved.[79] A few days later he wrote in his own hand a eulogy for 'our late dear and dread sovereign', in which he praised James's achievements as a young man ruling Scotland, his peaceful accession to the English throne, and his twenty-two-year reign, during which not a single peer had been executed – a pointed contrast to Tudor times. God had shown James his especial favour by saving him from several assassination attempts, including the Gunpowder Plot. In return James had been a good Christian, the best defender the church had known for many a year, and an excellent father to his son. He ended an exemplary life by achieving 'so strong a death'.[80] Although Laud may have exceeded that generous artistic licence granted to the writers of eulogies – the old king had in fact died badly in his own vomit, pus and excrement – he looked back on James's reign with sincere regret. But Laud had little time for mourning. Two days after he had penned the eulogy for the old king, Buckingham asked him to draw up a list of churchmen whom the new monarch might promote, with 'O' for orthodox or 'P' for Puritan beside each name. Almost at once the die for the new reign was cast.

IV

'A cloud arising'

On 9 April 1625, a fortnight after James's death, and four days after drawing up the list of churchmen, Laud wrote in his diary:

> Saturday. The Duke of Buckingham, whom upon all accounts I am bound for ever to honour signified that a certain person, moved through I know not what envy, had blackened my name with his Majesty King Charles laying hold for that purpose of the error into which, by I know not what fate, I had formerly fallen in the business of Charles, Earl of Devonshire. . . . The same day I received a command to go to the Right Reverend the Bishop of Winchester, and learn from him what he would have done in the cause of the church.[1]

In this rather cryptic diary entry are discernible three of the themes that were to characterise Laud's rise over the next eight years, during which he gained a pre-eminence in both church and state that few Englishmen have enjoyed before or since.

The first theme was the need to retain the king's favour in the face of accusations that Laud was overly ambitious, such as that old but still most galling charge touching the Mountjoy marriage, or the accusation that Laud was 'popishly affected' which Henry Burton sent the king a few weeks later. Since Charles dismissed Burton, who had been Clerk of the Closet when he was Prince of Wales, the Bishop of St David's received a clear sign of the new monarch's support.[2]

The second theme apparent in the diary entry was Laud's dependence on Buckingham. During the first three years of the new reign Laud was more the duke's man than he was the king's. Buckingham exerted a far greater influence over Charles, a much weaker character, than he ever had over James. The favourite committed England to a long series of expensive military adventures, first against Spain, and then against France. When they failed through bad leadership, bad planning and bad luck, Buckingham and Charles had to return to parliament to ask for new taxes to pay for further hare-brained escapades. Parliament refused, and by trying to impeach the duke precipitated a constitutional crisis.

Against this political background of botched offensives, addled parliaments, and widespread distrust developed the third theme, that of the rise of the Arminians. As the diary entry shows, Buckingham sent Laud to ask the advice of Lancelot Andrewes, Bishop of Winchester, one of the church's wisest elder statesmen. If Andrewes was not as close a mentor as Neile (whom Burton also accused of being popishly inclined), it was quite clear that the new administration believed that the Arminian wing of the Anglican Church was now the orthodox one. Over the next three years Arminians moved out of the universities into the centre of national affairs through a series of *causes célèbres*. While this process frightened Laud, who at times supported his more radical allies with a distinct reluctance, it enhanced his own power by discrediting his opponents in the king's eyes.

Nonetheless, for the first eight years of the new reign, as Laud's power increased his fears waxed and his health waned. As he confessed in 1626, after the Montagu case propelled him and his Arminian circle out of the relatively safe waters of Oxford University into the stormy seas of national controversy: 'Methinks I see a cloud arising and threatening the Church of England. God of his mercy dissipate it.'[3]

For many people the most obvious and immediate cloud threatening the commonwealth was the Duke of Buckingham. They thought that his hold on the new king was virtually complete. It was as if Charles had let another succeed to the throne as he would have done had his elder brother, Prince Henry (who was nearly the same age as Buckingham), not died in 1612.

Sensing the changes in the political winds, Laud had shifted his loyalties from Williams to Buckingham, well aware that the new king did not like his father's Lord Keeper, who had advised him that legally he could not continue the old parliament but must hold elections for a new one. This rift delighted Buckingham because (as Williams's friend and biographer John Hacket put it) he 'loved not that anyone should stick too long in a place of greatness'.[4] The split between his old mentor and new sovereign also benefited Laud: Buckingham not only appointed him his confessor, but gave him complete power over the church patronage that he controlled.[5]

While Laud's rise had been due to Buckingham's favour, in the first two years of the new reign no one thought of him as one of the king's intimates.[6] In many respects this is surprising, for Charles and Laud had much in common, sharing, for instance, a love for order, hierarchy and decorum.[7]

The bishop may even have felt James's death more deeply than did his son, for as we have seen he composed a moving eulogy for the late monarch.[8] A few weeks later, whilst trying to adjust to the bereavement, Laud noted in his diary: 'in my sleep His Majesty, King James, appeared to me. I saw him passing by swiftly. He was of a pleasant and serene countenance. In passing he saw me, beckoned to me, smiled, and was immediately withdrawn from my sight.'[9]

Although Laud did not officiate at James's funeral, he almost certainly took part in the massive procession of some nine thousand people which took more than an hour to walk from Somerset House in the Strand to Westminster Abbey. If he heard the two-hour sermon that Williams preached eulogising the late king, the chagrin he surely felt on listening to his rival's wit and erudition must have been balanced by the pleasure he derived from Williams's tactless allusion to Moses's stutter, for the new monarch suffered from such a speech impediment. On balance it is unlikely that Laud enjoyed the ceremony. 'All was performed with great magnificence,' an observer noted, 'but the order was very confused and disorderly.'[10]

Magnificent confusion! James was buried as he had lived – and in a fashion that Laud and Charles were determined should continue for not a moment longer than necessary.

The opening of parliament gave both men the chance to call a new tune. Even though the speech that Charles, who stuttered badly, gave to both houses was short and hesitant, the sermon that Laud preached on 19 June in the Chapel Royal in Whitehall came through loud and clear: 'The king is God's immediate lieutenant upon earth,' he began. 'And the power which resides in the king is not any assuming to himself, nor any gift from the people, but God's.' He went on to tell the members of parliament that 'All judges and courts of justice, even this great congregation . . . receive influence and power from the king.' Anticipating the absolutism of Louis XIV, Laud declared, 'The king is the sun. He draws up some vapours, some support, some supply from us. It is true; he must do so. For if the sun draws no vapours it can pour down no rain.'[11] With his characteristic concern for unity, Laud told the congregation that if they did not accept the divine right of kings then the whole order of the cosmos would be shattered: take but degree away and discord would certainly follow.

Many members of parliament did not agree. They felt that Laud's brand of divinely sanctioned obedience would end in military adventures abroad and papism at home. So the Commons refused to vote taxes for the former and spent much of their time angrily debating the growth of the latter, until the king forced them to adjourn to Oxford, purportedly because of an outbreak of plague in London.

Adjourning parliament did little to stop the plague and nothing to quiet people's religious fears, and if anything the case of Richard Montagu, Archdeacon of Hereford and vicar of Stanford Rivers, Essex, exacerbated the latter.[12] In 1622 Montagu came across some Catholic missionary tracts which he felt impelled to answer with the curiously entitled broadsheet *A*

Gagg for the New Gospell? No a new Gagg for the Old Goose. Montagu's tone angered his enemies, who, he charged, 'prate so much and perform so little'. He upset the Calvinists who dominated the established church, by pointing out – quite correctly – that neither the 1595 Lambeth Articles nor the 1604 Hampton Court Conference committed Canterbury to Geneva. Worse still, many Calvinists believed that the new gag Montagu had devised for the Papists allowed them to say far too much. He failed to make the obligatory condemnation of the pope as the Antichrist, and by narrowing the doctrinal differences between the English and Roman churches opened the possibility that the Whore of Babylon might not be utterly beyond redemption. Such whiffs of popery alarmed the most sensitive Puritan nostrils. Thomas Yates, fellow of Emmanuel College, Cambridge, and Samuel Ward, a radical preacher from Ipswich, petitioned parliament to ban Montagu's diatribe. They referred the matter to Archbishop Abbot, who gently chided the author, 'Be of no scandal or offence. Go home, review your book.'[13]

Montagu went home and wrote a second book, *Appello Caesarem.* Perhaps he chose this title because the last time he had presented a copy of his writings to James I, the king had declared, 'If this be popery, then I am a Papist.' Most members of parliament did not agree, and after Henry Sherfield called Montagu's works 'very dangerous and seditious', they ordered the rector to appear before the House of Commons. On 7 July a Commons committee condemned Montagu for insulting parliament and the king, and for sowing religious dissension. But before they could agree upon a punishment, Charles announced that Montagu was a royal chaplain, and thus exempt from any parliamentary censure.

The Montagu affair helped turn Arminianism from a subject of donnish disputes confined mostly to the universities, into the cause of a schism that swept the realm.[14] James had tried to nip the problem in the bud in 1617 by enjoining the heads of the Cambridge colleges that 'no such seed grow in the university'. Two years later he attacked Arminianism through the delegation he sent to the Synod of Dort in Holland. Thus Arminianism developed a vaguely anti-monarchical tinge.

Montagu changed all that. By playing on James's fears, he convinced the king that the Puritans were really subversives who wanted to destroy the religious *via media* the King had favoured since coming to England. By appealing to Caesar, Montagu associated Arminianism in many Englishmen's minds with authoritarian kingship. By positing that Catholicism might not be utterly evil, he handcuffed Arminianism to Rome. Such, at least, was the opinion of its opponents. But most Arminians defined themselves not as being sympathetic to Catholicism, but as being adamantly opposed to the Calvinistic doctrine of predestination.[15]

Initially Laud played little part in the Montagu affair. It had been the radicals from the left who first brought *A Gagg for the New Gospell?* to public attention. There is no evidence that Laud took advantage of Abbot's embarrassing failure to quiet the controversy when it first started. In parliament Neile did far more to defend Montagu than Laud, who never rose to speak on his behalf. The controversy frightened the bishop, who after the session ended went for a holiday, staying with his old friend and former student Francis Windebank at his country house in Hurst, near Reading.

But Charles would not let his bishops duck the issue. In response to royal pressure, Laud, Buckeridge and Howson of Oxford certified to Buckingham on 2 August 1625 that Montagu 'is a very good scholar and right honest man; a man everyway able to do God, his Majesty, and the Church of England great service'. Thus the Commons must not be allowed to persecute him.[16] They went on to say that Queen Elizabeth and King James had quite plainly established that only the monarch and the Convocation of the Church of England had the right to discuss religion, it was no business of parliament.

Three days after signing this letter, with no excuse left to keep him in Oxford, the new Bishop of St David's started the arduous journey to Wales, reaching Brecon on 21 August. Here he preached on Sunday, spending the next couple of days 'very busy'. The sixty-mile journey across some very rugged country to the bishop's palace at Abergwili, just outside Carmarthen, was especially tiresome. On the second day his coach turned over twice, once with Laud inside.

On arriving at Abergwili, Laud's first official act was to consecrate the chapel he had ordered built at the palace for the bishop's use. He had paid for it out of his own pocket, and designed it to resemble an Oxford chapel, naming it in honour of St John the Baptist 'in grateful remembrance' of his old college. He wrote a special service of consecration in Latin, not English, which appealed to his love of the classics whilst not offending the susceptibilities of his flock, most of whom spoke only Welsh. This inability to communicate with his people was perhaps one of the few advantages that being a Welsh bishop offered Laud. He immediately advertised that his chapel was open for the ordination of suitable candidates for the ministry. Only one young man turned up, and he was woefully unqualified. Laud spent several days in the nearby market town of Carmarthen, where he preached to the assize judges. On 10 October, 'I went on horseback up to the mountains. It was a very bright day for the time of year, and so warm that on our return I and my company dined in the open air at a place called Pente Cragg.'[17]

It was as if the bishop were taking a well-earned rest after the two months he had spent working hard trying to put his diocese in order. But compared to his previous visit the records of his episcopal activity in 1625 are slight, which might be explained by the fact that during the late summer and early autumn Laud seems to have been experiencing a great deal of personal strain.[18]

Even before he left for Wales Laud fell, 'I know not how', badly injuring his shoulder and hip.[19] Since he had lived for several years in the president's rooms at St John's he must have been familiar with their layout, and can hardly have tripped over a step. Could he have fainted due to some emotional reason? If the dreams Laud noted are anything to go by, he was without doubt an exceedingly worried man. Whilst still in England he dreamed that Lady Buckingham had a row with her husband, and might have miscarried. In Brecon he dreamt of going to bed with the duke. A fortnight later, on 4 September, 'I was very much troubled in my dreams. My imagination ran altogether upon the Duke of Buckingham, his servants and family. All seemed to be out of order; that the Duchess was ill, called for her maids and took to her bed. God grant better things.' A week later he had two nightmares one after the other. In the first he imagined that his protégé Dr Thomas Price 'was ungrateful to me'. In the second he dreamed that Sir Sackville Crowe, a Gentleman of the Bedchamber, had died, 'having not long before been with the king'. The latter dream must have been particularly painful, for it came only weeks after he had dreamed about Charles's death, and only months after James had actually passed away. Two weeks afterwards Laud recorded another set of dreams. The first involved a marriage 'of I know not whom at Oxford', while in the second John Thornborough, Bishop of Worcester, appeared with head and shoulders covered in white linen, and offered to meet him at Ludlow.

Laud's waking life and nocturnal anxieties reflected one another. On the evening of 28 August, after consecrating St John's Chapel at Abergwili, he had a premonition that he had done so on the anniversary of the Baptist's beheading. He rushed to look it up, and was disappointed to find that the anniversary was on the morrow, until he remembered that 28 August was an even more auspicious day, for it was then, fourteen years earlier, that James had heard the disputed election to the presidency of St John's and had 'with great justice delivered me out of the hands of my powerful enemies'.[20]

What all this anxiety means one cannot say for sure, except that it reveals Laud as a man worried to the point of neurosis. In Wales he was particularly concerned about falling victim to implacable enemies. Three of the dreams touched upon his mentor, one involved a marriage (surely a remembrance of the painful Mountjoy affair), two touched upon death, one even that of the king, while Bishop Thornborough could well have been wearing a shroud. Could it be that Laud felt uneasy about his own relations with Buckingham? A bachelor, uncomfortable with women, as Buckingham's confessor Laud could not have been unaware of the nature of the favourite's relations with James. Could the ensuing dream which emphasised the duke's heterosexual activities as a father and husband have been a form of unconscious compensation?

Whatever the reasons for the bishop's emotional concerns about Buckingham, he certainly had good political reasons to be worried. On 12 August Charles dissolved parliament to save his friend from the Commons' wrath. Laud was afraid that his enemies – who were far more numerous in his fears than in actuality – might use his absence in Wales to poison the king's mind against him. In fact the opposite happened. On 25 October the king dismissed Williams as Lord Keeper, ordering him to surrender the great seal, symbol of that ancient office, to Sir John Suckling, the Controller of the Household, and an officer so insignificant that none failed to recognise the slight. As the Venetian ambassador noted, Laud's great rival fell because 'he ventured to speak and advise the king contrary to Buckingham's advice':[21]

Cheered by the news of Williams's downfall, Laud set out for England on 11 November. He stayed with his friend Sir John Scudamore at Holme Lacy, Herefordshire, for several days, before going on to Francis Windebank's house for a few weeks. He moved to Hampton Court for the New Year, before returning to the prebend's house at Westminster, into which he had finally moved, having had to surrender the rooms he normally occupied at Bishop Neile's London seat, Durham House, to the French ambassador. It was a sign of Laud's growing independence from his old Oxford patrons that for the first time in his career he now had a house of his own in the capital.

In London the political climate was deteriorating, less because of the activities of religious radicals such as Montagu than because of the failure of the Cadiz expedition. Unable to blame the king personally for this military débâcle, loyal subjects had to seek scapegoats and explanations, which they quite naturally sought in religious terms. Notwithstanding Laud's royally commissioned prayer, 'Lord, turn our enemies' sword into their own bosom', the attack on Cadiz ended in a disgraceful rout, when the British landing force looted the main Spanish naval wine stores and got vilely drunk.[22]

In contrast the assault on the Church of England took place in a far more sober fashion at Westminster Abbey, York House, and within the Houses of Parliament.

The prevalence of the plague and the refusal of Henrietta Maria, the French princess whom Charles had married in May 1625, to take part in a Protestant ceremony, delayed the coronation for over a year. It was a ritual that meant much to the new king, who on New Year's Day 1626 appointed a commission that included Laud and Abbot to draft plans for the ceremony. Laud did much of the commission's work; he had a private audience with the king on 18 January to discuss the service, and five days

later presented him with a book outlining the details. Charles was adamant
– and Laud surely delighted – that Williams was to play no part in what
would in many ways be the most important day in the king's life. He
ordered Williams to nominate one of the prebends of Westminster to take
his place as dean. Rather than suggest Laud, the obvious candidate,
Williams sent the king a list of all the prebends to choose from.[23]

To no one's surprise Charles selected Laud to play the part traditionally
given to the Dean of Westminster. At ten in the morning of 2 February
1626 he welcomed the king as he entered the Abbey's great west gate, and
presented him with Edward the Confessor's staff. He was one of the bishops
who accompanied the king to the throne. After the five-hour ceremony,
during which Abbot anointed the king and placed the crown upon his
head, and Bishop Senhouse of Carlisle preached a sermon on the uncannily
prophetic text 'Be faithful unto death and I will give you the crown of life',
Laud offered Charles the coronation regalia, which he accepted before
returning them to the Abbey's safekeeping. For the king it had been a
moving day, the memory of which would motivate him until the moment
of his death. For Laud it had been a perfect one: the plague was over; he
had played a part far beyond that of a junior bishop by administering the
communion wine to the king. With rare satisfaction that evening he noted
in his diary that never had he seen a ceremony 'performed with so little
noise and so great order'.[24]

Having played so prominent a part in the coronation Laud and his
religious allies were sure of the king's support in the debate over Montagu's
writings that began eight days later at York House, the Duke of Buckingham's London residence. It was held at the request of two leading
Puritan peers, the Earl of Warwick and Lord Saye and Sele. At the opening
session Dr John Preston, Master of Emmanuel College, Cambridge, and
Bishop Thomas Morton of Lichfield attacked Montagu's writings as being
Catholic. Lord Saye and Sele and Sir Edward Coke urged the Church of
England to accept the Calvinist doctrines laid down at the Synod of Dort.
'No! No!' Buckingham cried out, 'away with it, we have nothing to do with
that synod.' When the conference reassembled on 17 February it was quite
clear that Buckingham had come out in favour of the Arminian position.

The York House conference has been seen as a pivotal event in which
the crown committed itself reluctantly to Arminianism. In fact, the meeting
was much more of a charade than a conversion.[25] There was absolutely no
chance that Buckingham could have convinced Charles – who in most
other respects was putty in the favourite's hands – to change his faith. A
month before the conference the king had commissioned Bishops Neile,
Andrewes, Buckeridge, Laud and Montaigne of London to examine
Montagu's works. Not surprisingly this packed committee wholeheartedly
endorsed the rector's views as being completely compatible with those of

the Church of England, recommending that the king order all further debate on the matter ended. 'Go to His Majesty's gracious favour,' the commission advised Montagu. Surely they were buoyed up by the secret conversation that Laud, Neile and Andrewes had reputedly had two years earlier with Matthew Wren, Prince Charles's chaplain in Madrid, who assured them that the prince was far more committed to their religious viewpoint than was his father. Because of Calvinism's emphasis on individuality and personal faith, its disregard for order and deference towards authority, and its disinterest in either harmonious worship or the beauty of holiness, it is hard to see how that faith could have had much appeal for Charles, even as a young man. Certainly as he grew older he never displayed the slightest interest in the concept of predestination; his faith in the certain salvation of kings was as confident as Rubens's portrayal of James's accession into heaven on the ceiling of the Whitehall banqueting hall. In sum, then, the York House Conference changed neither Charles's nor Buckingham's faith, but rather brought their religious views into greater prominence at a time when parliament was increasingly concerned about the growth of Catholicism.[26]

The king and his advisers had recognised that the moment parliament met, the outcry against the spread of popery would reach fortissimo. In early January Charles commissioned Laud to give the sermon at the opening of parliament on 6 February, and may have selected the text, Psalm 122:2–3, 'Jerusalem is like a city that is at unity in itself.' Laud told the members of both houses that while neither church nor state could flourish without the other, at present the relationship between the two was badly askew. 'The time is now come,' the bishop maintained, 'that the civil courts are much too strong for the ecclesiastical.' He attacked Calvinism by arguing that its doctrine that 'no bishops, no governors, but a parochial consistory to govern the Church, defied Christ's teaching', and was thus against 'monarchy in the state'. Few in the congregation could have failed to be reminded of King James's adage: 'no bishops: no kings'. After telling them that God had first given King David complete legal and judicial power, Laud ended his provocative homily with the conciliatory hope 'that the king and his people may now, and at all times, meet in love, consult in wisdom, manage their council with temper, entertain no private business to make the public suffer'.[27]

The bishop's long sermon had little effect, except, possibly, to further irritate the House of Commons. Even though on 10 February Sir John Eliot vituperatively blamed Buckingham for the fiasco at Cadiz – 'our honour is ruined, our ships are sunk, our men perished, not by the sword, not by the enemy, not by chance, but by those we trust' – the first weeks of the 1626 parliament were remarkably placid. 'Our Parliament talks much, but does little,' the London letter writer John Chamberlain noted on 7 March.[28]

Perhaps Chamberlain was thinking of Laud's defence of the king's arrest of the Earl of Arundel delivered to the House of Lords, which one modern authority has described as 'one of the most foolish speeches of a long career'.[29] Nonetheless Laud shared Chamberlain's view that very little had been accomplished. 'We are in a very busy parliament, and yet we have sat six weeks and I cannot give you any account what we have done,' Laud wrote to Scudamore on 18 March. 'There is nothing yet come to any issue.'[30]

The letter which Laud wrote to Scudamore a week later showed how quickly and drastically parliament's mood changed. 'I hold you a very lucky man that you be not at this time a member of the House,' he told his friend. 'I doubt much if things go on a fortnight longer in the course they are now in, that all will be stark naught. So bad indeed that it is not fit for me to write what I think.'[31]

Three things had produced this massive deterioration: first, the king's desperate need for money, and the Commons' reluctance to vote taxes; second, an attempt to impeach Buckingham; and third, the exacerbation of religious controversy by the sermon which Bishop Goodman of Gloucester preached to the Convocation of the Church of England on the first Sunday in Lent.

Goodman was not a controversialist who loved the cut-and-thrust of debate. Neither was he an Arminian. On the contrary he was, as a contemporary put it, 'a harmless man that was hurtful to himself'. Without fully thinking of the consequences the Bishop of Gloucester delivered a discussion of transubstantiation which came perilously close to the Catholic interpretation of that divisive subject. Responding to public protests, Charles referred the sermon to a committee consisting of Abbot, Andrewes and Laud, who reported that Goodman had advocated nothing contrary to the doctrines of the Church of England. To demonstrate their support they recommended that he be invited to preach before the king to elaborate upon his arguments and confound his critics. Laud, not Abbot, delivered the committee's report to the king, which clearly reflected his and Andrewes's views – and Abbot's decline. As one Cambridge don observed sardonically, 'the archbishop is sick of political gout'.[32]

In return for his support, Charles insisted that the bishops protect Buckingham in the House of Lords. On the afternoon of 22 April he summoned fourteen of them, including Laud, to reprimand the Lords for not doing enough to save the favourite. Telling them to 'follow the directions of our consciences', he left them in no doubt as to which way their consciences should point.[33] Laud did not respond to the challenge by speaking in the upper chamber (for although he was a good preacher he was a poor debater). Instead he drafted speeches for the king's use urging the Commons not to delay in voting taxes whilst the Thirty Years War raged on the Continent.[34]

As his irritation with the Commons increased, so Charles's support for the duke and his Arminian allies grew. On 1 June, following the death of the Earl of Suffolk, he forced Cambridge University to elect Buckingham as its new chancellor. The election was as close and nasty as had been Laud's to the presidency of St John's fifteen years earlier. The Head of Clare Hall drove one fellow from his sickbed to vote for the duke, who just won by 108 votes to 103.[35] Neither the narrowness of the victory nor the brutal fashion in which it was obtained diminished the king's joy or the duke's gratitude.[36] Laud promptly used both to try and improve discipline at the university, an endeavour that many Puritans found far from appealing. According to Simonds D'Ewes the 'Arminian party', whom he defined as 'the enemies of God's grace and providence', had elected Buckingham.[37]

Victory at Cambridge did not avert defeat in Westminster. 'For Parliament business we are in as hot skirmishes as ever we were, and for my part I cannot look for my good end,' Laud wrote to Scudamore on 10 June.[38] The end came quickly – and badly – five days later. After rejecting a request from the Lords for more time with a curt 'Not a minute,' Charles sent parliament packing on 15 June.

Laud played little part in the 1626 parliament. His attempt, hours before its dismissal, to try and improve relations between the Lords and Commons was an indication of his lack of influence at Westminster. But his role in defending Goodman, and helping Buckingham get elected chancellor, showed the extent of his influence in the royal councils at Whitehall. This was apparent in the declaration Charles issued on 17 June explaining his reasons for dissolving parliament. By declaring he would not tolerate 'the least innovations in the Doctrines and Discipline of the Church', the king clearly sided with the Arminians, whom he called 'his sober, Religious and well-affected subjects'.[39] Three days later he nominated Laud to the lucrative diocese of Bath and Wells (which he let him hold *in commendam* with the well-paid prebend's stall at Westminster), and asked him to preach at court the following 15 July.[40] As his text Laud selected Psalm 74:22, 'Arise, O God, maintain thy cause', telling the congregation how lucky they were to have such a monarch as Charles, who kept one eye raised to heaven and the other down upon his subjects. Far from being offended, this image of omnipotence (modified by a pronounced squint) delighted the king, whom the preacher assured, 'Your merit, and nobleness of your heart will glue the hearts of your people to you.' Charles promptly ordered the sermon printed.[41]

The little man had won. 'Arminianism is grown so famous,' lamented the Earl of Norwich, 'the whole world had gone Arminian.'[42]

As was so often the case with Laud's career, disappointment soon soured the sweetness of success. Two weeks after his formal election to the bishopric he admitted to Scudamore that while he had been anxious to 'fasten on to any indifferent thing to get out of Wales', he had just heard that Winchester had fallen open on the death of Lancelot Andrewes. 'But now, as God hath disposed of business, it is likely to prove my hindrance. For being so lately preferred, I know not how in modesty to be a present suitor again.'[43] Laud's reactions to Andrewes's death were complex. While there is no doubt that part of him mourned the passing of 'the most worthy Bishop of Winchester, the great light of the Christian World', another side almost wished that Andrewes had vacated his office a few months earlier so he could enjoy it. Being compensated with Andrewes's position as Dean of the Chapel Royal was but a paltry morsel.[44]

Although Laud intended visiting Bath even before he was formally elected, there is no firm evidence that he ever set foot in his diocese as bishop.[45] In fact the main influence he exerted there came a decade later when as Archbishop of Canterbury he raged against many of the same offences that he had committed during his tenure at Bath and Wells.[46] In October 1627, for instance, he dismissed Walter Bushell from the keepership of the palace, notwithstanding a memo he had previously written arguing that such a termination was dubious legally. The previous April Laud leased Buckland Manor for three lives, and three months before Compton Dando at the ludicrously low rental of £2 a year, even though later from Canterbury he was to condemn such exploitation of church resources.[47]

Charles had not, of course, appointed Laud to Bath and Wells to improve the diocesan finances or minister to its people. The promotion was for services past and future, the most important of which was to 'tune the pulpit' by using the church and its considerable influence to bolster the government's policies.[48]

It was quite obvious that some preachers were playing particularly cacophonous tunes. Peter Smart, a prebend of Durham, on 27 July 1628 from the cathedral pulpit called the altar 'a damnable idol', and all those who bowed before it 'spiritual fornicators'. For good measure he added that bishops were 'Rome's bastardly brood, still doting on their mother, the painted harlot of Rome', and defined an Arminian as an 'arch-heretic and enemy of God'. Laud's friend John Cosin sent him a copy of the sermon with the warning that there had been 'a great noise about it, and tongues begin to wag'. (He added the equally painful intelligence that their mutual friend Dr Augustine Lindsell had just passed twenty-one stones which had nearly 'stoned him to death'.) Laud dragged Smart before Star Chamber, which fined him £400, confiscated his church livings, and imprisoned him during the king's pleasure.[49]

The bishop was quite convinced that it was agitators such as Smart who had done so much to bring about that 'breach of Unity which is grown so great and common among all sort of men', and which the king's September 1626 injunctions to the clergy tried to curb. Drafted by Laud, approved by the privy council and issued in the king's name, these injunctions stressed the ideal:

> Church and State are so nearly united together that they may seem to be two bodies, yet in some relations they may be accounted but as one in as much as they are both made up of the same men which are differenced only in relation to Spiritual and civil ends. This nearness makes the Church call on the help of the State to succor and support her, whensoever she is pressed beyond her strength. And the same nearness makes the Church call in the help of the State, both to teach that duty which her members know not, and to exhort them to, and encourage them in the duty that they know.[50]

This passage is worth quoting at length because it shows clearly the view of church–state relations which Laud and Charles shared, and for which both of them, in part at least, died. Charles liked Laud's draft so much that on 2 October he let him know through Buckingham that he intended making him his next Archbishop of Canterbury.[51]

In the meantime, because Abbot stubbornly refused to die, Laud had to be content with the deanship of the Chapel Royal. If it did not pay as well as Canterbury, and certainly lacked its prestige, it did at least bring its incumbent into regular contact with the king. Whenever King James had entered the chapel the dean had to stop the service, no matter what point it had reached, and start a brief anthem to give the preacher time to reach the pulpit to deliver the sermon, the only part of the office that interested James. Laud objected to this practice, telling the new king that it was disorderly, that it put too much emphasis on preaching, and that it denigrated the liturgy. Charles not only agreed but thanked his new dean for correcting his errors; for the good of his soul the king did not want to feel too comfortable in the presence of his confessor.[52]

In February 1627 Robert Sibthorp, vicar of Brackley, Northamptonshire, preached a sermon at the county assizes that discomforted his allies while angering his enemies. He told the judges that the king could do 'whatsoever pleaseth him. Where the word of the King is there is power.' Alluding to the current attempt to collect a forced loan to make up for the taxes that parliament had refused to sanction, Sibthorp argued 'That if a prince impose an immoderate, yea even an unjust tax, yet the subject may not, thereupon withdraw his obedience and duty.' This sermon might have remained no more than the unrecorded rantings of an ultra-Royalist rustic had not William Murray asked Archbishop Abbot to approve its publication. But since William Murray was the nephew of Thomas, the king's old tutor, he may have been setting an ambush for the archbishop. Heartened by the tide of anti-Catholic feeling caused by the recent discovery of a secret conclave of Jesuits in Clerkenwell, Abbot refused to license the sermon. Most likely at Murray's request, Charles intervened by inviting the country vicar to preach at court.[53] In this sermon Sibthorp declared that 'The King is not bound to observe the Laws of the Realm concerning the Subjects' rights and Liberties', and that anyone who disagreed did so 'upon pain of eternal damnation'.[54] Charles told Laud, Neile, Buckeridge and Howson to read the sermon to see if it should be printed. They asked Abbot for his objections and Montagu for his advice, and spurned the former by taking the latter's advice and recommending its publication.[55] After it appeared under the provocative title *Apostolic Obedience*, Charles made Laud and Neile privy councillors as a special mark of his favour.

In October Abbot's enemies persuaded the king to suspend the archbishop and to commission Laud, Neile, Buckeridge and Howson to carry out his duties. The fallen primate was bitter. Principally he blamed Buckingham, who had, he maintained, grown so powerful that by now 'all the keys of England hung at his girdle'. He went on to hint that somehow the king was responsible for his downfall.[56] While it was difficult for any seventeenth-century Englishman – even a disgraced archbishop – to blame an anointed sovereign (especially after he had done the anointing in God's name), Charles's actions in the Manwaring case suggest that, once he decided to get rid of Abbot, he, not his adviser, was the moving force behind the vendetta.

Even Laud felt that Dr Roger Manwaring, rector of St Giles-in-the-Fields, had gone too far when he twice preached at court that anyone who did not obey the king, for instance, by refusing to pay the forced loan, was surely damned eternally. Laud opposed the printing of these sermons because they 'would be very distasteful to the people'. Charles did not agree (or else did not care), and ordered their publication under the title *Religion and Allegiance*.[57] Afterwards Laud and his friends had no doubts about the margin of their victory over Abbot. As Peter Heylyn crowed, it 'did so disanimate and deject the opposition Party, that the balance began visibly to turn to the Church's side'.[58]

Although Laud was delighted to be rid of Abbot (he was reportedly the first bishop to sign the order of suspension, for his more senior colleagues shrank from endorsing this traumatic step), the Sibthorp affair worried him deeply, particularly before it became clear which way the king would turn. This anxiety may explain the rash of dreams that the bishop noted in his diary in early 1627 – that his dead mother returned to stand by his bed, that Williams chased him on horseback through the night, that he saw his dead friend Sir George Wright, and that he was reconciled to

Rome.[59] As always Laud hated to start a controversy – which might explain why, once he believed that he had been forced to join it, he fought with great ferocity and gave little quarter. And after he had won the good fight, his mental condition, both awake and asleep, improved greatly: in April the king made him a privy councillor; in May Charles promised to elevate him to London after Montaigne vacated the bishopric; in July Laud wrote to Scudamore, 'I am in good health, though I have much ado with a tedious journey.'[60]

The journey to which Laud alluded was the expedition to the Ile de Ré, off La Rochelle, where Louis XIII was besieging his rebellious Huguenot subjects. The English government had assembled a large fleet of a hundred ships carrying seven thousand troops to restore Frederick and Elizabeth to the German territories from which the Catholic powers had expelled them eight years before. Neither the king nor the duke ever really explained how fighting off the Atlantic coast would affect events in central Europe. Eschewing geography they put their trust in theology by asking Laud to compose a special prayer for the expedition's success.

While Buckingham was trying to cope with the malignant effects of the French, the weather, and his own incompetence, Laud remained in London attempting to fill in for him. In August he annotated the draft of the king's reply to Sir John Suckling's petition objecting to the new statutes for Norwich Cathedral, and handled Bishop Theophilus Field's request to be transferred to a better-paying diocese than St David's.[61] 'My Lord,' Field wrote to Buckingham, 'I am grown an old man, and like old household stuff, yet to be broken in oft moving. I desire it then but one for all be it Ely, or Bath and Wells; and I will spend the remainder of my days Writing a History of your Good deeds.'[62] Laud responded to this charming jobbery by suggesting that Field be allowed to hold another living in addition to St David's. He forwarded to the king the report from Sir Dudley Carleton, British ambassador to the Netherlands, that English and Scots ministers there were not using the proper form of worship; Charles replied that he was 'much troubled' by the news, and wanted Carleton to persuade the Dutch authorities to stop the practice.[63]

People were starting to realise that the Bishop of Bath and Wells was now a person of consequence. In August, for instance, the Mayor of Wells wrote to him about Martin Lucas, a Dunkirk pirate, who had escaped from the town prison – a matter which would normally have been the Secretary of State's responsibility.

In much the same way, the bishop would not normally have been concerned with the complaint of James Harrington, a fellow of Wadham College, Oxford, who wrote telling him that the warden was punishing him unfairly. Not unexpectedly Laud sided with authority, for university discipline was an interest that came naturally to him.[64]

In August 1627 in the king's name he commanded the vice-chancellor and heads of college at Cambridge to send him copies of all orders they had issued since 1558. This fiat greatly irritated Cambridge, particularly as the university had just made him an honorary Master of Arts.[65]

Oxford was far less hostile to the intrusions of one of its own sons. In April 1628 a disputed proctors' election went to the king, who referred the matter to Laud. On his recommendation Charles instructed the Chancellor of Oxford, the Earl of Pembroke, that the old system was 'a nursery and seed plot of faction and contention', and should be replaced by a new formula wherein the proctors rotated amongst the colleges on a twenty-two-year cycle. Since the injunctions that were sent to Oxford, and which the university promptly adopted on New Year's Eve, were written in Laud's hand there can be no doubt about their true authorship.[66] The bishop was able to persuade Charles to reform the universities for two reasons. First, the king believed that the Church of England could never flourish unless academic discipline was taut enough to produce first-rate ministers. Second, in Buckingham's absence Laud was at court more often and had greater access to the king. Serving His Majesty was not, however, without its pains. At Hampton Court Laud pulled a muscle, and was in agony for several days until the king ordered him out of bed to come to Newmarket: 'I made an hard shift, not without pain and some danger, to wait upon his Majesty.'[67]

After Buckingham's return from France in utter defeat the king needed Laud more than ever. Of the eight thousand men who had sailed from England with the Bishop of Bath and Wells's prayers for their safe return, the duke brought home only three thousand – and a thousand of them were too feeble to walk ashore.[68] The public were outraged. One person called it 'the most shamefulest overthrow the English have received since we lost Normandy'. Another, whose anger obviously outran his poetic talents, wrote:

> And now, just God! I heartily pray,
> That thou wilt take that slime away.
> That keeps my Sovereign's eye from viewing,
> The things that will be our undoing.[69]

But unlike the vast majority of his subjects Charles did not blame Buckingham for the fiasco. Instead the two tried frantically to raise money for yet another invasion of France, appointing Laud to a Blue Ribbon committee to study ways of doing so, and to prepare for the forthcoming parliamentary session.

As usual Laud did not play much of a role in Charles's third parliament, in spite of the fact that Abbot, on the king's orders, had surrendered his proxy to him. He was a poor parliamentarian, being inclined to preach too long and too loftily for most members' tastes. Sure that his motives were of the highest Laud was incapable of descending to the give-and-take that successful parliamentary management demands. Although he tried to prepare himself for the coming session by studying parliamentary history and procedures, his homework did nothing to divert members' wrath away from the Arminians.

The new parliament started much as had the old ones – with high hopes, lofty words, and an elevated sermon. Laud preached on Ephesians 4: 3, 'Endeavouring to keep the unity of the Spirit in the bond of peace', stressing the familiar refrain: 'Unity, then, both in Church and common-wealth, is so good that none but the worst break it, and even they are so far ashamed of the break that they must seem holier than the rest.'[70] The description of those who opposed the king's wishes as rank hypocrites redeemed only by a grudging realisation of their own duplicity so pleased Charles that he ordered it printed. 'These times are for action,' he sternly told both houses, 'not tedious consultations.'[71]

Initially parliament seemed to heed Charles's threats and Laud's warn-ings, particularly after the government started to persecute recusants with unusual vigour. Always inspired by a little Papist-bashing, the backbenchers voted the king five subsidies. It was said that when Charles heard that they had been passed unanimously, he wept for joy.[72] His happiness quickly evaporated as the Commons turned their attention to the duke. Even before the start of the session Laud had anticipated such a shift in a memorandum he wrote opposing calling parliament in the first place. They would never, he wrote, vote taxes, 'which are due by the law of God, nature and the nation' without demanding something in return. 'Thus the powers of the Crown are parted with, and the Prerogative diminished.' He was also worried that the Commons would question the right of church courts to decide what he believed were ecclesiastical matters.[73] While in a second memorandum, written a few weeks later, Laud seemed to have accepted the king's decision to call a parliament, he warned against accepting its constitutional pretension by writing a long historical analysis of Magna Carta. Far from being a seminal document, he argued, the charter 'had an obscure birth by usurpation, and was fostered and showed to the world by rebellion'. Because Edward III had confirmed Magna Carta in November 1359, the king could with equal ease revoke it whenever he pleased, and his people must vote him taxes 'freely' and 'without dispute'.[74]

This view did nothing to endear Laud or his allies to the Commons. Even before members voted the five subsidies, they complained about the licensing of Montagu's and Sibthorp's sermons. On 28 April Sir Benjamin Rudyerd told the Commons that Magna Carta should be reissued to remind people that the king had no right to imprison people without trial. In

private Laud reacted to this speech by noting on his own copy that the
important thing was for people to trust the king and his advisers.[75]

The painful truth was that by the early summer of 1628 few members
of parliament fully trusted the king's ministers, particularly in matters of
religion, which the crown tried to declare out of bounds for public debate.
When Arminianism was first raised in the Commons, one member asked,
'How can we make Laws and not debate religion?' At the time the most
important law that parliament was trying to make was the Petition of
Right. Although religion was not one of the four major grievances the
petition tried to address, it was a major component of the political climate
that produced the passage of the petition on 7 June 1628. Laud joined
with the other bishops in urging the king to assent to the petition with the
traditional Norman-French phrase, 'Le roi le veult', and so leave no doubt
as to its legality.[76] Nonetheless, immediately after the wild celebrations that
greeted its passage, the Commons turned their attention to religion. On 9
June they censured Roger Manwaring for preaching that those who
opposed the forced loan (a chief grievance of the petition) would burn for
ever in hell, even though Laud testified that the king had ordered the Bishop
of London to license the publication of the offending sermon.[77] Soon
afterwards the Commons passed a remonstrance condemning the growth
of papism and Arminianism and Buckingham's incompetence, sentenced
Manwaring to be fined £1,000, to acknowledge his faults, and be
imprisoned during His Majesty's pleasure. Two days later they sent a
deputation to the king asking him to have the common hangman publicly
burn Manwaring's books.

Instead of turning to his executioner, Charles resorted to his Bishop
of Bath and Wells, who advised against accepting the argument, first raised
by the Commons in their remonstrance of 11 June, that ministers should
be punished for royal policies that did not work, because to do so would
mean that no honest man would dare advise the crown frankly for fear
of retribution. The bishop firmly rejected parliament's contentions that
recusancy was on the increase, or that Arminianism was but 'a cunning
way to bring in popery'. Charles agreed. On 28 June he adjourned parliament and announced he would pay the fines of all whom the Commons
had imprisoned. The following month he formally pardoned Manwaring,
and gave him the living of Stanford Rivers, Essex, just vacated by
Montagu's promotion to the bishopric of Chichester.

Even though a strained hamstring prevented Laud from attending the
first week, the 1628 parliament taught him a great deal.[78] In anticipation
of the session he had drawn up a set of political theories which questioned
the validity not just of Magna Carta, but of parliament itself: all the latter
was good for was causing trouble, prejudicing the royal prerogative, and
meddling with the church – none of which, he maintained, could be justified

by the Great Charter, which in fact quite clearly guaranteed the church's privileges. The parliamentary session confirmed Laud's view that his and the church's, even society's, survival lay not with the Commons at Westminster but in the crown in Whitehall. As his good friend Bishop Richard Corbet so aptly put it:

> His Majesty may wonder more to see
> Some that will be king as well as he.
> A sad presage of danger to the land,
> When lower gain the upper hand,
> When Prince and Peers to Peasants must obey,
> When Laymen must their Teachers teach the way.[79]

V

'Nothing but trouble and danger'

Whatever may have been Charles I's faults, lack of loyalty to those who flattered him could not be counted amongst them. A few months after Richard Corbet warned of the dangers of social anarchy, Charles made the poet Bishop of Oxford. Neither did the king forget Laud's loyal services, nor the fact that the Commons had bitterly attacked him and Neile on 11 June 1628 as notorious Arminians (there were few better ways of winning royal favour than incurring the Commons' opprobrium). Thus on 2 July, a week after the king adjourned parliament, he appointed Laud Bishop of London. The move perturbed Laud, for although the promotion pleased him (the two previous Archbishops of Canterbury had been promoted from London), he was concerned for the future. 'God make it happy,' he wrote in his diary, 'for I expect nothing but trouble and danger.'[1]

Charles was anxious to have a loyal prelate installed as Bishop of London, and he personally ordered Secretary of State Conway to complete the paperwork without delay.[2] He thought that Laud's predecessor, George Montaigne, had been 'a man inactive' and 'one that loved his ease too well to disturb himself with the concernments of the church'.[3] Strangely enough John Milton agreed with this judgment, describing Montaigne as 'a canary sucking and swan eating prelate'.[4] Montaigne, whose greatest historical achievement may well have been getting Charles and Milton to agree on something – if only his own incompetence – also demonstrated the workings of seventeenth-century ecclesiastical promotions. In order to make vacant the important see of London, the king had to make Montaigne Archbishop of York, because he refused to accept the diocese of Durham, which, though venerable, was junior to London. That the king was willing to pay a high price to obtain Laud's services in London made the new bishop's power obvious to all. As Richard Montagu noted, 'My Lord of London can do what he will.'[5]

On taking over as Bishop of London Laud immediately instituted a visitation of his diocese. He sent commissioners out to all the parishes armed with a list of 123 questions which left no stone unturned. They asked about preaching, church attendance, recusancy, the position of the altar, the keeping of parish records, witchcraft, drunkenness, and even the supervision of widows and surgeons – the former being apparently as great a threat to men's morals as the latter were to their health.[6] Even though Montaigne had conducted a similarly comprehensive visitation the previous year, when some 84 per cent of the parishes had replied before the deadline, Laud prosecuted more clergymen for Nonconformity and neglect of duty in his first year than Montaigne had in the whole of his seven-year tenure.[7] The new bishop paid especial attention to Essex, which was, in his eyes, a hotbed of Puritanism. Of the ministers patronised by the Barrington and Masham families, five were suspended, one investigated, and eleven forced to flee abroad. An imprisoned minister complained, 'Now is the time come when not myself, but all of my judgment are cast out as men utterly unprofitable and unfit to God.' Roger Williams agreed; as he escaped to Massachusetts he wrote, 'It was a death to me when Bishop Laud pursued me out of this land, and my conscience was persuaded against the national church, and ceremonies and bishops.' In December 1630, the same month that Williams sailed for Boston, John Humphrey, Deputy Governor of Massachusetts, concluded that in England 'The Bishop of London hath silenced many godly men of late.'[8]

While Laud was able to harry several leading Puritans out of Essex, elsewhere in his diocese he was less effective. For instance, he and his staff managed to question but eighteen of London's seventy lecturers, only one of whom they forced to leave the city. As usual Laud focused on the details, about which the visitation reports provide a great deal of information. In 1632 he tried to reform the system of censorship by ordering the Stationers' Company to stamp his imprimatur on all books printed in London. Even though the Stationers complied, these restrictions failed to prevent the appearance of seditious works.[9] When the Lord Mayor of London issued a set of instructions for the better keeping of the sabbath (a goal which Laud warmly supported), he endorsed his copy of the edict with the words 'My jurisdiction is encroached.'[10] This attitude did not help the implementation of the privy council's order that the Lord Mayor and the Bishop of London should work together to enforce the proclamations against the eating of meat in taverns on Wednesdays and Fridays.[11] The bishop and the City quarrelled over trivial matters, such as the prosecution of a woman for selling apples on the sabbath.[12] Equally ineffective was Laud's own order that mothers who murdered their babies should not be allowed to pass them off as stillborn at the inquest.[13]

In sum, Laud's activities as Bishop of London anticipated his record as Archbishop of Canterbury. For the first time in his career he was able to carry out his ecclesiastical duties while remaining in the capital, able to serve the king politically – although he did take a couple of months off in the summer of 1631 (when governmental business slackened) to travel around his diocese and visit the clergy.[14] As Bishop of London Laud angered many people without producing any substantial long-term results. He fulminated, yet he rarely created. He stood on his dignity, but all too often he ended up appearing undignified. Take, for instance, the consecration of the church of St Katherine Cree in London on 17 January 1631. As a minion proclaimed, 'Open, open ye everlasting doors that the King of Glory may come in,' the west door swung open to reveal a short, red-faced little man who, constantly bowing and throwing handfuls of dust in the air, strode with as much dignity as was possible under the circumstances up to the high altar. According to a widely circulated and believed report, he ritually cursed all who might profane the newly consecrated church and blessed those who helped rebuild it, whilst the congregation cried 'Amen! Amen!' After preaching a sermon, Laud bowed several more times to the altar, then lifted the napkin from the communion bread, which he licked, before bowing thrice and blessing the wine.[15]

During Laud's first few months as Bishop of London national politics were building up to a crescendo, which climaxed with the assassination of the Duke of Buckingham in August 1628. During the summer of 1628, following the passage of the Petition of Right, the dismissal of parliament and the realisation that the king would do nothing about Buckingham, England seemed to seethe with frustration. A London mob murdered Dr Lambe, the duke's physician, as he walked home from the theatre, vowing that the next time they would get his notorious patient. There was a riot in Carmarthenshire over the duke, who was widely rumoured to be bedevilled with a nosebleed so violent that not even the Lord Keeper's mace placed across his neck could stop it. The ghost of Buckingham's father was reported to have been seen walking the battlements of Windsor Castle warning of the dangerous drift of affairs, which John Rous, the diarist, thought had 'caused men's minds to be incensed, to race and project'.[16] Even Buckingham recognised the perils of his situation. Taking Laud aside, he implored him to see that the king looked after his widow and children. When the bishop asked what was the matter, the duke replied that he was convinced someone would try to kill him.[17] He was not, however, troubled enough to wear the padded jerkin that many of his friends had begged him to use. Thus on 23 August John Felton, a discontented army officer, was easily able to stab Buckingham to the heart when he came down for breakfast at Captain Norton's house in Portsmouth high street.

Even though the overwhelming majority of Englishmen hailed Felton as a hero, the murder of his patron upset Laud deeply. The two men had been drawn together by the attraction of opposites. Buckingham admired the bishop's stolid respectability, Laud liked the duke's flamboyant charm, and perhaps there was a latent sexual attraction between them. Three days afterwards Laud called his friend's murder 'the saddest accident that ever befell me, and should be to all good Christians'.[18] He believed that in drinking Felton's health Alexander Gill, usher of St Paul's School, was devoid of 'all humanity'.[19] He wrote to the Dutch theologian Dionysius Vossius that he was sure that his patron had gone directly to heaven.[20] He told Scudamore that Buckingham's death was 'the saddest news that I ever heard in my life . . . I have passed a great deal of heaviness, yet I have cause to expect more to come.' The crime made Laud question his own political, and even physical, survival: 'Now the court seems new to me, for I mean to turn a new Leaf in it for all those things that are changeable.'[21]

While Laud's diagnosis was correct, his fears were groundless, for the duke's death marked a turning point in Charles's reign from which the bishop benefited greatly. According to one story, three days after the favourite's murder Charles assured Laud that 'He looks upon him now as his Principal Minister.'[22] The bishop won the king's gratitude by rushing to console Lady Buckingham, for he and Charles were among the few men in the land to mourn the duke's death sincerely. The king did not, however, make Laud or anyone else his prime minister, for as Anthony Weldon, the contemporary historian, astutely recognised, 'After [Buckingham's] death the very name of favourite died with him, none singly engrossing the king's care and favour, but a regular motion was set to all officers.'[23]

During the following decade three themes characterised royal government. First Charles was not an active monarch. Rather than deal with the minutiae of government he preferred to spend his time with his wife and her mainly Catholic friends, and in collecting art and patronising drama. The king's withdrawal into the little world of the court upset many of his ministers, who complained about the lack of direction from above. Laud agreed with Sir Francis Windebank's complaint: 'The truth is that you pull down as fast with one hand as you build up with the other. What appearance can there be of success when you fix upon nothing?'

The second theme that emerged following the removal of the favourite who had virtually monopolised politics for a decade, was the rapid growth of factions. The most important one centred around Sir Richard Weston, the Earl of Portland and Chancellor of the Exchequer, who advocated a pro-Spanish foreign policy. A second group, led by Henry Rich, the Earl of Holland, and strongly linked to Queen Henrietta Maria and her recusant friends, favoured a pro-French foreign policy. Last, and least powerful, there was Laud and later Sir Thomas Wentworth. While Laud and Wentworth had few political allies, the duke's removal may well have helped in the long run, by allowing Laud to become more his own man, and also by thwarting a possible move against the Arminian faction. Just before he was murdered Buckingham confessed to Dudley Carleton that he was determined 'to walk new ways, but upon old grounds and maxims, both of religion and policy, finding his own judgment to have been misled by account of his youth and persuasion of some person he began better to know'.[24]

The third theme, which took longer to develop, was the departmentalisation of royal government and the growth of spheres of ministerial responsibility. Each of the king's ministers had fairly clearly delineated portfolios, the details of which Charles left to them whilst setting – or more often drifting into – major policy decisions. This form of government increased Laud's powers, for his portfolio, basically religion and education, was broader and more unambiguous than most, and one in which the king took an active interest.

The fundamental shift in royal government from the dominance of the favourite to what has often been called the personal rule did not take place immediately, but evolved over several months, being confirmed by the breakdown in March 1629 of the king's relations with parliament. The process started in late August 1628, when Charles reacted to his favourite's death by ordering the expedition that Buckingham was to have led to set sail for the relief of La Rochelle under the command of Robert Bertie, Earl of Lindsey. He also ordered Laud to see that prayers for the expedition's success were said in every church in the land, a request that the bishop had to decline by pointing out that only the Archbishop of Canterbury had such a national jurisdiction. But neither Laud's private devotions nor Abbot's public promulgations were a match for Lindsey's incompetence. Unable to relieve La Rochelle, the fleet returned home in disgrace.

Once again military failure dictated the calling of parliament. The king and his ministers recognised that the Commons were bound to demand the redress of their grievances before voting taxes, so they tried to mend as many political fences as possible. Much to Laud's annoyance the king invited Abbot back to privy council meetings, and received him with great public favour at Whitehall. He also withdrew his support for Montagu's divisive polemic, *Appello Caesarem*, and appointed the Calvinist Provost of Queen's College, Oxford, Barnabas Potter, as Bishop of Carlisle. While such concessions doubtless worried Laud, he went along with the tactics adopted by the privy council in December 1628, conceding to any attacks that parliament might make against recusants while holding firm against those on Arminians.

Assaults against both were launched in the second week of the 1629 session. On 30 January the Commons attacked Papists as 'an open enemy' and Arminianism as 'a subtle and more dangerous underminer of the religion of Almighty God'.[25] Laud was an obvious target for parliamentary wrath. Even though on 3 February Sir Humphrey May, Chancellor of the Duchy of Lancaster, told the Commons that both Laud and Neile had 'on their knees and with tears in their eyes' assured the privy council that they were not Arminians, few believed the testimony of this royal appointee, for the very good reason that such flamboyant gestures were utterly out of keeping with Laud's character. If they were not Arminians as Jacobus Arminius might have defined that term, they certainly were according to the lights of many of their contemporaries. So the attacks on the Bishop of London continued. The Commons criticised him for 'the licensing of bad books', which John Selden called 'a crime'. Three weeks later they passed a set of articles on religion which castigated Laud as one who 'hindered the preferment of them that are orthodox, and favoured such as are contrary'.[26]

Because the king failed to adhere to the agreed tactic of giving ground to parliamentary attacks on recusants while resisting those against Arminians, and kept on adjourning sessions from week to week, the Commons' unhappiness with the crown's religious and financial policies grew during the late winter of 1629, climaxing in the famous fracas of 2 March. As Black Rod hammered on the door demanding admission in the king's name to announce that His Majesty had ordered parliament adjourned for yet another week, and as Benjamin Valentine and Denzil Holles held the Speaker in his throne so the session could continue, Sir John Eliot introduced a resolution condemning all Arminians, together with those who paid taxes contrary to the Petition of Right, as capital enemies of the state. Once Eliot's motion was passed, the Speaker was allowed to leave his chair, and the chamber doors were unlocked to let the members go home, before closing again, this time, many thought, for ever.

These shocking scenes greatly angered the king, who leapt to Laud and Neile's defence. 'There is a very great wrong done to two Eminent Persons who attend our Person,' he told the House of Lords on 10 March.[27] Few believed him. Indeed, at a time when no loyal subjects could possibly blame the sovereign for the ills within the realm, other scapegoats had to be found. 'The hatred against the Lord Treasurer [Weston] and the Lord Bishop [Laud] increases,' the Venetian ambassador wrote home a couple of days later, 'they being the king's chief favourites.'[28] Seditious pamphlets castigated both men. One called all bishops 'spiritual dogs' who conspired in 'a treasonous and evil working for the popish infidels' church'.[29] Another, posted in front of the Dean of St Paul's house, warned: 'Laud, look to thyself, be assured thy life is sought, as thou art the fountain of all wickedness, repent thee of thy mountainous wickedness before thou be taken out of the world. And assure thyself neither God nor the world can endure such a vile counsellor or whisperer to live.' Laud took such threats very seriously, and spent months trying to discover the perpetrators.[30] After all, a mob had just murdered Dr Lambe, and a lunatic had stabbed Buckingham. 'Lord, I am a grievous sinner,' prayed the bishop, 'but I beseech Thee deliver my soul from them that hate me without a cause.'[31]

As the king's *de facto* minister of religion, Laud handled myriad public problems as well as his own personal concerns. At Charles's command he drafted new statutes for Norwich Cathedral and orders to be issued in Archbishop Abbot's name commanding all clergy to leave London and return to their livings unless required at court.[32] The king charged him with the collection of contributions for the relief of Huguenot refugees, and ministers who had left the Palatinate.[33] On 9 December he held the Bible as Charles swore to uphold the treaty with Spain, a 'peace disliked by everyone', as one ambassador noted.[34]

In return for his services Laud was able to influence the king. He had Matthew Wren, an Arminian ally, promoted, and persuaded Charles to allow Bishop Owen of St Asaph's to tithe unharvested corn.[35] There were, however, limits to Laud's influence. He could not get his candidate Edward Stanley made Warden of Winchester College, because the king preferred another man.[36] Neither did he have much luck with the appointment of bishops, largely because Charles insisted 'that young men should not be commended'.[37]

At the start of the personal rule the chief result Laud had on the crown's religious policies was the two sets of orders issued in late 1629. At the time there was widespread support for these injunctions, due in part to a reaction against the Commons, who many felt had gone too far on 2 March. Thus in November 1629 forty-one clergymen from Essex – generally considered the most Puritan county in the realm – petitioned Laud that they were worried about 'a want of general conformity', and begged him 'not to be lax unto us'.[38] Heartened by such requests, early in the following month he persuaded the king to issue a set of injunctions ordering all subjects to accept the church's teachings.[39] Both Laud and Charles personally revised the various drafts of these injunctions. The day after the first set of injunctions were promulgated, Laud convinced the king to issue to all bishops a second set, based on those originally put out by Queen Elizabeth. Since only the Archbishop of Canterbury had the authority to promulgate instructions so widely, they were dispatched over Abbot's signature on New Year's Day 1630. They ordered bishops to reside in their dioceses unless needed at court, to visit each parish at least once every three years, not to ordain unworthy candidates for the priesthood, to ensure that children were taught the catechism, to supervise lecturers properly, and to send the archbishop a detailed report on their activities every year.[40]

Charles and Laud hoped that the injunctions to the clergy and to the bishops would still religious controversies, for it is quite clear that after Buckingham's murder and the dissolution of three parliaments, defeats abroad, and tumult at home, more than anything else Charles wanted peace and quiet. Laud agreed. Domestic tranquillity based on unity had been a constant theme of his sermons. 'I have always moved every stone that these thorny and perplexed questions might not be discussed in public before the people, lest we should violate charity under the appearance of truth,' Laud wrote to Vossius in the summer of 1629, adding, 'I have always counselled moderation lest everything should be thrown into confusion by fervid minds.'[41]

There is no doubt that Laud considered the minds of the Feoffees of Impropriations to be particularly fervid. This was a pity, for in doing so he failed to see how much they had in common with him, perhaps because, as he confided to Vossius, 'For the present I have little to hope and much to fear.' Both Laud and the Feoffees agreed that laymen held far too much of the church's property, and that one way of restoring the church spiritually was to revive it economically. The Feoffees had been formally founded in 1625 as an endowment to repurchase church income that had fallen into secular hands and use it to support first-rate ministers. While Laud agreed in principle with the Feoffees' aims, in practice he thought them 'a cunning way, under a glorious pretence, to overthrow the Church's Government, by getting into their power more dependency of the clergy, than the King, and all the Peers, and all the Bishops in all the kingdom had'.[42]

The attack on the Feoffees, who were first regarded as a fairly beneficial group, began on 11 July 1630, when Peter Heylyn, fellow of Magdalen College, preached a sermon at St Mary's Church, Oxford, on the text 'But while men slept, the enemy came and sowed tares among the wheat'. Even though Laud had defended Heylyn a couple of years earlier in a quarrel with the Regius Professor of Divinity, Dr John Prideaux, and the two men afterwards became such close friends that Heylyn wrote Laud's biography, it is unlikely that the young don opened the offensive at the bishop's request. Most likely Heylyn persuaded Laud that the Feoffees were in fact a problem by sending him a printed copy of the sermon. As reluctant to start fights as he was eager to pursue them, once adopted, to the bitterest of ends, Laud brought the Feoffees to the king's attention. Charles referred the matter to his Attorney General, William Noy, who summoned the Feoffees to appear before the Exchequer Court for holding property as a corporation without a royal charter. Finding the accused guilty on the technicality in February 1633, the court dissolved the Feoffees, and sequestered their assets to support aims that Laud found far more congenial. He was delighted with the verdict, noting in his diary that the Feoffees 'were the main instruments for the Puritan faction to undo the Church'.[43]

The Exchequer was not the only court that Laud employed to enforce his religious policies. As a member of the Courts of High Commission and Star Chamber he used them not only as legal bodies with powers of enforcement to further his religious policies, but as public forums to vent his own righteous indignation. Some transgressors got what they deserved. For praying 'Lord, open the eyes of the Queen's Majesty, that she may see Jesus Christ, who she had pained with her infidelity, superstition and Idolatry,' the Court of High Commission suspended Nathaniel Bernard from his London lectureship; after he made 'an humble submission' they restored him to his post.[44] Others were not treated so leniently. In January 1630 Dr Alexander Leighton was charged before Star Chamber for writing *Sion's Plea against the Prelacie*, in which he called bishops 'Sataned', 'Men of Blood', and 'enemies to the State'. Laud voted that Leighton be imprisoned during His Majesty's pleasure, fined £10,000, degraded from the ministry, pilloried, whipped, have his ears cut off, and be branded on the cheek SS for 'Sower of Sedition'.[45]

The same month as the unfortunate Dr Leighton appeared before Star Chamber, the vestry of St Edmund's Church, Salisbury, voted to remove a stained glass window that depicted God as an old man creating the world, on the grounds that it was idolatrous. Henry Sherfield, the town recorder, also thought the window was obscene, for it contained 'a naked man, and the woman naked in some part'.[46] John Davenant, the Bishop of Salisbury, was not so sure, and he ordered that the window be left alone. Untroubled by such doubts Sherfield took matters into his own hands by climbing up a ladder, pikestaff in hand, to smash the window. Notwithstanding Davenant's reluctance to prosecute, the bishop's chancellor brought Sherfield before Star Chamber, which in February 1633 committed him to prison, fined him £500 and ordered him to repair the window and apologise to the bishop. Characteristically Laud voted for an even harsher punishment, not so much because he was opposed to iconoclasm, as because Sherfield had defied the authority of a bishop, albeit a Calvinist one.[47]

Perhaps the most famous Star Chamber case (and certainly the one with the most serious long-term consequences) that Laud heard involved William Prynne. A member of Lincoln's Inn, and the author of nearly two hundred books, Prynne would scribble for three hours, break for beer and a bread roll, and then return to his labours, writing in such a hurried hand that one government censor explained (rather unconvincingly) that he had only licensed his manuscripts for printing because he could not read them. In 1633 Prynne published a particularly tedious tract entitled *Histriomastix, a Scourge of Stage Plays*, in which he castigated, *inter alia*, the theatrical profession, by defining 'women actors' in the index as 'notorious whores'. Laud was outraged, because of the queen's well-known love of appearing in amateur dramatics, and because as a student he too had taken part in such productions. He was already familiar with Prynne, who had tried to circumvent his power, as the Bishop of London, to license books, and he helped the prosecution by showing the king an extract of the diatribe's most offensive parts. In public he called *Histriomastix* 'A scandalous book against the State in an infamous manner' whose author was guilty of 'infamous treason'.[48] In private he noted that Prynne 'hath in many ways mistaken me, and spoken untruth of me'.[49] These attacks not only hurt Laud but frightened him badly, for he associated Prynne with Leighton, and thus with assassination threats. He was surely relieved when Star Chamber sentenced the impertinent barrister to be imprisoned for life, be pilloried, have both his ears cut off, be fined £5,000, and to lose his Oxford degree and membership of the bar.[50]

The three major cases of Leighton, Sherfield and Prynne, as well as several other minor ones, illustrate why Laud's attempts to use the courts to improve England's religious climate failed. He was the guiding force behind many of these prosecutions. Nathaniel Bernard appeared before Star Chamber at Laud's instigation. In other cases his friends initiated prosecutions. Although Heylyn first brought the Feoffees and Prynne to the attention of the authorities, Laud welcomed their appearance in the dock.[51] A year before Prynne's Star Chamber hearing, when the barrister was defending some rioters from Suffolk, Laud declared from the bench, 'We must not sit here to punish poor snakes, and let him go scot free.'[52]

While Laud's motives for trying to use the king's courts to punish the ungodly may – in his own eyes, at least – have been of the highest, he did it with a venom that belied any good intentions. His zest was as unsavoury as it was unchristian. His enthusiasm was as extravagant as his claims. While certainly tedious and overwritten, by no stretch of the imagination could *Histriomastix* be considered, as Laud maintained, a work of 'high treason'.[53] Just as extravagant was the bishop's reprimand delivered a year later to the minister who appeared before the High Commission wearing a velvet-lined coat, that 'this is a great sin and will bring down the judgment of God on this land'.[54] When another minister, William Slate, appeared before the same court wearing large ruffles that extended up to his elbows, Laud threatened that if he ever saw him dressed so extravagantly again he would seek out some canon law 'to take hold of him'.[55] As a judge Laud used the law for his own ends far too frequently whenever he was personally involved in a case. Behind the barbaric punishments he voted on Dr Leighton was his fear of being assassinated. He was sure that Leighton had gone around telling people to 'kill all the bishops', and believed he could well have been responsible for the rash of anonymous fliers that appeared all over London threatening Laud's life.[56] By overreacting Laud exaggerated the threat from fanatics like Leighton and Prynne. No more than five hundred to a thousand copies of their books were ever in circulation.[57] Indeed, when he first appeared before Star Chamber Prynne was remarkably abject and contrite – in contrast to the consistently obdurate Leighton – and only when he realised he could expect no mercy did he become intransigent, calling Laud an 'exceeding fiery, insolent, violent, implacable, malicious and revengeful spirit' who he hoped would end in 'misery, ruin, if not hell itself'.[58] When a defendant touched a raw nerve Laud was implacable. The only explanation for his hounding of Sir Giles Allington for marrying his own niece contrary to canon law was that it painfully reminded the bishop of the Mountjoy affair.

While posterity has by and large condemned Laud's activities in Star Chamber and High Commission as a blot on his career, they were widely supported by his contemporaries. 'It was spoken like a bishop indeed,' effused the Cambridge don Joseph Mead about Laud's speech at Allington's trial.[59] The University of Oxford was only too happy to strip Prynne of his degrees, while Lincoln's Inn entertained the king and queen at an expensive banquet and masque to apologise for the insolence of one of its former members.

But in the long run Laud's use of secular courts for essentially spiritual ends hurt him. His bullying tactics created martyrs – men whom the public remembered, and victims with long memories for revenge. He forgot his own advice that spiritual unity 'proceeds from charity'.[60] Despite the fact that Sherfield had swung his pikestaff with so much enthusiasm that he fell off the ladder and hurt himself, many men were sure that in smashing the Papist window he had been doing the Lord's work. The courts were too blunt and too crude an instrument to achieve Laud's goals. All too often they failed to reveal the full facts of a case. Because Laud failed to grasp that the Sherfield affair was a squabble within the urban oligarchy of Salisbury rather than a wholesale attack on the Church of England, he supported Bishop John Davenant even though he was a Calvinist.[61] As an instrument of moral reform, a court can only work when there is such a degree of consensus that the expulsion of the recalcitrant is a threat that they profoundly fear. But Laud picked on people who basically did not want to belong to his group, while failing to frighten many of the waverers into remaining on his side. The threat of being harried out of the land held few terrors for men who did not particularly want to stay.

Following Buckingham's removal there is no doubt that Laud desperately wanted to remain in royal favour, and that he and Sir Richard Weston rapidly emerged as the king's most powerful counsellors. The Commons recognised this development less than six months after the duke's murder when they attacked the pair in their tumultuous resolution of 2 March 1629.

According to Edward Hyde (Laud's friend), Weston was 'a man of big looks and a mean and abject spirit'. No one could doubt that he was an efficient administrator, who had learned much, if not more than his mentor, Lionel Cranfield, Earl of Middlesex, about restoring the crown's finances. In a sense Weston and Laud had much in common, one being concerned with an economic crisis, and the other with an ecclesiastical one. But they were protégés of two political rivals who continued the conflict from one political generation to the next: ten years earlier Buckingham had helped impeach Cranfield, and Williams had befriended Weston.

During the 1630s the animosity between Laud and Weston vented itself in several different ways. When the king granted Laud two hundred tons of timber from the royal forests to build the new quadrangle of St John's, Weston ordered that it be taken from 'decayed trees'. Several times Laud complained to the king about Weston's 'falsehoods and practices that were against me', prompting the Lord Treasurer to complain, 'That little bishop would monopolise the king's ear for he is ever whispering.'[62]

One of Laud's problems was that he could neither work with nor leave alone people whom he disliked and with whom he felt ill at ease; nor could he accept his enemies' friends. Unlike his old student Windebank, he could not bridge the gap to those who stood in the middle. Convinced that those who did not stand wholeheartedly with him must be malignantly against him, he alienated moderates such as Sir Francis Cottington, the Chancellor of the Exchequer. This inability to tolerate neutrals, together with his gruff lack of tact, conspired to keep Laud an outsider, both at court and within the government. It is no surprise, therefore, that Sir Thomas Wentworth became his closest ally.

Wentworth was a Yorkshireman who had learned the vital importance of quite literally having friends at court in 1621 when he was ignominiously forced to leave the bench in the middle of a trial on the arrival of the new commission of the peace from which enemies in London had removed his name. This proud man was addicted to efficiency. For Wentworth, making things work well was far more important than working well with people. During the 1620s he tried to use parliament to improve the efficiency of the government, but he failed, for parliament was too weak an institution, and anyway as a legislature could not oversee the daily operations of the executive. As his father had told him, 'we live under a prerogative government'.[63] So in the 1620s he came over to what many saw as the other side, changing his colours to pursue the same goals.[64] Charles never trusted or liked Wentworth – at least not until after he allowed his faithful servant to be executed. The king kept him away from court, first appointing him President of the Council of the North, and then Lord President of Ireland. Thus Wentworth needed friends at court desperately.

At first glance the ruthless country gentleman, whose many enemies called him 'Black Tom', and the insecure little red-faced prelate seem a particularly odd couple. Wentworth was twenty years younger than Laud, and never accepted the role of protégé which the bishop normally insisted his younger friends, such as Heylyn, assume towards him. Wentworth was a firm Calvinist who did not agree with Laud's views on predestination.

The bishop never served as his Confessor, yet many other things bound the two together: both shared a love of efficiency; one needed a link to the centre, and the other a confidant in the provinces. They were at ease in each other's presence, and shared a common sense of humour, giving their enemies private nicknames that seemed to make their friendship an even more precious protection against a hostile world. For instance, in a long letter of October 1632 Laud gleefully recounted an accident that had befallen Cottington whilst out hunting. Six weeks earlier the Chancellor of the Exchequer had stolen Laud's pen during a privy council meeting and put it in his breeches pocket. It fell down inside the lining, painfully pricking him 'where exactly I'm not sure', recounted the bishop gleefully.[65] On another occasion Laud punningly wrote to Wentworth of their mutual enemy Richard Boyle, Earl of Cork, who was trying to subvert ecclesiastical appointments, 'God bless the church from any that is as foul as a Boyle or as light as a Cork.'[66] 'I hear that you have knighted a Lincolnshire gentleman, one Mr Smith,' Laud teased his friend; 'he will deserve it for I hear that he is valiant in one kind of combat. He was censured in High Commission Court for getting two sisters with child.'[67] Like many people, Laud found that laughing at things which frightened him – whether ministerial ambitions, aristocratic pretensions, or human sexuality – made them less daunting.

During the 1630s Laud sent Wentworth some 130 letters in which, at great length, he discussed his plans and confessed his anxieties. In many ways this correspondence replaced his diary as an outlet for his most personal worries, being written, Laud admitted, 'with so much mirth and freedom'.[68] It became the core of a relationship that started as a political convenience based on the need for good communications and an ally, and became that prop – that intimacy with another being – which all of us need in walking life's ultimately lonely road.

Most seventeenth-century Englishmen would have agreed that few men were lonelier than the king. Answerable only to God, the ultimate responsibility was his alone. 'Kings are ordained of God for the good of his people,' Laud preached on 27 March 1631, the sixth anniversary of Charles's accession. The bishop went on to call Charles 'a wise, and just and religious king . . . made by God . . . to meet the great difficulties of his time at home and abroad, that so his people . . . may live and flourish in peace and plenty'. Such statements clearly reflect Laud's opinion of Charles the king. If his attitudes towards Charles the man were different he did not reveal them, even to his diary, so long as Charles continued to support him. After all he had much in common with the king. Both loved detail, believing that if the sum of the smallest parts was right then the whole must be too. After visiting York, Charles sent the Dean and Chapter a letter ordering that the arrangement of the pews in the Minster be changed.

Since the letter was written by Laud's secretary, William Dell, it seems likely that the bishop originated it.[69] Unlike the king, Laud was willing to work hard, and unlike many other ministers he was willing to confine his activities within the boundaries set by Charles's departmentalisation of government. When, for instance, Charles's sister Elizabeth of Bohemia asked Laud to intervene with the king in foreign affairs, he refused, saying that they were outside his bailiwick.

Charles and Laud shared a common sense of place, hierarchy and order: both felt that as a king and a bishop respectively they were ultimately answerable to God, and must support each other. Thus when the king wrote that episcopal incomes 'hath been so diminished that they suffice not to maintain the bishops that live upon them according to their place and dignity', Laud was in total agreement.[70] With his own hand he corrected a letter the king sent to the Dean and Chapter of Christ Church, Oxford, listing all the addressees in the correct order of precedence, before adding that His Majesty expected to be obeyed – a rebuke that was hardly necessary. Laud often added such barbs in the king's name, upsetting the loyal and having no effect on the recalcitrant.

Shared values, common hatreds, mutual fears made strangely good bedfellows. Both Charles and Laud needed each other, and yet their relationship remained one of public convenience rather than private friendship. Even though Laud displayed little interest in art for art's sake, he tried to manipulate the king's passion for painting to achieve his political goals. In May 1637, for instance, he commissioned the French sculptor Le Sueur to cast life-size statues of the king and queen. With a telling insight into his master's insecurities (that may have come from his own lack of stature) Laud told the sculptor to make the short sovereign well over six feet tall.[71]

While Charles was happy to use Laud as the royal family's vicar, he never made him his confessor. Laud might baptise the king's children (an honour normally accorded only to the Archbishop of Canterbury) but he was never allowed to keep the king's conscience. Charles made men bishops only in their late middle age because he wanted them to have some sense of gravitas, of dignity, and of distance. He wanted dedicated men, whose chief, indeed, whose only interest was the church, and thus he shared Laud's view that priests should remain single.

Neither the queen nor her friends agreed. Indeed, soon after making a public pronouncement in favour of clerical celibacy Laud had to conduct the marriage of Thomas Turner, an old pupil of his from St John's and one of his chaplains, to the daughter of his friend Sir Francis Windebank, in order to help dissipate the ill will that his remarks had generated, particularly at court. A fierce little bachelor, reared in the highly intellectual milieu of the university, Laud disliked the world of the court. 'What a great courtier you are grown of late, and how cold a friend,' he once reproved Sir John Lambe.[72] The court was sophisticated and frivolous; he was provincial and serious. 'The sands of the River Loire are not more changeable than the friendships of the court,' lamented Secretary of State Conway.[73]

The bishop tried to extend the limits of his influence with the king and the court by trying to place allies in positions of power so as to be better able to bridge the gap between his world and theirs. He first managed to do so in 1632. 'Mr Francis Windebank, my old friend, was sworn Secretary of State,' he wrote in his diary on 15 June, 'which place I obtained for him of my gracious master King Charles.' Less than four weeks later he was able to note with equal satisfaction that William Juxon, another old friend and protégé from St John's, was 'at my suit sworn Clerk of His Majesty's Closet, that I might have one that I might trust near his Majesty, if I grow weak or infirm as I must'.[74]

Physical infirmities, and the emotional strain of trying to walk across the quicksands of Caroline politics, greatly distressed Laud, an insecure man at the best of times. And for him these were, in many respects, the worst of times. 'Dies erat Veneris,' he noted in his diary, 'the days were poisonous.' That day, 14 August 1629, 'I fell sick upon my way towards the Court at Woodstock: I took up my lodging at my ancient friend's house, Mr Francis Windebank. There I lay in a most grievous burning fever, till Monday, Sept. 7, on which day I had my last fit. I was brought so low that I was not able to return to my own house at London, till Tuesday, Octob. 29.'[75] Laud was so close to death that he could not perform his official duties. With the sense of shame that energetic men often feel at being incapacitated, as chancellor he apologised to Oxford University for his inactivity by expressing the fear that 'my successors should have cause to say that I had been unworthy to the office'.[76] He was not well enough to return to London until mid-October, after which he had a relapse, possibly as a result of the journey. He managed to get out of bed on the 24th to go and see the king at Denmark House, before having another bout of fever which 'was so fierce that my physicians, as well as my friends, gave me for dead, and it is a piece of a miracle that I live'.[77] Laud suffered several relapses as he forced himself to return to duty, and seems to have lost a fair amount of weight. After he had to attend the king at Charles's express command on 25 January 1630, he noted that 'the day was not a day of choice for a thin man to go abroad'.[78] Laud did not recover fully until 21 March 1631, Palm Sunday, surely a day fraught with omens, since it marked the end of what he was convinced had been the climax of his mid-life.

Although he was weak in body, for most of the time Laud's mind remained as energetic as ever. As he lay hour after hour on his sickbed, chafing at his incapacity, he thought deeply about his life, his career, and his church. He saw a Church of England much decayed in power and wealth because avaricious bishops had squandered her resources, and greedy laymen had purloined her heritage. The growth in the number of lecturers controlled by secular corporations, and the increase in private chaplains who were in danger (as Laud himself showed in the Mountjoy affair) of becoming rich men's theological flunkies, had done much to lessen the church's proper control over true doctrine. To remedy such abuses Laud was more than ever convinced that firm action was vital. Thus in December 1629, before his health was fully recovered, he got the king to issue a set of injunctions to the clergy, and persuaded him to order Archbishop Abbot to send another set of instructions to the bishops the following New Year's Day. Both documents, which were essentially Laud's work, were remarkable achievements for a sick man, and drafting them may well have delayed his complete recovery. But with their completion came a sense of inner peace. 'It is true, My Lord, God hath restored me, even from death itself,' the bishop wrote to Archbishop James Ussher of Armagh, adding that 'having renewed my lease, I should pay Him an income of some service to His Church'.[79]

Even though Laud continued to suffer brief bouts of sickness, after mid-1631 he had as much energy as before. 'I have recovered my health', he wrote in July, 'beyond expectation.' He now pursued his goals with the enthusiasm that Charles usually reserved for the chase, gaily writing to Windebank in 1632, 'We took another conventicle of Separatists in Newington Woods upon Sunday last, in the very brake where the king's stag should have been lodged for his hunting the next morning.'[80]

He had recovered his health, won friends at court and in influential places, developed a working relationship with the king, devised a clear agenda for the future that was built upon a sound historical foundation. All that remained was for Abbot and the Calvinist old guard to formally step aside and let the new Arminian light shine through. This opportunity came on 4 August 1633 when Abbot died early in the morning. Two days later Laud visited the king, who as he walked through the door greeted him with the words, 'My Lord's Grace of Canterbury, you are very welcome.'[81]

VI

'The little man is come up trumps'

As primate of England Laud enjoyed considerable powers in his own right. His attempts to exercise these powers to reform the church will be the subject of this chapter. Chapter VII will discuss the broader powers Laud had as one of the king's leading ministers. Laud's role as an educator, principally as Chancellor of Oxford University, will be the subject of Chapter VIII. Of course, the distinction between the three areas is both artificial and far from clear, changing over time. Charles had appointed Laud to Canterbury, and – as Abbot had learned to his cost – could strip a primate of most of his authority. But when the king made Laud his archbishop, everyone realised that, whatever the source of his power, he was now, more than ever, a man to be reckoned with.[1]

Such a recognition was immediate. The morning that Abbot died someone, most probably David Codner, an English Benedictine posing as a courtier in the queen's household, sidled up to Laud at Greenwich and offered to make him a cardinal. Laud promptly informed the king. Eleven days later the same anonymous figure repeated the offer, and once more Laud told Charles.[2] The story, which Laud noted in his diary, is perplexing. The offer was unofficial, for there was hardly time for it to have come from Rome. Moreover no one in the queen's household would have had enough influence with the pope to be able to guarantee a cardinal's hat even to so spectacular a convert as the Archbishop of Canterbury.[3]

Even village drunks recognised Laud's elevation. In the new primate's home town of Reading, Ludovic Bowyer babbled that the king had issued a warrant for Laud's arrest, and that he was a traitor who had paid the pope £17,000 for his promotion. Apprehended by Constable Edward Johnson, and censured by Star Chamber, Bowyer promptly escaped from custody. 'And God forgive him,' Laud noted, leaving the distinct impression that he had no intention of emulating the Almighty's benevolence.[4] A more sober commentator compared the new primate to the Bishop of London who had burnt so many good Protestants during Bloody Mary's reign, praying 'God not to send a Bonner to persecute the Church'. Another observed that Laud had donned Abbot's clothes 'before we were sure he was in fact asleep and key cold'. The Venetian ambassador best expressed the widespread concern that the appointment might engender 'immoderate heat', by reporting (quite erroneously) that the king had ordered Laud to do nothing without the privy council's approval.[5]

The offer of a cardinal's hat may have added to Laud's own sense of unease, for he had dreamed of succumbing to Rome. He reported the proposal to the king with alacrity, telling Charles that 'he would not suffer that, till Rome were other than it is'.[6] The pomp of his formal election on 29 August 1633, and his installation on 19 September, which he marked with a sumptuous banquet at Lambeth Palace, did not improve his morale, for he abhorred such gastronomic marathons.

Even the pleasure he received from the congratulations of his friends was qualified. He responded to Sir Thomas Roe's best wishes by describing his new appointment as 'that troublesome place whither I am going'. 'I hope', he added, 'you shall find me the same man at Lambeth as you did at London.'[7] Wentworth's best wishes for 'many happy days' as archbishop elicited some deep-rooted yet half-recognised fears. Laud replied:

> But truly, My Lord, O look for neither nor for many, for I am in years and have had a troublesome life; not for happy, because I have no hope to do the good I desire. And besides I doubt shall never be able to hold my health there one year. . . . In truth, my Lord, I speak seriously, I have had a heaviness hang upon me ever since I was nominated to this place, and I can give myself no account of it, unless it proceed from an apprehension that there is more expected from me than the craziness of these times will give me leave to do.[8]

Just before Laud confided these fears to Wentworth, Charles made perfectly clear what he expected from his new archbishop. In September 1633 he sent the primate two letters. The first ordered him 'to use all such Ceremonies and offices, and to carry yourself with the same State & dignity, and to assume such privileges & precedence as your predecessors'.[9] The second started with a broadly defined goal: 'There is nothing dearer to us than the preservation of True religion, as is now settled and established in our kingdom.' The king went on to list fourteen specific objectives: bishops were to reside in their dioceses, to visit their parishes, and to be careful whom they ordained. They should curb the growth of lecturers, preserve church property, and send their archbishop an annual report by 10 December.[10] Since William Dell, Laud's secretary, drafted Charles's second letter, this correspondence surely represented the king's and the arch-bishop's common objectives. Even though with hindsight we know that in the long run their programme was a disastrous failure which helped to bring both men to the block, in the short term it appeared to be a resounding success. In 1636, after reviewing Laud's career, the Earl of Dorset told the Earl of Middlesex, 'I concur as well as you do that the little man is come up trumps.'[11]

One of the archbishop's failings was that he placed too much import-ance on trivial matters. For instance, if the alien churches were a real problem, they certainly were not as important as the attention he gave them would suggest. To attract skilled Protestant refugees from France and the Low Countries to settle in England, Queen Elizabeth had allowed them to set up their own churches, and to ply their trades in English towns without having first served an apprenticeship. Because these alien churches were an effective link to the immigrant population, and acted as a welfare agency with the richer members helping out their poorer compatriots, the government was happy to see them flourish. Indeed, in 1625 and 1631 the privy council ordered prosperous Walloons to continue attending (and thus financially supporting) their own church in Norwich and not to go to the local Anglican services.[12]

In March 1633 Laud reversed this eight-year-old policy by having the privy council order an investigation of the alien churches, on the strength of which in April 1634 he asked the French and Dutch churches in Kent what liturgy they used, and how many of their members had been born in England. About nine months later the archbishop decreed that the French and Dutch churches must say their liturgies in English, and that only those born outside the realm could worship in the alien churches, which meant that their children had to attend Anglican services. This crude attack on their families and heritage prompted the immigrants to petition the king, often with considerable support from the local authorities (who were anxious to keep the poor rate down). Even the intervention of the king's friend, the Huguenot hero the Duke of Soubise, was of little avail. By insisting 'My injunctions must be obeyed,' Laud made the slight compro-mises he offered seem all the more paltry.[13]

The dispute over alien churches was unnecessary for, with the passage of time and the assimilation of the native born, the problem would have solved itself. The churches were not, as Laud told the king, 'great nurseries of inconformity'. Indeed, as he had to admit in the same report, they had no connection with English Nonconformists. Between 1633 and 1645 membership in alien churches fell from 10,789 to 4,312.[14] Perhaps the archbishop's high-handed treatment of the alien Protestants, and more important their allies in the local urban elites, contributed to anti-episcopal feeling in Kent, London and East Anglia. Without a doubt his rudeness to the local worthies of Canterbury, and later of Norwich, increased the gentry's irritation that he did not entertain them as well or as often as had his predecessors.[15] Of course, harassing immigrants, bad manners and even niggardliness in hospitality to local worthies were not enough to cause a revolution in either church or state. But they were enough to persuade men to stay put when called upon in the hour of need. As one insulted aristocrat explained, 'It's an ill dog that's not worth whistling.'

Many of those who did come running when whistled in the crisis of the late 1630s and early 1640s were the dogs of war, English and Scots mercenaries who, after serving the Protestant cause in Europe, returned home to fight against king and bishops. Together with their compatriots in trade, they had their own chaplains, particularly in the Low Countries and Northern Germany. Thus with hindsight, at least, it is ironic that when in March 1633 Laud first asked the privy council to investigate the way Englishmen and Scots worshipped overseas, he did so in order to prevent them from becoming 'a perpetual seminary to breed and transplant men ill affected to the government into this kingdom'.[16]

Dudley Carleton, the British envoy to The Hague, first brought the problem to Laud's attention four years earlier. The British regiments in the service of the Netherlands were using a bastardised Anglo-Dutch liturgy, which Carleton thought produced little discipline, much debauchery and even more drunkenness. Laud, who always believed that the correct prayer book was an elixir which could cure most of life's ills, wrote to Secretary of State Conway on 20 February 1628 asking him to request the king to prohibit the hybrid liturgy.[17] Even though Charles admitted to being 'much troubled' by the deviation, his government was able to do nothing.

Another British ambassador to The Hague, William Boswell, raised the issue again in a letter he wrote in March 1633 describing the state of the English church at Delft, which was, he believed, of a 'most insufferable and most dangerous consequence'.[18] Laud used this intelligence to get his ally, Sir Francis Windebank, to raise the matter at a meeting of the council, which ordered the prelate to investigate the spiritual state of all English merchant churches overseas, as well as that of the mercenary regiments. Eager to comply, the archbishop soon discovered that the church at Hamburg did not own – let alone use – an Anglican prayer book, an omission glaring enough to prompt the king in council to order that all Englishmen abroad must follow the established form of service, that the Archbishop of Canterbury must approve the appointment of all regimental padres, and that mercantile churches abroad should come under the jurisdiction of the Bishop of London.[19] The following year the archbishop attempted to implement this policy by sending Mr Beaumont, 'a man learned, sober, and conformable', to take over the church at Delft, which had been rent by sectarian conflicts.[20] Even though Beaumont had been instructed to report the names of trouble-makers to the Bishop of London, there was in fact very little the authorities at home could do to control

Englishmen abroad. Take the case of John Davenport, one of the Feoffees, and minister of St Stephen's, Coleman Street, who in late 1633 fled from London to Amsterdam, where he became co-pastor of the English church.[21] When Laud pressured the Dutch authorities to deport him, Davenport escaped to New England; he became minister at New Haven, where he flourished until his death in 1670.[22] As Laud had to confess to Boswell in 1638, he was disappointed by how little they had achieved with English churches on the Continent.[23]

The archbishop had scant regard for those who went to America. 'They have thrust themselves out, and cut themselves off, and run a madding to New England,' he declared, 'and I know some that went out like fools.'[24] He did try to ensure that only conforming, and thus presumably non-maddened, members of the Church of England defected to the New World, by having the privy council instruct ships' masters to send them the names of all immigrants they proposed carrying across the Atlantic. When this system proved unworkable, the council ordered masters to give bonds that they would not transport anyone who had not taken the oath of supremacy, and that they would hold morning and evening prayers every day at sea. This, Laud hoped, would stop the immigration of persons of 'idle and refractory humours, whose only and principal end is to live without the reach of persons of Authority'. He even tried to ensure that the inhabitants of Bermuda used the Anglican liturgy and book of homilies, and received reports about the state of the established church in Newfoundland.[25] Laud was behind the decision to set up a sub-committee of the council on plantations, and was himself a member of this body. But apart from establishing the precedent that the Bishop of London should be in charge of Anglicans abroad, it had little lasting effect. He received only two communications dealing with affairs in New England, where his influence was far less than his later Puritan detractors would have us believe.[26]

The same could not be said about Ireland.

Laud was rare amongst royal advisers in that he saw his master's dominions – England, Scotland, Ireland, Wales and even New England – as a whole, and paradoxically he did much to divide them still further. He first became seriously interested in Irish affairs when William Bedell, Bishop of Kilmore, wrote to him about the state of the Irish church. The Irish were not interested in 'the inward and true reason of things: they are sensible in the purse', Bedell told Laud, citing examples of how church courts preyed upon the people, and how civil lawyers rode roughshod over the rights of bishops.[27] 'The estate of the Church is very miserable,' Bedell added. 'The people . . . were obstinate Recusants.'[28] Horrified, Laud wrote back, 'My Lord, we live in times in which the church is overgrown not only with weeds within it, but with trees and bushes about it, which . . . drop sourly upon whatsoever is good in it.'[29]

No one could doubt that the Church of Ireland was in a parlous state. For years English travellers had reported on the decay of its buildings. One of them (who was apparently unaware of how fond the Irish were of horses) wrote home in disgust that most of their churches were like stables. In Dublin horses were actually kept in St Andrew's Church, and the crypt of Christ Church was used as a tavern. In Meath over half the livings of the established church had been impropriated by laymen, many of them Catholics, who used the money to support their own priests. At the start of the century it had been reckoned that one archbishop held three other bishoprics, and seventy-seven livings, all at the same time.[30]

There was little that Laud could do to alleviate this state of affairs until the summer of 1633, when the king made him Archbishop of Canterbury, and Sir Thomas Wentworth became Lord Deputy of Ireland. For the next half-dozen years Laud acted as Wentworth's liaison with the king. He read letters from the Lord Deputy aloud to Charles, who dictated his instructions back to Dublin. For much of the time the archbishop did his job well. He relayed messages accurately, and with judicious editing soothed the relations between two prickly men who needed one another as much as they disliked and distrusted each other. For instance, when Charles refused to give Wentworth the earldom he desperately wanted, the archbishop conveyed the rejection so delicately that the Lord Deputy did not leave the king's service because of thwarted pride. Because Laud provided his friend with links to the crown far better than any of his predecessors had enjoyed, he helped make Wentworth's tenure in Ireland a very significant although not a particularly successful one. In return for this assistance Wentworth acted on Laud's behalf in Ireland, and thus allowed him to have a much greater influence on the church there than that exercised by any Archbishop of Canterbury before or since. The first item on Laud's agenda for the Irish church was the improvement of its financial state, which he concluded was far worse than the Church of England's. Pluralism and absenteeism were so rife among the Irish clergy that he said, 'I am almost ashamed on my calling.'[31] But he could hardly blame Irish ministers for wanting to hold more than one living, for, as a group of them petitioned him, 'in the whole Christian world the rural clergy have not been reduced at such an extremity of contempt and beggery as in Ireland'.[32]

After Wentworth persuaded the Dublin parliament to pass legislation limiting the amount of time for which church lands could be leased to laymen, the archbishop began to hope that 'the Church of Ireland will begin to flourish again'.[33] There is no doubt that an energetic bishop, such as John Bramhall of Derry, could make significant financial improvements. It was said that in the province of Armagh alone he recovered church land worth between £30,000 and £40,000, a figure so incredibly large that only Bramhall's many enemies could bring themselves to believe it, particularly in view of the fact that in his own diocese of Derry he was able to recover only £1,000.[34] Even so it cannot be doubted that during these years the economic condition of the Church of Ireland improved: in Derry alone some £3,339 was spent to this end. But the account books cannot tell the whole story; ultimately what counted were the men.[35]

For centuries Ireland has been a graveyard for enterprising Englishmen and a snug haven for mediocre ones. In trying to improve the quality of the clergy there, Laud was beset with place-seekers who were, he complained, driven by the 'fretting cankerworm of ambition'. On arriving in Ireland they all too often reacted to the poverty of their livings and the inhabitants by falling into indifference, indolence and alienation. Many 'went native', marrying Catholic women. Some livings were so poor that they could not support a minister even at that desperate level of poverty suffered by most of his flock.[36] Irish bishops were so ill paid, even by Welsh, let alone English standards, that even had they wished they could have done little to help solve the church's economic problems.

Ironically the most serious impediment to producing men well disposed to the king's service was the king. At heart, Charles's main interest in Ireland was as a source of patronage; over half the letters he personally wrote on Irish affairs were on this topic. Since he insisted on appointing only 'men known to him by services done', by the end of the decade all the Irish episcopal bench was composed of Englishmen with few contacts and even less influence in Ireland.

Laud realised that the reform of the Church of Ireland required an improvement of institutions as well as men. At his urging in December 1634 Wentworth forced the Church of Ireland's convocation to adopt a set of canons based on the Anglican Thirty-Nine Articles in place of the Calvinist ones that they had used since 1615, and the following year he overcame Archbishop Ussher's objections and persuaded Convocation to establish a Court of High Commission.[37]

One of the most promising instruments for the long-term improvement of the Church of Ireland was Trinity College, Dublin. It had been founded in 1592 for the promotion of civility, learning and Protestant piety — virtues which its English sponsors believed to be synonymous, at least as far as Ireland was concerned. Unlike Oxford and Cambridge, during the next generation Trinity College did not flourish, because it was, as Laud observed, 'as ill governed as any college in Christendom or worse'.[38] When Ussher offered Laud the chancellorship of Trinity College in 1634, he warned that 'the Fellows there were so fractious that nothing could please them'. The archbishop, who may have found the challenge of taming fractious dons, particularly Calvinists with Cambridge degrees, an alluring one, accepted. He managed to get rid of Provost Robert Ussher by promoting him to the remote but far more peaceful archdeanery of Meath, and appointed as his successor William Chappell, sometime fellow of Christ's College, Cambridge. But Chappell could not stop the squabbling. When he tried to appoint fellows to administrative posts on the basis of ability rather than length of service, the senior ones countered by accusing one of his nominees of refusing to wear a surplice for college chapel. Such charges always impressed Laud, who dismissed the Nonconformist. As usual he pinned his hopes for reformation on regulation, and drew up a set of statutes which he implemented in June 1637. They strengthened the powers of the provost, and made fellowships tenable for life. While the statutes may have saved Trinity from destroying itself in academic civil wars, they did not fulfil the hopes that their author expressed to Wentworth: 'and I think, as you do, that religion and civility in that kingdom will much depend on the reformation of that place.'[39]

Laud understood Ireland's church and people even less than he did its university. For one thing, the Church of Ireland was not the Irish church. Ireland was overwhelmingly a Catholic nation. It was not, as Laud and most Englishmen seemed to think, a land where the problem of recusancy was especially bad: 'so many Romanists', the archbishop lamented, 'swarm there.'[40] The established Protestant Church of Ireland was basically Calvinist in belief, in part because it had not been subjected to the Arminian influences from Oxford, and because its beleaguered members reacted to the overwhelming presence of Rome by moving as far to the left as they could. Thus the articles which they adopted in 1615 stressed predestination, original sin, and the primacy of scripture without once mentioning bishops. By pressuring this vulnerable minority, by reprimanding its bishops, by telling the clergy that the king was 'very ill satisfied' because they did not wear vestments to preach, Laud (and Wentworth) alienated Ireland's Protestants from their natural allies in England. So they helped produce the crisis of 1641 that precipitated the Civil War, and drove many Protestants out of the Church of Ireland.[41]

As the archbishop's emphasis on wearing the right vestments for services showed, he set great store by symbolic deeds and correct ceremonial. 'They are small things, but wilful contempt of them, and breach of public order, is no small offence before God,' he declared, adding that 'without ceremony it is not possible to keep any order or quiet discipline'. He believed that there was an intimate connection between 'The outward sense of God' and 'the inward'.[42] Symbols and ceremonial have always had a profound effect on men's actions. Many of our political fights are over symbols. They form a shorthand that by blurring distinctions allows those who are in general agreement to remain united, and by oversimplifying each party's position makes compromise and concession even more difficult to attain.[43] Seventeenth-century men attached great importance to religious symbols. Enoch ap Evans of Clun, Shropshire, even murdered his mother and brother in a quarrel about whether Communion should be taken kneeling, standing or seated.[44] While symbols did not usually drive men to murder, they did, as the Bishops' Wars (a symbolic name if ever there was one) proved, prompt them into taking up arms.

The most impressive visible symbol that illustrated Laud's view of the relationship between form and substance was St Paul's Cathedral. His attitude (which he shared with Charles) was clearly expressed in a letter that the king sent to the Lord Mayor and Aldermen of London requesting donations for the rebuilding of the cathedral. After defending the importance of good works (a none too subtle dig at the Calvinistic belief in predestination), the letter went on:

> It has always been our care Since we came to the throne not only
> to defend the true faith which we profess, but also to maintain the
> Church and Clergy in their proper jurisdiction, and dignity and
> professions; and withal to encourage and enable our subjects, in
> all places, to reedify, repair and beautify their churches, that respect
> and outward appearance being a good effect and clear evidence of
> their zeal.[45]

Quite clearly both king and archbishop were expressing their conviction that if the church as a building was in good condition, it must also be in good repair as a spiritual institution.

No one could deny that the fabric of St Paul's was in such a bad state that it was 'a scandal to the nation'.[46] Lightning had damaged the spire and roof in 1561, the nave had become a short cut for meat porters carrying freshly slaughtered, dripping carcases from Smithfield Market, it was a playground for children, a job shop for unemployed clergy, a place where writers of news letters could garner the latest intelligence, and a rendezvous where ladies of the oldest profession found bountiful business. Young men in search of work went there, as did respectable young women to court young men.[47] In all respects, St Paul's had become a public convenience – quite literally in the case of one Lucett, a yeoman from Warwickshire who was charged before High Commission for performing a bowel movement therein. In his defence he explained that he had done so in a quiet corner, out of necessity and from ignorance.[48] No wonder Laud felt that the church did not get the respect that was its due.

The initiative to restore St Paul's, however, came from the king, who in 1631 established a commission of some fifty prominent people, including Laud, and three years later sent commissioners to every county to solicit contributions. By promising a first payment of £1,000, and then £500 per annum for the next three years, and offering to sell crown lands to restore the west of the cathedral, Charles persuaded others to contribute. Altogether he managed to raise some £40,000.[49]

In this process Laud served as the king's loyal lieutenant. The personal letters urging contributions he sent to the bishops of his province, the City of London, the Mayor of Carmarthen, and the Justices of the Peace for Wiltshire have survived. Although he told the bishops they should collect without 'pressing any man beyond that which he shall please voluntary and cheerfully to give', from his own purse he happily donated between £1,000 and £2,000.[50]

So eager was the archbishop to raise money for the restoration of St Paul's that he cut ethical corners. By persuading the king to donate all fines levied by High Commission he corrupted it 'from an ecclesiastical court for the reformation of manners to a court of revenue'. Writing in the king's name he warned Mary More, a widow who 'absolutely refused to give anything', that she did so 'upon peril of our utmost displeasure'.[51] Laud had forgotten that widows are best persuaded with gentleness to give their mites. In contrast John South of Kelstern, Lincolnshire, was granted a pardon for incest, reputedly after donating £2,300 to St Paul's, while Thomas Curtis was restored to his living at Martock, Somerset, from which he had been dismissed for adultery, after making a similarly large donation. Just as unseemly was Laud's response to Martha Hellwys, whose husband had not paid her the alimony High Commission ordered. Even though she was destitute he refused to let her have the £500 her husband had paid in fines to the court for several adulteries, on the grounds that the money was already earmarked for St Paul's.[52]

The way that the money was spent on rebuilding the cathedral elicited as much criticism as did the manner in which it was collected. Inigo Jones designed the west front in the Palladian style, using as his model the facade of Il Gesu, the mother church of the Jesuits in Rome. No wonder the Puritan physician John Bastwick fulminated that he was 'making a seat for a priest's arse to sit in'.[53]

Puritan rantings notwithstanding, contributions for the restoration of St Paul's poured in. In the first year of the full-fledged campaign £16,000 was collected. Although this dropped after the initial enthusiasm wore off to £9,342 in 1636 and £10,444 in 1637, by 1639 it had gone back up again to £16,000. The fact that in a year that saw the collapse of the Laudian hegemony people were still giving generously to St Paul's shows the profound importance of symbols in rallying the faithful during a crisis.[54]

A particularly potent symbol was the altar – or as many Englishmen preferred to call it, the Communion table – and its placing. If it were located in the middle of the church, with the minister saying Communion facing the congregation, and often serving them the bread and wine in their seats, he was more like a waiter than the bridge to the Almighty he seemed to be when, standing with his back to the people, he raised the Host to Heaven above the altar placed at the east end, as the light streamed down.

Laud insisted that the altar must not be placed in the middle of the church: 'It is not fit that the people sit above God's table or be above the priest.' Altars in parish churches should be at the east end, as they were in cathedrals; 'the daughter should be like the mother,' he wrote, 'so that there may be uniformity.' The archbishop feared that if the altar were left in the middle of the church, parishioners would sit around it and gossip, that schoolmasters would use it for their lessons, boys to dump their satchels on, and churchwardens to cast their accounts, until there was no difference between the Lord's table and that in any man's kitchen.[55] The altar should be the centre, the focus of the church and its worship. One reason why he ordered that the Earl of Cork's family tomb in Dublin Cathedral be pulled down was that it overshadowed the altar and prevented it from being moved to the east end.[56] Quite simply, Laud believed that 'the altar is the greatest place of God's residence of earth, greater than the pulpit'. Thus he was horrified to learn that the vicar of Welwyn, Hertfordshire, was using a tombstone as the Lord's table.[57] Moving the altar to the east end, surrounding it with rails, and treating it with reverence and veneration, implied that ceremony was far more important than preaching. With equal sincerity many Englishmen were convinced that such veneration was Papist, perhaps treasonable, particularly whenever Laud's followers hung the canopy of state, the symbol of royalty, over the altar.

Since Edward VI's time the altar had usually been placed in the middle of the church.[58] While declaring the position of the altar 'no matter of great moment' so long as the Sacrament was ministered reverently, the Elizabethan injunctions of 1559, which were reconfirmed in 1604, suggested that the altar be kept in any convenient place, and moved to the lower end of the chancel for Communion. Laud did not appear to realise that the Oxford colleges where he had been bred up in religion, and the Chapel Royal where he had slaked his ambitions, were exceptions to this rule. Thus on becoming Dean of Gloucester in 1615 he insisted on moving the altar to the east end of the cathedral. He was most annoyed when Bishop Williams of Lincoln reproved the vicar of Grantham for stirring up 'a needless controversy' by moving the altar to the east end of his church (and for genuflecting so often and so enthusiastically that one member of his flock put out his foot causing the vicar to trip and hurt his back).[59] Laud could well have been behind the 1627 proposal to revise the Elizabethan injunctions, for one of his first acts on becoming Archbishop of Canterbury was to replace the old altar in his chapel at Croydon with a splendid new one (costing £33) which he moved to the east end.[60]

The case of the altar at St Gregory's, London, gave Laud an opportunity to attempt to establish a national policy on altars. In late 1632 the Dean and Chapter of St Paul's, surely acting on the instructions of the Bishop of London, as Laud then was, ordered the adjacent parish church of St Gregory's to move its altar to the east end of the church. Five parishioners appealed to the Court of Arches. The judge, Sir Henry Marten (who had been appointed by Abbot), was sympathetic, and the parishioners might have won had not Laud managed to move the case to the privy council. Here the king heard it on 3 November. Ruling against St Gregory's, Charles announced 'his dislike of all innovations' and ordered churches to follow the example of St Paul's and the Chapel Royal.[61]

The problem was that for many Englishmen moving the altar to the east end of the church was a distressing innovation. As an example, for at least seventy years the altar at Beckington, Somerset, had stood in the middle of the parish church.[62] When Bishop William Peirs of Bath and Wells told them to move it, and to put a rail around it, the parishioners refused. Two churchwardens, James Wheeler and John Fry, were summoned to appear before the bishop's court, where Dr Arthur Duck interrogated them. Being rich and powerful men who had the solid backing of the parish, and the rector, Alexander Huish, Wheeler and Fry appealed to the Court of Arches. For such impudence and for defying their bishop's authority, they were imprisoned for a year and forced to do public penance, as a result of which Wheeler died.

The Beckington and St Gregory's cases became *causes célèbres*, as potent as the Hunne case of 1517 that preceded the Reformation. They created martyrs. They demonstrated the limits of the powerful prelate's ability, and the inadequacies of the ecclesiastical machinery through which he had to operate to force people to do what they did not want to do. Such cases linked Laud with that Papist villain Cardinal Wolsey. Among the first items to be attacked, even before the archbishop's fall from power, were altars and the rails that surrounded them: the soldiers off to fight the Scots in 1637 chopped them up for firewood and out of spite.

To many Protestants altar rails were a particularly odious innovation because, as the rector of Beckington put it, they 'give admittance unto dogs, while Christians be kept out'.[63] When one Christmas Day at Tadlow in Cambridgeshire a dog stole the consecrated loaf from the altar, Laud was convinced that the outrage would never have have taken place had the Lord's table been surrounded by rails.[64] Such a conclusion was perhaps only possible from a man whose only pets were Persian cats and a tortoise, and who knew as little about the ability of dogs to jump fences as he did about his fellow countrymen's adherence to long-established and familiar symbols of their forefathers' Protestant faith. Protestantism – that was the key word for most Englishmen. As William Chillingworth, Laud's wayward protégé, put it in the title of the book he published in 1638, *The Religion of Protestants a safe way to Salvation*. For most Englishmen Protestantism was not only a sure way to salvation in the next world, but an equally sure means to survival in this one. As the Thirty Years War raged on the

Continent, they were convinced that an evil international Papist conspiracy was bent on bringing its rotten fruit to England, threatening true religion just as desperately as had the Armada or the Spanish Inquisition. In face of such massive subversion they must band together.

Having served as minister to British merchant churches in Sweden and Germany John Durie had seen at first hand the horrors of war.[65] The experience convinced him that Protestants must unite. In 1630 the Edinburgh-born minister, who had been educated at Sedan, Leiden and Oxford, came to England carrying introductions from the British ambassador, Sir Thomas Roe, and leading German Protestant ministers. Charles gave Durie a chilly reception, passing him on to Abbot and Laud, who were nearly as frigid. Durie retired empty-handed to the Continent in July and resumed his quest of uniting Lutherans, Calvinists and Anglicans, but with little success. All he could show for his labours when he returned to England to seek the archbishop's help in November 1635 was a pile of debts. Laud wrote him letters of recommendation to the leaders of the German Lutheran and Calvinist churches, and when Durie pointed out that he needed money to go to the Frankfurt Diet to deliver them, offered him a living in Devon worth £20 per annum.[66] So Durie rode two hundred miles through the winter to his new living, only to find the incumbent still alive. Even though the archbishop's mistake was an honest one, he was unsympathetic when the travel-worn Durie returned asking for another position. Laud told him that he could not give to every good cause, that he had done enough for him already, and that if his predecessor, Abbot, had not wasted Canterbury's resources there would have been no problem finding him a fat vicarage worth £140, or even £160, a year.[67]

Ecumenicalism had a much greater appeal for Laud intellectually than financially. As he told the Jesuit Father Fisher, the various Christian faiths were 'members of the Catholic Church, which is spread over the face of the Earth'.[68] If this church was Catholic enough to include the Roman and Greek churches, then surely it had room for those of Luther and Calvin? But in reality it did not work out that way. Getting involved with continental Protestants might drag England into the Thirty Years War, which would mean calling on parliament to vote taxes – and presumably to impeach Laud. While he was happy to include in his Catholic community the Greek Orthodox faith, which was a thousand miles away, he was less inclined to include Lutherans and Calvinists, who were far closer both geographically and theologically. In any case he believed that Durie's objectives were unobtainable: they would, he wrote, 'produce good, if they could be carried out'.[69] Nonetheless the archbishop insisted that Durie, a Presbyterian minister, be reordained into the Church of England before he appointed him to the vicarage of Saxby, Lincolnshire. This time the living was vacant, but it was so paltry that it paid Durie less than he had to pay for the curate's stipend. Poorer in pocket, although not in zeal, Durie returned to Germany to spend the rest of his life pursuing the ephemeral dream of ecumenicalism, while Laud continued to follow the almost equally elusive goal of reforming the Church of England.

No one could deny that the Anglican Church needed reform. At Langley, in the diocese of Lincoln, the churchwardens stripped the lead from the church roof and melted it down.[70] When some of the molten lead spilled on the ground and flowed into an open grave, they dug up the coffin, which they burnt with the corpse inside it to recover the precious metal. At Llanidloes, Montgomery, the vicar cut up the surplices for tea towels, and allowed pigeon shooting inside the nave. At Rye gunpowder was stored in the chancel, and a recalcitrant servant was whipped there. A brewery stood in Chester Cathedral close. At Stratford-on-Avon pigs and chickens were allowed to root and roost in the chancel, where they manured Shakespeare's tomb. Further south at Knotting, Bedfordshire, the church-wardens staged cock fights in the chancel, which were attended by crowds of enthusiastic gamblers.[71] At Lancing, Sussex, pigeons flew through the broken windows and left droppings in the church.[72] Such details do not, of course, tell the whole story. No institution as large as the seventeenth-century Church of England, no matter how efficient, could be completely free of blemishes. But such incidents profoundly affected Laud, who (as his annual reports to the king showed) saw things not as a generalised whole, but as the sum of the particulars. Even though there was in fact far more support for Laud and his reforms at the grass-roots level than has been supposed, largely because the surviving records and the investigatory machinery highlighted opposition, cases of disobedience, such as that at Beckington, as opposed to those of compliance, stood out.[73] Indeed, any deviation from his rigorous norms would have upset Laud, who wanted a degree of conformity so high as to be virtually unattainable. He remembered vignettes, and even though he feared that at times they might be 'too homely', by using mundane images he communicated 'my just indignation' to ordinary men and women. As he put it in one of his most powerful commonplaces, 'But this is the misery, 'tis superstition now-a-days, for any man to come with more reverence into a church, than a tinker and his bitch come into an ale-house.'[74]

To keep irreverent tinkers and their bitches out of the church (where either might snatch the bread from the altar), and to keep the church from becoming no better than an ale house, Laud pursued four main policies. First, he attempted to enhance the Church of England's economic position. Second, he tried to reduce outside interference in the church's affairs. Third, he wanted to use and improve the church's administrative machinery, and, fourth, he wanted to educate a cadre of dedicated disciples who would carry on his good work after he was gone.

Certainly the Church of England was in poor financial shape. Its income had failed to keep up with more than a century of inflation, and much of it had fallen into the pockets of laymen. Thirty-six per cent of the livings in England had been thus impropriated, which meant that every year revenue worth between £232,000 and £325,000 was lost to the church.[75] The consequences of diverting an average of between £23 and £35 per annum from each parish were obvious. In the Isle of Man, where 90 per cent of the livings were worth less than £4 a year, only two or three of the seventeen priests were literate, the diocese being, Laud noted, full of 'many unlearned and unworthy ministers'.[76] As he concluded, 'The Clergy must needs be as ignorant as their means.' Clerical incomes were unfairly distributed. The vicarage of St Mary's, Ashwell, Hertfordshire, was worth £520 per annum, while five miles down the road the incumbent at Royston had to make do with £5 a year.[77] The Bishop of St David's (as Laud knew only too well) had to scrape by on only £200 a year, less than a tenth of what his brethren at Ely, Durham and Winchester enjoyed. William Harrison noted in his *Description of England* (1577) that many parishes were so poor that they could not 'maintain a mean scholar let alone a learned one'.[78] Seven years later Archbishop Whitgift estimated that only 15 per cent of them were solvent enough to support any sort of scholar at all. The trouble was that in the following half-century not only did parishes get poorer but scholars became more numerous, more learned, and thus more expensive. The number of university graduates entering the ministry, who unlike their pre-Reformation counterparts usually had families to support, increased dramatically. In the diocese of Worcester, for example, the proportion of ministers with degrees rose by 84 per cent between 1560 and 1640.

While Laud recognised only too well that the Church of England had economic problems, the steps that he took to alleviate them were in fact not as far-reaching as has sometimes been thought. For example, while agreeing that a good clergyman must be appointed to the new chapel serving Putney and Mortlake, 'a place of great inconformity', he did nothing more than hope that the patron, the Earl of Wimbledon, would provide a sufficient stipend. Occasionally he suggested financial solutions, as at Peterborough, where he told the Dean and Chapter to use £310 from the leases of the manors of Castor and Sutton to repair the cathedral.[79]

Laud saw leases as a significant means of improving episcopal incomes. Even before he went to Canterbury he tried to prevent his fellow bishops from making excessively long leases in which they received a large premium, known as an entry fine, to compensate for the loss of real income that their successors would suffer as rents failed to match inflation.[80] In 1634, the king, at the archbishop's request, ordered that no bishop, prebend, or dean and chapter should make leases for longer than twenty-one years, and certainly not for the three lives that had been the practice, which had allowed them 'to enrich their families at the expense of their successors'. The weakness of this policy of focusing on improving diocesan income was that it directed attention towards the cathedral, rather than the parish church, where the need was the greatest.[81]

Another area where Laud tried to reform ecclesiastical revenues was the London tithes. For nearly a century they had not been adjusted to keep pace with inflation, so that the rector of St Martin's, Ongar, could complain that he only received £73. 7s. 10d. a year instead of the £1,600 that was his due. Because the City of London's courts, and not the Church of England's, heard tithe cases, and because parliament had on several occasions rejected attempts to bring them in line with the cost of living, a group of clergy petitioned Charles for redress. Although they had Laud's private support, and the king's public sympathy, their suit produced little more than a long set of negotiations and hearings, basically because the king did not wish to alienate the City any further since he desperately needed to borrow from it, and because Londoners were notoriously reluctant to pay for any church minister with whom they were not in agreement.[82]

Quite clearly there were limits to royal support in trying to resolve a problem that anyway was not so serious as Laud's activities would suggest. Between 1535 and 1650 the average income of ministers in London rose by 625 per cent as compared to a 650 per cent increase in the cost of living.[83]

One sure way a cleric could improve his own income was by holding more than one job at a time. This practice, known as pluralism, meant that the minister neglected at least one of his parishes, where a poorly paid and thus poorly motivated curate performed his duties while the minister pocketed the profits. Such curates served in between an eighth to a quarter of English parishes.[84] Some pluralists were notorious. Beside John Atherton's request that, in return for giving up his living at Huish Champflower, Somerset, on being appointed to a position in Dublin, his successor pay him £300 or else agree to marry his daughter, Laud sardonically noted, 'Excellent honest simony'.[85] His reaction to another pluralist from Ireland (where poverty made the practice a ubiquitous necessity) was equally droll. He wondered if the Archbishop of Cashel, who held sixteen livings at one time, would develop 'a sciatica in his conscience sooner than in his hips'.[86] However, Laud not only tolerated pluralism but practised it himself. While admitting that 'the clergy cannot be great when they have not to eat where they reside', he was personally a pluralist from whom livings had to be prised when he left the presidency of St John's, and who gave his old college several multiple livings. On several occasions he told parishioners that they must accept the appointment of pluralists since it was the king's pleasure.[87]

One reason for the financial pressures that produced pluralism was the impropriation of income by laymen, which raised the equally important question of control. 'I will not endure that any lay person (much less a corporation) have power to place or displace curates or beneficed priests at their pleasure,' insisted the archbishop. Thus when the villagers of Hammersmith collected £250 to build a chapel, and their representative, the Earl of Mulgrave, asked if they might appoint the priest, the archbishop replied, 'My Lord, I shall be very unwilling to give way to any popular nomination; but if the inhabitants will trust me with the nomination, I will see that they shall have an honest and painful man.'[88] Characteristically Laud turned a matter of procedure, which could be negotiated, into one of trust that allowed no compromise. He even had reservations about Queen Elizabeth's injunctions ordering clergy to set aside a proportion of their stipends in order to send poor young scholars to university, not because he opposed such a fine objective (he had himself attended Oxford on similar terms), but because he preferred to 'leave the Clergy free masters of their own charity'. He noted of the queen's commands, 'I doubt they are hardly of a binding force.'[89]

In practice, time and time again, despite high declarations that he would not 'give away a hair of my bishropic', Laud was obliged to render unto Caesar that which he would have preferred to keep, if not for God, at least for the Church of England. The law severely limited bishops' ability to interfere with the rights of laymen – and the king in particular – to exercise church patronage. So when Charles made Humphrey Peake lecturer of St Margaret's, London, Laud wrote sympathetically to the parishioners that there was nothing he could do about it.[90]

There was, however, a great deal that parishioners could do about the appointment and dismissal of lecturers – that, after all, was the whole point of paying for them in the first place.[91] Money would be raised to support a minister chosen for his preaching ability to give extra sermons, particularly on Wednesdays or market days. Since merchants could usually afford them, lecturers tended to be concentrated in towns: 90 per cent of London's parishes had them, for instance. While most lecturers were orthodox men, intent on reviving the faith – a goal that Laud shared – they had a degree of independence from episcopal authority, a licence that he abhorred. Thus the main objective of the injunctions that he had the king issue in 1629, and reissued in 1631 and 1634, was that lectures be given only by beneficed clergy, subject to the discipline of their bishop, who could deprive them of their livings. As with the Feoffees, Laud did not bother to try and seek a mutually agreeable solution.

Another instance where a jurisdictional dispute superseded a shared problem involved church ales. In many parishes, particularly in Somerset, a feast was held to celebrate the anniversary of the church's dedication. These occasions often degenerated into drunkenness and violence, so the justices of the peace and the king's justices on circuit would ban them. Chief Justice Richardson's renewal of the Somerset ban in 1632 outraged Laud, not because he approved of drunkenness in churches, but because the judge had issued the ban without first informing the local bishop.

Many people opposed church ales because they profaned the sabbath, which they believed should be kept holy as a day of rest, and of strenuous sermons. But for many folk Sunday was the only day they had for recreation. 'When shall the common people have leave to exercise, if not on Sundays, seeing they must apply their labour and win their living on all working days?' asked the king's order of 18 October 1633 reissuing the *Book of Sports*.[92] In many ways this book, which James I had first promulgated in 1618, was an eminently sensible edict allowing people to enjoy wholesome recreations after they had attended church on Sundays. But keeping the sabbath holy was an issue that aroused deep passions. The vicar of Olney, Buckinghamshire, was threatened with excommunication for trying to stop dancing after Sunday church, while the incumbent of Tunbridge Wells was nearly lynched for promoting sabbath sports and setting up a maypole.[93] Since quarrels over the sabbath sometimes reached the privy council, Laud should have been more sensitive to the issue, and should never have asked the king to order all ministers to read the edict from the pulpit.[94] Having to do so put them on the spot. Deeply resentful, most complied. Some compromised: one minister read the *Book of Sports* and then the Ten Commandments before telling his flock, 'You have heard the commandments of God and Man, obey which you please.'[95] A few refused, and were suspended from their livings. When one of them, Richard Culmer, asked Laud for a pardon, the archbishop supposedly replied, 'If you do not know how to obey, I do not know how to grant.' Once more the matter was turned into one of authority not faith, of priestly power not pastoral care. Laud summed up his attitude in a note he made beside a set of orders the Lord Mayor of London issued for the better keeping of the sabbath: 'My Jurisdiction encroached.'[96]

The church's administrative machinery limited Laud's efforts to protect and expand its jurisdiction. The Church of England was a vast bureaucracy, with all a bureaucracy's strengths and weaknesses. It produced huge amounts of paper, from the registers of baptisms, funerals and marriages at the parish level, to the annual reports the archbishops sent to the king. Like most bureaucracies it was committed to routine, to a quiet life, and was inimical to reformers such as Laud. As Archbishop of Canterbury he had to plough through a great mass of material – idleness was never one of Laud's faults. His energy meant that he got bogged down in the most trivial details – such as finding a good plumber to serve the needs of the archdeanery of Buckingham.[97] To handle all this business the archbishop had a clerk who read aloud incoming petitions, and then Laud dictated his answers. On 7 July 1637, for instance, he heard a petition to be allowed to attend a nearby church, rather than the parish church, which was two miles away from the petitioner's house (and presumably even further removed from his religious views), and a request from a young man that his case should no longer be delayed in the church courts. He referred both matters to Sir John Lambe, Dean of the Court of Arches.

Church courts operated at the provincial and diocesan level, dealing with legal matters such as wills and probate, and moral ones, such as adultery, bastardy, and fornication. In the former instance they performed a useful service, while in the latter they enforced generally accepted *mores*. By and large they operated efficiently, and often more impartially than secular courts, for they were run by a dedicated and well-trained set of officials. As early as 1626 Laud told parliament that he believed that the authority of the church courts should be increased.[98] They were his sort of tool – clean, cold and concise. On becoming Bishop of London, and then Archbishop of Canterbury, he quickly put his mark on the courts under his control. He was angry when attempts were made to delay cases before the ecclesiastical courts, telling Lambe in one such instance to 'take this business to heart'.[99] When a petitioner complained that the court of the Welsh Marches was stopping church wardens from bringing matters before ecclesiastical courts, the archbishop sent Sir John Bridgeman, Chief Justice of Wales, a curt letter hoping that this was not so.[100] The following month Laud had the king issue a proclamation permitting a bishop to grant an injunction from an ecclesiastical court, without a patent under the great seal.[101] Even with his friends Laud tolerated no infringement of the rights of churchmen or their courts. When Wentworth told him that he had dismissed a priest for paying a bribe to obtain an appointment without referring the offence to the court of High Commission, the archbishop told the Lord Deputy that his action was 'the most odious abuse . . . it is against the law of nature; for it hangs a man first, and tries his case afterwards'.[102] Though his anger certainly did not spring from any deep-seated concern for due process, he was right to preserve the integrity of church courts, for they were settled institutions, with regular procedures, as compared to the other instruments of church control, which operated occasionally, thus having only sporadic effect.

One such instrument was the visitation. Every few years a bishop would visit his parishes, or send out commissioners armed with long lists of questions, to assess the state of the diocese. Laud made strenuous efforts to obtain the right to visit Cambridge University, and to ensure that no part of his province was exempt from his jurisdiction as archbishop. Although he set great store by visitations, taking great pains in drawing up the questions, they tended to be superficial tools.[103] In the 1636 Sussex visitation only one of the 202 items found amiss was actually reported to the bishop, while in Kent the visitors' orders about Communion rails, kneeling, and altars were widely ignored.[104] At best the impact of visitations on stamping out Puritan education was 'marginal'.[105] In a day or two, no matter how thorough the questionnaires, an inspector could barely scratch the surface. Take the visitation Sir Nathaniel Brent, Laud's Vicar General, made in the summer of 1635. At Norwich he was concerned about the privy at the west end of the cathedral, and the failure of several priests to wear vestments. At Swaffham he reported 'few puritans at this place, but much drunkenness'. He threatened to dismiss Samuel Cobb, the schoolmaster at Oundle, for refusing to bow at the name of Jesus. At Derby he suspended three clergymen for celebrating clandestine marriages, and two more for being notorious drunkards (all of whom were reinstated the next day on the petition of their colleagues). He reported that in Gloucester Cathedral, which years before, as dean, Laud had tried to reform, there were 'many things amiss'. So superficial was Brent's lightning tour that he had to admit on 16 June, 'I have suspended a notorious popish school master in Ruardean in the Forest of Dean whose name I have forgotten.'[106]

Visitations were important sources of information that helped produce the annual reports on the state of the church in their provinces, which the archbishops of Canterbury and York sent the king every January. In most instances the information from visitations went to the bishop, who used it in his report to Laud. The archbishop took the composition of these reports seriously; his were far more detailed than were, for instance, Abbot's, or even Neile's from York.

Starting with Canterbury itself, the archbishop's annual report briefly listed problems diocese by diocese. Often the points made were trivial: 'a seditious lecturer at Ripon'; 'many giddy in matters of religion' in South Hertfordshire; 'the usual . . . a great resort of recusants at Holywell'. In his reports Laud never tried to provide an overview of the church; he failed to synthesise, to relate one year to the past, or to set goals for the future. But the reports do reveal an interesting facet of the church as a bureaucracy. In Sussex and Nottingham, at least, churchwardens – like wily taxpayers – quickly learned that so long as they filled out the forms correctly, and did not draw attention to any serious problems, the bishop and his officers would be unlikely to audit them.[107] In much the same way bishops quickly learned that if they admitted to major defects in their dioceses they would soon bring Laud or one of his minions down to find out what was wrong and whom to blame. Thus in 1636 the Bishop of St David's reported 'all things in order', while admitting that the vicar of Pengam had attacked holy days, so as to make his optimistic report seem credible. New bishops might first tell their superior that they faced serious problems, but after two or three years they would report that all was well in order to claim credit for having done an excellent job. So by the time the Long Parliament met, and started to attack episcopacy, the intelligence reaching the crown revealed a church that was prosperous, well-governed and contented.[108] Indeed, anyone reading these reports who was utterly ignorant of English history might be flabbergasted to learn that within a few years the happy, healthy church they described would face the most dangerous crisis it had yet known.

Ultimately the machinery that Laud used to reform the church was only as good as the men who ran it. He could bully, he could reward, particularly with the carrot of promotion. 'God speed you well in Derry', wrote Laud to Bramhall, who was travelling around Ireland sending back reports on the state of the church, 'you are in a good way for that bishopric.'[109] But often the archbishop had to lead, using his own officials, friends and followers.

Perhaps the most important of Laud's lieutenants was Sir John Lambe.[110] Born in about 1566 and educated at St John's College, Cambridge, Lambe first came to prominence in 1623 when the Mayor and Corporation of Northampton petitioned parliament about his overzealous prosecution as registrar of Peterborough of local Nonconformists. James I quashed the complaint by awarding Lambe a knighthood, and Bishop Williams made him his commissary at Lincoln. Three years later Lambe broke with Williams because he refused to help him prosecute a conventicle of Nonconformists, the details of which he secretly relayed to the privy council, much to Laud's delight. One of Laud's first acts on becoming archbishop was to dismiss Sir Henry Marten, a distinguished civil lawyer, from his post as Dean of the Court of Arches and put Lambe in his place. John Hacket, Williams's biographer (and thus a biased source) described Lambe as 'very officious . . . crafty . . . hated of all men . . . ravenous in taking fees'.[111] He certainly lacked his predecessor's independence: once he told the privy council, 'I serve under my Lord's Grace of Canterbury and what you will have me do I will do.' At heart a bully who would terrify opponents in court into submission, Lambe made up for his lack of originality by great energy and overweening ambition. Even though wags likened him to a wolf rather than a lamb, his loyalty and tenacity made him the ideal factotum for Laud.

In the day-to-day administration of church business the ubiquitous Dr Duck was indispensable. Born in 1580 and educated at Exeter College, Oxford, Arthur Duck was a Doctor of Civil Laws whom Laud appointed chancellor of the diocese of London in 1628, and of Bath and Wells in 1635. His hand quite literally appears everywhere, drafting letters for the king on church affairs, helping the archbishop in his squabbles over the position of the altar, visiting refractory Oxford colleges, reminding his master of friends to be rewarded and enemies who must be punished. Unlike Lambe, he remained in his master's shadow, settling the details while helping carry the immense burden of the archbishop's administrative load.

In the task of running the Church of England the selection of bishops was crucial. All of the eleven men first appointed to the episcopal bench during Laud's primacy were firm allies. Some, such as Matthew Wren of Ely and later Norwich, shared his harshness, being, as a Cambridge don put it, 'wonderful ambitious'.[112] A few, such as William Juxon (who succeeded Laud as Bishop of London in 1633), were milder men who could conciliate, and lead the flock with reason, rather than drive them with harsh words and sterile edicts. Only five of them were first appointed to the episcopal bench before 1637, when Laud's ecclesiastical policies had made themselves felt. Two of the five, however, Edmund Griffith of Bangor, and Roger Manwaring at St David's, were incumbents in places too far from the centre to exercise much influence. Because bishops were frequently moved from diocese to diocese, their influence was muted. On the other hand all the men appointed to the episcopal bench during Laud's primacy upset the balance that had existed within the established church for at least two and perhaps as many as three generations. His ability to influence the composition of the church at a less senior level was far more limited. Out of the 9,000 livings in the Church of England only 144 were in the Archbishop of Canterbury's gift, and since they fell open infrequently between March 1635 and February 1638 he was able to make only twenty-seven appointments, two of which went to his kinsman Richard Baylie.[113] Although Laud could, of course, attempt to influence the patronage exercised by others to further the careers of clerics who agreed with him, he does not appear to have done so – at least in the case of the Lord Keeper, the largest secular holder of advowsons.[114] Nonetheless, a distinguished historian has concluded that in promoting such men, in upsetting the *via media*, 'Archbishop Laud was indeed the greatest calamity visited upon the English Church'.[115]

That sweeping judgment perhaps exaggerates the archbishop's importance, but there is no doubt that his attempts to reform the church ended in failure. Thus on one level the question 'Could they ever have succeeded?' is an academic one, for the future was to prove Laud disastrously wrong.

One of the most effective ways of trying to shape the future, particularly in the long term, is through education. Laud hoped that his reforms at Oxford would produce generations of ministers ready to carry on his programme. His university reforms worked, the statutes at Oxford and Trinity College, Dublin, proving remarkably durable, but there is no evidence that the universities produced a flock of zealous ministers eager to carry the Laudian standard. If the post-Restoration and eighteenth-century Churches of England and Church of Ireland and the universities of Oxford and Dublin were Laud's legacy, then his educational policies cannot, by any stretch of the imagination, be called resounding successes.

Much attention has been paid to the archbishop's attempts to solve the Church of England's financial problems. He has been accused of 'trying to revive the Middle Ages, not only in ceremony, but also in economics'.[116] Ironically Laud's detractors have exaggerated his efforts, for although in his correspondence to Wentworth he talked a lot about reform, about 'Thorough', a vaguely defined attempt to promote the public good over private interests and thus create an ideal society, such aspirations were more an outlet for his frustrations than a concrete, realistic goal. Most of his attempts to reform the church financially referred not to the Anglican Church but to that of Ireland, a Protestant body so irrelevantly moribund in that Catholic nation that its resuscitation was far more likely to bring most Irishmen to revolution rather than to salvation. Frequently Laud's high aspirations were salves for disappointment. In the well-known letter he sent to Bishop Bedell of Kilmore, acknowledging that in reality pluralism could not possibly be abolished in the Church of Ireland, he wrote:

> And I wish as heartily as you, that there were a dissolving of
> pluralities, especially in bishoprics. But as these times are, this
> cannot well be thought on, till the means of the Church there be so
> settled, as that men may be able to live in some sort answerable
> to the dignity of their calling. For poverty draws on contempt, and
> contempt makes clergymen unserviceable to God, the Church and
> the commonwealth.

What at first glance might appear to have been a declaration of financial independence for the Church of Ireland (not England) was in fact a *cri de coeur* that it might survive: 'for God forbid that Church should be an incurable body,' the archbishop concluded.[117]

The limits of Laud's reforms may be seen in his own cathedral at Canterbury. A year after becoming archbishop Laud sent the Dean and Chapter of Canterbury eighteen questions on the state of the building. He was interested in mundane details. Were children allowed to play in the churchyard? Did the clergy wear square caps in church? What were the choristers' wages?[118] Using the king's directive he demolished stalls squatters had put up too close to the cathedral (which upset a lot of property owners), and restored the Arundel Tower, while improving the facilities for the choir. By moving preaching from a chapel at the back of the cathedral to the chancel he made the sermon-hungry Puritans attend the whole of divine service – much to their annoyance. To pay for all this he increased the cathedral's rentals and cut its charity to the poor.[119] He revised the cathedral's statutes, and ordered the chapter to appoint an archivist to catalogue and maintain their records. In spite of all these reforms he had to admit in June 1637, a month before the Scots crisis started, 'It troubles me not a little that I have taken so much care for the honour and peace of that Church, as I have done, and with so little success.'[120]

Laud's financial reforms had comparatively little impact for three reasons. First, they were intended to help the cathedral clergy, who played a far less important role in the church's pastoral life than those in the parishes, and who many Protestants thought were 'loitering lubbers'.[121] Second, the reforms threatened the vested interests of important segments of the nation, who resisted them with vigour, but without the desire for revenge that has been supposed. Third, the archbishop had to operate through the church's bureaucracy, which although comparatively efficient was hampered by legal restrictions, the greed of other men, and the sloth of its own servants. Like the centurion of the Bible, Laud believed that if he told men to do something they would do it automatically, that if he made statutes they would be followed, that if he sent questionnaires they would be answered honestly, and that men would obey rather than say yes and the next day carry on just as before. Laud failed to find common ground with his opponents. He neglected those groups within the church that supported his reforms. He relied on competition rather than co-operation. He struck things down and rarely put up anything in their place. All too often, as his attempts to visit Cambridge University showed, his victories were Pyrrhic.

In all his church policies his ideas and his actions contradicted each other. He maintained a fine intellectual commitment to ecumenicalism that today many churchmen find particularly attractive. But at the time his toleration for all Christians, including Catholics, was enough to scare many Englishmen, while his reluctance to support John Durie showed how shallow his support for ecumenicalism really was. Time and time again the minister who from the pulpit preached unity, from his study pursued divisive policies. Indeed, no state paper has survived in which Laud placed the need to maintain political unity before achieving his goals. He did, however, frequently recognise the political limitations on his ecclesiastical power, particularly as regards pluralism and the appointment of bishops. While Laud might declare that 'against the church I shall not serve', time and time again he had to give way to powerfully connected job-seekers, particularly when they had the king's support.[122] When forced to bow to the realities of court politics he sounded especially bitter. But he should not have been surprised, for he only had to look at his own career, with the disputed St John's elections, and his acrimonious encounters with Abbot at Oxford, to realise that the secular authorities had ultimate control over the church.

Thus after the Laudian tide receded men saw that the high claims His Grace of Canterbury made for the established church were built upon the sands of lay *Realpolitik*. When Scudamore asked him if enjoying impropriated church income was wrong, Laud, with that honesty he found possible only with the closest of friends, replied that such monies were due to priests by act of God, which no act of parliament could possibly excuse.[123] Had St Thomas More's ghost been able to read this letter he would surely have approved. Bishops, Laud maintained, ruled through divine power: the church was a separate institution that must ultimately render to God, not Caesar. In normal times such myths did not matter – ambiguity and contradictions smooth over civilisation's cracks. But as Laud (like Thomas More) discovered, when normality had broken down, men insisted on secure principles rather than vague compromise.

VII

'The Richelieu of England'

In April 1635, less than two years after Charles made him Archbishop of Canterbury, and less than two weeks after Lord Treasurer Weston died, Sir Thomas Roe wrote to Elizabeth, the exiled Queen of Bohemia, about William Laud as follows:

> This is the great man, made now of the Commissioners of the Treasury, and the First of the Junto in Foreign Affairs, and in the greatest esteem with his Majesty of any in my observance, and I will hope . . . that he will prove a happy instrument of the public, both at home and abroad.

Roe, who was one of the most perceptive men of his generation, had recognised that Laud was now a minister with powers and responsibilities that extended at home and abroad far beyond those normally exercised by an Archbishop of Canterbury. Following the death of his rival, Weston, and his appointment to a position where he could play a leading role in the formation of financial and foreign policies, there seemed to be no limit on his influence so long as he continued to bask warmly in the king's favour. Thus Roe concluded his letter to Charles's sister by advising her to cultivate Laud, to bring him around to her side and thus 'show him the way to make himself the Richelieu of England'.[1]

While Roe's expectations were, of course, unfulfilled, the archbishop's enemies feared his growing power. Unlike Cardinal Richelieu, however, Laud was not the king's chief minister, Charles was not a minor unable to rule on his own, nor was the English monarchy as untrammelled by legal and constitutional restrictions as that of France. After Buckingham's death the king was determined that no subject should ever again dominate English politics as he had done. He retreated to the world of the court; the queen replaced Buckingham in his affections and came to exert considerable influence. A careful man, with a small yet tidy mind, Charles departmentalised the work of government during the personal rule, allowing each

111

minister considerable latitude within his assigned area of responsibility. Although the archbishop talked of the desirability of having each of the crown's great ministers dependent on the king, in fact, if they went about their business, quietly doing their part to govern the realm, Charles allowed them considerable independence.[2]

Laud's own view of the politics of the 1630s stressed the significance of faction and confrontation. These certainly existed, but they were not as widespread as the archbishop believed. He had always seen politics in terms of great personal ties, of fights if not to the death at least to dismissal, ignominy, and perhaps the Tower. At Oxford he had seen Abbot and his cronies as his mortal enemies. As a junior bishop his erstwhile mentor, John Williams, became the *bête noire* who haunted him waking and sleeping. After Buckingham's murder, Lord Treasurer Weston became Laud's bugbear; following Weston's death, Sir Francis Cottington emerged as his bogeyman. If anything, as time went on, this fear that can only be described as paranoia got worse and became a subject of concern to his friends. 'For to confess a truth,' confided Wentworth to Windebank in June 1634, 'he is already, since he came to be his Grace of Canterbury, gotten forth out of our reach.'[3]

By the spring of 1634, however, it seemed to many of the king's councillors that it was Weston who was out of their reach. Signs of royal favour towards the Lord Treasurer were manifold. Weston's daughter had married Lord Feilding, Buckingham's nephew; his son had wed the Duchess of Lennox; on 7 January 1634 the king created Weston Earl of Portland.[4] Partly out of jealousy, and partly because they opposed his pro-Spanish foreign policy, the archbishop and Lord Keeper Coventry attacked Weston for selling off to the public, at ridiculously low prices, timber from crown forests that had been earmarked for the Royal Navy. 'But is it not a pitiful case that a gracious Prince should' asked the outraged archbishop, 'be left poor whilst so many enrich themselves?'[5] He brought the matter to the attention of the king, who evidently took it seriously enough to frighten Weston. Ill in bed at the time, Weston sent his son and daughter-in-law to Charles to defend him. Even Lady Buckingham, the favourite's widow, came to court for the first time in years to plead for the Lord Treasurer. It worked. When Weston was well enough to return to Greenwich Palace in early May, the king received him warmly, to the great confusion of his enemies.[6]

At this point Laud should have had enough sense to let the matter drop. Weston might have been turned into a good ally, and anyway the king needed someone with his financial abilities to help with the introduction of ship money. But with the academic's penchant for pursuing a vendetta long after it should have been allowed to die gracefully, the archbishop continued to rage against Weston and his ally Sir Francis Cottington, and even against

Windebank: he complained to Wentworth that Cottington 'hath tempted my old friend, the Secretary from me, and he is become his man'.[7] The feud between Laud and Cottington should never have come about, for the two shared many common goals. Once they had worked amicably together: Cottington had arranged the delivery of two hundred tons of the best timber for the St John's quadrangle, and had raised money for the restoration of St Paul's. Essentially, then, their quarrel, for which Laud was mostly to blame, was caused by the clash of both men's ambitions, and by the archbishop's insecurity.[8] The latter got worse in August when Laud heard of the death of William Noy, the Attorney General who had prosecuted Prynne in Star Chamber. Although as the Venetian ambassador noted, 'He is lamented by few,' Laud certainly mourned Noy's passing. 'I have lost a dear friend,' he noted in his diary, 'and the Church the greatest she had of his condition.'[9]

In order to redress the balance, the following month the archbishop and his allies struck back, persuading the king to dismiss Sir Robert Heath as Chief Justice of Common Pleas. Convinced that he was soft on Puritans, and would obstruct their reform efforts, they wanted Heath dismissed from the privy council, and so revived the familiar charge of selling crown lands to private buyers at give-away prices.[10] This time the allegations stuck, and the faction fight between Laud and Coventry, Weston and Cottington was tied at one round apiece. During the winter the former seemed to be winning on points, although, as far as Laud was concerned, at considerable personal cost. In February 1635 Charles made him a member of the privy council committees on trade and revenue, and on 1 March asked him to think about 'the great business' and to 'give him account'.[11] Nonetheless Laud was under considerable strain. 'I was never so busy as I am at the present, and am heartily weary,' he wrote to Wentworth on the 4th, telling Bishop Bramhall the same day that he never 'had less leisure in his life'.[12]

In one sense Weston's death nine days later on 13 March 1635 came as a relief to his enemies. 'I am delivered of the heaviest adversary I ever had,' wrote Wentworth. But it provided no respite from the burdens of work. The king's councillors were so divided (and the king was so irresolute) that no one had sufficient support to be made Lord Treasurer, and the king had to appoint a commission consisting of Windebank, Coke, Edward Montagu, Earl of Manchester, Sir Henry Montagu, Cottington and Laud. The commission was badly divided. Cottington blamed Laud for persuading the king to place the office in commission in order to thwart his own candidacy as Lord Treasurer, a post for which he was convinced that his experience as Chancellor of the Exchequer ideally suited him.

With his customary lack of sensitivity for other men's feelings, Laud lost no time in getting down to business. On 16 March as first commissioner he called the first meeting, which decided to sit every Tuesday, Thursday and Saturday afternoon.[13] Convinced that Weston had been lining his pockets at the public expense the archbishop demanded an audit of the accounts. 'What we shall find there I know not in particular,' he told Wentworth, 'but sure I am a hard estate.' Initially Cottington reported that during the past year the crown had a surplus of £53,358. 8s. 2d. Laud wanted further details. The Chancellor of the Exchequer procrastinated. Windebank sided with Laud, warning the king that the financial position was so serious that 'If your Majesty continue it in this way, your service will infinitely suffer.'[14] In fact the king's true annual deficit was running at about £18,000 a year, and the crown's debts totalled over £1 million.[15] Even though the audit turned up no evidence of peculation by Weston, it further strained relations between the commissioners and produced an immense amount of work. They received reports on the state of the customs revenue, royal lands, knighthood fines, recusancy fines, income from the royal mint, from the Duchy of Lancaster, from the farming out of the tin and the soap monopolies. Personally Laud examined disbursements from the public works, the customs, the soap monopoly, first fruits, recusancy fines, and annotated masses of papers dealing with crown loans, and abuses in the Office of the Pells. But most of these audits were too out-of-date to produce a useful picture of the crown's finances, and too detailed to give Laud much spare time.[16] 'I have not leisure since I meddled with the Treasury . . . the accounts are so many, so long delayed, so confounded, so broken, so all naught, that I have every day less hope than other to do any great good.'[17]

According to one diplomat Laud and Cottington quarrelled 'daily' and thus could do little to improve the king's revenues. 'In our commission,' Cottington told Wentworth (perhaps in the hope that he would intervene to alleviate his friend's obduracy), 'we run our business extreme ill, and so, if it continue, we shall spoil all.'[18] In the face of Cottington's superior financial knowledge Laud felt inferior, and thus he often became truculent in meetings; then the next day, full of remorse, he would apologise. Finding Cottington's frivolity particularly irritating, he fell into the traps his adversary set for him. For instance, the king wanted to build a ten-mile-long brick wall around his hunting preserve at Richmond Park. Both Laud and Cottington opposed the idea because it would cost £10,000; but when Cottington realised that the king was determined to have the wall, he changed his mind, telling the council that he believed the project was sensible and, even though it meant enclosing land, it was completely lawful. Anyone who thwarted the king's recreations, the chancellor told him teasingly, opposed the king's health, and might that not be construed as treason? Laud, whose hatred of enclosures was well known, complained to the king, who reproved him for intemperately leaping to conclusions and remarked, 'See how unjustly your passion hath transported you.'[19]

Laud and Cottington also clashed over the soap monopoly. In 1631 the Company of Soap Makers of Westminster, who were a front for the queen's and Weston's Catholic friends, won the lucrative soap monopoly, for which they agreed to pay the crown a royalty of £4 a ton. Most Protestant Englishmen found this new soap as odious as the faith of its manufacturers. There were even riots against it in London, while all over the country people made their own, illegal soap. Cashing in on public discontent, the old soap manufacturers tried to regain their monopoly by offering to pay double the royalty. The archbishop argued that the crown should accept their tender on financial grounds, but could only persuade Manchester to support him. Coke hedged, while Edward Sackville, Earl of Dorset, and Thomas Howard, Earl of Arundel, joined with Cottington and Windebank to oppose the change. Laud was livid: he wrote to Wentworth, 'You shall not need to bid me not to trust Cottington; for I assure you the business of the soap hath washed off all that from me. But is it possible that Cottington should have so shamefully betrayed you for Coventry, whom he hates deadly?'[20] However, the archbishop reserved his full venom for Windebank, who he was convinced had betrayed him after thirty years' friendship going back to St John's. Had he not obtained the Secretary of State's office for the ingrate? 'No one thing hath troubled me more,' Laud lamented.[21]

The third conflict between Laud and Cottington involved the case of Sir Anthony Pell, who sued Sir James Bagg for the £2,500 that he claimed he had paid him for his help in attempting to obtain the repayment of a £6,000 loan from the crown. The queen, still smarting from Laud's efforts to deprive her friends of the soap monopoly, supported Bagg, who had been Buckingham's factotum, by coming in person to Whitehall to watch the proceedings. Convinced that the defendant was guilty of taking bribes, the archbishop sided with Pell, while Cottington supported Bagg. Although the privy council split on political lines ten to nine against Bagg, the king ignored the verdict by keeping him as Governor of Portsmouth. The tide seemed to be turning against Laud. 'There is a mortal quarrel between the Archbishop and my Lord Cottington,' Secretary Conway reported in November, 'but Cottington hath gained the King's favour and the archbishop lost.'[22]

The battle ground that would determine which way the battle went was the appointment of a new Lord Treasurer. It was obvious to all that the commission was not working, and that the king would have to return to the normal practice of having one man responsible for the Treasury. There were three frontrunners: Wentworth, who did not particularly want the job, and whom the king wanted to keep in Ireland; Cottington, the best qualified, and odds-on favourite, whom the queen supported; and Juxon, the dark horse running in the church's colours.[23] During the Christmas season Laud took advantage of Cottington's absence from court, due to a bout of pneumonia and the gout, to have several tête-à-têtes with the king. He gave Charles a list of thirty-one bishops who had been Lord Treasurer between 1066 and 1470, to prove that there were ample precedents for appointing a prelate to that office. Indeed, he added, an unmarried priest enjoyed a distinct advantage: having no family to provide for, he would not be tempted to embezzle the crown's revenues as Weston had been.

Accepting these arguments, on 6 March 1636 Charles suddenly announced the appointment of Juxon as Lord Treasurer. ' 'Tis news indeed,' reported one gossip, 'we begin to live here in the Church Triumphant.' Another complained that now bishops 'swarm mightily about the court'.[24] Ecstatically Laud noted in his diary, 'No Churchman had made it since Henry 7 time. I pray God bless him to carry it so that the Church may have honour, and the King and State service and contentment by it. And now if the Church will not hold themselves up under God, I can do no more.'[25] Quite simply Laud had won, and won decisively. Cottington was to remain a nuisance – indeed, a threat who the archbishop dreaded would somehow make an alliance to bring Williams back from exile in Buckden. But for the next two or three years, of all His Majesty's privy councillors, My Lord of Canterbury was the first amongst a motley bunch of equals, who no longer fought each other with their old ferocity, not because they had learned to love each other for the good of their master's service, but because there was no point. If fighting broke out again it was obvious who would win.

Much of the credit for the comparative peace in ministerial politics over the next few years was due to William Juxon, who was, said the Venetian ambassador, 'a man of great integrity, not fanatical for any party'.[26] Even though his efforts to heal the rift between Laud and Windebank failed because of the former's intransigence (much to the latter's regret), Juxon did manage to bring quiet to the Treasury. Through his influence the transferral of the soap monopoly from the queen's friends to the Independent Soap Makers of London took place fairly peacefully, for he had sense enough to buy out the incumbents and so win Cottington's support.[27] The archbishop's resolution to 'sit quietly and let the business work as it will . . . never meddle more in it' undoubtedly helped Juxon settle the soap monopoly once and for all. 'So unless the Devil have a storm to raise that I see not,' Laud concluded sardonically, 'we shall once again be clean.'[28]

All this time, of course, the archbishop continued to rage in his letters to Wentworth against delay, 'Lady Mora', using the Latin word to refer contemptuously to the tactics of his opponents. He wanted 'Thorough', a fundamental reform which would modernise church and state, bringing efficiency to both. But a survey of the policies that he actually rendered to Caesar suggests that they were as limited in scope as were those he rendered to God, and that far from being some grand design, 'Thorough' was more the expression of the impatience of Laud and Wentworth, champing at bits through which they knew they could never bite.

In February 1635, for instance, Charles appointed Laud to the privy council committee on trade, whose membership consisted of Coke, Manchester, Arundel, Cottington, Vane and Windebank. The archbishop shared the widely accepted economic theory of mercantilism, opposing the export of wool and fuller's earth, while working to improve the quality of finished cloth exports. He tried to keep bullion in England, and once argued that transporting gold out of the realm was as serious an offence as counterfeiting – a crime punished by death. He accepted a highly regulated economy, supporting the guild system at a time when it was breaking down in the face of urban growth and the development of large trading companies.[29] Monopolies were, he believed, desirable, for they regulated trade while providing revenues for the crown. Thus he opposed the soap monopoly not because he was against the principle of allowing one group to control a market, but because it had been given to the queen's friends at the expense of the king's revenues. The archbishop had little time or patience for those who broke economic regulations; they lacked self-control. Thus he ordered Oxford's vice-chancellor to stop Mr Brown, the stationer, from undercutting the competition. When Star Chamber convicted John More in January 1634 for erecting thirty-seven buildings in the London suburbs contrary to royal proclamations, he voted for the harshest punishments. Ten months later he favoured the highest fines for Sir Anthony Roper, found guilty of enclosing 700 acres in Kent, explaining that such racketeering was 'one of the great mischiefs of this kingdom'.[30] When Thomas Lord Brudenell asked to be forgiven the £500 he had been fined for what he had the temerity to call 'a most benign and charitable enclosure', the archbishop was outraged: the peer who had evicted honest farmers in order to use the land for running sheep had, he said, 'devoured the people with a shepherd and a dog'.[31]

Fundamentally the archbishop's economic views were simple. At the Star Chamber hearing of one Archer, who was charged with buying up corn in order to hoard and resell it at a profit, Laud declared that the engrosser 'was guilty of a most foul offence . . . grinding the face of the poor'.[32] He explained that the food shortage following the poor harvest of 1630 was due to the deliberate policies of greedy speculators, and was not an act of God. As a man of God the archbishop could hardly blame the Almighty; as a minister of the crown he could not entertain the possibility that the government had lost (to borrow a phrase from a different culture) 'the mandate of heaven'.[33] Laud was convinced that regulation from the top was as vital in economics as it was in the church, the universities or the world of ideas – men were basically bad, and had to be made good.

Like all trite clichés, this was an idea whose power the sophisticated have all too often underestimated.

At a personal level Laud was sympathetic to merchants and their problems – after all, he came from merchant stock. He was friendly with Daniel Harvey, a London merchant who had an estate near the archbishop's country house at Croydon, whither Harvey would ride to discuss business, about which his host asked many penetrating questions. Harvey told him that although merchants did not mind paying tunnage and poundage – the Petition of Right notwithstanding – they resented the expense of having to unload cargoes for customs inspection and then load them again, and were even more irritated because Weston had not responded to the petition they had sent him begging relief. Laud promptly summoned Edward Hyde, the young lawyer from the Middle Temple who had drafted the petition. Hyde later recalled that the archbishop received him courteously, and that, as they strolled through the gardens of Lambeth Palace, asked a number of direct and penetrating questions. Laud was appalled to learn that Weston was trying to pressure the merchants into buying the right to collect customs revenues for an additional £40,000. But apart from expressing his quite genuine concern, which was augmented by an even more heartfelt loathing for Weston, there was nothing further that Laud could do.[34]

Laud could, however, do something to curb the spread of undesirable ideas by tightening up the censorship of books. In 1631, as Bishop of London, he ordered the members of Stationers' Company to put his imprimatur in the front of all their publications in order to show that his chaplains had read and licensed them. Although there were gaps in the system (Prynne managed to get ten of his works into print between 1636 and 1637), the percentage of books appearing with the episcopal imprimatur rose from 14 per cent in 1634 to 35 per cent in 1640. While Laud's censorship was moderately effective in normal times, it easily collapsed under the tidal wave of political pamphlets which appeared with the opening of the Long Parliament.[35]

Laud's view of human nature influenced his social policies. When he was Bishop of London he ordered that the Jacobean statute which tried to prevent the mothers of illegitimate children from passing off their murdered babies as stillborn be read at least twice a year in Middlesex, a county where the problem was particularly acute, 'so that the mischiefs that too often happen in that kind may by God's grace he prevented'. He had little time for those who fought duels: he argued that Peter Apsley, charged before Star Chamber for challenging the Earl of Northumberland, 'is no Christian', and should be fined £10,000.[36] He blamed the outbreak of the plague in 1637 on 'the carelessness of the people, and greediness'.[37] Laud quite simply – and simplistically – believed that if everyone kept, and was kept, in his place, then things would not go awry. Thus his solution to the dispute over the pews in Rickmansworth church was to order that the parishioners should 'be placed in the church according to their conditions, qualities and degrees'.[38]

Unfortunately in dealing with foreign policy such tidy platitudes did not apply, particularly when the pursuit of a goal abroad was confused and half-hearted. During Buckingham's time Britain conducted an adventurous foreign policy which involved her in wars that were as needless as they were unsuccessful. After the duke's assassination, the failure of Charles's third parliament forced him to make peace with France and Spain, and external relations took a back seat. 'To tell the truth,' the Venetian ambassador wrote home in May 1633, 'the government, just at present devotes scant attention to foreign affairs.'[39] In theory the restoration of his sister and brother-in-law Elizabeth and Frederick to the German Palatinate, from which imperial Catholic forces had expelled them a decade earlier, remained the chief goal of Charles's foreign policy during the first four years of the personal rule.

The archbishop and the exiled queen corresponded through their common friend Sir Thomas Roe.[40] She begged for Laud's help, and he sent her plainly noncommittal replies, which − with an author's touching belief in the efficacy of his own publications − he tried to sweeten by enclosing a presentation copy of his and Buckeridge's edition of Andrewes's sermons.[41] When she pressed him, Laud answered that he could do no more, because he was not a member of the privy council committee on foreign affairs.

Even after he was appointed to that body in March 1635 the archbishop did little to help the recently widowed queen, whose cries for help became more desperate, particularly as her brother's enthusiasm for her cause waned, and the Holy Roman Emperor and the Elector of Saxony signed the Peace of Prague in May 1635 declaring her family's lands and titles forfeit. The archbishop did agree to help collect money for refugees from the Palatinate, on whose behalf he sent letters to all the bishops in his province.[42] He sympathised with Elizabeth's horror at the hatred that her cause aroused, writing of one particularly nasty pamphlet that she sent him, 'I have in my time read much bitterness, but hardly have I seen so much gall drop from any man's pen.'[43] He was perfectly willing to perform minor services for her, such as helping Dudley Avery, the son of the queen's agent in Hamburg, get a foundation scholarship to Eton.[44] For several months he urged the queen to adopt the absolutely hopeless policy of trying to persuade the Holy Roman Emperor to accept her son Charles Louis's right to be one of the German Electors.[45] Desperate to revive her family's fortunes, Elizabeth sent her two sons, Charles Louis and Rupert, to England in 1635. From the start their visit was not a great success. After a stormy crossing of the Channel, the Royal Navy received them with cannon salutes at Dover, where one gun crew forgot to remove the ball, which just missed the princes and killed a couple of men nearby. On their arrival in London, Laud entertained them at Lambeth Palace, promising to read carefully the memorandum they had brought. It swayed few minds, and the princes returned home empty-handed.

By the end of the 1630s Laud was becoming increasingly concerned with the possibility that Britain might get more involved in a continental war. He established personal lines of communication with the ambassadors in Paris and Madrid, because, as he confided to Wentworth, 'I see all things of burden coming on'.[46] Time was to substantiate his fears, though not as far as foreign policy was concerned. Although external affairs took up a fair amount of his energies, eventually he had to admit to a 'weak understanding' of them.[47] Anyway, Britain had little influence abroad, largely because of the ineffectualness of the Royal Navy, the traditional instrument for exercising power overseas.

In some respects the decision taken in the middle of the decade to expand the Royal Navy was an expression of the king's frustration at being unable to intervene on land abroad.[48] John Selden, the great jurist, provided the intellectual justification for this policy. His bombastic legal treatise Mare Clausum proved to the satisfaction of most Englishmen (although disappointingly few foreigners) Britannia's right to rule the waves. Laud persuaded the king to release Selden from prison, and archbishop and jurist became good, albeit unlikely, friends. 'My nearer care of JS was professed, and his promise to be guided by me; and absolutely settled on Friday night,' the archbishop wrote in his diary on 2 February 1635.[49]

Another reason for Laud's supporting the expansion of the Royal Navy was the growing menace of piracy. He read the horrid details of pirate attacks on England which fill the state papers: Yarmouth was bombarded; King's Lynn lost twenty-five boats, and Ipswich five; two hundred people were captured in Cornwall to be sold into heathen slavery. His outrage on being presented with a petition from Dartmouth, the Devon port particularly susceptible to raids, was as typical as it was genuine. 'He gave the answer striking his hand upon his breast,' a petitioner reported home, 'that while he had breath in his body he would to the utmost of his power advance a business so necessary and consequential; and has assured me that His Majesty would take such a course as that within this twelve months not a Turkish ship should be able to put to sea.'[50] For the suppression of piracy, more than for any other reason, Laud supported the collection of ship money to build up the Royal Navy, calling the tax 'the most necessary and most honourable business both for the King and the kingdom that ever was set on foot in my memory'.[51] While the new fleet did in fact curb piracy, and ship money was not so unpopular a levy as later complaints would lead us to believe, the archbishop's part in shaping naval policy was limited and sporadic.

In much the same way, taken as a whole, Laud's policies were neither as logical, consistent or effective as his letters to Wentworth, with their high-sounding commitment to the principles of 'Thorough', and rooting out the delays of 'Lady Mora' and her malignant cronies, would suggest. There is no doubt that at a theoretical level both men were deeply committed: Wentworth once urged that the 'fanatic spirits' who opposed their goals 'should have their tongues bored, and if it be possible themselves whipped back into their right wits'.[52] Even though Laud agreed whole-heartedly, in practice his commitment to resolving concrete issues, such as the economic problems of the church, was more apparent than real, and focused mainly on the irrelevant Protestant Church of Ireland. Like those of most politicians, Laud's policies were neither as well thought out as his defenders would have us believe, nor as effective or as consistent as his enemies have maintained. As his diary reveals, he saw his most important goals in very concrete and specific terms, and as he pursued them he never forgot that, to remain in power, he must contain his enemies, cultivate his friends, and – most important of all – curry the king's favour.

For Charles and Laud the distinctions between the two religious extremes – Puritans on the left, as it were, and the Catholics on the right – were not so clearcut. The king once lumped the two together by arguing that 'the neglect of punishing Puritans breeds Papists', while three years later Laud signed an arrest warrant for John Fennen which blurred the difference between Catholic and Puritan by describing him as a 'Recusant, and a Separatist'.[53] Sometimes the archbishop gave the impression that all who opposed the crown were equally bad, no matter which side they attacked from. But because those on the left did so in a more raucous and public fashion they generated far more animosity. Laud surely agreed with the anonymous rhymester who believed:[54]

> A puritan is such a monstrous thing
> that loves Democracy and hates the king . . .
> A Puritan is he whose heart is bent
> to cross the king's designs in Parliament.
> Where whilst the place of Burgess he doth bear
> He thinks he owes but small allegiance there . . .
> So that with his wit and valour he doth trye,
> How the prerogative he may deny.

As Samuel Moore, Master of Trinity College, Cambridge, told Laud, the 'doctrine of predestination is the root of Puritanism, and Puritanism is the root of all rebellion, and disobedient intractableness in parliament, and all schism and sauciness in the country, nay in the church itself.'[55] One can

imagine the little archbishop's head nodding up and down in fervent agreement as he wrote back, 'And I like it well that you mean to have the
judgment of so many and such men.'[56]

Estimates vary as to how many Puritans there were in the land, particularly as the term was never clearly defined. Some have suggested that as
few as 4 per cent of the clergy were Puritans, others as many as 17 per
cent, the true figure probably lying in the middle.[57] Laud exaggerated their
importance. He was convinced that Puritans lurked in dangerously large
concentrations throughout the land. In 1634 he had the Court of High
Commission order every justice of the peace to ferret out all Brownists,
Anabaptists, Familists and Arians, wherever they could be found.[58] Many
Puritans had no respect for the niceties of the established church. 'A barn
with them is as good as a church,' Laud wrote.[59] He was convinced that
many Puritans were, quite simply, mad. After Robert Seal of St Albans told
him about the vision he had had commanding him to go to the Archbishop
of Canterbury and reprove him for the church's failure to preach the Lord's
Word, he noted in his diary, 'I believe the poor man was overgrown with
fancy. So I troubled not myself further with him.'[60]

But Laud did bother himself with those dangerous Puritans he believed
sane and sincere. For instance, his quarrel with the Godly sort in Gloucester
went back to 1615, when he was appointed dean of the city's cathedral.
In 1633 High Commission summoned John Workman, a leading Puritan
preacher from Gloucester, for giving a sermon before the assize judges that
attacked clerical abuses, superstitious images and dancing. To show their
support the city council voted to pay Workman's stipend as their lecturer
indefinitely. Angry at this snub Laud ordered several councillors to ride to
London, where they were fined £200, and he had Workman hounded out
of the diocese. Two years later the archbishop initiated an inquiry into the
running of the city's hospital, ordering the councillors to appear before
High Commission; the case dragged on at considerable personal expense
to the defendants until 1638. The previous year Laud had forbidden the
council to dismiss John Bird, master of the Crypt School, for failing to get
enough of his pupils into university. By the end of the decade it was said
that Gloucester Puritans were so upset by such harassments that a hundred
of them were ready to escape to New England.[61]

The archbishop's most famous – or notorious – clash with Puritans
involved William Prynne, Henry Burton and John Bastwick. Prynne and
Laud were old enemies. In 1634 the archbishop had the London barrister
hauled before Star Chamber for publishing *Histriomastix*, a long, tedious
attack on practically everything the splenetic author could think of,
including dancing, bonfires, actresses, make-up, fornication, religious art,
short hair on women and long hair on men, hunting, drinking toasts,
Jesuits, Jews, excessive laughter, maypoles, nuns, Papists and sodomy. Star

Chamber's sentence of life imprisonment, the pillory, having both ears cut off, a £5,000 fine, and the loss of his Oxford degree and membership of the bar did not keep the irrepressible lawyer down. Even in the Tower he was able to continue writing tracts, including *News from Ipswich* (1636). This pamphlet (which no one for a moment believed actually came from Ipswich) attacked Laud as the 'Arch-Agent for the Devil; that Beelzebub', and bishops in general as 'execrable traitors, devouring Wolves', and blamed the latter for a whole host of problems, including a large number of shipwrecks and unseasonable weather.[62] While someone with a better-developed sense of humour might have been inclined to accept the final indictment as proof of the *jure divino* powers of prelates, the archbishop once again dragged the barrister before Star Chamber.

William Laud and Henry Burton were even older enemies.[63] In April 1625 Burton had sent the new king a letter calling Laud and Neile 'popishly affected'. As a result Charles dismissed him from his post as Clerk of the Closet. Burton spent much of the next decade using his pulpit as rector of St Matthew's, Friday Street, London, castigating bishops. In 1636 he went too far, calling them 'anti-christian mushrumps' and 'caterpillars . . . that have devoured the fruits of the land'. Summoned to appear before Dr Duck, he locked himself up in his study, from whence he published the offending sermons, before being arrested and hauled before Star Chamber.[64] The experience had not taught Burton discretion. He told Attorney General Bankes that 'prelates are invaders of the king's prerogative royal, condemners and despisers of the Holy Scriptures, advancers of popery, superstition and idolatry and profanenesses. . . . They show neither wit, honesty nor temperance . . . being enemies of God, and the king and of every living thing that is good.'[65]

If Dr Bastwick was — as befitted a good medical man — not so sweeping in his diagnosis, he did pronounce it in capitals perhaps in the hope of showing that certainty which is so often expected from his profession. He called bishops 'POLECATS, STOTES AND WEASELS'.[66] In reply Edward Hyde called him a 'half witted cracked brained fellow . . . with some wit and much malice'.[67]

All these attacks cut the archbishop to the quick. 'The thing is full of sedition, and certainly made to stir up some to villainy,' he wrote to Wentworth about *News from Ipswich*, adding that Burton's sermons were 'a monstrous libel'. He had extracts made of the most inflammatory parts of the sermons, and requested the judges to rule against Burton's and Prynne's allegations that bishops had no right to visit without a commission issued under the Great Seal. The weather made things even worse. 'The heat has been as great here, to me nothing is more troublesome.'[68] So when the malefactors appeared before him at Star Chamber on 14 June 1637 Laud was both prepared and punitive; without doubt he approved the court's denial of Prynne's opening motion that the bishops leave the bench because they were interested parties. At the end of the hearing he felt that he had to give a speech defending prelates as being appointed by God, and as having governed the church since the days of the Apostles. Emphatically he denied that either he or the king wished to change the established religion. If the accused sincerely wanted to reform the church, why didn't they petition the king instead of resorting to 'mutiny'. There was not a sovereign in Europe more constant to true religion than King Charles. Laud then disqualified himself from voting on the sentence. And after the court voted the sentence, he gave them his 'hearty thanks'.[69]

It was a savage punishment. Star Chamber ordered the three to be fined £5,000, imprisoned for life and to have their ears cut off (they were particularly incensed that a little scar tissue had been left on the side of Prynne's head from the previous mutilation). The prisoners bore their mutilations heroically. According to the Puritan artisan Nehemiah Wallington, Burton wished he had enough blood to shed 'to swell the Thames'. Prynne declared, 'The more I am beaten down, the more I am lift up.' In an unusual display of professional courtesy Dr Bastwick gave the executioner the benefit of years of surgical experience by advising him how best to slice off his own ears, whilst asking, 'Shall I be ashamed of a pillory for Christ who was not ashamed of a cross for me?'[70] Such courage deeply impressed the crowd. It was said that 100,000 people lined the road to Highgate to watch Burton being led off to perpetual imprisonment. Yet hindsight may have exaggerated the importance of Prynne, Burton and Bastwick as martyrs. At the time the Venetian ambassador reported that at their 'brazen audacity . . . the wisest were disgusted', and only 'the senseless people, and those full of the spirit of faction had compassion on them'. Sir Robert Phelips, the parliamentary leader who had been imprisoned for attacking Buckingham, wrote to Laud congratulating him on dealing so firmly with the three troublemakers, whom he called 'lunatics'. As late as 1640 Wallington heard a man in a London street say that 'it were no matter if they had been hanged'.[71] While it is possible that in 1637 Prynne, Burton and Bastwick were not as popular, and thus Laud not as detested, as posterity would have us believe, it is certain that the case profoundly affected the archbishop. 'And, indeed, My Lord, if some speedy order be not taken, and a round one too, I shall have much cause to think that my life is aimed at,' he wrote to Wentworth, who replied that the trio's real target was not prelacy but 'the very life blood of monarchy itself'. Thus the case of Prynne, Burton and Bastwick helped fix in the archbishop's mind the misconception that those who opposed him were republicans who threatened his life. Within a few years many people became convinced that the trio were the widely supported victims of a villainous archbishop's malice. For Laud the results of both misconceptions were to prove disastrous. 'To neglect all Christian mildness, and fall upon the killing and massacring of these poor flies in the Star Chamber,' observed Bishop Williams, was 'a most unfortunate diversion'.[72]

Nearly as unfortunate were the consequences of Laud's quarrel with the religious centre that Williams in many ways represented.[73]

Following his dismissal as Lord Keeper in October 1625 for opposing Buckingham's foreign policy, the 'wonderfully ambitious' Welshman returned to Buckden, where as Bishop of Lincoln he had his palace, to build, plant trees, lay out a park and fish ponds, and – above all – to intrigue.[74] In 1628 Williams was secretly negotiating with Buckingham to be allowed to return to politics, and clashed with Laud over the placing of the communion table at Grantham. The duke's assassination in August of that year dashed the Welshman's hopes. Weston's death five years later revived them. As part of the general jockeying for preferment Williams sent Laud in December 1633 a rather stiff letter of reconciliation. After denying that he had ever favoured schismatics or Puritans, he asked the archbishop to intervene with the king on his behalf. Laud did so, and 'all I got by it for myself was a smart chiding', he replied to Williams, adding that he had never derived any pleasure from 'the differences that are fallen out' between them. Over the next year Williams twice tried to get the archbishop to intervene on his behalf, and on each occasion Laud's efforts grew more half-hearted as his anger increased, since he was aware that all along Williams was plotting against him privately with Cottington, while publicly fighting him over visitations.[75]

Williams objected to the Archbishop of Canterbury's proposal to inspect Lincoln on the grounds that the power had lapsed because it had not been exercised since Cramner's day, over a century before, and that the pope had anyway exempted the diocese. Not surprisingly Laud disagreed, and got Lambe to go through the medieval records at Lambeth Palace, before referring the case to Attorney General Noy, who heard it at Lincoln's Inn on 21 and 22 March 1634. Three days later Noy issued an order endorsing the primate's prerogative.[76]

While Noy did not side with Williams over the matter of visitations, for the past six years he had been protecting him from being prosecuted on an old charge of bribing witnesses. But after the Attorney General died in 1634, Williams recognised that the case would most likely come to trial, and tried to plea-bargain by offering to pay a fine of £4,000 and then £8,000 to dismiss the charges – which were pretty thin, for they included employing as his registrar at Lincoln John Pregion, even though he had been involved in a paternity suit. Taking Lord Haughton's advice that 'patience must be our virtue in these times', the Bishop of Lincoln made one more grovelling conciliatory overture to Laud. It did not work. By the end of the year, when it seemed that the king might accept Williams's offer,

Laud spent a week of long private conversations successfully persuading Charles to reject it.

Constant rebuffs combined with Laud's remorseless hatred to make Williams lose what little sagacity his choleric constitution allowed. As one letter writer put it, 'His Pride and Obstinacy in not submitting to the King in due time have undone him.' So to clear himself from the dubious charge of secret bribery the Bishop of Lincoln resorted to open cozenage. The Welshman concluded that if he was liable to be hanged on a trumped-up charge of stealing a lamb, he might as well try to purloin the whole flock. And hanged he very nearly was. 'I hear from London the Bishop of Lincoln is like to lose his head,' wrote one diarist.[77] Humble letters of apology in which he talked of his 'weariness of life by these misfortunes' no longer had the slightest effect on Laud, who was convinced that Williams was no better than an arsonist determined to burn the Church of England to the ground.[78] He made twenty-seven pages of hand-written notes on the charges against his enemy, and when the case came before Star Chamber in July 1637 delivered a long and intemperate speech.[79] If his diatribe began in sorrow at seeing a man of Williams's estate on trial, it ended in anger. The bishop, he declared, was guilty of 'a very foul crime, and a most odious and detestable fault . . . and if these things be suffered and may go unpunished, no state can stand'. Williams's offence of subborning witnesses was worse than murder, for instead of destroying one body it damned two souls. After assuring his fellow judges that the accused 'manifestly wrongs God', the archbishop voted that Williams should be fined £10,000, suspended from all his offices, and imprisoned during His Majesty's pleasure.[80] Because Star Chamber, a secular court, did not have the right to deprive a churchman of his livings, two weeks later High Commission summoned Williams. Once more both sides tried to work out a plea-bargain, perhaps under pressure from the king, who was always uncomfortable when two of his most important prelates fought.[81] But Williams rejected Laud's offer of an Irish bishopric in return for the surrender of all his English offices: he was convinced that once he was in Wentworth's clutches the Lord Deputy 'would cut off his head within one month'.[82]

Six days before Williams's hearing, Cottington came to see Laud at his country house in Croydon, the first time he had ever been there. As they walked through the garden in the summer evening he complimented the archbishop on his speech at the trial of Prynne, Burton and Bastwick: it needed saying; it expressed his own feelings exactly. But when Cottington raised the matter of Williams, who was his friend, Laud rejected his overtures, telling Wentworth a few days later that if 'that fierce mastiff' escaped it would ruin both church and state. Thus the prosecution of Williams prevented Laud from making any alliance with the political as well as the religious centre.[83]

For Laud the Williams affair reinforced that of Prynne, Burton and Bastwick – all four men were tried within a month. If they got away with their heinous crimes, he believed, 'no state can stand'.[84] In both cases the archbishop's deep-rooted paranoia was obvious. At the end of the year he told Wentworth that Williams had been 'a root of all the mischiefs which have befallen Church and State for some years past'. But there was a difference between the prelate and the Puritans. Williams was a politician ready – all too ready – to compromise, unlike the three fanatics who, the more they were beaten down, the more uplifted they became. Laud made the mistake of lumping the four men together, and so when the crisis came he had no one – not even the Roman Catholics – with whom he could ally himself. This astounded Laud's enemies, who for years had been convinced that he was not only in bed with the whore of Babylon but was her most enthusiastic and active pimp. The trouble with the Papist Jezebel, however, was that she appeared in far too many guises.

There was, for instance, Laud's godson William Chillingworth.[85] In 1629 he converted to Catholicism, but after a couple of years of studying in seminaries on the Continent decided to come in from the Roman cold. At Laud's urging he wrote an apologia, *The Religion of Protestants a safe way to salvation* (1638). The archbishop was afraid that the proofs of the work might be tampered with, 'for I know that the Jesuits are very cunning at these tricks'.[86] He had good cause for concern, for six months earlier someone had excised the Protestant commentaries from William Heywood's translation of Bishop Sale's *Praxis Spiritualis*.[87] In 1634 Laud tried to persuade recusants that they could take the oath of allegiance to the crown in good conscience, and had Sir Robert Lashfield dismissed from his court post as a Gentleman Pensioner when he was discovered trying to smuggle his daughter to a nunnery abroad.[88] The following year during a privy council meeting he warned the king that 'the papists were the most dangerous subjects in the kingdom', and in 1637 he ordered the vice-chancellor to stop students leaving Oxford to study in continental seminaries.[89] But there were limits to what Laud could do with country Catholics, especially because, as one of them, John Hilton, an alderman of Appleby, Westmorland, pointed out, 'Some Privy Councillors, aye, and the king himself had a wife a Recusant, yet they continued in their places.' Laud must have found the jibe especially galling because he had to read Neile's report on Hilton's impertinence aloud to the king, who told him to inform his fellow archbishop that he was 'pleased to remit these presump-tuous speeches'.[90]

For years Catholics had been a problem at court, and for Laud the problem was exacerbated by the fact that he loathed the place. Time and time again he gave vent to his hatred of court life. 'I have just come wearily from court,' he told Wentworth in one letter, sneering in another, 'you know the workings of a Court.'[91] He was ill at ease in the court's artistic milieu, calling Van Dyck's paintings 'vanity . . . shadows'. Worse still, he could not get on with the queen and the world of petticoat politics she had created about her since she arrived in England in 1625 determined to do her utmost to improve the lot of her new country's Catholics. Laud blamed Windebank's defection on backstairs intrigue: 'And this much can money and friends against honour [do] in movable courts.'[92] Henrietta Maria never liked Laud. A silly woman, she fell out with people for the most trivial reasons, writing Wentworth off, for instance, because he had ugly hands. Laud found it hard to deal with ladies, particularly those whose breeding made him even more conscious of his lowly origins. Only with a very few women who were the wives of his friends, and thus no threat, did he feel at ease, treating them, one recalled to her surprise, 'with great respect and civility . . . with kindness, full of reason'.[93]

A comparison with Father George Con, the papal agent to the queen, reveals Laud's inadequacies as a courtier. The younger son of a Scots noble, Con was a brilliant conversationalist who could charm the ladies. When he arrived in England in 1636 he gave Henrietta Maria a crucifix, a present from the pope, which she immediately hung about her neck. Con plied the king with gifts of works of art, agreeing with his patron at the Vatican, Cardinal Barberini, that it would be worth stripping Rome of its treasures to be able to restore England to the true faith. Laud warned the king against such ploys, telling him that 'if he wished to go to Rome the Pope would not stir a step to meet him'.[94] But when he tried to play the same game by having Le Sueur sculpt the statues of the king and queen for his Oxford quadrangle, he seemed more interested in the financial details than the artistic creation.[95] Even inviting Con to Oxford for a tour of St John's and a banquet did nothing to improve relations between the two men. Con thought Laud was 'timid, ambitious, inconstant and incapable of great designs'.[96]

There was nothing timid, however, about most Englishmen's reactions to the conversion of prominent courtiers and aristocrats to Catholicism. To prevent his own wife from defecting, Sir William Balfour beat up the priest who tried to convert her, a drastic but efficacious remedy of which Charles tacitly approved. Conversions were a public scandal that caused Laud great concern, and damaged his reputation even more. He could never understand why anyone would do such a thing, having in his conference with Fisher clearly drawn the line between Canterbury and Rome. To try and comprehend one such defection, he carefully went over the letter that Walter Montagu sent to his father, the Earl of Manchester, explaining his conversion.[97] But understanding did not prevent him from supporting the young man's banishment from court (perhaps because what had most impressed Montagu about Catholicism had been watching the exorcism of a group of Ursuline nuns in Loudon, France). When Kenelm Digby, the son of Everard Digby (who had been executed for his part in the Guy Fawkes conspiracy), converted, he sent Laud a long letter of explanation, to which the archbishop sorrowfully replied. In much the same tone he informed Charles of the conversions of Anne and Elizabeth, daughters of the late Earl of Falkland.[98] Ladies of quality were particularly susceptible to the Papist siren. After Lady Maltravers and Lady Katherine Howard converted, one courtier noted, 'Our great women fall away every day.'[99] Awkward in female company, all Laud could do was take consolation in the Venetian ambassador's conclusion that Con had taken advantage of 'the simplicity of women, over whose mind the last impressions are always the strongest', and then raise the matter with the king.[100]

After his wife went over to Rome, Lord Newport complained to the archbishop, who brought up the widespread problem of court conversions at a privy council meeting on 22 October 1637. In 'a full and free speech' he castigated the freedom given to Walter Montagu (now allowed back at court), Tobie Matthew, and the rest of the queen's set to help Father Con proselytise. Charles agreed, and said he intended doing something about it. When Henrietta Maria heard the news that night she was, as Laud noted, 'highly displeased with me', and demanded that her husband put a stop to the archbishop's meddling. He countered by proposing that the queen's chapel and those of Catholic ambassadors be closed to English subjects, which so upset her that she had to be physically restrained by Con. One suspects that for the next few nights there were some uneasy moments in the royal bedchamber until Henrietta Maria realised that discretion was wiser than petulance. In December she and Laud had a long conversation, after which 'we parted friends'. Ten days later Charles issued a proclamation prohibiting conversions.[101]

This was a victory, and at the time it seemed a substantial one; but very soon it proved to be Pyrrhic. The proclamation of December 1637 ended the uneasy truce which had been in force since 1634, when Laud and Henrietta Maria had discussed the visit of Gregorio Panzini, Con's predecessor as papal agent, and it created a deadly feud with the queen's set that became far more dangerous after the collapse of the personal rule enhanced the latter's influence in the king's councils.[102] While it is true that Charles sided with his archbishop against his wife in 1637, the fact that he was forced to do so did nothing to endear Laud to the king (who always resented those who forced him to make a painful choice). By taking on the court Catholics, Laud sowed the seeds of a bitter harvest that the Scots rebellion germinated, and the Long Parliament reaped.

While making him many powerful enemies, the archbishop's campaign against conversions won him few friends. His emphasis on stained glass windows, genuflecting, choirs, surplices, and the placement of the altar convinced many Protestants that he was quite literally a closet Papist who, as one London apprentice alleged, hung a crucifix in his private chamber.[103] Having in his conference with Fisher drawn the frontier between Canterbury and Rome with a precision that convinced him as completely as it failed to sway most other Protestants, Laud was particularly sensitive to such charges. Certain of his own innocence, he became all the more convinced of his opponents' malignity. Thus he objected to Ben Jonson's play *The Magnetic Lady* because of the character Parson Palate, 'our Popish Priest'.[104] When he told Charles that the Polish ambassador was spreading the story that he, Laud, was really a Papist it amused the king greatly – much to Laud's chagrin, for he would have preferred sympathy or, better still, righteous indignation, to laughter.[105] Recognising that he was in danger of being crushed between the proverbial rock of court snobbery and the hard place of country suspicions, he wrote to Wentworth, 'I doubt not that I have enemies enough to make use of this . . . I am between two great factions, very like corn between two millstones.'[106]

The relationship between Charles and the archbishop was crucial, for it was upon the king's favour that the power of any royal servant ultimately depended – as Abbot learned to his mortification. Charles departmentalised his government, letting each minister handle his own sphere of responsibility. After Buckingham's murder, no one favourite monopolised royal government, which in many ways returned to the older pattern where competing factions struggled amongst themselves for influence and the king's favour. Between 1629 and 1637 no one single item dominated royal business. Rather than dividing in order to rule, Charles mostly left his ministers alone. His government was basically reactive. The king was not a hard-working man. His ministers, as well as foreign ambassadors, constantly complained that 'no discussion about grave matters can be held'.[107] This meant that energetic, capable ministers such as Laud, who enjoyed the king's favour, could exercise considerable power. For instance, because the king could not bother to go through Wentworth's dispatches from Ireland, he had Laud read them aloud to him, which gave the archbishop far more influence over Ireland and its church than had been enjoyed by his predecessors. There were, of course, limits, as Laud recognised. 'I can do no more than I can do,' he explained to Wentworth; 'no man can serve a king further than he will be served.'[108] Charles would make bishops only of men whom he knew personally and whom he had heard preach at court. All too often Laud discovered that someone had gone behind his back and had persuaded the king to make some ecclesiastical appointment. But on major issues, the two men remained in remarkable accord. As the decade went on, and the archbishop learned the boundaries of his authority, he no longer referred small matters to Charles, or issued orders on such items with the injunction that they were to be done in the king's name.

For instance, in 1634, he got Charles to instruct the Reading corporation to clean up the mess left by the butchers' market at the end of Broad Street (where he had grown up); in contrast three years later he told Wentworth that if the Lord Chief Justice of Ireland could not stop the suit prohibiting the clergy of Cork and Ross from collecting tithes on fish, then he would have to refer the matter to Charles.

Defining the limits of the archbishop's authority helped Laud and Charles remain in basic agreement. They shared a common love of order and a belief in authority. Both were shy men, who may have recognised each other's insecurities, and the façade they erected to protect themselves from hurt, against a world that they regarded as basically hostile. If they did not like each other, they did not feel that it was necessary, or even desirable, that they should. Laud was the king's vicar. Charles believed that he could never, should never, become too friendly with the keeper of his conscience. For Laud it was never a choice between being the king's or God's good servant first, because in the halcyon days of the 1630s the two were synonymous.[109] Thus both men built their relationship, and their mutual policies, on two misconceptions. So long as their efforts seemed to be succeeding, and the king and all his ministers worked well together, the results were most satisfactory. 'If good sermons, or good plays, new Braveries, or fresh wit, Revells', wrote the poet Sir John Suckling, 'have any Rhetorique about them, here they are, I assure you, in perfection.'[110] But when their policies failed, and the sand upon which they had built the personal rule eroded, the consequences were catastrophic.

VIII

'To be your chancellor'

Of all the letters Laud wrote none caused him greater grief than the one he penned in June 1641 and sent 'To my very loving friends, the vice-chancellor, the doctors, the proctors, and the rest of the convocation of the university of Oxford'. Writing from the Tower of London, his life in jeopardy, Laud looked back on the achievements he valued the most, and which 'I hope after my death you will acknowledge'. He reflected on his work as an educator, and upon his attempts as the product of one great university, who tried to use Oxford, Cambridge, and Trinity College, Dublin, to shape his master's realms far more profoundly than would have been possible from any economic reforms. He thought of Oxford as his home, as the place where he had been the happiest, and most secure. Here he had enjoyed his most public triumph, and left his most enduring physical legacy. Throughout his life, which even before his downfall had never been a particularly happy one, the disgraced prelate concluded, 'there is nothing more hath so nearly touched me as the remembrance of your free and joyful acceptance of me to be your chancellor'.[1]

Laud loved St John's, and he never broke his university connections. For instance, his godson William Chillingworth, Fellow of Trinity College, continued to send him weekly newsletters about academic affairs. Oxford made Laud, and he could never forget it. Neither did the king, who referred university matters to the Bishop of London even before he became Oxford's chancellor; after all, education and religion were closely linked. So Charles had Laud investigate a disputed election at Trinity College, Dublin.[2] The bishop almost certainly persuaded the king to write to the vice-chancellor and heads of colleges at Oxford urging them to do something about the shanties in St Mary's between All Souls and Brasenose, and to their brethren at Cambridge ordering bear-baiting stopped in the town.[3] Bear-baiting and shanties! No wonder Laud was convinced that the state of England's universities left much to be desired, and he was delighted when Oxford elected him its chancellor in 1630.

The office fell vacant on 10 April 1630 with the sudden death of William Herbert, Earl of Pembroke. When the news reached Oxford, Laud's friends, led by Juxon and the St John's fellows, moved so fast that they had enough votes to elect their old president even before the vice-chancellor, Dr Accepted Frewen, galloped back from Andover in time for Saturday evening prayers. Despite his Calvinist-sounding Christian name, the vice-chancellor agreed to break the sabbath by calling a convocation for the following day. Overnight Pembroke's brother Philip, Earl of Montgomery, the new Earl of Pembroke, emerged as an alternative candidate, having the support of the Welsh at Jesus College (he had extensive lands in the principality), as well as the Calvinists, who Laud alleged were being led by Williams. Largely because Christopher Potter, Provost of Queen's (traditionally a Puritan college), abstained, Laud was elected by nine votes. Delighted, Charles confirmed the new chancellor by saying that 'he knew none more worthy of it'. Brushing aside the usual accusations of fraud and corruption, Convocation installed Laud as their new chancellor on 28 April. He was deeply honoured by the office, which 'was beyond my deserts and contrary to my desires, but, since it hath pleased God, by their love, to lay it upon me, I must undergo the burden as I may'.[4]

By long-standing tradition Oxford's chancellors played little part in the day-to-day running of the university. For all but two of the previous seventy-eight years they had been laymen, powerful in their own right, who protected the university from outside interference, helped it negotiate with the government, and acted as umpire in disputes too bitter to be resolved internally. Such a limited role was beyond Laud politically, academically and psychologically. The Arminians at Oxford had engineered his victory; now he was going to reward their expectations.

One of Laud's first acts as chancellor was to instruct the vice-chancellor (who was elected every two years from among the heads of college to run the university) to send him weekly reports on affairs at Oxford. 'I am given to understand,' he wrote to Dr Frewen on 28 May 1630, 'that formalities, which are in a sort the outward and visible face of the university, are in matter utterly decayed.'[5] The new chancellor decreed a plethora of small changes: tutors and scholars must wear caps and gowns on Sundays; undergraduates must stop poaching the king's game at Woodstock; convocations should not be called so frequently; greater care must be taken in setting exams since the king 'took great distaste' at one recent question; MAs must not haunt taverns; all BAs must raise their hats to masters and doctors; no boots and spurs were to be worn with gowns; and the vice-chancellor was to see that public oral examinations were held with all due decorum, since at present they were rife with 'the animosities and fractious contestation of young and hot heads'.[6] As usual Laud believed that if the university's outward and visible face was in good order then its real, inner heart would be healthy too.

Laud's enemies – who were never as numerous as he believed – did not accept the chancellor's growing influence without a fight. Even though one of his first actions on taking office was to reprove John Tucker of Oriel College for preaching a provocatively Arminian sermon, his efforts were half-hearted and unconvincing.[7] More consistent was his order of the following year that Dr William Page of All Souls be allowed to publish his *Treatise or justification of the bowing at the name of Jesus*. He may have done so in order to counter Prynne's attacks on this practice, or simply to get his own back on Abbot, who had tried to stop the polemic's appearance.[8] It was enough to goad Laud's enemies into action. Declaring that the Arminians were 'worse than the Turks', they counter-attacked in the summer of 1631. 'In this year there arose a great stew in the university by some fractious men,' recalled Laud, 'which laboured to disturb the government both in their sermons and in convocation and by secret plottings.'[9] The story was a familiar one. Thomas Ford, William Hodges and Giles Thorne preached a series of sermons attacking Arminianism. The vice-chancellor, Dr Henry Smith, imprisoned them, so they appealed to Convocation, and were freed by the proctors. Dr Smith referred the matter to the king. 'These late stirs are not of an ordinary nature, but strike at the very root of government, which now lies bleeding,' wrote Brian Duppa to Laud with graphic hyperbole, adding, 'The gangrene will spread further, for the university by these means is likely to be the seed plot of mutineers.' Laud found Duppa's warnings all the more convincing since Thorne had been a Balliol protégé of Williams.[10] After spending six hours hearing the case at Woodstock Charles expelled Ford, Hodges and Thorne from the university, dismissed the two proctors from their post, and would have deprived Dr Prideaux, the renegades' leader, of his Regius professorship had not the Earl of Montgomery (Laud's opponent in the chancellor's election) intervened on his behalf.[11] The chancellor's victory was complete: his enemies were so thoroughly routed that Laud could make fundamental and lasting reforms at Oxford.[12]

Even before he was elected chancellor Laud told his predecessor, the Earl of Pembroke, that there would be no peace at the university until the statutes were revised. 'So soon as I was admitted to the chancellorship,' he recalled, 'I thought it as my duty to reform the university which was extremely sunk from all discipline and fallen into all licentiousness.' After instructing the vice-chancellor to write to him every week, and making a promise (which he failed to keep) to reply to these newsletters with equal frequency, the archbishop appointed a committee to reform the university statutes, which over the years had become an awful hodgepodge. The sub-committee that actually did the work consisted of Thomas James, Bodley's librarian; Richard Zouche, Regius Professor of Civil Law; Peter Turner, Professor of Geometry; and Brian Twyne, an antiquarian from Corpus. In August 1633 the university's convocation approved a draft set of statutes, which they forwarded to Laud, who spent a year revising them before sending his version back to Oxford with instructions that they be put into effect without delay or further debate for a trial period ending in September 1635. The king, he said, was 'marvellously well pleased' with them. The following June Laud signed, and Charles sealed, a final version of the statutes, which remained in force virtually intact until the University Reform Act of 1854.[13]

The statutes built on existing Laudian reforms. They confirmed the practice of electing proctors in rotation amongst the colleges according to their size that he had introduced in 1628. They recognised the Hebdomadal Council, consisting of the chancellor, vice-chancellor, and heads of colleges, which met each week to run the university, and which Charles had instituted, at Laud's recommendation, in 1631. The new statutes introduced public oral examinations for degrees in place of the requirement of attending lectures and disputations. They tightened college discipline, and authorised the vice-chancellor's court, which was to meet every Friday in St Mary's Church, to punish the recalcitrant.

Laud introduced other reforms. He expanded the Bodleian Library, to which he gave the cabinet of coins, assembled by John Barcham, Dean of Essex, that became the nucleus of the university's collection.[14] He had the king appoint Joseph Crowther university lecturer in Greek, and persuaded Edward Pococke to return from his extensive travels in the Levant to serve as Oxford's first lecturer in Arabic.[15] When Pococke was in Constantinople on study leave, Laud wrote to Thomas Greaves, the Deputy Reader in Arabic, asking on what days he lectured, and if he needed any regulations passed to further the teaching of his subject.[16] To support instruction in Greek the chancellor took advantage of one of the most embarrassing typographical errors in the history of printing, the omission of 'not' from the Seventh Commandment in the Bible published by Patrick Young, the royal printer (so that it read 'Thou shalt commit adultery.'). He ordered Young to atone by buying a set of Greek type and, at his own expense, publishing at least one book a year in that language.[17] To assist the new Arabic lecturer Laud got the king to instruct every trading ship belonging to the Turkey Company to bring home at least one manuscript in Arabic or Russian, the Koran excluded.[18] Oxford University Press was not forgotten. The archbishop helped it obtain a set of Arabic type, and, in a move that would not be without its appeal today, ordered that everyone granted an honorary degree or given exemption from taking their finals pay £20 to provide subventions for scholarly publications.[19]

At heart Laud was a bureaucrat. He investigated, he drew up and dispatched questionnaires, he commissioned fact-finding committees and then carefully read their reports. He issued regulations, which he enforced. He punished, and, above all, he concentrated on the details. For instance, at Oxford he insisted that the teaching of Latin to divinity students be improved, and that second-year undergraduates spend less time studying Calvin.[20] The chancellor shut down Mr Croft's riding stables because he believed that the undergraduates were not strong enough to handle his large horses, and anyway would be better employed in their studies. He ordered that the new statutes should be displayed in the Bodleian, and be available for public use, and had a pocket version printed for students.[21] When one petitioned to be excused a term's residence for his MA degree Laud refused this comparatively innocuous request as if the whole future of English higher education was at stake, not wanting 'to create a precedent which may endanger the statutes and government'.[22] The chancellor insisted that all colleges hold Vespers simultaneously so that 'the prayers of the church, howsoever different in place, might be jointly put up to God in all places at the same time'.[23] Laud believed that a lot of small reforms would together achieve big results. Sometimes this policy worked; most often it did not. All too frequently in his schemes Laud had to use men who shared neither his faith, his fervour nor his foresight.[24]

Take, for instance, the problem of students and alcohol. From his own years as proctor he remembered only too well that undergraduates got drunk.[25] Soon after becoming chancellor he asked the privy council to investigate the plethora of taverns 'too much haunted by young gents and scholars', and they ordered Oxford to reduce the number of taverns to the statutory three. This was far too few to quench the students' thirst for beer, and the brewers' thirst for profits. During the rest of the decade some three hundred unlicensed drinking establishments were reported to be plying their trade about the university. Another hundred received licences from a local justice of the peace, a brewer, on condition that they buy only his beer. The city of Oxford would not co-operate with the chancellor's efforts to tackle the problem of student drunkenness, because they resented his high-handedness, as epitomised in the charter that he obtained giving the university the right to search private houses for robbers, whores and students living outside college.[26]

Many colleges disliked Laud's reforms because they strengthened the university's powers at their expense. While recognising the importance of the colleges (he had, after all, been President of St John's for a decade), Laud defended himself from such charges by pointing to abuses at the college level. When he heard that the statutes and finances at All Souls were in a mess, and that the fellows were more concerned with fashion than scholarship, he appointed a committee to visit the college. They reported that 'some things are very much out of order there', prompting the chancellor to stipulate to Dr Richard Astley, Warden of All Souls, that only senior fellows be made dean and bursar, and that all members of the college 'use not long undecent hair, nor wear large falling bands, nor boots under their gowns, nor any like unstatutable novelty in their apparel'.[27]

The situation at Merton College called for more radical remedies. In early 1637 a quarrel between two fellows was referred to Laud, who sent the college a detailed questionnaire. The answers prompted him to dispatch a group of visitors, John Bancroft, Richard Baylie, John Lambe, Arthur Duck and Gilbert Sheldon, to inspect Merton. They discovered a mare's-nest: places sold, meals missed, lectures not given, Latin neglected, students whoring or else drunk on the warden's favourite double-strength ale. By dismissing two of the fellows who favoured reform, the warden, Nathaniel Brent, thwarted the chancellor's efforts. By the time Laud sent another inspection team to Merton in July 1640, it was too late for him to make any lasting changes.

The task of stamping out abuses at college level was made more difficult because Laud was not able to find out about them. All Souls only came to his attention because a dispute amongst the fellows was referred to him in his capacity as the college's visitor, and not as university chancellor. He heard about Merton's problems through a secret correspondence with Peter Turner, a senior member of the college, and university professor of Geometry, who had done Laud good service in revising the statutes.

Only at one college, St John's, where the chancellor had contacts, friends and influence, was he able to call the tune – and that largely because he paid the piper. With an enthusiasm that amounted almost to nepotism he gave his old college eight advowsons, allowing them to appoint their own men, particularly those from Reading, to rich church livings.[28]

Without doubt, Laud's most lasting contribution to St John's was the quadrangle he built. It is still a monument that all – no matter what else they might think of the archbishop – can applaud. Serene, perfectly proportioned, over the centuries it has been an academic oasis from which young men from St John's have ventured much strengthened to face the worst the world can offer. Laud first decided to build a new quad in August 1630. The following March he calculated that it would cost him £1,055. On 15 April 1631 the President and Fellows formally accepted his generous donation, appointing one of their number, John Lufton, to oversee the construction, which began on 31 July. It took five years to finish. Plans were changed, the first set of masons went bankrupt and asked for more money (which Laud paid them). He inspected the site on several occasions, and ordered sides built so that the quad would be 'absolutely uniform without the least eyesore'. He drew up the regulations for the new library built at the end of the quad, which included a special room for rare books and scientific instruments. The building was not completed until July 1636, when its total cost came to more than £5,000, nearly five times the original estimate, all of which Laud quite cheerfully paid.[29]

While the details of the new quadrangle were the work of stonemasons such as Richard Maude, William Hill and Jack Jackson, and its slightly Flemish style owed much to Inigo Jones and his pupil Nicholas Stone, Laud was responsible for the project's overall motifs – classical, authentic, restrained and self-confident. On the east side he placed eight busts representing True Learning, Astronomy, Architecture, Music, Poetry, Mathematics, Philosophy, Literature and Rhetoric. Opposite them were the busts of True Religion, Piety, Temperance, Fortitude, Justice and Prudence, Faith, Hope, and Charity. And presiding over them all at the end were Le Sueur's statues of the king and queen.

Just as the art of Charles's court is in many ways the truest representation of the king's personality and political attitudes during the 1630s, so too the art that Laud endowed at Oxford was a profound indication of his feelings and ideas. This was as true about the St John's quadrangle as it was about the plays which he commissioned to celebrate the visit of the king and queen to Oxford in August 1636 to open it.

In the first play, *The Floating Island*, written by the university orator, William Strode, rebellion breaks out in the realm of King Prudenius, who, with his minister, Intellectus Agens, goes into exile to give the rabble full licence.[30] Led by Irato, Desparato, Hilario, and Sir Amorous, they elect Fancie their queen, but after the country degenerates into anarchy they beg King Prudenius and Intellectus Agens to return. Having learned their lesson they humbly acknowledge their fault, and the Epilogue concludes, 'The Isle is settled, Rage of Passions laid, Phancy to Prudence bows.'

The following day William Cartwright's *The Royal Slave* took this theme of the need for law and order one stage further by reminding the academic audience assembled at Christ Church that they too must be leaders in improving the commonwealth. Cratandar, a Persian slave, had, according to the supposed custom of his people, been made king for three days before his execution. But rather than follow the example of his hapless predecessors by squandering his last three days in licence and debauchery, he used his scholarly wisdom to benefit the commonwealth – much to the anger of his fellow slaves, who had come to expect an orgy every time their world was turned upside down. The lesson was quite clear. As Laud told Charles on another occasion, 'the two universities are the great nurseries' for good and able men, 'and if they that are there to be trained up are irregularly bred, it will not be possible to uphold good order and discipline in the church'. In this instance the archbishop was, in fact, referring to Cambridge – a university which he never really understood, or liked.

The government had been worried about the state of affairs at Cambridge for several years. One reason why the king nominated Buckingham to be Cambridge's chancellor in 1626 was to try and tighten up university discipline.[31] In 1630 the king issued a proclamation that if any Cambridge scholar was in danger of marrying the daughter of an innkeeper, or of any tradesman, the university authorities could banish the girl to at least five miles from the town in the hope that a long walk across the Fens would cool the most ardent passions. In May 1631 the king ordered the university to reduce its fees to the level the Elizabethan statute laid down. Since the university sent Laud an amended copy of their fee schedule, it seems likely that he initiated this royal edict, as he did those of 1632, the first of which forbade bullbaiting at Cambridge, while the second prohibited the secret election of college heads.[32]

A few Cambridge men approved the interventions of Oxford's most powerful graduate. Laud helped John Cosin get elected Master of Peterhouse, where he placed a cross over every chapel stall, and bought a silver incense holder for £14. 19s. 6d.[33] The Master and Fellows of King's College were quite happy to petition the king to ask Laud to settle a dispute with their sister foundation at Eton over the vicarage of Windsor.[34]

Most members of the university, however, deeply resented the archbishop's growing power, particularly when he claimed the right to visit them. He first did so in May 1635, prompting the vice-chancellor and heads of colleges to issue an interim denial in July, with the request that they be given more time to formulate a definite response.[35] Laud repeated the claim in December, warning the university, 'If you think these delays to make me forget or forgive the business, you will find yourselves deceived.' The evening the vice-chancellor received this warning, he called together the college heads, and they agreed to ask for more time for a final reply. The archbishop appeared to soften his tone, writing back on 30 December, 'so wishing you a happy new year, and all fair passage in your government, I leave you unto the grace of God, and rest your very loving friend, Canterbury'. Four months later, on receiving the university's formal answer, the archbishop's tone was very different: 'I plainly see you have no purpose to submit to my metropolitan visitation, but had rather the king should hear it.'[36]

Charles heard the case concerning the archbishop's right to visit the university, on 21 June 1636, with Laud standing on his right, and the Earl of Holland, Cambridge's chancellor, on his left. Opening for the plaintiff, Attorney General Heath cited Henrician and Elizabeth statutes, as well as precedents from the reigns of Edward I, Richard II and Edward IV, to prove that his client had the authority to visit any university in the land. Mr Gardiner, the Recorder of the City of London, conceded that as a general principle bishops could visit every three years and archbishops once in their tenures. 'I may visit as often as I will,' interrupted Laud. When Gardiner cited papal bulls to prove that the archbishop's powers were not unlimited, he once again interjected, 'I dare say that the Pope doth as much to beat down Bishops as any puritan doth in England.' The debate became even more acrimonious when Laud insisted that he must visit Cambridge because the state of affairs there had got completely out of hand – there were at least three unconsecrated college chapels in which surplices were not worn – and that if he went through the usual channels it would be too late, and 'the University will be past remedy'. Laud rejected Holland's compromise solution that as Cambridge's chancellor he commission the archbishop to visit the university with an emphatic 'No, I would desire to have my own power,'[37]

On this unyielding note the case went to judgment. Charles accepted the privy council's unanimous recommendation that the archbishop could visit Cambridge whenever he liked so long as he had the monarch's permission.[38]

Laud's victory over the universities (for the same day he won a similar but amicable judgment against Oxford) was as complete as it was hollow. He had insisted on the right as one of principle. There should be no corner of the king's religious realms through which the primate's writ could not run. For this reason he brushed aside the claims of Winchester College, St Paul's Cathedral and the Bishop of Lincoln, that they were exempt from his jurisdiction. But in fact he did very little with the powers he had bought at so high a political cost.

Of course, he had plans. For Cambridge Dr Cosin drew up a reform programme, which, as usual, concentrated on the details: members of the university must wear gowns according to their degree, they must not flaunt gaudy stockings, nor extravagant neck and wrist cuffs. But this was hardly an agenda that justified alienating men as powerful as the Earl of Holland, who, as Laud had to admit, 'is not well pleased with me'.[39]

Between the legal right to do something and the actual ability to execute that right lurked a number of impedimenta, including the church's own bureaucracy, men who did not share Laud's goals, energy or ambitions, and those whom he upset needlessly. The further away from his locus of power a problem was situated, the less chance he had of doing anything lasting about it. The greater the vested interests he threatened, the smaller his hope of getting his own way. For instance, at Oxford he could achieve things at St John's which he could never do ten minutes' walk away at Merton. The gap between Laud's aspirations and his ability to achieve them had two main results. First it forced him to concentrate on obtaining the right as a matter of principle to do something, rather than the power as a matter of fact to achieve it. Second it made him, almost in frustration, concentrate on the symbolic issues. Both policies alienated more people than they rallied to his cause, for supporting different principles divides more than it unites, while uniting against a common enemy may produce the strangest of bedfellows.

Such thoughts, however, were far from anyone's mind in August 1636, when Charles and Henrietta Maria led a state visit to Oxford to open the new quadrangle at St John's. It was the apogee of Laud's career, not merely as a university chancellor, but as primate of the Church of England as well as a royal minister.

For Laud it was a glorious time. It had been one of those rare English summers of cloudless skies and no rain, the sort of weather that on winter nights for years afterwards is nostalgically remembered by all except those who have to wrest a living from parched fields.[40] Charles signed Oxford's new statutes on 3 June, and on the 21st the king in council confirmed the Archbishop of Canterbury's right to visit both universities.[41] The quadrangle was finished, the new Arabic lecturer appointed, everything was ready for royal inspection. Laud ordered the proctors to ensure that none of the undergraduates had long hair (prompting one father to summon his son home to save the lad's locks), and persuaded the heads of colleges to budget £200 for entertainments and dramatic presentations.[42] 'The churches or chapels of all the colleges are much beautified, extraordinary cost bestowed upon them, most of them new glazed,' reported one letter writer, adding that 'all their communion tables are fairly covered with rich carpets.'

The archbishop set out for Oxford from his summer house at Croydon in grand style. Six horses drew his coach, which was attended by fifty cavaliers. He spent two nights at Sir Thomas Roe's place at Cranford, having specifically asked his old friend not to go to any great fuss for his entertainment. The next night he spent at Cuddesdon, where he lodged in Bishop Bancroft's newly built episcopal palace, before riding on to Oxford.

The following Monday, 29 August, was set for the royal entry.[43] For Laud it could not have been a more auspicious day, being the Feast of St John the Baptist, and the twenty-fifth anniversary of James's decision confirming his election to the presidency of the college named after Our Saviour's harbinger. That afternoon outside St John's a large crowd from all over the university gathered to welcome their chancellor, and as the university bell struck one, the sign for all students of quality to join them, they rode up the Woodstock road to meet the mayor, twenty aldermen, and some sixty retainers. Here, at about two o'clock, town joined gown to welcome the royal party with official speeches from the vice-chancellor and the city recorder. Then everyone lined up for the formal procession into Oxford. Two trumpeters led the way, followed by leading citizens, the aldermen, the proctors, some twenty-five learned doctors, and the Bishops of Winchester, Oxford, Norwich and London. Escorted by two beadles, Laud preceded the coach carrying the royal party. Behind them came Lord Chancellor Coventry and Sir Francis Cottington, followed by those citizens and students who had lined the route to watch the procession pass, before joining it to participate in the festivities. It was an impressive show. Taken to see it at Christ Church when he was four, Anthony Wood, Oxford's historian, would talk about it for the rest of his life.[44] He watched the university present the king with a bible, and the queen with a pair of gloves and a copy of William Camden's *The True and Royal History of Elizabeth, Queen of England*. (Heylyn says she got a Protestant bible, something most of her subjects believed she sorely needed.) That evening they saw *The Floating Island*, a play by William Strode, the university orator (see p. 138). Apparently most courtiers found it heavy going: the Earl of Caernarvon remarked that 'it was the worst that he ever saw but one he saw at Cambridge'.

Fortunately Laud never learned of this back-handed compliment. At eight the next morning he and the king attended a sermon at Christ Church, and at nine went on to a convocation that made Charles Louis, the Prince Elector of the Palatinate, an honorary MA, entering him on the books as a member of St John's in tribute to Laud, who gave a sweet Latin speech of welcome. Laud spent the rest of the morning showing the king around the Bodleian Library, where he pointed out his own donations. He also showed the king a bust of His Majesty, which, he joked, would stop the students stealing books since they were now under royal protection. (It has, alas, never worked.) Charles found it all so interesting that he was reluctant to leave for his next appointment at St John's. Because Henrietta Maria was still getting dressed in her rooms at Christ Church, the Earl of Pembroke's son, William Herbert, was called upon to make a short extemporaneous speech (which the undergraduate from Exeter College did well enough to be awarded an MA the next day). When the queen was ready, the royal party went to St John's, where they inspected the new quadrangle before sitting down to 'a stately and magnificent dinner', as one guest recalled, 'at which all the Gallantries and beauties of the kingdom seemed to meet'.[45] Few had seen such a banquet, even in those days of massive feasts. Laud spent £2,666. 1s. 7d. from his own purse to set before the king and queen, princes, proctors, professors, courtiers, councillors, dons, drones and hangers-on a feast that included seven stags, sixty-three bucks, seventy-four rams, two lambs, five oxen and one calf, and which lasted, course after course, and drink after drink, for five hours. Afterwards there was a short but doubtless welcome break, which the king and queen spent in the president's lodgings. Laud led them to the hall for yet another dramatic presentation (see p. 138), which the queen liked so much that she asked if she could borrow the costumes so she and her ladies could put it on. That night the archbishop noted in his diary, 'and all passed happily'.[46]

After bidding the royal party goodbye in Christ Church quadrangle at nine the next morning, the chancellor entertained the heads of colleges at

St John's, then departed for his summer estate, staying at Cuddesdon and Henley-on-Thames along the way, and leaving his steward behind to pack up and pay the bills. On 8 September Laud wrote to Wentworth, 'I am now back to Croydon, from my weary, expenseful business at Oxford. Yet most glad I am it is passed without any noted blemish that I yet hear of.'[47] After so grand a triumph there is something petty about this reaction. Even more small-minded was the relief that he noted down in his diary a few days later that hardly any of the plate and furnishings he had borrowed for the royal entertainments had been stolen: 'I lost but only two spoons, which were of mine own plate, and but little of my linen.' What could be more revealing! Laud had been oblivious to the larger matters, while focusing on the smaller details. When Thomas Brown, the proctor, preached at Christ Church before him, the royal family and the whole university on the text 'Blessed be the king that cometh in the name of the Lord', Laud apparently never noticed the pun, but instead noted that it was 'an excellent sermon . . . which gave great content'.

IX

'More vinegar than oil'

By 14 October 1636 the excitement over the royal visit to Oxford had died down. The king and queen had moved on to Winchester and Henley-on-Thames, lectures had returned to normal, dons to their studies, the archbishop back to Croydon, and his steward had paid most of the bills. That night Laud wrote in his diary, 'I dreamed marvellously that the king was offended with me, and would cast me off, and tell me no cause why. *Avertat Deus*. For cause I have given none.'[1] For a man at the pinnacle of his power and influence it was a remarkable dream. If dreams are, as Freud argued, 'the royal road to the unconscious', then this one suggests some deep inner torment, some guilty secret so painful that it tortured the most hidden parts of Laud's mind. So the thirty-two dreams that the archbishop recorded might provide an entrée into his personality, complementing what we know about it from the records of his waking life.

To attempt to obtain the fullest possible understanding of their subject is a paramount duty of all biographers. But in Laud's case this goal is especially important, for his personality had a profound effect on both his policies, and their failure, and his own subsequent emergence as a scapegoat. Thus it might be worthwhile to pause in our analysis of Laud's public life and career in order to examine more closely the inner man. As Bishop Fuller, one of the earliest historians of the Laudian church, astutely observed, in his public dealings this very private man was wont to 'infuse more vinegar than oil'.[2]

There are no forms of evidence more ephemeral than dreams. Trying to make head or tail of one's own dreams is difficult enough, without dealing with those of someone long dead. Yet from the beginnings of civilisation dreams have fascinated people.[3] Many sixteenth- and seventeenth-century Englishmen, among them John Foxe, Francis Bacon, William Sancroft, Richard Baxter, Ralph Verney, Sir Harbottle Grimston and George Foxe, recorded their dreams, convinced that they were often 'the speaking of God to man'.[4] According to the second-century Roman writer

144

Artemidorus, whose *Onirocritica* was the most popular dream book in early modern England, dreams were either a revelation of God's will, or were produced by physical stimuli, such as over-eating or eating certain foods. Artemidorus recognised three types of dreams that today would be described as day-residue, symbolic and anxiety dreams. Two thousand years earlier Plato had defined wish-fulfilling dreams as occurring when 'certain of the unnecessary pleasures and appetites I concur to be unlawful' come to the surface 'when the reasoning and human and ruling power is asleep'.[5] These authors, with whom Laud was surely familiar, were writing in remarkably modern terms, although they did not, of course, use our modern terminology. Neither did they fall into the trap of trying to analyse the dreams for their latent content – for their supposedly real, yet hidden, meaning, best discovered through free association with an analyst.

Without doubt an analyst would have eagerly noted the dream that Laud had in 1627, in which his mother appeared to him whilst he was in bed, 'and drawing aside the clothes a little, looked pleasantly upon me; and that I was glad to see her with so merry an aspect'. Thirteen years later, when things were not going so well for the archbishop, 'I dreamed that my father (who died 46 years since) came to me; and to my thinking he was well and as cheerful as ever I saw him.'[6] Laud was the youngest child of a large family. 'My mother had ten, I was the tenth, and was paid to the Church, and there are but myself and my half brother left,' he told Wentworth.[7] Even though he furthered William Robinson's career, helping his half-brother become Archdeacon of Nottingham in 1633, they were never close; no letters between the two have survived.[8] Laud also got his nephew Edward Layfield made Archdeacon of Essex, and helped his cousin Elizabeth Webb in an Irish suit. But basically his involvement with relatives was limited.[9]

In a very real fashion Reading and Oxford were substitutes. On New Year's Eve 1633, 'as I was at my prayers', Laud felt that the Almighty was telling him to find the best 'way to do the town of Reading good for their poor, which may be compassed by God's blessing upon me, though my wealth be small'.[10] He helped the corporation obtain a new charter, got the king to order the cleaning up of the offal that butchers were dumping in Broad Street near the house in which he had grown up, and took great pains to ensure that the grammar school was able to recruit a good master. If he was a dutiful son to his home town, then on behalf of his old college he sometimes seemed a rapacious nepotist. Personally he was most generous to St John's, and to Oxford University, working hard to present the former with advowsons that would further the careers of its fellows, whom he treated with remarkable forbearance. Once he excused William Lufton from being absent from his parish at Ibstock, even though 'He is a hot man, and his spleen such' that Laud feared he might assault the vice-chancellor.[11]

Such private mildness belied the public image of Laud as 'a fellow of mean extraction and arrogant pride'.[12] He could be remarkably warm with his friends, as Heylyn's character-sketch shows:

> Of Stature he was of low but strong Composition. So short a trunk never contained so much excellent treasure, which therefore was to be the stronger by reason of the wealth which was lodged within it. His Countenance cheerful and well bloodied, more fleshly than any other part of his body, which cheerfulness and vivacity he carried with him to the very Block . . . Of Apprehension he was quick and sudden, of a very sociable Wit and pleasant Humour: and one that knew as well how to put off the gravity of the place and Person, when he saw occasion, as any man living whatsoever. Accessible enough at all times, but when he was tired out with multiplicity and vexation of business.[13]

To those with whom he felt at ease, or to whom he had some long-standing tie, Laud could be surprisingly kind. Take the case of Stephen Dennison, curate of St Katherine's, Leadenhall Street, who in a sermon called the congregation 'Frogs, hogs, dogs and devils . . . knaves, villains, rascals, queens, she-devils, and pillory whores'. High Commission suspended him from preaching, but within three months Laud and Juxon lifted the sentence because Dennison seemed to have overcome his emotional problems.[14] Laud treated another errant minister, John Hales, from Eaton, whom he had known at Oxford, with equal leniency. Rather than dragging the poor man before High Commission for attacking the church's authority, the archbishop called him to Lambeth, where they spent a whole day walking about the palace grounds discussing Hales's views. Hales admitted the error of his ways, and Laud made him one of his chaplains, and eventually a prebend at Winchester.[15] Such a conversion was, admittedly, based in part on coercion (as well as ambition). If Hales had not seen the light as they strolled through the garden, then surely his mentor would not have spared the rod. Edward Hyde, who first got to know Laud as they too perambulated in the palace garden discussing a mercantile petition the young lawyer had been instructed to present, noted that 'the greatest want the Archbishop had was of a true friend, who would seasonably have told him of his Infirmities, and what the People spoke of him'.[16]

Sir Thomas Wentworth, Laud's closest friend, could never perform this role, if only because he too was a proud man, equally unconcerned about public opinion. There was no question that the two needed each other. 'If I fail you, I'll fail myself,' Laud wrote to his friend, adding in another letter, 'My Lord, I am very much bound to you for the constancy of your love towards me.'[17] They shared each other's hopes, fears and frustrations. 'A vent is sometimes necessary,' Laud wrote of their correspondence.[18] They discussed emotional and physical pains, swopping medical advice as do men who dread the encroachment of old age. They needed each other in order to succeed in their jobs, and to salve each other's disappointments. It was a friendship that worked because it was conducted at a distance between two equals who, had they been geographically closer, might have demanded from each other the deference which they insisted upon from most other people with whom they had to deal.

Laud and Wentworth became scapegoats not so much because they were seen as the architects of the crown's failure but because as individuals they made enemies needlessly through the infusion of vinegar. A profound sense of insecurity helped make the archbishop, at least, behave in this fashion, especially when he felt that people did not like him, and that secretly, behind their well-kept hands, they were sniggering at his physical appearance, or his humble origins (as did Lucy Hutchinson, whose father had been Lieutenant of the Tower of London, and who thought that Laud's 'mean extraction' might well have produced his 'arrogant pride'). Insults drove the archbishop to a cruelty that was almost pathological. For calling him 'the little meddling hocus-pocus' Laud voted that Lambert Osbaldeston should be fined £5,000 by Star Chamber, that his living be confiscated, and that he should have his ear nailed to the pillory before his pupils at Westminster School. When Thomas Shepard asked the archbishop to rescind the ban on his preaching, he refused, becoming very angry 'as though blood would have gushed out of his face'.[19] Perhaps Shepard did not approach the prelate with sufficient humility, and exhibited the bad manners which prompted Laud to vote that Lord Morley be fined £20,000 for calling Sir George Theobalds 'a base rascal . . . a dung hill', and punching him in the royal presence. But there was something needless about Laud's infusions of vinegar. One of his first acts on becoming Archbishop of Canterbury was to inform Richard Sterne, fellow of Bennet College, Cambridge, that he had been selected for the high honour of preaching the St Paul's Cross sermon. But instead of ending the pleasant duty of giving someone good news on a friendly note of congratulation Laud concluded with the stern warning: 'And hereof fail not, as you will answer the contrary at your peril.'[20]

As the little archbishop travelled about the land in such great pomp, he made the disastrous mistake of appearing ridiculous. John Bastwick caricatured him proceeding through the realm, escorted by forty or fifty mounted attendants shouting 'Room, room, for my Lord's Grace' as costermongers' barrows went flying, and children at play were trampled underfoot to make way for this little, low, round, red-faced man.[21] Herbert

Croft, Bishop of Hereford (and thus a far more friendly witness), seemed to suggest that there was much truth to Bastwick's description:[22]

> When first I chanced to see him enter at court, there was such a shifting of places, such withdrawing of each side, that I expected some extraordinary greatness to pass by, but seeing his little dimension only pass by, I wondered why each one retired themselves for fane of, yet when by chance he perceiving about struck me with his piercing eye, I then rather wondered how they durst stand so near.

Even though religion played a central role in Laud's life and career, and he had been nurtured on biblical stories such as the Annunciation, which taught that dreams were a way by which God talked to men, only one of the archbishop's dreams involved religion. On 30 January 1625 he noted, 'Sunday Night, my dream of my Blessed Lord and Saviour Jesus Christ. One of the most comfortable passages that I ever had in my life.' The intensity of this experience, which hints at an almost sexual nocturnal passion, contrasts markedly with the restrained and highly intellectual nature of Laud's written devotions. The dream is mystical; his recorded prayers are thoughtful. Both his public and private devotions are urbane, well-written, polite. He talked with his Maker rather like a young don conversing with the senior fellow of his college, respectful of the superior's position and careful for his own future elevation. His devotions lack the soul-searching guilt that we associate with the Puritans, and which is often found in his diary. The prayers that the archbishop composed for specific events, or topics, such as war, peace, sorrow, death, the plague, were based on scripture, and lacked the personal touch. The one he composed on Buckingham's assassination – an event which shook him to the core – reads as if it were written by a stranger, and not the duke's grief-stricken friend and protégé.

Just as Laud's prayers failed to distinguish between the public and the private, so his religious policy failed to make the same distinction.[23] He wanted windows into men's souls – or rather, he wanted their souls to be kept outside so all could see them revealed in the correct performance of public ritual.

In much the same way the repressed nature of his religious feelings suggests an intense sense of unease with his Maker to which one wag cruelly alluded by describing the archbishop as 'mighty, but not Almighty'. Without doubt Laud loved God, but at a distance, and not on His terms. As well as being a sign of his own social unease, Laud's insistence that bishops operated *jure divino* was a declaration of independence not just from the crown, but, in a way, from God himself, that echoed James I's famous claim that the holders of his office 'are not only God's lieutenants upon earth, and sit upon God's throne, but even by God himself are called Gods'.[24]

Laud conveyed this opinion in 'A book in Vellum, fair written, containing the records which are in the Tower, and concern the Clergy. This book I have got done at my own charge, and have left it in my study at Lambeth for posterity. Junii 10, 1637.'[25] It is still there, in the palace record office, for posterity to read. But far more revealing than the 248 pages of precedents going back to 1272 defending clerical privileges, is the iconography of the title page. It shows a building, surely symbolic of the church. Underneath are the arms of Oxford and Cambridge universities, and of the Bishops of Bath and Wells, St David's, and London, supporting the title 'Iura et Privilegia Clero Anglicano ex Parliamentarum Rotulis'. Beside this heading 'The Rights and Privileges of the English Church from the Records of Parliament' are the two figures of Antiquity and Truth (the latter a rather attractive naked lady). Above them all proudly stand the arms of the Archbishop of Canterbury, and nowhere can be found any allegorical mention of God or the king.[26]

The vellum book's emphasis on the past, with its mainly Catholic precedents, suggests why Rome tantalised Laud. It was the oldest church, the original one. No matter how much Protestants might argue that it was really the pope who had lost his way, the Reformation was a revolution – a breach that Laud deeply regretted.

> 9 March 1627. I dreamed that I was reconciled to the Church of Rome. This troubled me much, and I wondered exceedingly how it should happen. Nor was I aggrieved with myself, only by reason of the errors of that Church, but also upon the scandal which from my fall would be cast upon many eminent and learned men in the Church of England. So being troubled at my dreams, I said with myself that I would go immediately, and confessing my fault would beg pardon of the Church of England. Going with this resolution a certain priest met me, and would have stopped me. But moved with indignation I went on my way. And while I wearied myself with these troublesome thoughts, I awoke. Herein I felt such a strong impression that I could scarce believe it was a dream.[27]

Laud was, quite clearly, not a Roman Catholic. His conference with the Jesuit Fisher is a classic and fundamental defence of Canterbury against Rome.[28] His reluctance to help the ecumenicalist John Durie in any meaningful way shows little commitment to reconciliation. And yet, Rome, after all, was the original Catholic church. For an authoritarian such as Laud, the pope could well have appeared as the original symbol of episcopal authority. If, as Laud maintained, Anglican bishops ruled *jure divino*, how much stronger was the claim of St Peter's successor to be the rock on which

Christ commanded that his church should be built? Quite obviously Rome, with its rituals, style and self-confidence, appealed to Laud just as seductively as it would to his disciples of the Oxford Movement three centuries later. Could it not be that subconsciously, at least, Laud realised that there was a grain of truth to the Puritan charges that he was indeed a closet Papist?

Some of Laud's dreams were so unpleasant he could hardly bear to reveal the details even to his diary: '20 November 1636. Sunday Night: My fearful Dream. Mr Cobb [a servant] brought me word, etc.'[29] A decade earlier he recorded, 'I was very much troubled in my dreams. My imagination ran altogether upon the Duke of Buckingham, his servants and family. All seemed to be out of order.'[30] The anxiety behind the nightmare he had on 21 December 1626 is obvious: 'I dreamed of the burial of I know not whom, and that I stood by the grave. I awakened sad.'[31]

Death and disease were constant themes in Laud's dreams, nine of which involved these morbid preoccupations. He dreamed that Lady Buckingham had a miscarriage, that Sackville Crowe, a Gentleman of the Bed Chamber, had died of the plague, 'having not long before been with the king'.[32] A couple of years later he dreamed of a Mrs Grove, possibly a long-dead friend of his mother.[33] Two months afterwards, on 9 February 1627, 'I dreamed that I was much troubled with the scurvy, and that on the sudden all my teeth became loose; that one of them especially in the lower jaw, I could scarcely hold it with my finger, till I called out for help, etc.'[34]

Such dreams about sudden disease should not surprise us, for unexpected death was a constant, even in the highest circles of Stuart life. Just before Laud dreamed that Sackville Crowe had died, a footman caught the plague, forcing the court to flee from Windsor to Beaulieu.[35] Throughout his life physical ailments constantly troubled Laud. Days after the dream about losing his teeth (which Freudians would interpret as the fear of being castrated), Laud 'began the cure for a certain itch'. Laud nearly died on several occasions as a child, and once as an undergraduate. As President of St John's, whilst riding back from an abortive trip to curry favour at court, he fainted just outside Oxford, and had to be slowly and painfully nursed back to health at Sir Francis Windebanke's house. In August 1630 he fell ill of 'a burning fever' that 'was so fierce that my physicians, as well as my friends, gave me for dead, and it is a piece of a miracle that I live'.[36] Once he ruptured himself by over-energetically swinging two weighty tomes – the titles of which were not, alas, recorded – like Indian clubs in his study in order to keep fit. In middle and old age he was in frequent pain from a pulled leg muscle. 'My Lord, I am very weary, not only of writing letters, but almost of everything else,' was a constant complaint to Wentworth. Yet in spite of his dreams about death, the fear of dying never seems to have been a major concern in Laud's waking life. At the end he died bravely, welcoming martyrdom. 'Though I walk through the valley of the shadow of death, yet I will fear no evil,' he prayed a few weeks before his execution. 'O Lord I am weary and heavy laden.'[37]

Part of Laud's psychological burden was the constant fear of betrayal and rejection. He dreamed that he went over to Rome, that courtiers mocked him in the Tower, that Williams taunted him, the king disowned him, 'K.B.' rejected him, 'L.M.St.' shunned him, and his protégé Dr Theodore Price betrayed him.[38] All these dreams prove what the documents of Laud's waking life already show. 'I am resolved to go on steadily in the way that you have seen me go,' he wrote to Wentworth, 'so that if anything fail of my hearty desires for the king and the Church's service, the fault shall not be mine.'[39] To his Maker he prayed, 'O Merciful God, since thou hast ordered me to live in these times in which the rents of the Church are grievous, I humbly beseech Thee to guide me, that the divisions of men may not separate me from either thee or it.'[40] Such sanctimoniousness, of which many examples have survived, betrays an extremely insecure man, who tried to conceal his insecurities with bombast, bullying, and ferocious punishments in Star Chamber, and by focusing on the details, by attending to the surface, such as rituals and symbols, in the hope that the substance would somehow mend itself.

Throughout his life Laud constantly felt that he was threatened by enemies, whom he often vaguely defined, and sometimes named. In 1624 he wrote in his diary, 'So may God bless me his servant, labouring under the pressure of them who always wish me ill.' Born in 1573, Laud had grown up in Tudor England, where fear of conspiracies and treasons was widespread.[41] Psychologically he needed a bogeyman lurking in the shadows to do him harm, for this would enable him in good faith to wage the fights which he abhorred, and yet relished. At Oxford he had feuded with George and Robert Abbot. After falling out with John Williams, Laud fought his mentor with as much venom asleep as he did awake.

On 3 October 1623 he recorded in his diary, 'Friday, I was with my Lord Keeper; to whom I found some had done me very ill offices. And he was very jealous of Lord Buckingham's favour.' A couple of months later, 'I did dream that the Lord Keeper was dead . . . his lower lip was infinitely swelled and fallen, and he rotten already. This dream did trouble me.'[42] Even after Charles had stripped Williams of the Lord Keeper's office and banished him back to his diocese of Lincoln, the prelate still continued to haunt Laud's dreams. On 14 January 1627, 'I dreamed that the Bishop of Lincoln came, I know not whither with iron chains. But returning loosed from them, leaped on horseback, went away; neither could I overtake him.'[43] Five years later, on 13 July 1633, on the way back from Scotland, 'I dreamed that my Lord Lincoln came and offered to sit above me at the Council Table, and that Lord Holland came in and placed him there.'[44] It

was as if at night Laud was frightened that somehow Williams would free
himself from the bondage to which he had persuaded the king to chain
him; and thus by day Laud had to do all he could to ensure that his rival
never managed to return to power and overtake him. So Laud had Williams
dragged before Star Chamber, which sentenced him to be fined heavily,
and imprisoned during His Majesty's pleasure. Only asleep could be admit
to himself that by hounding his vanquished enemy he was disobeying
Christ's injunction to turn the other cheek. The following March the archbishop's friend Sir George Wright, who had just died, appeared to him in
a dream within a dream, and 'whispering in my ear, told me, that I was
the cause why the Bishop of Lincoln was not admitted into favour, and to
Court'.[45]

Laud's best-known dream, of 21 August 1625, revealed the relationship between his subconscious and conscious fears:

> That night, in my sleep, it seemed to me that the Duke of
> Buckingham came into bed with me; where he behaved himself
> with great kindness towards me, after that rest, wherewith wearied
> persons are wont to solace themselves. Many seemed to me to
> enter the chamber who saw this.[46]

When in 1644 Prynne published this dream in his *Breviate of the life of
William Laud, Archbishop of Canterbury, extracted for the most part
verbatim out of his Diary, and other items out of his own hand*, he
suggested that Laud was guilty of 'uncleanness'. The primate angrily
retorted that 'there was never fasn'd upon me the least suspicion of this
sin in all my life'. Could he have protested too much? After all, as the
duke's confessor and an intelligent observer of court life, Laud must have
been aware that Buckingham's' relationship with the king started as a
homosexual affair.[47]

Laud's diary does not support his assertion that he was utterly above
suspicion. 'My Lord Buckingham was pleased to enter a near respect to
me,' he wrote on 19 June 1622, 'the particulars are not for paper.' Five
years earlier Laud confessed to his Maker, 'I wandered out of my way from
thee into a foul and strange path . . . O Lord, for my saviour's sake, forgive
me the folly and strengthen me against the weakness for ever.'[48] His diary
shows that he committed the act that caused him so much guilt 'cum E.B.'.
It is full of similar cryptic references to his 'unfortunatenesses' with 'T.',
'S.S.', 'P.B.', 'E.M.', 'A.D.' and 'E.B.'[49] Beyond the fact that the pronouns
show that all these individuals were male, none of them have been identified; neither have those who appeared in his dreams. 'Towards the
morning [of 4 August 1635] I dreamed that L.M.St. came to see me the
next day, and showed me all the kindness I could ask for.' Again, 'I dreamed
that K.B. sent to me in Westminster Church that he was now as desirous

to see me, as I him,' Laud recorded in his diary on 6 June 1633. 'I went with joy, but met another in the middle of the Church, who seemed to know the business, and laughed; but K.B. was not there.'[50] A year later he confided to his diary, 'My ancient friend E.R., came to me, and performed great kindness, which I may not forget.'[51]

What all this means one cannot say for sure, and in a sense it does not really matter, for there is no doubt that both asleep and awake Laud was a very troubled man. The nine diary references to 'K.B.' suggest an intensely painful relationship. Laud's dreams, as well as his waking life, reveal a man tormented by guilt almost at times to the point of neurosis. He touched on some dreadful enigma on the night of 11 September 1625: 'I dreamed that Dr Theodore Price admonished me concerning Ma. 3, and that he was unfaithful to me, and discovered all he knew, and that I should therefore take heed of him and trust him no more.'[52] He alluded to some terrible secret – perhaps the same one – in a letter to his confidant, Sir John Scudamore, of September 1626: 'One thing there is which I have many times feared, and still do, and yet I doubt it will fall upon me. I cannot trust my letters with it: but if it come, I will take my solemn leave of all contentment. But in that way I shall ever rest your loving friend.'[53]

To friends such as Scudamore, Laud was a warm, decent man. To his enemies, who in comparison were legion, he was 'that little active wheel that sets all the rest at work by his active motion'.[54] Far more than most human beings, he was a mass of contradictions, an enigma who tied himself up in riddles, which a biographer can try to unravel with much fascination and little success. Such confusion could be the result of a surfeit of riches, for few men have revealed themselves in their diary and letters as fully, and yet as ambiguously, as Laud did. Intellectually his ideas were in contradiction. Emotionally parts of his mind fought one another, fearful that at any moment some hidden secret chasm would open to swallow up all that he cherished. So perhaps it would be fairest to leave the last word on the archbishop to a friend. 'He is an excellent man,' wrote Sir Thomas Roe in 1634, 'for he is very just, incorrupt, and above all, mistaken by the erring world.'[55]

X

'*Who's the fool now?*'

On the evening of 9 March 1638 the king's jester. Archie Armstrong, went out to the White Lion tavern in Westminster for a few drinks.[1] It was a particularly difficult time to be the royal fool, for there were very few laughs to be had at court. 'The king in the present state of affairs,' wrote the Venetian ambassador that same day, 'is not loved by his subjects.'[2] About twelve months earlier Charles had ordered the introduction into Scotland of a revised prayer book on which Laud and some of the Scottish bishops had been working for at least a couple of years. Bringing Scotland into religious conformity with England had long been a goal of the king's, and it was one that Laud ardently endorsed. Both men were equally surprised when on the prayer book's first use in St Giles's Cathedral on 23 July 1637 the congregation rioted.[3]

The crown did not back down. Instead it insisted that the Scots adopt the new prayer book. With equal stubbornness, many of them signed a covenant to resist until not only had the liturgy been withdrawn, but episcopacy itself was abolished. Laud supported the king's resolve, for he was convinced that these Covenanters (as the defiant Scots Presbyterians quickly became known) were out to destroy not only himself, but true religion and monarchy itself.

During the winter and early spring of 1638 from north of the border bad news was followed by worse. 'We find our authority much impaired,' complained a royal proclamation of 9 February.[4] Five days later Charles's adviser on Scottish affairs, the Earl of Traquair, cautioned him that if he insisted on ramming the new prayer book down the Covenanters' throats he would need a standing army of some 40,000 English soldiers. The king brushed aside all such depressing warnings, which prompted the Venetian ambassador to report, 'At court, however, they try as much as possible to suppress such bad news.'[5]

Thus it is not surprising that after trying — and presumably failing — to cheer up the gloomy court, Archie the Fool needed a dram or two.

154

Indeed, he had far more than a couple, for according to John Sharpe and Robert Terr, two other customers in the White Lion, in his cups he shouted out, 'My Lord of Canterbury is a monk, a rogue and a traitor.' Then, as if he were addressing Laud, he asked, 'Who's the fool now? Did you not hear the news from Stirling about the liturgy?'[6]

When Laud learned of the incident he complained to the king, who referred the matter to the privy council. They might well have ordered the fool to be flogged, but at the archbishop's request they commanded that he be ceremonially thrown out of the palace. He was taken to the porter's lodge, his coat was pulled up over his head, and quite literally he was kicked out. Archie brushed off the mud and returned home to his native Northumberland, where he wrote a best-selling – although to modern tastes extraordinarily tedious – book of jokes. Archie's expulsion changed nothing: it was the action of a government too frightened to take a joke even from one licensed to make them. Although Laud was unfairly blamed for the new prayer book and for the crown's ineffective attempts to force it on the Scots, within a few years most people had but one answer to the jester's jibe of 'who's the fool now?'

The question of revising the Scottish prayer book was an old one going back to the previous reign. In the 1570s, a generation before he came to the English throne, James VI did much to limit the powers of the Scots nobility over the church, and established a weak form of episcopacy to administer what was in many respects a Presbyterian kirk. In 1614, a dozen years after leaving his native land, he proposed liturgical changes, and got the National Assembly of the Kirk meeting at Perth to accept the Five Articles, which instituted kneeling during Communion, saints' days, private communion and baptism, and confirmation by bishops. When James proposed further reforms, including a new prayer book which Bishop William Cowper of Galloway had drafted, the other bishops protested. The king had sense enough to leave well alone, announcing in 1621 that he had no intention of changing religion north of the border.

Here matters rested until the late summer of 1629, when Dr John Maxwell, a minister from Edinburgh, came to London with a draft of the 1619 prayer book. He may have brought it on his own initiative, but more likely he did so at the request of some of the Scots bishops. Charles referred the matter to Laud, who told Maxwell that 'if His Majesty would have a liturgy settled there, it should be best to take the English liturgy without any variation, so that the same service book might be used in all his Majesty's dominions'.[7] Maxwell replied that the Scots bishops would not tolerate having an alien version imposed upon them, and even though Charles supported Laud's view the matter was allowed to drop. Laud seems to have been quite happy, if he could not get the whole loaf, to have nothing at all, boasting, 'I held that business for two, if not three years at least.'[8]

In the summer of 1633, after several cancellations, Charles went to Scotland to be crowned. Laud was a member of the royal party. It was his first trip north of the border since he had accompanied King James as an ambitious college president in 1617, and he made himself as obnoxious to the Scots as he had on his previous visit. On 18 June, three days after being admitted to the Scottish privy council in Edinburgh, Laud attended the coronation at Holyrood Abbey.[9] John Spalding, clerk of the Bishop of Aberdeen's consistory court, recorded that all the bishops wore surplices and genuflected during the service, and that an altar decked with candles had been placed at the east end of the abbey, and a crucifix hung on the wall.[10] During his visit the king had conversations about revising the prayer book with several Scots bishops, who opposed accepting the English version lock, stock and barrel. As before, Laud wanted to ignore their objections, but Charles demurred, explaining that he had 'no intention to do anything, but that which was according to honour and justice and the laws of that kingdom'.[11] As was his habit after losing on a major matter, Charles compensated by winning on a petty one. On 15 October he issued a set of regulations for 'the better ordering of divine service' at the Chapel Royal, Holyrood, commanding the immediate use of the English form of worship.[12] According to the seventeenth-century historian John Rushworth, the king promulgated these regulations (which were extended the following year to all cathedrals and college chapels) at Laud's bidding – a charge that years later, as a prisoner in the Tower, he emphatically denied.[13] On the other hand, Laud had both the power and the will to do so. The king had just made him Archbishop of Canterbury, and two months earlier, on his own authority, Laud had ordered Scots as well as English mercenary regiments in continental service to worship according to the English liturgy. Laud admitted that the English prayer book was to be used in the Chapel Royal 'for example's sake'.[14]

In October 1634 the king issued a warrant strengthening the powers of the Court of High Commission in Scotland, which like its English counterpart punished those who opposed the established church.[15] Next Charles announced the creation of a new bishop for Edinburgh, much to the irritation of the burghers, who disliked his candidate, William Forbes, who had a reputation for being popishly affected, as much as they resented having to pay for the extensive renovations to St Giles's Cathedral that its promotion to an ecclesiastical seat required.[16] Then the king ordered all members of the Scots Privy Council and Lords of the Sessions, and their staffs, to take communion according to the English form in the Chapel Royal at least twice a year. Finally he formally instructed the committee of bishops, whom he may have appointed the previous year when he visited Edinburgh, to 'draw up a liturgy as near that of England as might be'.[17]

In response to the last request the Scots bishops sent John Maxwell, who had just been promoted Bishop of Ross, to discuss the new prayer book with the king. On 28 September 1634 Charles gave him a printed copy of the English Book of Common Prayer with annotated suggestions and alterations, which he may have dictated to a clerk. Maxwell returned with this version, which he and his fellow bishops spent six months revising. When they sent the product of their labours back to the king in the following spring they also wrote to Laud explaining that although they wished to do all they could to obtain 'a full Conformity in the Churches' of England and Scotland, 'this must be the work of time'.[18] Charles read their edition, which he ordered printed with some minor alterations. Meanwhile the Scots bishops had second thoughts, so they sent the king another draft, which he referred to Laud and Bishop Matthew Wren. In April 1636 he rejected the second set of Scots revisions, in favour of those from Laud and Wren, with their increased emphasis on the communion service. So the Scots bishops sent Maxwell back to London to request yet another set of changes. Some of them Charles accepted; others he turned down, with his usual lack of tact, as typical of 'the diversity, nay, deformity' of Scots worship.[19] The following month the king issued a proclamation, to be read aloud in every marketplace in Scotland, that the new prayer books should be published, and that every parish should use them, buying at least two copies.

All those in England who had been involved with the revisions of the prayer book must have felt pleased with the fruit of their labours as the final edition came off the press in March and April of 1637. Never before had the government in London consulted Scots opinion so extensively before deciding on a course of action. Its mistake, however, was not a lack of consultation, but talking to the wrong people. Scots bishops were not as powerful as English ones. Unlike the latter, they had not helped to bring about the Protestant Reformation, which prompted one contemporary to call them 'but a chip off the old block papacy'.[20] Scotland's bishops were a much later creation that the crown foisted on a fundamentally Presbyterian church. They lacked the social standing of their English brethren. Charles's order of July 1637 that the Archbishop of St Andrews be given the same precedence in Scotland as the Archbishop of Canterbury enjoyed in England much offended the Caledonian aristocracy. Scots bishops were, as another contemporary observed, 'neither fish nor flesh, but what it please their earthly God and king to make them'.[21]

Their king was able to make them many things – as Adam Bellenden, Bishop of Dunblane, learned only to well. When Charles heard in 1634 that Bellenden had omitted parts of the English prayer book from the services he conducted in the Chapel Royal, he asked Laud to write conveying his extreme annoyance. The archbishop added that such obstinacy had cost him the bishopric of Edinburgh, to which the king had just appointed David Lindsay. Two months later, after telling Bellenden that the king did not accept his excuses, Laud added, 'I doubt not if you continue to do that which his Majesty looks for in the course of the church, and which is most just and fit to be done, but that you will easily recover his favour, and find the good of it.' Bellenden learned the error of his ways speedily enough to be promoted the following year to Aberdeen (where the new bishop once again offended the king by ordering a fast, prompting Laud to observe wryly that 'he hath overshot himself').[22]

Other bishops were far more compliant. John Spottiswoode, Archbishop of St Andrews and Primate of the Scottish Church, was so Erastian that he boasted that the new prayer book 'is formed so nigh to the English as we could', a claim that gave credence to the widely held belief that he had once laughingly bragged, 'If the king would turn papist we were behooved to obey.'[23] For his part in drafting the revisions, James Wedderburn followed Bellenden to the bishopric of Dunblane, while Thomas Sydserff (who supported the royal cause so enthusiastically that a fellow minister described him as 'a violent, virulent man'), was promoted to Galloway. In revising the liturgy the crown ignored the advice of uncooperative prelates, but relied instead on the four Laudian appointments to the fourteen-member Scottish episcopal bench: Maxwell, Wedderburn, Sydserff, and Whitford of Brechin.

Had any of these four bishops read the letter that Robert Baillie, minister of Kilwinning kirk, Ayrshire, sent to a friend on 2 January 1637, he would surely have been surprised. 'The proclamation of our new Liturgy is the matter of my greatest affliction,' wrote the Presbyterian divine. 'I am greatly afraid that this apple of contention will banish peace from our poor church hereafter for ever.' Any one of the four Laudian bishops might have called Baillie an alarmist: after all, the very similar canons of 1636 had been accepted with hardly a murmur of protest. The previous year Charles had sent Laud and Juxon a copy of the canons, by which the Scots church was governed, with instruction to revise them 'as near as convenient may be to the Canons of the Church of England. And to that end you, or either of you, may alter what you find fitting.'[24] They did so zealously. The new canons were quite radical: communion must be taken kneeling, altars had to be placed at the east end of the church, no one could teach children without a licence from his bishop, and all men should remove their hats during divine service. Even though such reforms stank of Rome to nostrils far less sensitive than those of most people north of the border, Laud sent them to Maxwell with the hope that they 'will be of great use for the settling of that Church'.[25] Charles was reported 'well pleased' with the printed version, except for the many typographical errors. 'Young, the printer is the greatest knave that I ever dealt with,' said the Earl of Stirling.[26] Never had any ecclesiastical reform been introduced into Scotland with so little consultation; even James would have convened a job lot of ministers and dons to endorse them. But Charles went blandly ahead and proclaimed the enactment of the new canons on 23 May 1635 with the sweeping assertion that 'The king's power . . . is the highest power under God.'[27]

Even the king's supporters feared that there might be repercussions to the introduction of the new canons, 'which perchance at first will make more noise than all the Cannon in Edinburgh Castle', wrote Juxon to Maxwell, adding, 'but when men's ears have been used a while to the sound of them they will not startle so much at it, as not at first; and perchance find them as useful for preservation of the Church.'[28]

Thus after the canons were received with virtual silence the government in London quite reasonably assumed that the new, and less radical, prayer book would be accepted in much the same way. They could not have been more wrong.

There were, admittedly, warning signs. The introduction of the new prayer book was postponed from Easter to midsummer 1637 to give people time to get used to the innovation. According to Robert Baillie, after the announcement that every church in Edinburgh had to use the liturgy the following Sunday, 23 July, 'The whole body of the town murmurs and grudges all week exceedingly.'[29] Nonetheless on the appointed day Dr Hannah, Dean of St Giles's Cathedral, started morning service without taking any special precautions. Almost at once 'the inferior multitude began in a tumultuous manner to fill the church with uproar'.[30] When the bishop entered the pulpit to quieten them they pelted him with three-legged stools. So the Archbishop of St Andrews had to slip out through a side door to get help from the civil authorities, who managed to clear the church, allowing the clergy to finish divine service as the mob outside howled in protest, beating at the doors and throwing stones through the windows. Afterwards the ministers were lucky to get back to their lodgings. Perhaps taking precautions would have made no difference. Bishop Whitford of Brechin read the new service with a brace of pistols laid on the lectern, and his wife and servants standing guard with loaded blunderbusses. If he sat down to lunch afterwards happy that stern measures had made the people see sense, the attack on his church by an angry mob a few hours later can have done nothing to improve his digestion.[31]

Quite simply the new liturgy was an immediate and immense disaster. It was, as Henrietta Maria observed years later when a widow in exile in France, 'that fatal book'. Who, then, was responsible for its introduction?

John Hacket, Bishop Williams's biographer, who was as unreliable in his judgments as he was partisan in his conclusions, had no doubts. He recorded that three years after agreeing not to extend the Articles of Perth, Laud came to James with a revised version of the Scots liturgy and canons, 'but I sent him back with the frivolous draft he had drawn', the king recalled.[32] A modern authority, E. R. Adair, has agreed: 'that Laud was the driving force behind the changes introduced into the Scottish Church there is no doubt.'[33]

Some particular evidence supports this view. For instance, when Maxwell revived the idea of the new liturgy in 1629, Laud urged the adoption of the English version in its entirety. He had conversations with the Scots bishops during his visit to Scotland in the summer of 1633, and could well have pressured the king into ordering work started on the new version the following May.

As a general rule Laud enthusiastically endorsed the ideals of uniformity and the reform by statute. At the same time as the prayer book was being revised, he updated the statutes of Oxford University, and insisted that the alien churches in England, together with English and Scots merchants and mercenaries abroad, and members of the Church of Ireland, all worship in the same established fashion. The archbishop could not have put it better than his best friend. 'I hold it not fit,' wrote Wentworth to the Prolocutor of the Church of Ireland, 'nor will suffer that the articles of the Church of England be disputed.'[34] More than any other of Charles's ministers, Laud saw the king's dominions as a whole, and he conducted an extensive correspondence with Irish and Scots bishops. Yet he never appeared to like the Scots personally. Because the University of Oxford's statutes forbade them to hold fellowships, it is unlikely that he got to know any Scots well as a young man; certainly he grew up sharing the prejudices widely expressed by the jingle of the day:

> Bonny Scot, we all witness can,
> That England hath made thee a gentleman.

On the other hand the archbishop's contacts with Scots bishops such as Maxwell, Bellenden and Wedderburn were so close that it has been suggested that this small group of ambitious, anglicised prelates were really responsible for the new prayer book.[35] This seems doubtful. The Scots bishops were never very influential, and anyway Laud and Juxon permitted them very few revisions of which they did not fully approve. If they let the new liturgy talk of 'presbyters' rather than 'ministers' it was because the two English prelates believed the former to be synonymous with 'priests'. A letter which Laud sent to Wedderburn, the most influential Scots editor of the liturgy, on 20 April 1636 shows how hard it is to allocate responsibility precisely. After starting by saying that 'His Majesty was much troubled . . . and . . . hath commanded me to write' ordering that the revisions to the statutes of deacons and priests be dropped, the archbishop went on to ask

Wedderburn to send him his suggestions regarding another set of revisions, and 'I will not fail to give you my judgment.'[36]

Years later, Laud denied any blame for the introduction of the prayer book and canons: 'I never meddled with them, but at such time, and in such a way, as I was called and commanded by his Majesty.' Sometimes he blamed the Scots bishops: 'it was the fault of their own prelates.' More often he returned to the king: 'I did nothing but as I was commanded and warranted by His Majesty. . . . I inserted nothing without his Majesty's knowledge.'[37] Because at the time he wrote those words Laud was a prisoner in the Tower, about to be tried for his life, and thoroughly disillusioned with Charles I, his testimony is suspect. It cannot even be tested against other contemporary evidence, for his diary and letters are peculiarly silent about the prayer book until after the St Giles's riot. However, the Covenanters exaggerated Laud's influence so wildly in their indictment, that he was quite right at his trial to dismiss their allegation that he was the sole author of the whole liturgy as 'much ado about nothing'.

In sum, therefore, it is impossible to say whether Laud was chiefly responsible for the implementation of the new prayer book. But in a sense that does not really matter: the question 'king or minister?' is badly posed. It was not a case of either Charles or Laud, but rather the combination of the two men working on and with each other, reinforcing each other's resolve, and augmenting each other's weaknesses, with one taking the initiative and the other setting the pace as they egged on a few Scots bishops to fill in the details. When he was an old man, Bishop Sydserff remembered that he and his friends were 'so lifted up with the king's zeal, and so encouraged by Archbishop Laud, that they lost all restraint'.[38] Thus while a zealous prosecutor – and there were none so full of vindictive zeal as the archbishop's covenanting enemies – might try for a verdict of guilty (if only by association), the safest judgment that the jury of history should return on Laud's part in introducing 'that fatal book' is the appropriately Scottish one of 'non-proven'.

Once Charles is put in history's dock the jury's decision might be very different, if only because the prayer book was the last in a series of blunders in his dealings with Scotland. Because he was born in Scotland and spent the first three years of his life there, Charles felt he intuitively understood that country, even though he knew little about it. Thus he brought to his handling of Scottish affairs a fatal combination of ignorance and a firm belief in his own expertise.

At the start of his reign, the new king ordered Archbishop Spottiswoode to wear an English surplice for James's funeral. Rather than don such Papist rags the primate of Scotland refused to attend the burial of the master he had served faithfully for two decades. At the time few Englishmen worried about Spottiswoode's protest. Like the initial reluctance of the

Edinburgh ministers two years later to comply with the king's order to administer Communion only to those kneeling, it seemed a token thing, easily brushed aside. At first the Scots appeared to be a compliant bunch. Unlike their brethren at Westminster, the Edinburgh parliament not only voted their new sovereign the large tax he requested in 1625, but sent him the sort of fawning letter of congratulation that Charles, like James, enjoyed (unlike his son, James never really believed such protestations).

Encouraged, Charles instituted two reforms that in many ways anticipated the personal rule, and even the introduction of the prayer book. First he decreed that no member of the Scots privy council could also sit on the Court of Sessions, Scotland's supreme court. This upset the seventeen magnates who sat on both bodies, for it forced them to chose between one or the other. While the reform of the Court of Sessions was merely ineffective, Charles's second reform, the Revocation Edict of July 1625, was downright dangerous. It cancelled all grants of land made by the crown since 1540, including church estates confiscated at the Reformation. Although few landowners actually lost their property, many were fatally alienated from the crown.

Two factors limited the damage done by the two reforms: the king's indolence and the Earl of Menteith's energy.[39] Over the next decade Charles showed little interest in the land of his birth. Laud egged him on to alter the liturgy. His wet nurse asked for arrears of her pension. He told St Andrews University not to give an honorary degree to one Bostock, an Englishman from a bad family, and instructed the Chapel Royal to limit its purchases of communion plate to 'all that is necessary, but no more'.[40] Charles personally annotated only one of the 2,500 letters sent out by the Secretary of State for Scotland in his name during the first ten years of his reign.

The king was happy to leave the conduct of Scottish affairs in Menteith's capable hands. William Graham, seventh Earl of Menteith, was born in about 1591, the scion of an ancient Scots aristocratic family. He first attracted Charles's attention when he came to London in 1626 as a member of the delegation to protest against the Revocation Edict. Because Menteith was able to modify the edict, and thus make it more acceptable, Charles appointed him president of the privy council two years later. The secret of the earl's success was an ability to placate the nobility while maintaining a precarious working relationship with the kirk, and retaining royal favour. But in 1633 he fell from favour, largely because of his enemies' machinations at court.

Perhaps some conflict between the growing powers of a distant, blundering crown and a threatened feudal nobility was inevitable. Certainly England and Scotland were such different nations that making them work together demanded far greater abilities and much more knowledge than the government in London possessed. The prayer book was as much an attack on Scottish nationalism as it was a Papist threat to the faith of the kirk. As Robert Baillie put it, Scotland did not want to be turned into a 'pendicle of the diocese of York'.[41]

Some Scots leaders tried to duck the issue. On the Sunday that the prayer book was first read, most of the privy council found excuses to be out of town (Traquair went to a kinsman's wedding). A few nobles, including the Earl of Rothes and Lord Balmerino, used the occasion to stir up the riot at St Giles's for their own ends.[42] Thus by convincing a large number of Scots that it 'was going to change the whole constitution of that church and kingdom', the government in London managed to unite kirk and commoners, burghers and aristocrats, labourers and landlords in opposition against them.[43] Therefore the new liturgy was part of a much wider issue extending far beyond Laud's sphere of influence. It was consistent with the king's overall policies on Scotland, which provoked a reaction that anticipated that in England by three years, and that in Ireland by five. But in all three countries loyal subjects could not blame the king, even if he was at fault. Loyal folk needed a scapegoat, and they found one *par excellence* in Laud.

The St Giles's riot caught most Englishmen unawares. As Clarendon recalled, 'there were very few in England who heard of any disorder there, or anything done there that might produce any.'[44] Before the summer of 1637 most Englishmen knew little about Scotland, and cared less. The king's initial reaction to the riot was to blame the Scots privy council for allowing it to occur in the first place, and for not punishing the perpetrators immediately afterwards. Laud informed them, on the king's instructions, that 'His Majesty takes it very ill that the business concerning the establishment of the service book hath been so weakly carried.'[45] 'What resolution will follow up on this is not yet known,' noted one Scots aristocrat at the end of the month.

In September Charles reprimanded the Scots privy council for giving in to the opposition, which he wrote off as no more than 'a needless noise'. 'Either we have a very slack council or very bad subjects,' he said.[46]

It did not take the English government long to conclude that they had both. By September sixty-eight petitions against the new prayer book had been sent to the Scots privy council. The government reacted by ordering the petitioners to leave Edinburgh, and the council to move to Linlithgow. This produced further rioting on the part of 'the rascally people of Edinburgh'. The people of Glasgow rioted in sympathy, while the sober merchants of the capital were annoyed at losing the profits they usually enjoyed from being the seat of government. As winter forced many petitioners to leave Edinburgh and return to their homes, they left behind a committee know as The Tables to maintain pressure on the government there, which was growing ever more demoralised. 'I am in all things left alone,' complained Lord Treasurer Traquair, asking, 'Shall I give way to the people's fury?'[47] While the government in Edinburgh was indeed frightened and irresolute, most Scots thought them 'peremptory and absolute'.[48] Worse still they were Papist. As one ageing aristocratic roué explained, 'If I have lain with never so many whores, I will never lie with the whore of Babylon.'[49]

Who then, people asked, was playing the pimp? The king could not possibly be a whoremaster, so it must be Laud. In January 1637, when Robert Baillie heard that the prayer book was ready, he told a friend that it was all a conspiracy by Laud against 'our gracious prince'. Even after he had learned of Charles's full involvement, Baillie could not bring himself to blame the king, and two years later he went off to fight for his sovereign trusting 'to die in the faith of Christ and hearty love of King Charles'. According to the Spanish ambassador, by the winter of 1637/8 the archbishop was generally thought to be 'the *primum mobile* of the whole machine . . . who controls the king's will absolutely'.[50]

Even before the St Giles's riot Laud was angry with the Scots. He wrote to Traquair on 4 July 1637 saying 'that I was much troubled to see things there in such a way. For I thought that we had happily come to an end of those troubles.' He was not, however, referring to the liturgy, but to a mundane legal challenge to church property rights. In addition Laud was deeply involved with the trial of Prynne, Burton and Bastwick, and that of Bishop Williams, who, he was sure, were out to destroy not just himself and episcopacy 'but the very life blood of monarchy'.[51] The archbishop was thus hardly in the best frame of mind for dealing with another, far more serious crisis from north of the border. As he concluded to Traquair, 'This hath been one of the heaviest terms that ever I endured.'[52]

Laud took the riot very much to heart. 'The very bitter news . . . from Scotland,' wrote the Venetian ambassador on 17 August 1637, 'has exceedingly afflicted and depressed the Archbishop of Canterbury.'[53] Eleven days later Laud asked Wentworth, 'when will this end? What do you think will become of me when I am thus used? Is this not an excellent reward for my service?'[54] Convinced that stern measures immediately taken would have stopped the troublemakers in their tracks, he blamed the Scots privy council for their irresolution, and even hinted that Spottiswoode and his fellow bishops were at fault for not putting some backbone into the secular authorities. How could any reasonable man object to the new prayer book? Had not everyone been fully, more than fully, consulted? If 'one man out of a humour dislikes one thing, and another another, by that time everyman's dislike were satisfied, I doubt there would be little left to serve God with,' the archbishop declared.[55] Laud considered the complaints that the new liturgy was Papist, and the charges that he was a crypto-Catholic, to be particularly unfair. Was he not working on the final revisions to his conference with Fisher? Had he not done so much to stop conversions at court that he had crossed the queen?

Like a wounded animal the archbishop retreated to his lair to lick his wounds, muttering to Wentworth that 'this canker is grown to be a wolf in the very breast of the kingdom'.[56] And then, after advising Gilbert Sheldon, Vice-Chancellor of Oxford, 'to be very mindful of the waspishness of these times . . . and not to stir up the least trouble in church and university', Laud hit back. Since at this time he had the nightmare about marrying the king to a widow and being unable to find a prayer book, it could be that the strain of the Scots rebellions reopened the wound of the Mountjoy marriage and goaded him into taking drastic action. He urged Charles to take a hard line with the Scots and send the troublemakers home. Taking his advice, Charles ordered the petitioners to leave Edinburgh, while publicly denying that either he or the liturgy was the least bit Catholic.[57]

On 9 February 1638 the king took the sternest measures attempted so far by issuing a proclamation that the Scots must stop all organised opposition to the prayer book or be charged with treason.[58] 'It does no way satisfy them,' Traquair reported with massive understatement. Immediately the Scots drew up a Covenant pledging their lives to resist not just the new prayer book, but the rule of bishops. Within days, tens of thousands of them had signed the pledge, some with their own blood. One of the Covenant's authors called 28 February 1638, the day it was first published, 'the glorious marriage day of the kingdom with God'.[59] Scotland was convinced that by refusing to accept what had already become known as 'Laud's liturgy', she was doing God's will – perhaps even the king's – and certainly not the archbishop's. For Laud the Covenant was the beginning of the end.

After Menteith's fall from power in 1633, Charles came to depend on John Stewart, first Earl of Traquair, to administer Scotland. By the standards of the king's Scots servants Traquair was an able man about whom his enemies always believed the worst, and his friends rarely the best. He and Laud had been friends for a decade, and the archbishop was convinced that Traquair was the man best able to help reform the Scots church – indeed, he was the only layman brought into the discussions about rewriting the liturgy. Once the storm broke, Traquair urged the king to back down. At Laud's urging, Charles called Traquair to London in February 1638, where in several interviews he begged the king to withdraw the prayer book, since England lacked the huge standing army of forty thousand soldiers he estimated would be required to make the Scots accept it.[60] Rather than take unwelcome advice, Charles, as usual, changed his advisers. He sent Traquair back to Scotland – by his own account he departed 'with great unwillingness' – and turned away from Laud to seek Hamilton's counsel.[61]

In moments of crisis Charles instinctively found the weakest reed – and then clung to it for dear life. Of all his subjects there were few weaker reeds than James, third Marquis (and later first Duke) of Hamilton, whose nickname, 'Captain Luckless', is a good indication of his reputation. Educated at Oxford, he inherited his father's title the same month as Charles came to the throne, and soon became a favourite of the new king.[62] Laud never liked the duke, whom he suspected of supporting radical Presbyterian ministers in Ulster, and defrauding the Scots treasury of money 'by handfuls'.[63] After Buckingham's murder, Charles made Hamilton Master of the Horse, and encouraged him to lead a disastrous expedition of volunteers to the Continent to help the Swedish king Gustavus Adolphus. Though he raised impressive numbers of troops, Hamilton's capabilities as a commander stopped short of actually bringing them into battle, and most of them died of hunger or disease. This did not diminish him in the king's favour, however. As Buckingham proved after the Ile de Ré, military débâcles made the royal heart grow fonder. Thus when Charles decided in the spring of 1638 to resort to firmer measures in dealing with the Scots, he quite naturally turned to the one Scot who possessed military experience, influence in his native land, and the king's regard. In truth the only things that Hamilton lacked were ability and self-confidence.

Realising the dangers involved, Hamilton had a series of conversations with Charles in early May to work out a precise set of instructions. The king signed the final draft on the 16th. The duke was charged to force the Scots privy council, on pain of dismissal, to publicly support the liturgy; to raise an army and personal bodyguard; to refuse to accept any petitions of protest; to threaten the Scots with an English punitive expedition; and to make clear that all who opposed these steps 'must be proclaimed traitors'. Charles was taking a much harder line than Spottiswoode or Traquair advised; indeed, the latter privately warned Hamilton to do all he could to ensure that the king did not continue 'in his follies'.[64] But the only concession Charles offered was to reform the Scots currency. He was convinced that if he appeased the Covenanters he would become as powerless as the Doge of Venice, a mere figure of fun, and was thus 'resolved to hazard my Life, rather than suffer authority to be condemned'.[65]

All along Laud urged his master not to yield an inch to the Covenanters. 'No question', he noted in his diary, 'but there's a great concurrence between them and the Puritan party in England. A great aim there to destroy me in the King's opinion.' But by now it was obvious that Charles was setting policy, and that the archbishop was merely encouraging his master to do what he would have done anyway.[66] A clear indication that Laud's influence was waning came minutes after the king and Hamilton agreed on the final draft of the duke's instructions. Charles summoned Laud, Spottiswoode, Sydserff, Whitford and Maxwell. 'Canterbury desired humbly by way of question of his Majesty for what he was called,' Hamilton recalled; 'his Majesty answered to hear and bear witness what had passed.'[67] To hear and bear witness – that was all the king now required of his archbishop and bishops. Laud alluded to the demotion when he wrote to Wentworth, 'I wholly agree with you that a prince puts a great prejudice upon his own affairs, if he continue a servant longer in any great employment than he will give him trust and power to execute. . . . I cannot but fear I have seen all the best of my days.'[68]

XI

'The beast is wounded'

In the autumn of 1638 Sir William Boswell, the British ambassador to the Netherlands, sent Laud a pamphlet entitled *The Beast is Wounded*. Its anonymous author bitterly attacked the archbishop for his religious policies and for forcing the new prayer book upon the Scots. Laud professed not to be hurt by such calumnies. 'I thank God I trouble myself not with these things,' he told Boswell. 'But I am very sorry for the public which suffers much by them'[1] He was, however, worried enough to ask the ambassador to send him all such libellous pamphlets published in Holland, and even offered to pay for their shipping to England. Boswell obliged. With what must have bordered on masochism, Laud – as was his habit – read all the splenetic diatribes from those whom he called the 'fierce factions in Amsterdam', telling Boswell that he thought they were 'extremely full of very base falsehoods'. In truth these attacks hurt him so much that the only person to whom he could mention them was the king; he did not even confide them to his diary. A few months later he may have been alluding to such libels when he tried to comfort Bishop Thomas Morton of Durham with the thought that as a bishop he must expect people to scheme against him. 'These times are so full of danger,' concluded Laud, 'that I know not whom to believe.'[2]

Laud was hurt and angry. The Scottish crisis helped bring about the collapse of the departmentalised form of government of the 1630s, and allowed the queen's Catholic friends to gain more power as the king, who had spent much of the previous decade secluded at court, started to play a larger part in shaping national policies. Laud's fears became even more morbid, his expectations still more pessimistic. He tried to compensate for the erosion of his influence in the king's councils by becoming an ultra-loyalist. And thus he turned for comfort to his roots, as old men often do, finding in making gifts to his home town and settling the affairs of Oxford University a solace that he could no longer gain from handling the affairs of either church or state.

Nevertheless, the pamphleteer was right. The anonymous charges hurt, for by 1638 the archbishop was only too painfully aware that he had been sorely wounded.

The process was well underway by 23 May 1638, when the Marquis of Hamilton set out for Scotland with an extraordinarily heavy heart. Not even the death of his wife, with whom he had been on notoriously bad terms, could cheer him. After arriving in Edinburgh and talking to the Covenanters, he advised the king to raise a fleet and an army to crush the rebellion. 'I expect that not anything can reduce that people to obedience, but only force,' agreed Charles, as he set about recruiting six thousand soldiers and a fleet to convoy them to the Firth of Forth. The king did not put all his trust in the sword: he relied on duplicity. While announcing that he had suspended the Scottish High Commission and the new liturgy, and that he would call a parliament and General Assembly of the Kirk for the autumn, he secretly advised Hamilton 'to flatter them with what hopes you please'.[3]

After failing to persuade the Scots to swear to a more moderate Covenant, and being unable to work with the General Assembly of the Kirk that met at Glasgow, Hamilton had to admit defeat. 'I have done my best,' he wrote to the king from Scotland, 'though next to hell I hate this place.'[4]

Laud shared Hamilton's feelings entirely. 'Never were there more gross absurdities, nor half so many committed in any public meeting, and for the National Assembly never did the Church of Christ see the like,' he wrote to Hamilton, adding that Alexander Henderson (who had just been elected to chair the Assembly) was 'a most violent and passionate man, and a Moderator without moderation'.[5] The archbishop was fully aware of what was going on north of the border, since in May Charles appointed him to act as his liaison with Hamilton. In addition Dr Walter Balcanquhall, the Dean of Durham, sent Laud first-rate intelligence about 'the tumultuous violent proceedings in Scotland'.[6] Although the king wrote the occasional general letter, mainly in the hope of encouraging Hamilton, he had Laud draft the detailed orders, such as the instructions for handling the Assembly. The archbishop found the work burdensome. 'My frequent letters to my Marquis of Hamilton by His Majesty's command lie heavily upon me,' he admitted.[7] But instead of giving the archbishop any respite, Charles asked him to work with Wentworth to co-ordinate plans for obtaining Irish troops to suppress the Scots, and to prevent the spread of the Covenant among Ulster's Presbyterians.

The archbishop and the Lord Deputy confided their deep sense of depression and pessimism to one another. A month before the king sent Hamilton to Scotland, Wentworth warned that 'there is a necessity imposed upon us, and we must bend and bow unto it'.[8] Laud replied that he was fully aware 'that his standing is slipping', and two months later he told

Bishop Bramhall of Derry that the Church of Ireland could expect little help from him in the future.[9] By early summer the archbishop's spirits touched rock bottom:

> It is not the Scottish business alone that I look upon, but the whole frame of things at home and abroad, with vast expense out of little treasure, and my misgiving soul is deeply apprehensive of so small evils coming on. God in heaven avert them. I can see no cure without a miracle.[10]

A month later his spirits had not risen an inch. 'The Scottish business is extremely ill indeed and what will become of it God knows, but certainly no good,' he told Wentworth on 20 July (incidentally agreeing with John Pym, who that very day wrote to a friend that it was 'a time which threatens great change and trouble').[11] The archbishop was convinced that Williams was in league with the Covenanters, and would somehow persuade the king to commute the Star Chamber sentence against him. Worse still, his enemies at court had joined Scotland's Presbyterians and England's Puritans to destroy him: 'Holland speaks now with great liberty against me,' he lamented, adding that the arrival of the queen's mother that autumn could only exacerbate things, for apart from adding to the crown's financial burdens, the scheming Frenchwoman would increase her daughter's malignant influence in the king's councils. As an indication of his concerns for the future Laud told Wentworth to burn his letters after he had read them. 'Warm your hands on the flame of it,' he wrote at the end of one, adding that another was 'to be sacrificed to Vulcan'.[12] So depressed did Laud become that by October he made himself physically ill and had to take to his bed for a week, explaining that 'as things go I have no joy left'.[13]

His influence was waning nearly as fast. While in late 1637 and early 1638 Venetian diplomats reported that Laud was the king's sole adviser on Scottish affairs, by the end of August Gustinian noted that the archbishop 'does not now enjoy the customary abundance of the royal favours', and 'if the trouble persists he may lose them entirely'.[14] While the Venetians may well have exaggerated the precipitousness of the archbishop's decline, there is no doubt that at times he had to resort to fishing for sprats, such as arresting Captain Napier, a Scots mercenary who was supposed to have said that the English were mad to think that an army of 40,000 men would be enough to hold down his people, and that 300,000 was a more realistic figure. It was a tribute to Laud's energies – which always exceeded his sense of proportion – that he managed to track down some thirty-seven such treasonable utterances.[15] But neither diligence nor concern for detail enhanced the archbishop's influence. At the end of the year a correspondent warned Hamilton that Laud 'meddles in no business concerning Scotland . . . but . . . to give his opinion as a privy councillor'.[16]

The trouble was that the English privy council never had much say in Scottish policy. Charles did not formally place the crisis on the whole council's agenda until July 1638, even though it had cropped up three or four times in the committee on foreign affairs – which says something about how the English government regarded the Scots. In July the king informed the council about the background to the crisis and of his intention to 'proceed with rigour', but did not seek their advice. Although Laud had urged Charles to refer the crisis to the council as a whole, when he established a council committee for Scottish affairs he did not appoint the archbishop to it.[17]

Apart from adding to Laud's sense of hurt the omission made no difference, for by now the king was handling matters that before he would have left to his ministers. In October, for instance, he gave Secretary of State Windebank a detailed set of proposals on raising troops to fight the Scots, and the following month discussed with Hamilton – and not Laud – the appointment of a new Dean of Durham, the strategically important diocese on the Scottish border.[18]

Gradually Laud started to turn against his whole instinct and training, and to blame the king. He began to do so obliquely by attacking the king's taste in art, and then complaining about Charles's extravagance, particularly towards his wife. In May 1638 he directly criticised the monarch privately in a letter to Wentworth for not accepting his oft-repeated advice to take swift and resolute action against the Covenanters. A few months later he softened this position by writing that the Scots had taken advantage of the king's easy and sweet nature.[19]

Most Englishmen agreed that the one group determined to take advantage of the king's nature was the queen and her Papist friends at court. When in 1625 the pope had given Henrietta Maria a dispensation to marry a heretic, he told the young Frenchwoman that she must emulate Bertha, the Frankish princess whose marriage to Ethelbert, King of Kent, a thousand years before had paved the way for St Augustine's conversion of England. Henrietta Maria spent her last night in France in a convent being constantly reminded that it was her duty to protect England's Catholics: those were her mother Marie de Medici's parting words.[20]

The marriage of Charles and Henrietta Maria had started badly, with Buckingham doing everything he could to make sure he continued to monopolise Charles's affections. After the duke's murder the marriage improved. The royal couple started a family, and during the 1630s the king turned his back on the world of parliament and politics to retreat into that of the court. He had plenty of time for his wife and her friends, a group of mainly Catholic courtiers who favoured a pro-French foreign policy. Until the outbreak of the Scots crisis their influence was confined to backstairs intrigue and to converting prominent people to Rome. Laud recognised the danger of such spectacular conversions, and in December 1637 persuaded the king to issue a proclamation forbidding missionary activities. Very soon, however, it turned out that the proclamation damaged Laud on all fronts. While these conversions deeply worried most Englishmen, who unfairly blamed them on the archbishop, Henrietta Maria and her friends blamed him for persuading the king to promulgate the proclamation in the first place. Very soon afterwards Charles distanced himself from the archbishop and tried to ingratiate himself with his wife by telling her in public that Laud 'is a man of great goodness, who wants everything his own way'.[21]

The court Catholics were determined to take full advantage of the crisis in Scotland. Father Con, the papal agent to the queen, and the king's good friend, believed that the growing opposition of Scots and English Puritans would make the crown more dependent on recusants at home, and governments abroad. The English crown might even need subsidies from foreign monarchs to rule without calling parliament, even though this would make it dependent on alien paymasters – as was to happen in the 1670s. Con told Charles that the Prayer Book Rebellion was part of a wider international Calvinist conspiracy, and that if he took firm steps to stamp it out in Scotland the pope might send him financial aid, even troops. He warned that France would take advantage of the crisis by trying to revive the 'Auld Alliance' between Paris and Edinburgh.[22]

The crisis in Scotland emboldened Catholics in England. On 22 March 1638 the Spanish ambassador prompted a minor riot by staging a Maundy Thursday procession through the streets of London, with priests bearing crucifixes and lighted candles. The following month Father Con felt confident enough to push the candidacy of Wat Montagu to succeed Sir Richard Acton as the queen's secretary. Although Charles chose neither Montagu nor Laud's candidate, Sir William Howard, his selection of Sir John Winters, who had close links with the Jesuits, was a good indication of the way the political wind was blowing. Con took it as an indication that the time was ripe to push for a bishop for England's Catholics and a cardinal's hat for himself, neither of which the king, with Laud's backing, would countenance. Indeed, the archbishop was so opposed to Con's promotion that he joined forces with Father William Price, leader of the English Benedictines, to lobby the pope against it.[23]

The arrival of the queen's mother in October 1638 further complicated matters. 'This is but a new beginning of evils,' complained Laud, and he went on to blame the difficult old dowager for the wet and windy autumn weather.[24] She added her considerable skill in meddling to the machinations of the pro-French party at court, which brought her into conflict with Con as well as Wentworth, both of whom favoured Spain. Had Laud been better able to deal with court intrigues, he might have formed an alliance with other Hispanophile politicians, such as Pembroke, Leicester, Northumberland, and Cottington, who shared his views about the need to stop pussy-footing with the Scots.[25]

Because it was that crisis which led to the Bishops' Wars, then the Civil War, and finally to the archbishop's execution, in retrospect the Prayer Book Rebellion seems by far the most important issue. But at the time its significance was not so obvious: for Laud Bishop Williams lurking in his palace at Buckden, and the realisation that the queen and her friends were gaining influence at his expense, seemed far more imminent threats. Although fatal, this misjudgment was entirely understandable. Laud had always had some bogeyman lurking in the shadows. His hatred of Williams went back nearly two decades, and after the archbishop's fall from grace his rival behaved very much as Laud had feared. Scotland was a distant threat, particularly compared to the queen and her Papist friends, who muddied the waters right at the centre of power, making things so complicated that they diverted the king's attention, and took up much of the archbishop's energies. As Caroline Hibbard has so convincingly shown, 'They subverted Laud's authority over religious policies, but in such a way that he got the brunt of the blame for their activities.'[26]

Ironically, as Laud became more closely identified with Rome he in fact took a much firmer line against Catholics. He ordered the Vice-Chancellor of Oxford to stop Jesuits recruiting undergraduates for their continental seminaries, and supported the privy council's efforts to tighten up the collection of recusancy fines.[27] As we have seen, he got the worst of both worlds from the proclamation against conversions – the public's ingratitude and the queen's hatred. Puritans normally applauded the judicial mutilation of recusants nearly as loudly as they did the public hanging, drawing and quartering of Catholic priests. But they did not give the archbishop any credit for voting in May 1638 in Star Chamber that William Puckering should be pilloried, have both ears cut off, be branded with the letter 'L' for libeller, have a hole bored in his tongue and be fined £10,000 for alleging that the king favoured Papists and persecuted Puritans.[28]

Laud won equally little credit for the publication of *A Relation of the conference between W. Lawd and Mr Fisher, the Jesuite* in 1639, some seventeen years after the debate actually took place. It was, he explained in the dedication, intended to refute those who had attacked him unfairly. 'And how of late', he wrote, 'I have been used by the scandalous and scurrilous pens of some bitter men (whom I heartily beseech God to forgive), the world knows.'[29]

While recognising the roots of his problem, the archbishop was unable to do much to resolve it. *A Relation of the Conference* was an academic book, too long, too intellectual, and far too full of learned references to have much appeal to general readers, who were all the more convinced that its author was a Papist. Like his monarch and his fellow ministers, Laud was a poor communicator. None of them took full advantage of the printed word or personal relationships to communicate between the centre and the various localities that made up the realm. Basically they did not bother to court public opinion: convinced that it should not count, they came to believe that it did not count. Therein lay not just Laud's problem, but that of his master's government. In the archbishop's case, however, it grew even more intense because his irascibility, his tendency to use vinegar, not oil, in human relations, meant that he was rarely understood, and hardly ever gained credit for his good intentions and Protestant achievements.[30]

Laud spent much of the summer of 1638 revising 'at broken hours as my leisure would permit' the manuscript of his Protestant *tour de force* for the press, and afterwards worried about how it would be received.[31] 'I am once more going to be a fool in print,' he told Wentworth. When the book came out he sent copies to all his friends. Naturally he presented the king with a copy (which so impressed Charles that he recommended it to his daughter at their last meeting just before his execution).[32] Laud sent copies to Wentworth; to the Lord Deputy's factotum, Christopher Wandesford; to his secretary, Sir Philip Mainwaring; to his legal and financial adviser, Sir George Radcliffe; and (perhaps as a peace offering), to his obdurate enemy, Lord Cork. He also gave copies to Richard Baylie, President of St John's, to Archbishop Ussher, Sir William Boswell, and Bishop Bramhall.[33] When the latter sent him a note of thanks, saying how much he had enjoyed the book, Laud replied with that obsequious gracelessness of which authors far more experienced than he are too often guilty. 'I must fear,' he wrote to Bramhall, that his praise 'proceeds rather from your affection, than any merit of the thing'.[34]

As the crisis in Scotland intensified and the court Catholics became more powerful, Laud had to carry the burden of his administrative responsibilities even though the pattern of governing through fairly well-defined and decentralised departments was breaking down. With considerable success, he spent many hours raising money for the restoration of St Paul's Cathedral, as if doing so were a way of protecting the established church from the growing threats of both Puritans and Papists. 'The truth is that God hath blest you with great fortune, & you have a noble and generous way with it,' the archbishop wrote to the magnate Sir Arthur Ingram, 'and therefore I pray you to open your hands freely to this Magnificent Work.'[35]

The archbishop also served as a liaison between the government and Sir Thomas Roe, the veteran diplomat, who was on a mission in Germany to try and drum up support for the restoration of the Palatinate. As the crisis in Scotland worsened and the Catholic partisans of France and Spain grew more powerful at court, central European affairs took a back seat.

Laud had to work hard to get the king or the privy council to pay much attention to Roe's mission, and by March 1639 confessed to his friend that 'I never thought from the beginning that any good could come of it'. Afterwards the archbishop's main concern was to have Roe recalled so he could take over as Secretary of State from Sir John Coke, who was ailing politically as well as physically. The fact that on 3 February 1640 the king replaced Coke with Sir Henry Vane, an enemy of Wentworth's, suggests that Laud's influence was equally shaky.[36]

The one place where the archbishop still exercised the power he had always enjoyed was Oxford. As the problems in Scotland intensified, and as his position at court weakened, Laud turned to Oxford as an escape, and also to do what little he could in the time left to him to help the university he loved above all others.

As Oxford's chancellor Laud had to deal with a mass of problems. He tried to stop Oxford students transferring to Cambridge, where the residency requirements for a degree were more lenient. He attempted to prevent large carts from damaging the road between the university and London. He dealt with pluralism by college fellows, drunkenness at the Westminster School old boys' reunion dinner held at Christ Church, the allegedly Papist licensee of the Mitre tavern, the appointment of a new librarian for Trinity College, the schedule of fees charged by the vice-chancellor's court, and the Earl of Denby's bequest establishing a herb garden at the university.[37] His old foe Nathaniel Brent, the Warden of Merton, whom he described as 'very foul', took up much of his time, although he was unable to reform that college.[38]

In many of his dealings with Oxford Laud displayed a peculiar attitude. It was as if Oxford was a microcosm for the wider political world. If Oxford was in good shape, so too must be the wider world. Indeed, as the outside world deteriorated, it became all the more important to make sure that standards did not fall at Oxford.

There was, for instance, the case of Proctor Lawford, whom on 13 April 1638 some undergraduates insulted by hissing and stamping their feet as he was finishing his sermon at St Mary's. Was Laud thinking of a similar fracas in St Giles's Cathedral when he wrote to the vice-chancellor that if the ringleaders were not sent down and the rest severely punished 'we shall have the youths break out oft into insolencies'?[39] Unconvinced that 'the whipping of two or three boys is sharp enough for such an offence', he told the vice-chancellor and the heads of colleges that their decision not to administer the flogging in public was 'a disgrace' and a 'great disservice' to the university. Laud's conclusion that 'The truth is if not exemplary punishment be not laid upon some of them, it will be of more dangerous consequence' quite clearly mirrored his criticisms of the king's handling of the crisis in Scotland.[40] In much the same way the

chancellor was thinking about external events when he wrote to the university the following month complaining about some controversial examination questions that they had set: 'If the worst enemy I have in the kingdom
had studied to do me a shrewd term, they could not (as times are) have
found a way more cunningly to have wounded me than this.'[41]

As the crisis worsened, university affairs became sillier. 'They grow
foolish at Oxford,' was the comment of one letter writer.[42] When Edward
Corbet, a proctor and fellow of Merton, petitioned to be excused from
bowing at the name of Jesus during university prayers, Laud angrily denied
his request, telling the vice-chancellor that 'if such may be kicked out, you
may bid farewell to all decency and order'.[43] The following October Laud
told the vice-chancellor and heads of colleges that they must see that the
university statutes were fully observed, particularly with regard to wearing
the correct dress for services at St Mary's. He explained that 'there is a
great necessity to hold up good order in the brokenness of these times'.[44]
In May Laud was outraged to learn that Edward Moore of Christ Church
refused to remove his hat to Edward Fuller, the university proctor, thus
provoking a fist-fight, and that Dr Samuel Fell, Dean of Christ Church,
had actually sided with Moore. He accused Fell of being 'a sudden, hasty,
and weak man, and most unlike a man that understands government'.[45]
Quite clearly those who allowed inferiors to get away with refusing to raise
their hats were just as bad as those who were unwilling, perhaps incapable,
of doing anything about the hooligans who threw stools at the preacher
when he used a new prayer book.

Laud's tenure at Oxford, together with the growth of the Arminian
faction at the university, undoubtedly did much to make it the centre for
the Royalist armies during the Civil War. He sent the Bodleian Library
several hundred manuscripts, scouring the Middle East for works in Arabic
and Greek. So grateful was the library that it has carved the name of
'Gulielmus Laud' on the tablet of benefactors for all readers to see as they
walk upstairs. While the archbishop almost certainly would not have been
amused to read his name immediately before that of 'Oliverus Cromwell',
one suspects that the merchant in him would have been quietly pleased
to be ranked with donors as generous as 'Fundatio Gulbenkianaea' and
'Edmundus S. De Beers'.[46]

Laud also remembered his old college. He gave St John's the advowson
of Hanborough, and the living of East Codford, Wiltshire, which was
worth £300 a year, as well as an astrolabe, books and manuscripts on
Greek, Arabic, mathematics, and a Concordance of Foxe's *Book of
Martyrs*, which had been finely bound by Nicholas Ferrar's Anglican
community at Little Gidding.[47]

Nor did Laud forget his home town. In 1640 he gave Reading corporation land in Bray, Berkshire, worth £200 a year. Every two years the

proceeds were to be used to help promising young lads who had just finished their apprenticeships to set themselves up in business, while in the third year the income was to be employed to provide dowries to four or five servant girls who had served their mistresses well for at least five years. Twenty pounds was to be spent augmenting the salary of the minister of St Lawrence's Church (in which parish Laud had been born), and a like amount to enhance that of the master of the grammar school (where he had been educated). An additional £8 was to be spent entertaining the President and Fellows of St John's on their annual inspection to see that the terms of the gift were being properly carried out, and – with a nice sense of relative worth – £2 should go to the corporation to cover their administrative expenses.[48]

Laud hinted at his reasons for making these most generous donations to Reading and Oxford in the letter he sent announcing the gift of the Bray estate: 'I have a great longing in myself to do some good for the town of Reading,' he explained. It was as if Laud, who was in his mid-sixties, was casting the balance sheet of his goals and achievements. He recognised that his life and his career were coming to a close. 'For my own part, I do not see "thorough" yet, and fear I never shall,' the archbishop confessed to Wentworth.[49] It was time for him to rediscover his roots, and to repay his debts. Like a man knowing that his job is about to end, he started to tie up whatever loose ends he could; if they did not include the English church, or the Scots Covenanters, then by default he had to settle those things, no matter how small, that were still within his orbit. True to form, he concentrated on the details, although with far less hope than before that if they were right then the whole would also come right. And so he tried to improve the minister's stipend in his first church, and the quality of the teaching in his old school, while ensuring that the president and fellows of his old college were entertained in the style to which he wanted them to remain accustomed.[50] For Laud, as things changed, the old order became more precious; and as the country drifted towards war, the virtues of peace seemed above price.

For Charles the threats posed by the Scots rebellion were very different. The king had decided to take up arms against the Covenanters as early as June 1638, when he confided to Hamilton, 'I expect not anything can reduce that people to obedience but force only.' The king rejected Traquair's warning that it would take a standing army of 40,000 troops to make the Scots accept the prayer book, in favour of Wentworth's and Laud's advice that the Covenanters were acting under pretence of religion in order to establish a republic. In December, at the archbishop's insistence, Charles started his military preparations in earnest. He sent Sir Jacob Astley as his Sergeant Major General (then a senior commissioned rank) north to inspect and train the militia, and ordered the Lord Lieutenants of the northern counties to drill their trained bands. As Laud noted, England's defences were in a deplorable state, which the king's extravagances and lack of determination did nothing to improve. 'I despair utterly of any thrift,' he wrote to Wentworth, as Charles lavished money on his wife that was desperately needed to outfit the Scots campaign.

The king decided on an ambitious four-pronged attack on Scotland, involving a direct invasion from the south combined with landings on the east and west coasts. Charles appointed the Earls of Arundel and of Essex to command the army, and, to please his wife, made her friend the Earl of Holland General of the Horse, instead of the far more experienced Earl of Northumberland. The latter wrote sourly to a friend, 'we sit daily in council, but to little purpose.'[51] To complement its military preparations the government waged a propaganda campaign, the chief result of which was to convince itself of the rightness of its own cause.[52]

While Laud played little part in devising these military preparations, he did all he could to support them, his zeal fuelled by a deep hatred of the enemy. He was convinced that Alexander Leslie, general of the Covenanting army, was the bastard of a serving wench and could neither read nor write, having started life as a pedlar.[53] Maintaining that Leslie and his lackeys were engaged in 'traitorous conspiracies', he begged the bishops of his province, as well as the civil lawyers of Doctors' Commons, to give 'greater sums in an ordinary way' to pay for the defence of the realm.[54] And give they did, the clergy contributing £24,395.

The church supported the crown with their prayers and preaching as well as their purses. On 27 March 1639, the day that Charles left London to join the Northern Army, Henry Valentine, a royal chaplain, gave a sermon at St Paul's wishing him every success, which was immediately published under the title God Save the King.[55] When His Majesty arrived in Durham, Bishop Morton preached before him in the cathedral. Comparing the Remonstrance that the Covenanters had published the previous month setting out their case to papal bulls, Morton concluded that the authors of both would receive 'everlasting damnation'.[56] The speech entitled 'A Full Confutation of the Covenant' that Henry Leslie, Bishop of Down, gave in September 1638 was translated into Latin so, Laud explained, that 'it might be enabled to travel abroad into other countries, and make known the hideousness of this Scottish Rebellion'.[57]

Laud believed that he was in danger. He asked Roe to purchase weapons from overseas – which were of such inferior quality that thirty of them blew up on the first firing.[58] He also armed his own servants with swords and had them scour the back alleys of London for subversives such as Captain John Napier and his accomplice, one Farloe.[59] Although convicted once again by Star Chamber, Bishop Williams refused to bow in total surrender. In Oxford one Francius, a mysterious atheist from Poland or Transylvania, was reported to be trying to subvert the undergraduates, while in Amsterdam the Covenanters had managed to stir up trouble in the English church, where – to cap it all – the minister Laud had handpicked to go to Holland, Sampson Johnson, was accused of Socianism (a form of Unitarianism), which the archbishop described as 'that horrid and mighty monster of heresies'.[60]

In the spring of 1639, as both sides were preparing for war, the Royalist poet Sir John Suckling wrote telling a friend in Norfolk that 'this Northern Storm (like a new disease) hath so far pos'd the Doctors of State, that as yet they have not given it a name'.[61] By the summer, however, Dr Robert Sibthorp was able to tell Laud's agent, Sir John Lambe, that 'some style' the conflagration in the north 'the Bellum Episcopalae'.[62] As the crisis worsened people were beginning to recognise that something was fundamentally wrong in the land, and that somehow bishops were chiefly to blame. In a simile that echoes the Shakespearian image of the storm in nature reflecting the discordance in the body politic, Thomas Smith wrote to Captain Pennington in January 1639 that 'the last great lightning has done a world of mischief over England, and the people are so generally molested with predictions and rumours of supposed vision, as if they were all struck with a panic fear. . . . The truth is that we do already see the beginning of much evil, and have cause to fear much more.'[63]

A similar pessimism prevailed in Scotland. Alexander Erskine wrote from Edinburgh the following month, 'Zeal of religion transports men beyond themselves and they think that all which they have done is for the good of religion, and pray that His Majesty may think so, for they pretend that all their actions are warranted by the laws of his church and country.'[64] Another Edinburgh correspondent shared this sense of crisis, without such a degree of ambivalence about opposing the king, perhaps because he was more willing to blame the bishops: 'We are busy here preaching, praying and drilling, and if his Majesty and his subjects in England come hither, they will find a harder welcome here as before, unless we be made quit of the bishops.'[65] Episcopacy very quickly became *the* issue. It was reported that if the bishops tried to return to Scotland 'the women will beat out their brains with stones'.[66] So unpopular did they become that in the streets of Edinburgh God-fearing Covenanters called black and white dogs 'bishops', throwing stones at the curs because their coats reminded them of prelates' vestments. From the city's pulpits ministers usually referred to Laud as 'the Priest of Baal and the Son of Belial'. Tavern conversation was even more intemperate: one drunken shoemaker castigated bishops as 'the Fire brands of Hell, the Panders of the Whore of Babylon, and the instruments of the devil'.[67] In their official propaganda the Covenanters blamed Laud, their Remonstrance of March 1639 alleging that he 'did negotiate with Rome about the form of our service-book'.[68] Thus by the time the

Scots troops marched south to save the king from the king's bishops, they were able to ignore the contradiction through the use of slogans – which have always been a good way of inculcating irrational conclusions. 'God bless his Majesty and the Devil confound his bishops,' the soldiers shouted to each other as they pitched their tents near Berwick.[69]

The idea that bishops in general, and Laud in particular, were to blame for the crisis that seemed to engulf the land quickly found adherents in England. In early 1639 Attorney General Bankes examined Mr Harris, a solicitor who had declared that as long as Laud lived there would be no parliament, that the archbishop could not stand the sight of a Scotsman, was destined to fry in hell, and was the cause of all the taxes.[70] The authorities arrested Godfrey Cade from Southwark for stating that Laud, 'the Pope of Lambeth, had caused the Scots war, had plucked the crown off Charles's head and trampled it underfoot, and used to birch the king's arse'. Cade maintained that he had been drunk when he made these remarks.

More sober – and far less vulgar – poetasters took up the theme:[71]

> What will you fight for, for a book of Common Prayer?
> What will you fight for, for a Court of High Commission?
> What will you fight for, for a mitre gilded fair?
> Or to maintain the prelates' proud ambition?

So asked one set of anonymous verses posted in the royal camp at Berwick. Another was more directly aimed at Laud:[72]

> But now brave England be thou bent
> To banish all that brood.
> And make your Lambeth lad repent
> That never did you good.

XII

'A foul business it is'

When on Wednesday, 27 March 1639, the twenty-third anniversary of his coronation, Charles I rode north to join his troops on the border and crush 'the Scottish Covenanting rebels', Laud prayed, 'God of his infinite mercy bless him with health and success.'[1] The archbishop's diary gives the impression that such prayers now represented the triumph of hope over experience. Mounting unpopularity not only hurt Laud deeply, but made him increasingly and openly contemptuous of what he regarded as the king's pusillanimity.

The archbishop fell ill, admitting to depression. Three days after Charles left London, Laud wrote to Wentworth, 'I have been extremely weakened, I scarce know how. And it may be my mind works upon me more than I think it doth, being no way satisfied with almost anything here.'[2] It was an indication of his desperate readiness to clutch at straws that he interpreted the return to Lambeth Palace's gardens, after an absence of several years, of the nightingale who used to sing there during his first (and far happier) two years as archbishop, as an omen that things would improve.[3] They did not. 'A foul business it is,' he said of Scotland in a letter to Roe at the end of May, 'and grown a dangerous one to us. I pray God preserve the King and make him happy in the settling of it.'[4]

When the crisis first erupted Laud appeared stunned, and, apart from urging the king to take resolute action, too shocked to mount a major counter-attack himself. The outbreak of military activities appeared to galvanise him into activity – as fighting so often does. He soon came to realise that if God were to preserve the king His church must do its share by taking resolute action. Thus he helped get Wentworth recalled from Ireland, and after his friend persuaded Charles to summon the Short Parliament, did all he could to use the Church of England's Convocation to maintain an unyielding stance. In so doing he played into his enemies' hands. By acting like the tyrannical ogre that they believed he had always been, he made a foul business even more dangerous.

181

In May of 1639 Laud was convinced that dangers threatened from every direction. The Covenanters, acting under pretence of religion, wanted to destroy him in particular, and monarchical and episcopal government in general. The Puritans were in league with the Scots. Bishop Williams was still lurking in the background, whispering in the king's ear, a spider weaving his wicked webs. The queen and her snobbish Papist friends were out to subvert the established church, while all the time sneering at the humble yet honest origins of its bishops. Even the king, Laud began to admit, was part of the problem.

A case in point was the commission the king appointed to rule England while he was off fighting the Scots, which consisted of Northumberland, Laud, Juxon, Cottington, Windebank, and Henry Jermyn (the queen's pet).[5] It was far too divided by old animosities to provide the strong leadership that the realm needed to weather the crisis, and was further hampered by the fact that, on the king's express order, it had to visit the queen and await her pleasure every Sunday.[6]

Laud gave public expression to his private fears in the speech he gave on 22 May 1639 during the Star Chamber trial of Sir Piers Crosley, who was accused of libelling Wentworth by alleging that he had been involved in the murder of Robert Esmond. Such attacks on the Lord Deputy were very dangerous, the archbishop said. They were in effect attacks on the Almighty, since the Lord Deputy was the king's deputy, and the king was God's lieutenant.[7]

Even more serious than wild accusations of murder was the refusal of the City of London to lend the crown money. This forced Charles to make a truce with the Scots at Berwick on 15 June 1638, whereby both sides agreed to disband their armies, and the king promised to attend the next General Assembly of the Presbyterian Kirk.

Few had anything good to say about the Treaty of Berwick. 'Episcopacy orthodox in England, heretical in Scotland,' thought Sir James Douglas. 'Lord Have mercy on our souls!'[8] As Sir John Suckling recognised, 'Necessity, not good nature, produced the treaty.' Laud disliked it from the very first. His immediate reaction was to pray that 'God would make it safe and honourable to the king and kingdom'.[9] When it became obvious that this would not happen, he was even more critical, convinced the worst sort of people would take control north of the border, that parliament was bound to be called to Westminster, where they would attack or even impeach him, and doubtless abolish episcopacy. In sum, he was sure that Charles was pursuing policies that would inflict lasting damage on the monarchy. The archbishop was particularly concerned about the plight of the Scots bishops, who had fled to England and were now virtually destitute, with no chance of returning home. He tried in vain to get English bishops to provide them with livings worth at least a £100 a year. Even though he blamed the Scots bishops, more than anyone else, for not warning him beforehand of the opposition to the new liturgy, he felt aggrieved that afterwards the king did nothing to support them in exile. As Laud's complaints about Charles became shriller, he no longer voiced his unhappiness solely to Wentworth, a friend as good and discreet as his diary. He complained freely to Roe, and even to public groups such as the Dean and Chapter of Exeter, to whom he wrote that 'the king can have neither honour nor safety' by signing the Treaty of Berwick.[10]

Soon after signing the treaty, Charles agreed with Laud's verdict and decided that the only way he could regain security and honour was to recall Wentworth from Ireland. After years of languishing in that backwater for English ambitions, Lord Deputy Wentworth was delighted to leave Ireland, and, after so many disappointments, he was even more pleased when Charles made him Earl of Strafford. But the king's exaggerated hopes cooled his new peer's elation. 'I find a great expectation is drawn upon me, for which I am most sorry,' Wentworth admitted to a friend, 'and the nearer I come to it the nearer my heart fails me.' But to a large extent Strafford had only himself to blame, for he (like Laud) had been telling the king that the Covenanters were using religion as an excuse to abolish bishops and then set up a republic. With copious professions of loyalty, both men urged upon Charles simple solutions to the complex problems facing the realm.[11]

Even though Strafford was reputed to have more influence with the king than any other minister, and Laud was clearly delighted to have his friend back in England, the earl did not get his own way, nor did he work as closely with the archbishop as many had anticipated. While the queen and her friends favoured a pro-French foreign policy and Wentworth wanted a pro-Spanish one, both agreed that the Earl of Leicester should succeed Sir John Coke as Secretary of State. Laud schemed behind the scenes to oppose the idea, for he was convinced that Leicester was a Puritan, and, after the Countess of Carlisle reported that she 'heard the Queen use strange violent persuasion of the king', Charles appointed Henrietta Maria's ally Sir Henry Vane the new secretary.[12]

Strafford's return to England marked a significant and unexpected decline in the archbishop's influence. While previously Charles had confined discussions about the Scots crisis mostly to Hamilton and sometimes Laud, he now opened them up to a much wider group both in the government and at court. The archbishop complained that he was being abused at court 'every day', and recognised that the public blamed him for the growing influence of the queen and her Papist friends. One afternoon in November 1639 he called his chaplain, Peter Heylyn, to his upstairs study. He was staring at a piece of paper which, he said, with tears in his eyes, was a letter announcing the defection to Rome of yet another person of quality, this time from North Wales. He knew that people would blame him and his fellow prelates for the conversion, even though he had done all he could to stop such activities. Then, Heylyn later recalled (perhaps with more emotion than veracity), the archbishop gazed tearfully up to heaven and made him promise that when he became a bishop he would do all he could to root out Catholic missionaries.[13]

Laud, like most of the privy council, had consistently opposed calling parliament. In late 1638 he warned Strafford that it would end ship money, cripple the church, and fetter the king at home and abroad.[14] His friend did not agree, for he had been able to control parliaments with great success in Ireland. Even though the majority of the privy council advised against doing so, Charles went along with Strafford's recommendation, telling them on 13 December that he had decided to summon a parliament for the following April. When he asked for their help in case this parliament proved to be 'as untoward as some have been', to a man the councillors – Laud included – pledged to 'assist him with their lives and fortunes'.[15]

After arguing about the decision for at least six weeks in the committee on Scots affairs, the king seemed to lose interest in events. He turned his attention to the court and to the Christmas festivities that included the last great Caroline Twelfth Night masque, Sir William D'Avenant's *Salmacida Spila*. This magnificently silly piece of escapism centres around a storm which ravages the realm. Various figures, including a mad lord, an invisible lady, and an ageing Hibernian, try to quiet the tempest, but fail. Then the king and queen come on stage and join hands, to bring peace to England as the 'Chorus of the Contented People' sing:[16]

> All that are harsh, all that are rude
> Are by your harmony subdued.
> Yet so unto obedience wrought
> As if not forced to it but taught.

Not only did this masque distract the king away from the very serious political problems that threatened the realm, but by pushing Laud back into the hostile world of the court, it further eroded the archbishop's power while enhancing that of the queen and her friends. For Laud the storm in the theatre of royal make-believe mirrored the reality of the natural order, as well as his dwindling fortunes. Two days after Christmas there were terrible storms. Two boats moored outside Lambeth Palace were sunk, and some chimneypots were blown down on to the roof above the archbishop's chamber, causing the roof to collapse on to his bed. Fortunately Laud was at Whitehall at the time, having been prevented by the bad weather from taking a ferry home across the Thames. The same storm blew over the pinnacles and weather vane on his country house at Croydon, making a twenty-foot gash in the roof, and brought the archbishop's coat of arms crashing to the floor in smithereens. At St John's the battlements tumbled into the room in which were stored the manuscripts that Laud had given to the college.[17] These storms made a great impression on the archbishop. Could they be omens that the divinely ordained great chain of being was about to be shattered? Was degree to be taken away and would discord follow? Was the visit from his father in the nightmare of 24 January 1640 that Laud recorded with unusual detail a warning of some sort, or was it an attempt to return to the orderly, paternalistic, and very safe world of childhood?[18]

> He asked me what I did here? And after some speech, I asked him how long would he stay with me? He answered he would stay till he had me away with him. I am not moved with dreams: yet I thought fit to remember this.

A remarkable incident involving Oxford suggests that Laud was indeed seeking to return to an earlier, more comfortable world. In February 1640 an Oxford MA (whom he would not name, but knew and trusted) wrote to him complaining about drunkenness at the university, particularly on the part of noblemen's sons. The chancellor was outraged. 'And it troubles me more than any other letter I have received for many a day,' he wrote to Vice-Chancellor Frewen. Invoking the familiar theme that the university was a microcosm for the commonwealth, Laud told Dr Frewen that if he could not maintain discipline he would 'destroy all'. Perhaps the tension under which he was labouring was responsible for this remarkable outburst. 'For young noblemen, when they are in the university, must be kept to a university life in some measure, or their example will spoil the rest,' he said.[19] Could it be that the licence permitted the high-born revived painful memories of his earlier days, when dashing young blades surely snubbed the earnest and oversensitive scholar from Reading? Was he suggesting that the rot in both state and university came from the top? Was he feeling pressure from those members of the House of Lords who sensed that the ending of the personal rule gave them the opportunity to enjoy the power that was theirs by virtue of their rank? Or was it just that he recognised that the queen and her sophisticated friends were winning?

Of the queen's power there was no doubt. Even though in December Laud had been able to persuade Charles to curb the activities of Count Cardinal Rossetti, within a few weeks, thanks to Henrietta Maria's wheedling, the papal legate was publicly back at his old tricks.[20] In January 1640 Laud was unable to prevent the queen from getting another of her friends, Sir John Finch, made Lord Keeper and Baron Fordwich.

Thus throughout the land anxieties about religion grew apace. In East Sussex the Arminian Justice of the Peace Edward Burton told Laud that 'the puritan faction is grown so strong', before begging him not to let anyone know that he was sending the archbishop reports, for if it came out it would be the end of him in the county.[21] (So impotent had Laud become that he could no longer protect his intelligence agents from the wrath of their peers.) The freeholders of Northamptonshire petitioned against new taxes, against new ceremonies and in favour of the old religion.[22] 'All places and sorts of men here are full of discontents and complaints . . . and not without great cause,' Bishop Bramhall warned Laud from Londonderry.[23] All too often such complaints were directed against episcopacy. 'I believe hierarchy must down,' Lady Brilliana Harley told her son.[24]

Laud felt so threatened that he persuaded Bishop Hall of Exeter to tone down some of the more strident claims he made in the manuscript of his pamphlet *Episcopacie by Divine Right Asserted*.[25] The archbishop recognised that events were approaching the crossroads. 'This year must bring forth some great Good or Evil. And a great part of the good hoped for will depend on the temper and well ordering of parliament,' he told Roe. 'I pray God send us to see better times.'[26] Always willing to help the Almighty do what he was convinced was in both their interests, the archbishop complained to the king that Edward Bagshaw, a Bencher of the Middle Temple, was giving aid and comfort to the Covenanters by delivering a series of lectures questioning the legal right of bishops to sit and vote in the House of Lords, and the powers of High Commission. Charles agreed, telling Lord Keeper Finch to ban all lectures on controversial topics. The offending lawyer came twice to Lambeth to talk the matter over with Laud, who refused to heed, threatening instead to haul him before High Commission. So Bagshaw had to leave the Middle Temple, and, as his students lined his way cheering, he rode off to Barking where he was overwhelmingly elected to parliament – yet another sign of Laud's growing unpopularity.

The elections to the Short Parliament were, as Windebank noted, 'very tumultary', and they revealed a great deal of public discontent. There were few seats that went uncontested. Candidates associated with the government were at a distinct disadvantage. For example, William Dell, Laud's secretary, was defeated at Canterbury, where the archbishop might have been expected to retain considerable influence, and had to scurry around to find a safe seat in the rotten borough of West Looe. Even though Laud managed to get his own nominee, Sir Edward Herbert, the Solicitor General, returned for Reading, he met with a surprising degree of opposition from the burgesses.[27] Laud prepared for the coming session by going through the state papers to see what powers the king had to control parliament, annotating one paper with the words 'something will be demanded'[28] – a masterpiece of understatement.

The first parliament for over a decade began auspiciously enough on 13 April 1640. Strafford had just returned from Ireland (on a ship appropriately named the *Confidence*), where he had persuaded the Dublin parliament to vote the king taxes. As Charles was rowed to open the session in the royal barge, which had been specially refurbished (at a cost of £620), the balladeers sang:

> We may be assured of this,
> If anything hath been amiss,
> Our king and state will all redress
> In this good parliament.

Laud did not share their high hopes. He was worried when John Pym rose in the house on 17 April to condemn the growth of church courts, the spread of popery, illegal taxes, monopolies, and the abuses of Star Chamber.[29] The archbishop cannot have been pleased that four of the twelve bills introduced in the Short Parliament were intended to reform the church. This legislation got nowhere, for on 5 May, much to Laud's relief, Charles dissolved parliament.

The king called a meeting of the privy council for six that morning. After some discussion they voted to end parliament immediately, the only opposition coming from Lords Holland and Northumberland. After Windebank was sent to the Speaker's house to break the news personally, the council committee on Scotland met at seven.[30] Strafford and Laud were present at this meeting, but they both missed the earlier one, the former because of ill health and the latter because of a misdirected message. This meant that two more hardliners were present to help form policy at the Scottish committee, which urged the king to follow up the dissolution of parliament by taking stern measures against the Covenanters. Venture all he had, urged Strafford, who allegedly advised the king to use an Irish army to destroy the Scots. Laud agreed. 'By the law of God you ought to have substance,' he told the king concerning his need for money, 'and ought to have it, and lawfully to take it.'[31]

In retrospect there is no doubt that ending what a contemporary called 'this short lived, or rather ... still-born parliament' was a mistake that had serious consequences for Laud.[32] The king's reasons for dissolving parliament were obscure, and may have had something to do with internal disputes amongst the councillors, hopes of financial aid from Spain, or fear that parliament might turn its attention to the Scottish business.[33] But the abrupt decision, made so precipitously that two important councillors were not given time to attend the meeting, and the Speaker had to be woken with the news at dawn, should not surprise us. It was inherent in the king's original decision of the previous December to call a parliament, when Laud advised him to get rid of it 'if the Parliament should prove peevish'.[34] Laud became extremely angry when the Puritan Lord Saye and Sele dared oppose

his motion to postpone the Lords' business for a day until 18 April to
allow the bishops to attend Convocation, and the pair had so heated an
exchange that one reporter described it as 'a remarkable passage'.[35] The
fact that this rather routine motion should have created such a fracas in
the Upper House – hardly a haven for radicalism – was an indication of
the bishops' loss of power. During the rest of the parliamentary session the
archbishop kept to his hard line. In mid-April Edward Hyde went to
Lambeth Palace to warn Laud of the dangers of dissolving parliament. He
met the archbishop walking in the garden, and begged him to do all he
could to advise Charles against such a calamitous step, since at heart very
few members were disaffected against church and king. The archbishop
scoffed at his friend's warnings, telling Hyde that he was exaggerating the
danger while minimising the strength and malignancy of the opposition.[36]

Events proved Laud wrong. Ending parliament produced a storm of
protest. Even Royalists, such as Sir Henry Mildmay, thought it took place
'to the much sorrow of all good men'.[37] Public opinion had no doubt about
whom to blame. 'It is indeed reported', wrote Sir Thomas Peyton to Henry
Oxinden, 'that the Archbishop was the chief cause of breaking the Parliament.' Some gentlemen law students agreed. Caught drinking toasts to
Laud's confusion in a tavern in Chancery Lane, they were brought before
the privy council, yet let off through the intervention of the Earl of Dorset,
who explained that they were really drinking to the downfall of Laud's
enemies.[38]

There was no such ambiguity in the broadsheets that began pouring
off the presses in 1640, and which Laud collected and read with mounting
indignation. 'So odious has he grown that we believe he stinketh in the
nostrils of Almighty God,' said one, while another constructed 'WELL AM
A DIVIL' as an anagram of William Laud. A third, found posted on the
Royal Exchange, urged all London apprentices to meet on 11 May to
march on Lambeth Palace.[39]

The plan had been mooted even before the dissolution of parliament,
for a London servant lad had been reported as urging that Lambeth Palace
be burned to the ground, preferably with the archbishop inside.[40] So Laud
had enough warning to mount a couple of cannon in his gatehouse, and
take refuge in Whitehall Palace, before a mob of about five hundred arrived
at Lambeth at midnight on 11 May demanding Laud's person. They
stormed the palace but did little damage, apart from breaking down the
door, and scaring the daylights out of the government in general and the
archbishop in particular. 'My deliverance was great,' he noted.[41] Wild
rumours swept through the city. Many expected that rioting would break
out at any moment, and that Laud, like Dr Lambe, would be murdered as
he walked the streets. The size and strength of the mob grew in men's fervid
imaginations.[42] On the privy council's order the militia were mobilised, but

they were of little use; some regiments became exhausted, particularly the Surrey contingent guarding Lambeth; others mutinied and stormed the White Lion Prison, freeing the ringleaders of the mob.[43]

The government believed that stern measures were called for. They issued a proclamation ordering the arrest of the rioters, whose recaptured ringleaders the king and council examined personally. In his own hand Charles wrote the warrant authorising the Lieutenant to the Tower to torture John Glover, a London apprentice, on the rack to wring from him the names of his accomplices.[44] Soon afterwards another rioter, Thomas Bensted, was hanged, drawn and quartered for trying to open the Archbishop of Canterbury's front door with a crowbar – one of the most elastic definitions of treason known to the majesty of English law – to Laud's apparent satisfaction.[45] From every side, from Williams, whom he was trying to get sent to Ireland, even from the Earl of Holland, Laud felt himself threatened by enemies. 'They cannot', he declared, 'be content with anything but an unsettled confusion.'[46]

And thus, to confound them, to produce settled order, the archbishop resorted to one of the few weapons left in his armoury – the Convocation of the Church of England.

By a centuries old tradition, whenever the crown called the first two secular estates, the Lords and Commons, to meet in Westminster, the third ecclesiastical estate met in convocation. Its first session opened in the chapter house of St Paul's Cathedral on 14 April, the day after parliament met, with a sermon preached on Matthew 10: 16, 'Behold, I send you forth as a sheep in the midst of wolves.' The text neatly summed up Laud's view of the church's current predicament and its immediate mission.[47]

By an equally old tradition, whenever the king dissolved parliament he also ended Convocation. But in May 1640 things were different. Later, as a prisoner in the Tower, Laud gave the impression that only with considerable reluctance had he gone along with the king's order that the Convocation should continue meeting even though parliament was no longer in session: 'I confess I was a little troubled.'[48] Contemporary documents suggest more caution than moral or legal qualms on the part of the archbishop, who ordered the privy council and law officers to rule that Convocation could continue in session because it had been called by a different set of writs than those used for parliament.[49] It took Laud only five days to recover from whatever reservations he might have had to draft in his own hand a set of instructions from the king telling Convocation what to do next.[50]

There were two unfinished items of business on its agenda: the passing of subsidies worth £20,000 over six years, and the revision of the canons by which the church was governed.

On 15 April, the second day that Convocation was in session, the debate on the new canons began. It was, Laud maintained years later, remarkably open and free. By the end of May Convocation passed six new canons, which the king confirmed the following month, with instructions that every minister should preach at least once a quarter a sermon promoting them. The canons were conservative, even reactionary. The first declared that the king ruled by divine right, while the second attempted to take the wind out of the opposition's sails by maintaining that he did so by scriptural authority. Three canons addressed the current political crisis: the king had the right to call and dismiss parliaments; any subject taking up arms against the king was damned and would suffer eternal hell-fire; it was the duty of all subjects to pay their sovereign taxes whenever asked. The only – and very half-hearted – attempt to placate the opposition, who were worried by the bishops' ability to manipulate convocation, came in the canon which declared that all those who advocated popery or democracy were guilty of treason against God and the king. And, as if to underscore the point, Laud got the common hangman to publicly burn some two hundred books seized from a Papist. Many members of Convocation wanted to go further than the canons: a committee of clergy passed a resolution supporting the railing off and veneration of altars placed at the east end of the church.

Without doubt the most controversial legislation that Convocation passed was the requirement that all priests, bishops, students, and university graduates had to take an oath by 2 November 1640 accepting the 'Doctrines and Disciplines and Government of the Church of England', and promising not to change them. Although this sweeping pledge was so vague that it soon became known as 'the et cetera oath', there was no doubt that it included a promise to maintain episcopacy, something which concerned many people deeply. 'The et cetera oath was the first thing that threatened me,' recorded the Puritan divine Richard Baxter. Sir Simonds D'Ewes thought it would drive all godly ministers to New England.[51] With the simple-mindedness so characteristic of those who put their trust in loyalty oaths, Laud believed that the best way of rooting out his enemies – who he was sure were dishonourable cheats – was to put them on their word of honour to reveal themselves for what they were. Thus in late 1639 and early 1640 he used oaths to root out the opposition not just in Convocation, but before High Commission, and among Ulster's Presbyterians.[52] There is no doubt that he believed Convocation had done well in passing the canons. 'I hope', he wrote in his diary soon afterwards, they 'will be useful to the church'.[53]

The passage of the canons was part of a wider attempt to reassert the church's authority, which took petty and spiteful forms. When Bishop Wren ordered the Mayor and Aldermen of Norwich to attend morning service in his cathedral, he sat them in a draughty pew under the public gallery. To add insult to injury someone dropped a bible, which broke the mayor's spectacles, a sailor defecated on an alderman's robe, while another man spat on another alderman's head.[54] More salutary were the archbishop's attempts to purge Oxford University Press's list of theological tomes that favoured Presbyterians, his continued efforts to reform Merton College, his encouragement of the publication of Bishop Hall's defence of the divine right of bishops, as well as all sermons supporting the king's authority.[55] In a sense all these efforts were part of the church's efforts to support the king and his army, who for the second time in just over a year were about to fight the Scots.

Before Charles left for the wars, Laud acted as a link between the central government and his friend Edward, second Viscount Conway, who commanded the royal army in the north. He tried to get the king to allocate the duty levied on coal shipped from the port of Newcastle to strengthening that town's fortifications, which everyone agreed were the key to holding the north. He failed, and his influence decreased all the more after the queen gave birth to a son, Prince Henry, and the plague forced the court to move from Hampton Court to Oatlands, where there was not enough room to lodge the archbishop. 'This business hath made me such a courtier that I am heartily weary of it,' he complained to Conway.[56] While Laud developed an unhealthy interest in espionage, he had to confess that war 'is a business quite out of my way'.[57]

It was equally unfamiliar to General Conway and his army. Conway described his troops as 'men that are fit for Bedlam or Bridewell'. His Sergeant Major General, Sir Jacob Astley, agreed that they were 'all the arch-knaves of the kingdom'.[58] Wherever they went, soldiers seemed to cause trouble. At Oxford they brawled with the students, inflicting bloodshed, much to Laud's indignation. The arrival of the king at their main camp did nothing to improve morale. After the Scots crossed the river Tweed at Coldstream, Charles became so desperate that he resorted to the archaic expedient of summoning a Grand Council of Peers to advise him. They insisted that he must call a parliament. Meanwhile Charles had to negotiate with the Covenanters, which filled Laud with gloom, for he felt that Scottish promises were 'not worth three of their lice'.[59] To Caledonian purses, at least, the treaty that they signed with the king at Ripon on 26 October was worth a lot more: he agreed to allow the Covenanters to occupy the counties of Northumberland and Durham, and pay them a subsidy of £860 a day for their pains. Then he rode south for the denouement.

There can be no doubt that the crisis that the king and his ministers faced at the end of 1640 was deep, desperate – and for Laud mortally dangerous. While historians may be able to trace its origins back for generations, if not centuries, for contemporaries as astute as Edward Hyde it was a recent phenomenon.[60] One day the sky was as blue as when the royal family strolled amongst the quiet gardens and quadrangles of Oxford University, then suddenly dark clouds appeared above the northern horizon, the heavens turned black, and the storm broke in all its fury. 'The state of things in this kingdom is very doubtful and uncertain,' noted Robert Woodford in his diary on 14 May 1640. Two days later William Hawkins wrote to the Earl of Leicester, 'I never knew the subjects of England so much out of order.'[61] Men such as Benjamin Cox, incumbent of Sandford, Devon, who in normal times were highly conformable, started to act strangely. Bishop Hall of Exeter told Laud that Cox had preached against episcopacy: 'We begin already to find the effect of the Scottish Schism,' was the bishop's sad conclusion.[62]

The crisis originated less from the king's policies than from the utter failure of those policies, and their failure was far more complete outside England than within its borders. The two great events that produced the English Civil War, the Prayer Book Rebellion and the Irish rebellion, began outside England. True, the Covenanters were reacting against a religious policy that Laud advocated, but as has been suggested, he took little part in the decision to introduce a new prayer book, and to force it on the Scots no matter what the cost to England. In any case the liturgy was only one of the issues behind the Scottish rebellion. Like the Irish rebellion four years later, the rebellion in Scotland was as much a matter of resistance to growing English influence as it was a matter of religion.

In 1639 and 1640 an unpopular and ineffective government was asking a great deal from its subjects, certainly far more than it had ever demanded before. It had already ordered people from inland counties to pay ship money. It had fined those who transgressed forest laws that only the most assiduous of antiquarians knew were still in force. It had piled new duties on the already over-burdened justices of the peace, while chipping away their prerogatives and perquisites by pandering to monopolists, such as Sir Giles Mompesson, to whom it had given the lucrative right to license ale houses. Equally over-burdened, and under-rewarded, were churchwardens, who every day seemed to be beset with another duty, one more hectoring command, or a further charge on their own purses or the parish rates. While stained glass windows, altar rails, vestments might or might not be idolatrous, all parishioners agreed that they were expensive.[63] But the sacrifices the government demanded from its subjects in 1639 and 1640 were far greater than merely paying to refurbish the church, build up the Royal Navy, paying a fine for not becoming a knight, or enforcing a lot of bothersome regulations from the crown: quite simply, being sent off to fight the Scots meant hazarding one's life for an unpopular cause.

In the past the troops levied by Charles's government had mainly been riff-raff, such as those sent to perish at Cadiz; although mourned by their nearest and dearest, they were hardly missed in the communities from which they were conscripted. Or else they were volunteers, often rootless men, motivated by the hope of pay or loot, or by zeal for the Protestant cause. But to fight the Bishops' Wars the government called upon the county militia: ordinary tenant farmers, led by the gentry, who had a considerable stake in society which they were loath to lose, particularly in so unpopular a cause as fighting the Covenanters.

Thus it is not surprising that they marched north with extreme reluctance, misbehaving themselves with a licence unusual even for English soldiery. All too often their violence was directed at symbols. There were riots in Colchester, Wisbech and Baldock, the latter prompted by the discovery of a man and woman fornicating – an activity of which in normal times most soldiers thoroughly approved. In Devon and Buckinghamshire levies murdered officers whom they suspected of being Catholics. The Essex militia smashed the stained glass windows at Hadham, and burnt altar rails in Chelmsford, Great Holland, St Osyth, Elstead, Ickleton and Radwinter, where not even the gift of a barrel of beer from the dean could dissuade them from their righteous duty. The Suffolk militia took to wearing white sheets over their uniforms to parody bishops' surplices.[64]

Violence was not confined to the army. During a christening in Halstead church, Essex, a couple 'of poor and silly men' snatched the prayer book from the priest, kicked it up and down the aisle, and ripped the vestments off the parish clerk's back.[65] Perhaps the most serious outbreak of violence took place in London, where, Laud wrote, a mob of 'very near 2,000 Brownists' stormed St Paul's whither High Commission had moved after the attack on Lambeth Palace, ripping up the books, smashing the furniture, and 'crying out that they would have no bishops or High Commission'.[66]

All these outrages took place in an atmosphere of intense crisis. After recounting the attack on Lambeth Palace, John Castle told the Earl of Bridgewater, 'what a wild sea this poor ship is driven'.[67] The dispatches of the Venetian ambassador were even more hysterical. In a description of the assault on Lambeth Palace he exaggerated the size of the mob fourfold, before reporting the completely false story that seven thousand people had burnt to the ground the archbishop's country house at Fulham (actually it was in Croydon).[68] Equally fantastic rumours swept through the land. At Cambridge the Cam was said to be running as red as blood, while men were seen fighting in the sky above the college rooftops. It was widely reported that nightmares so troubled Prince Charles that he could not sleep. When his father asked him what was the matter, the prince replied 'My grandfather left you four kingdoms, and I am afraid your majesty will leave me never one.'[69]

By 1640 the intense political crisis threatening the realm had become focused on symbols. This should not surprise us. For one thing the discredited old order had defined many of its policies in symbolic terms – altars, altar rails, Star Chamber, High Commission, surplices, and *jure divino* rule. Symbols often come to the forefront at times of crisis, but there are limits to what symbols can do. Like flags they can rally the troops, but they cannot explain why the troops have been rallied, and what they should do to resolve the crisis that brought them together in the first place.

Whom could Englishmen blame for the seemingly sudden collapse of the relative calm and tranquillity of the 1630s? Themselves? That was out of the question. Certainly not the king, who as a divinely ordained person was an extension of both God and their collective selves and thus was clearly above reproach. What about the Scots, against whom the government, counting on an ancient tradition of prejudice, hoped they would turn? To their surprise, many Englishmen found they had far more in common with the Covenanters than they anticipated, certainly a great deal more than they had with the Catholics, who seemed daily to be growing in power and royal favour. Like other societies in crisis, England turned to theories of conspiracy for an explanation.

Anti-clericalism had long been a force in English history.[70] It was rather like a chronic infection that remains dormant in the body politic until some accident, a broken limb or concussed pate, causes it to flare up. One can see anti-clericalism in the descriptions of those ecclesiastical rogues who rode to Canterbury with Chaucer's pilgrims. Before the Reformation, the last great upheaval in English history prior to the Civil War, it surfaced in the Hunne case, and the hatred of Cardinal Wolsey. Perhaps it is inherent in Christian doctrine. Very few priests can completely practise what the Bible tells them to preach, and if the church grows rich and they become ostentatiously powerful, this intellectual gap becomes a chasm of hypocrisy. But just as the anti-clericalism of *The Canterbury Tales* focused on those who abused their positions, such as the sleazy pardoner or the dandified friar, while praising the devout country parson, so at the end of the personal rule complaints about clerics centred on bishops, who were seen as epitomising all that was wrong with the church.

During the parliamentary struggles of the 1620s the attacks on bishops were, to paraphrase Sir John Eliot, on the men and not the order. In 1629 Prynne described bishops as 'the Watchmen, the Governors, the Bulwarks of our Israel, the Lights, the Eyes, the Seers, yea Overseers of our Church'.[71] A decade later many people thought that Prynne, Burton and Bastwick were mad dogs howling in the wilderness. But as Laud had to admit to Bishop Hall in November 1639, very recently 'some of a milder and subtler alloy' had started to attack bishops.[72] The following spring Edward Bagshaw, the Middle Temple lecturer, told Laud that until twelve months ago he had never heard anyone complain about bishops. While Bagshaw could have been muting his criticisms to try and keep his job, it is unthinkable that a dozen months before any trader would have dared hawk the ballads that almost everyone seemed to be singing in London's streets:[73]

> Since Bishops first began to ride
> In state so near the crown.
> They have been aye puft up with pride
> And rode with great renown.

During what a group of Huntingdonshire clergy described to Laud as 'these anti-episcopal and unsettled times', bishops made first-rate villains.[74] The scriptural basis for their authority was debatable, particularly in a period of intense scriptural debates.[75] They had popish connections that belied Bishop Montagu's flippant jest to Bishop Cosin, 'it will never be well till we have our own Inquisition.'[76] They had unpopular secular functions, backed up by church courts, High Commission and Star Chamber. They were associated with failed royal policies. And they were new men, selected for their academic qualifications in a society that normally allotted power and promotion on the basis of birth, connection, estates and kin. For 'a low-born man to be exalted high . . . all at once', wrote Lord Brooke in his *Discourse Touching the Nature of Episcopacy* (1641), 'must create as great a chasm in politics, as such leaps do in nature'.[77] Perhaps this is why Laudian bishops took comfort in the theory that they, like the king, ruled *jure divino*, or, as John Pym put it with more wit than charity, 'they wrestled Religion like a waxen nose, to the furtherance of their ambitious purposes.'[78]

Anti-episcopacy combined with a far wider and more deep-rooted fear of Catholics to fuel the crisis. So profound was the fear of a Papist conspiracy that even Laud accepted it. In the summer of 1640 Sir William Boswell sent the archbishop from Holland details about the rumoured Harbenfeld Plot, a vague and fantastic scheme on the part of an ill-defined group of conspirators, who were reputed to include Sir Tobie Matthew, Captain John Reade, the Earl and Countess of Arundel, Endymion Porter, Windebank, the Duchess of Buckingham and the Countess of Newport, to poison the king with 'Indian Nuts'.[79] Without hesitation Laud accepted the story unreservedly. 'The danger seems imminent,' he told the king, who agreed completely.[80]

Many Englishmen came to a very different conclusion about whom to blame, reverting back to their Tudor forebears' view that the body politic was a dangerous place rife with treason and conspiracies. Because hysteria and a sense of crisis had blunted their critical faculties, the allegation that Laud was a crypto-Catholic was perfectly credible. Because out of the whole villainous tribe of bishops the archbishop was the obvious arch-villain, in the over-heated popular imaginations he – and his co-conspirator, Strafford – made scapegoats *par excellence*:[81]

> Landless Will of Lambeth Strand
> And Black Tom, Tyrant of Ireland,
> Like Fox and Wolf did lurk,
> With many rooks and magpies
> To pluck out good king Charles his eyes.
> And then be Pope and Turk.

So went one of the popular songs, almost certainly whistled by Richard Beaumont, the London apprentice lad who started the rumour that Laud had a crucifix above his altar to which he secretly bowed. Such wild charges fell on fertile ground: in Bristol it was widely rumoured that the archbishop had actually become a Papist. A Berkshire justice of the peace reported the same story, adding that the county believed that 'it was Bishop Laud who was the cause of the ruin of all this army, and that the king was ruled by him'.[82] Father Chaissy, the queen's Franciscan chaplain, and Count Rossetti informed the Vatican that they had talked with Laud in the chapel at the Venetian embassy about his going over to Rome – a story that would have to be taken as yet another hysterical fantasy of the times, were it not found in two independent sources.[83] Could the Venetian ambassador have been alluding to the same possibility when he wrote home (quite erroneously) that the archbishop was so hated that he had had to take refuge in the queen's court?[84] Certainly William Claybrooke, the Church of England priest who converted to Rome, claimed that he had done so at Laud's command.

As the crisis fuelled by the failure of the king's policies, the Scottish invasion, the long-standing fear of Catholics, and the tidal wave of anti-episcopacy which sprang up almost overnight, came to boiling point, and threatened to spill over, scalding Laud alive, the archbishop grew ever more desperate. His private complaints that he was tired, surrounded by enemies, that all was lost, reached a crescendo. As he settled his affairs in the small amount of time he believed he had left, any incident was fraught with significance. On the evening of 27 October 1640, a week before parliament was due to meet, the archbishop went to his study at Lambeth to sort through some manuscripts that he was going to give to Oxford University. He found that the full-length portrait of himself (most likely the one by Van Dyck) had fallen face down on the floor, the string that held it to the wall having somehow broken. Laud was deeply worried. Buckingham's portrait had fallen down in just that way immediately before his murder. So this sad, embattled man turned to the one friend he could still trust, writing in his diary, 'I am almost every day threatened with my ruin in Parliament. God Grant this be no omen.'[85]

XIII

'The sty of all pestilential filth'

When someone told Laud that 3 November 1640, the date set for the opening of parliament, was also the one hundred and eleventh anniversary of the start of the Reformation parliament which had ushered in the greatest revolution England had known since the Norman Conquest, destroying Cardinal Wolsey, the proud and powerful prelate whom Laud most closely resembled, and suggested that the archbishop persuade the king to move the opening to a more auspicious date, Laud scoffed at such fears.[1] In public, at least, the prayer that he wrote to mark the opening session reveals a sense of guarded optimism. Laud asked the Almighty 'to bless this great Assembly and all their counsels', as well as the sovereign, whom he described as 'a good, a gracious, a just, a pious, and prudent king'. He hoped that parliament would behave in a fashion 'which becomes an obedient, a religious, a moderate, a free and a wise people', in order to achieve 'the safety of the kingdom and the settlement of true religion'. Interestingly enough, from his first draft Laud erased a reference to the fact that this parliament 'hath been much desired'. Privately he was preparing for the worst.[2]

This was only prudent, for as one letter writer noted after describing the state opening of parliament, 'Our clergy begin to apprehend some danger, seeing the people so much against them.'[3] Thus on 6 November the archbishop collected some eighty-one rare manuscripts in Greek, Latin, Arabic and Italian to send to the Bodleian Library, where they would be safe. A week later he gave Reading £100 for apprenticing poor but honest lads, adding that he had not tried to influence the election of their burgesses to parliament this time, 'because I found that there was a great deal of causeless malignity cast upon me, for I know not what'.[4]

Four days after the opening of parliament the Commons placed religion at the top of their agenda. 'Let religion be our *primum quaerite*, for all things else are but *etceteras* to it,' declaimed Sir Benjamin Rudyerd on 7 November. Sir John Holland agreed that 'In redress of our grievances those

197

of the Church ought to have priority.'[5] John Pym tried to focus their attacks on the issue of popery: on schemes to unite with Rome and to ally with Spain and to alter established religion, and upon English clerics who were willing to sell their birthrights for a mess of papal pottage. Initially the Commons' memory for grievances was far shorter, going back to the canons of the previous May. On 9 November the Lower House accepted Francis Rous's motion that no member of the convocation be allowed to preach before them, and a couple of weeks later they refused to take communion at St Margaret's, Westminster, until the altar rails had been removed.[6] Here they were fed a steady diet of sermons, mainly from Puritan ministers who had felt the Laudian lash, exhorting them to 'pluck up every plant that God hath not planted'.[7]

Four external forces prompted the Commons to root out the man who the preachers declared was the greatest tare of them all – petitions, the Scots, Bishop Williams, and the desire of Prynne, Burton and Bastwick for revenge.

In the first week of the new session parliament received some twenty petitions. Peter Smart protested against his imprisonment for preaching a sermon in Durham Cathedral against popist rituals, Francis Nichols, a Northamptonshire gentleman, complained he had been jailed for merely wearing a hat during a sermon, while a group from Newcastle requested parliament to order the common hangman to burn the new canons, and Mrs Prynne, Mrs Burton and Mrs Bastwick begged for the release of their husbands, who were imprisoned in Jersey, Guernsey and Scilly, respectively.[8]

The Commons immediately granted the wives' requests, instructing the governors of Jersey, Guernsey and Scilly to free the prisoners, who returned in great triumph to the capital at the end of the month. A procession of a hundred coaches and four thousand people on foot escorted the martyrs into London, which, one observer noted, 'galled the bishops exceedingly'.[9] Suffering made the three vengeful, their popularity more potent, and both forces combined to render Laud fatally vulnerable.

The archbishop had other enemies. On 16 November the Commons sent Black Rod to the Tower to free Bishop Williams, who the following day, attended by six bishops, returned as a conquering hero to take his seat in the House of Lords. Even though this was the first time the Lower House had directly overruled the king's authority by releasing a prisoner without his permission, Charles had a long midnight conversation with Williams a few days afterwards, and ordered all court decrees against him cancelled.[10]

The most powerful force working upon parliament was the least noticed.[11] After the Treaty of Ripon allowed the Scots army to occupy the two border counties, and guaranteed them a subsidy of £860 pounds a day (which also ensured parliament's virtual protection from royal dissolution without redress of grievances), the Covenanters sent commissioners to Westminster. When they arrived on 16 November, parliament welcomed them warmly, and Charles soon had to accept most of their demands. Compared to parliament, which may not have been as united or as well led as has been thought, the Scots had no doubt as to their objectives.[12] 'Episcopacy itself is beginning to be cried down and a covenant Cried up and the Liturgy to be scorned,' wrote Robert Baillie, one of the commissioners, to his home kirk; 'it is thought good to delay it till the parliament have pulled down Canterbury and some prime Bishops, which they mind to do so soon as the king has digested the bitterness of the Lieutenant's censure.'

The Commons had impeached Strafford a week before, and now he lay a prisoner in the Tower. Five days later they voted to set up a committee on religion to consider Laud's impeachment. Its chairman, Sir Edward Dering, declared that 'A Pope at Rome will do me less hurt than a patriarch may do at Lambeth,' to which another member added, 'Let us then endeavour a thorough reformation.'[13]

How did the archbishop react to this reformation which, as Thomas Knyvett noted, 'goes on again as hot as toast'?[14] At about the time of the opening of parliament, Laud took a very hard line against Thomas Wilson, a Puritan minister from Kent, threatening to arrest him if he dared come out of hiding. 'His Grace will either have more Grace, or no Grace at all,' Dering, a leading Kentish gentleman, observed sardonically.[15] But soon afterwards the archbishop recognised that the government must make concessions – preferably cosmetic ones. Thus on 11 November the crown issued proclamations ordering all recusants to leave London and the court, and declaring 8 December a national day of prayer and fasting.[16] Such a gesture of appeasement might have prompted the Earl of Northumberland to write to the Earl of Leicester that Laud, Windebank and Cottington 'are certainly in very great danger of being ruined'.[17] Three days later, on 29 November, sensing his vulnerability and aware that the Commons were to discuss the canons the following day, Laud tried to agree terms with his enemies, using his friend the constitutional lawyer John Selden as an intermediary: 'If we have erred in any point of legality unknown to us, we shall be heartily sorry, and hope that error shall not be made a crime,' he wrote, offering to surrender ship money, and to 'humbly beseech his Majesty for licence to review the Canons and abrogate them . . . to preserve the public peace'.[18]

But it was too late for concessions to preserve either the public peace or the Archbishop of Canterbury, particularly since the king was becoming reconciled to Williams, whom he saw as an alternative to his old, discredited ministers. Thus on 4 December Charles allowed the Commons to interrogate them on their role in Star Chamber hearings, a surrender which hurt Laud deeply.[19]

Worse was to come. On 11 November Alderman Pennington led a deputation of fifteen hundred Londoners to parliament to present a petition containing some fifteen thousand signatures calling for the abolition of bishops, root and branch. Within two months, thirteen counties had sent similar root and branch petitions, and within six months the Commons had received suits, many subscribed with over a thousand signatures, from half the counties in the land.[20]

The Scots commissioners wanted to destroy Laud before they abolished the bishops, for they were sure that his ruin would lead to the latter's destruction. For the Presbyterians who formed a bridge between Edinburgh and Westminster it was a heady moment. 'God is making here a new world,' exulted one of them, Robert Baillie.[21]

It took only six December days to undo Laud's old world. Nathaniel Wickins, Prynne's servant, testified that the archbishop had threatened him with perpetual imprisonment unless he betrayed his master, and Calvin Bruin, Peter Lee, and Richard Tolburne of Chester said that he had not only fined them, but solicited a bribe after they had visited Prynne in the town gaol – a charitable act widely regarded as a Christian duty. Prynne himself appeared before the Commons demanding that they reverse his Star Chamber conviction and let him sue for damages – which the House promptly voted.[22] In full cry, the following day, 16 December, they repealed the canons of May 1640 'as being against the King's prerogative, the fundamental laws of the realm, the liberty and property of the subject', and established another committee to see if Laud, the canons' undoubted author, was guilty of treason. Most informed sources never doubted the verdict. 'I believe that there is no question that the Archbishop will be accused of high treason,' one member of parliament wrote to his father.[23]

Adding to the pressure, the next day the Scots commissioners declared Laud 'an incendiary', and told the Commons that he was 'the prime cause' of the new liturgy that contained 'many Dangerous Errors in matters of Doctrine'. After it was alleged that he had compared Puritans to dogs – to the latter's distinct advantage – Dr Bastwick presented the House with a petition outlining his grievances.[24] 'So now you see we fly at all,' a member concluded, 'tomorrow we shall desire the Lords to sequester the archbishop.'[25] And so they did.

The Commons assembled well before dawn on 18 December. Having heard at seven a report of the previous day's conference with the Scots commissioners, Denzil Holles – who twenty-one years earlier had held the Speaker in his chair so the House could pass a resolution condemning Arminianism – rose to demand Laud's impeachment. The primate was responsible for the Scots war. He had introduced innovations into the

established church. He had brought in popery. He wanted to turn the
nation 'into slavery'. In short he was guilty of high treason. Harbottle
Grimston, the member for Colchester, was even more intemperate, calling
Laud 'the sty of all pestilential filth that hath infected the State and Government . . . the very broker and Pander of the whore of Babylon . . . the great
and common enemy of all goodness and all goodmen'. Their rhetoric
convinced the Commons, who on Pym's motion voted the archbishop a
traitor, and ordered Holles to go to the Lords and arrest him.[26]

Laud's immediate reaction was one of bitter surprise. After the Earl
of Essex and Lord Saye and Sele cut off his initial protests, he withdrew
from the upper chamber. 'I was accused by the House of Commons for
high treason, without any particular charge laid against me,' he wrote in
his diary. It was all the work of a rabble of seditious Brownists, who were
upset because he had lawfully punished their schisms. 'And though I pitied
them, as God knows, from my very heart,' he added with more than a
trace of sanctimoniousness, 'their malignity gave me over.'

The Lords handed the archbishop over to the custody of James
Maxwell, Black Rod. At the prisoner's request they allowed him to return
to Lambeth Palace to pick up some papers. Here he had a short and sad
conversation with his friends and steward, and was given 'much comfort'
to find that the psalms appointed for Evensong were numbers 93 and 94:

> Lord, how long shall the wicked, how long shall the wicked
> triumph? . . . Understand, ye brutish among the people: and ye
> fools, when will ye be wise? . . . Blessed is the man whom thou
> chastenest, O Lord, and teachest him out of thy law; . . . But the
> Lord is my defence; and my God is the rock of my refuge.

Convinced that the end was nigh, that evening the archbishop wrote in his
diary, 'God make me worthy of it, and fit to receive it.' He described how,
as he was being rowed from Lambeth Palace to Maxwell's house at Charing
Cross, hundreds of his poor neighbours came out to pray for his safe
return, 'For which I bless God and them.'[27]

For the rest of his life Laud had little for which to bless his Maker,
because the good folk he reported praying for him were almost unique in
the realm. The archbishop's troubles piled one upon the other. On 4
January 1641, on Pym's motion, the Commons authorised the committee
on religion to consider possible reparations against Laud, and ten days
later they heard Bastwick testify that the accused had stated that the Church
of Rome 'did not err in Fundamentals'. Other enemies followed the good
doctor's lead.[28] On 3 February three ministers testified that the archbishop
had thrown out their appeals against being suspended for refusing to read
the Book of Sports from their pulpits, and had told them, 'If you know
not how to obey, I know not how to grant.'[29] Four weeks later Isaac Knight

testified that when he explained to the archbishop that he could not take
the *ex officio* oath in good faith, he was told that 'the walls of the Fleet
[Prison] should satisfy his conscience'.[30] On 21 June it was alleged that
Laud had tried to allow the nuns of Douay to import their lace – which
was nearly as odious as their faith – into England duty-free, and eleven
days later that he had solicited a £200 bribe in a High Commission case.

This wave of long-remembered grievances turned public opinion
against Laud. In early January Sir John Temple wrote, 'Concerning my
Lord of Canterbury, there is now *altum silentium* so inconsiderable that
he is as no man.' But exactly a month later another correspondent reported
that the archbishop would surely be brought to trial, and 'will be found
very deep in capital crimes'.[31]

Laud's appreciation of his predicament also oscillated. In mid-January
he was reported to be confident that he would be pardoned. The following
month he reacted to the rumour that a group of powerful aristocrats had
persuaded the king to free him in return for dismissing him as archbishop
and as a member of the privy council by remarking bitterly, 'So I see what
justice I may expect.'

There was not a chance that the committee on religion and, more
significantly, the Scots commissioners would have accepted any such
arrangement, particularly after Charles pardoned the condemned Jesuit
Father Goodman, which was widely taken as a precedent for freeing Laud
and Strafford.[32] On 26 February 1641 Pym presented to the Commons the
committee's report recommending that the archbishop be impeached on
fourteen counts. The first charged that 'he hath traitorously endeavoured
to subvert the fundamental laws and government of this kingdom', the
second that he had attacked parliament's privileges, and the third that he
had tried to subvert justice. The rest of the articles elaborated on these
themes, adding that he had assumed papal powers, rewarded the 'popishly
affected', and conspired to reconcile Canterbury and Rome. The Commons
accepted the articles without objection, the only discussion being a trivial
question about the correct form of the archbishop's name.[33]

Sir Henry Vane took the charges to the Lords, who ordered that the
archbishop be brought from James Maxwell's custody to the bar of their
house. After the clerk had read out the indictment, Laud replied, 'My
Lords, this is a great and heavy charge, and I must be unworthy to live if
it can be made good against me,' before denying his guilt.[34] He was then
returned to Black Rod's custody.

Having impeached the archbishop on charges that they agreed involved
the heinous crime of setting himself up above the king, parliament was
determined that Laud must not be allowed to escape. So they ordered his
transfer from Black Rod's custody to the Tower. After the Lords granted
his request for a few days' grace so that his quarters there could be made

ready, Laud left Maxwell's house on 1 March to make the journey from Charing Cross and through the City. Black Rod would not permit the prisoner to travel at night, when no one would see him, since escape would also be easier under cover of darkness. Instead he made the journey at noon, when he hoped that people would be indoors having lunch. At first, he recorded, 'all went well, till I passed through Newgate Shambles, and entered Cheapside'. Here the archbishop was recognised, and a mob of apprentices and riff-raff jostled his coach with taunts of 'Little Willie, art thou there?' The jeering crowd grew rapidly, and at the Exchange a riot almost broke out. 'And so they followed me with clamour and railings even beyond barbarity itself, not giving up even until the coach was entered in at Tower Gate.'[35]

Although Strafford too was a prisoner in the Tower, parliament did not allow the two friends to meet, not even after the earl went on trial for his life on 22 March. When it became apparent that the Lords would not convict him on the flimsiest of evidence, the Commons forced through an act of attainder ordering his execution.

On his last night on earth Strafford asked the Lieutenant of the Tower if he might be allowed to see Laud. On being told that it was impossible without parliament's permission, he suggested that permission was not really necessary if the Lieutenant was present at the meeting to hear all that was said. When he was told that he must ask parliament, the proud earl refused, saying, 'I have gotten my dispatch from them, and will trouble them no further.' Instead he asked his chaplain, Archbishop Ussher, to request Laud to pray for him that night, and to bless him as he was marched past his cell out to the place of execution. Laud agreed. He told Ussher that while his conscience bound him to do the first, and his duty and obligations of friendship the second, he was terrified that he might not be strong enough to watch the earl being led out to his death.

The next morning, on his last walk to Tower Hill, Strafford paused outside Laud's window. The archbishop appeared. 'My Lord, your prayers and blessing,' asked the condemned man. 'He turned towards me, and took the solemnest leave that I think was ever by any at distance taken one of another,' the archbishop recalled. Laud lifted his hand to give the final benediction, and then fell to the ground in a swoon. 'Farewell, My Lord, God protect your innocency,' Strafford said as he walked to his death.[36]

It was a moving scene, one of those moments that are imprinted on every schoolchild's memory of history. It was one to elicit sympathy from all but the most implacable foes of the earl and the archbishop. Perhaps because he felt that he had failed Strafford both as a friend and as a priest by fainting during what were in effect the last rites, Laud fell ill of 'a tertian ague'. His failure was so painful that he could not bear to record it in the history he wrote of his trial and troubles.

During the last few months Laud had been under intense pressure. On 3 January, realising that the king was trying to transfer clerical patronage away from him to Williams, he signed a letter to Charles as 'Your Majesty's most humble Servant, though unfortunate'. This became his usual valedictory.[37] Lord Brooke's threat to pull down St Paul's so that 'no stone were left upon another' deeply worried him, while the appointment of a Lords' committee on bishops chaired by Williams quite literally made him sick.[38]

In many ways Strafford's execution was the moment of truth. For his friend the archbishop wrote a heartfelt epitaph: 'Thus ended the wisest, the stoutest, and everyway the ablest subject that this nation hath bred these many years.' For his sovereign – who he knew had cravenly accepted Williams's self-serving advice to break his sacred word to the earl by signing the attainder, and had then sent him a sanctimonious, self-centred prayer – Laud had only ill-concealed contempt: he called Charles 'a mild and gracious prince, who knew not how to be, or be made great'.[39]

Two of the most remarkable features about the first few months of the Long Parliament were the indecent haste with which Charles discarded his old ministers, and the speed with which religion came to dominate the public's thoughts.

In the last couple of months of 1640 the king allowed the Long Parliament to purge his leading ministers. Laud, Wren and Strafford all ended up in prison, while Lord Keeper Finch fled to Holland, and Sir Francis Windebank, after hiding from the Commons' sergeant under his bedclothes, escaped to France. Charles made no effort to protect them. Perhaps he blamed them for the disasters that had befallen him since the St Giles's riot; certainly he was coming increasingly under the influence of the queen and her Catholic friends, who had little love for Laud.

Of course, the king was trying to form policies in an extraordinarily difficult and complicated time, during which – it must be admitted – he was not the only Englishman to panic or do silly things. When two fat members of parliament happened to tread on the same floorboard simultaneously, causing it to break with a crack like a gunshot, the rest of the House instantly dived for cover. The Commons had, fortunately, recovered enough of their senses a few weeks later to greet with peals of laughter Sir John Clotworthy's proposal for a bill that all Jesuits be gelded.[40]

In those days of intense excitement, when the presses produced a flood of political and radical pamphlets, when plots were imagined on every side, and when so many communications were sent about the realm that the Letter Office's profits doubled, three motifs of dissatisfaction may be discerned.[41] The first was a regional, a local sense of wanting to be left alone. Once the Long Parliament destroyed the old order, this theme lost much of its impetus. The second was a legal and constitutional motif, which in retrospect may seem more important than it was at the time, largely because posterity has attributed its own goals to seventeenth-century Englishmen. Even though legal and constitutional arguments became more significant in 1642 than they had been in 1641, they were never as powerful as the religious motif. As Sir Benjamin Rudyerd told the House of Commons on 7 November 1640, 'religion hath been for a long time, and still is, the great design of this kingdom.' Religion – or rather, the religion of the Protestants – was the goal on which most seventeenth-century Englishmen concentrated. They paid comparatively little attention to the means to that end.[42]

That the English Civil War started, continued and ended as a war of religion should not surprise us. After the Reformation all the major wars that Englishmen fought, or wanted to fight, from the Armada to the conquest of Ireland, from the wars for Dutch independence or Huguenot rights to the Thirty Years War, were essentially wars of religion. In times of peace men saw their lives in religious terms; in times of war they comprehended their deaths in much the same way. Not just worship, but work, hierarchy, marriage, sex, child-rearing, sickness, wounds and adversity were understood within a religious framework. So it was only natural that they should have seen the crisis that started with an attempt to change the way Scots worshipped in the same light.

But religion was not a convincing explanation for why this crisis had come about. Beyond the occasional day of prayer and fasting, and the all too frequent three-hour sermons, Englishmen were not prepared to scourge themselves personally for the malady that existed within the body politic. The king – whom the radical MP Sir Simonds D'Ewes described as 'our great and gracious Prince' – could not possibly be at fault, for if it was the anointed head who was responsible for the body's ills then undoubtedly the whole must die.[43] Once more people not only needed a scapegoat to explain away the dangerous conspiracies that seemed to threaten them at every turn, but also a victim whose death would purge the cancer which imperilled the body politic.

Months before he described Laud as 'the Sty of all pestilential filth'. Harbottle Grimston told Sir John Bramson that he was determined to destroy the archbishop.[44] It was quite clear that Grimston was convinced that Laud was the evil genius responsible for all that troubled the common-wealth. From him stretched a web of wickednesses that explained seemingly unconnected crimes from one end of the realm to the other. Thus Grimston called the archbishop 'the only man, the only man that hath raised and advanced all those that, together with himself, have been the author and cause of all our ruins, miseries and calamities'. The venom, the hatred that Grimston felt for Laud, which was shared widely enough for the House unanimously to order his arrest, clearly emerges in this speech. Laud, he maintained, was the embodiment of all evil, and the foe of all goodness.

Thus, he concluded, 'it is not safe that such a viper should be near his majesty's person to distil his poison into his sacred ears.'[45]

In the Houses of Parliament at Westminster, and in the king's council chamber at Whitehall, Laud and all his policies fell suddenly and dramatically. The plausibility of *jure divino* bishops melted well before the winter snows of 1641, for by the spring the king had not merely rescinded the canons of the previous May, but limited the authority of diocesan chancellors. Parliament attacked the rights of deans and chapters, ordered communion rails taken down and the altar table placed in the middle of the church, they abolished the Court of High Commission and the powers of other ecclesiastical courts quickly fell into abeyance. 'I care not a straw / For the Bawdy Law,' boasted *The Pimp's Prerogative* that summer. When the incumbent at St Saviour's, Southwark, refused to remove the altar rails seven men rushed in during communion and pulled them down in a 'violent and tumultuous manner'.[46] No one, it seemed, not even Royalists, bothered to defend the archbishop or his reforms. Lay Anglicans such as Lord Falkland condemned him for 'the destruction of unity under pretence of uniformity', while friends such as Chillingworth did not mention him in their Royalist propaganda.[47] At worst cartoonists drew him as an ogre dining off a meal of Prynne's severed ears. At best contemporaries thought him irrelevant or a figure of fun. 'As for poor Canterbury,' Baillie wrote home in March, 'he is so contemptible that all cast him out of their thoughts as a pendicle at the Lieutenant's [of the Tower] care.' Some laughed when the mob attacked Laud on his way to the Tower. 'Being St Taffy's Day he had great store leeks attend him,' wrote Thomas Knyvett, 'to make him pottage this Lent.' Commentators who previously had never dared mention his lack of stature, particularly because the king was also sensitive about being short, now invariably referred to 'Little Laud'. As they cast Strafford as the villain they increasingly turned Laud into a buffoon. He became so insignificant so quickly in many people's imaginations that after Strafford's death in May 1640 it was widely believed that 'all things will run smooth', and the king 'will not stand at anything'.[48] The problem was that ending the Laudian regime, putting him out of sight and thus out of mind in the Tower, was comparatively easy – religious courts were abolished, altar rails torn down, and surplices were stored away (sometimes with potions to ward off the moths just in case they were ever needed again). Finding something to put in their place, however, was more difficult.

In normal times the outs might be expected to replace the ins, and, while people changed, policies would stay much the same. That was Laud's assumption. Thus on 28 June, after talking to Juxon, he concluded that he would never be restored to a position from which he could help his university. Accordingly he resigned the chancellorship of Oxford, writing:

My present condition is not unknown to the whole world yet by few pitied or deplored. The righteous God best knows the Justice of my sufferings, on whom both in life and death I wiil ever depend; the last of which shall be unto me most welcome, in that my life is now burdensome unto me, my mind attended with variety of sad and grievous thoughts, and soul constantly vexed with anxieties and troubles, groaning under a burden of a displeased Parliament, my name aspersed and grossly abused by the multiplicity of Libellous Pamphlets, and my self debarred from wanted access to the best of Princes, and it is a Vox Populi that I am Popishly affected.

Accepting his resignation, three days later Oxford elected the Earl of Pembroke as its new chancellor. 'God bless the university therewhile, and grant they may never have need of me, now unable to help them,' Laud noted, relieved that as he shrank into obscurity, overshadowed by great events, he was no longer a liability to the place where he had been bred up.[49]

The king's intransigence combined with pressure from outside parliament, particularly from the Scots, to destroy any chance of moderate episcopal reform. With his usual lack of tact Charles had a royal chaplain preach at court that Presbyterianism was a faith 'fit only for Tradesmen and Beggars'. Soon afterwards the king told parliament that he was utterly committed to bishops.[50] Williams, who believed that regulating episcopacy was tantamount to demolishing it, chaired a Lords committee to examine the possibility of a weak Presbyterian system in which bishops were answerable to diocesan committees of laymen and clerics. The proposal was defeated, because the pressures for total abolition were mounting so fast.[51]

They came from two sources. The first was the gigantic campaign that produced the flood of root and branch petitions. While the unpopularity of the Laudian bishops was in part responsible for engendering this massive outpouring, it explains neither the move to abolish all bishops, good and bad, Laudian, Williamites or neutrals, nor the sustained nature of this pressure, nor the fact that parliament did not finally abolish bishops until 1646, and then mainly in order to expropriate their lands to pay for the war.[52] Even Clarendon, the most astute observer of the Great Rebellion, had to explain the growth of the root and branch movement in the vaguest of terms. 'All that envy and animosity against the Church seemed to have been resolved in a desire', he wrote, 'to remove the bishops from their votes in the Lords' house, and from any office in secular affairs.'[53] People had lost faith in clerical institutions in general, as evidenced by the flood of petitions to the House of Lords in 1641 to hear ecclesiastical cases.[54] One member of parliament accused bishops of having plotted treason ever since

St Augustine's day, while another denounced them as 'prejudicial to the honour of the nobility and gentry'.[55] Bishops were not merely a flawed ecclesiastical body, but with their votes in the House of Lords they constituted a serious political block to reform, particularly as the year drew on and opposition leaders recognised that public opinion was reacting against their radicalism by swinging back to the king. Even before the outbreak in the autumn of 1641 of the Irish rebellion, with its horrid tales of Catholic atrocities, bills were introduced in parliament for the abolition of episcopacy. Charles's appointment and promotion in October of seven moderate bishops, most of whom had connections with Williams, did nothing to assuage the demands for root and branch abolition of episcopacy. By the end of the year, as the political climate worsened, mobs started to prevent the bishops from entering the Lords. When twelve of them, led by Williams, signed a petition protesting at their exclusion, a wave of indignation led to their arrest and imprisonment in the Tower. After Charles went with an armed guard to the Commons on 5 January 1642 to arrest the five leading opposition members of parliament, only to find that the birds had flown, he left the capital. Events drifted towards war, or rather the king pushed them in that direction by bringing constitutional issues to the fore. Not until after the first Civil War did episcopacy become the paramount issue it had been in 1641.

There is, of course, no doubt that episcopacy and religion played an important part in the events immediately leading up to the English Civil War. Yet Laud himself can have had no direct part in them. Imprisonment turned that harrier of Puritans, that scourge of the Feoffees, that Papist bogey into yesterday's man. It was as if the Laudian seed had been planted in the stony ground of the personal rule, only to spring up and wither way during the first heady days of the Long Parliament.[56] Admittedly 'Little Willie' was the perfect hate-figure, the ideal scapegoat upon whom the commonwealth's ills could be hung, but he was too small a force to help produce the war. Indeed, the decision to go to war, the initiative that led to the raising of the royal standard at Nottingham on 22 August 1642, came not from the opposition but from the king, who saw in war a simple solution to the complex dilemma that faced him and his realm. As Henrietta Maria put it, 'to settle affairs it was necessary to unsettle them first.'[57] Laud no longer mattered. 'The processes against the Archbishop', Sir John Coke had recognised fifteen months earlier, 'are asleep.'[58] Englishmen had far more important matters to think about than an archbishop from yesteryear.

As a prisoner in the Tower, Laud lost not just his freedom to come and go as he pleased, but the ability to direct his own life. Gradually the few powers he retained when he went into confinement were whittled away, and his finances dwindled. But for a man in his late sixties and early seventies, whose health had never been robust, he bore his predicament with remarkable fortitude.

Although he lost his liberty, Laud did not lose his office as Archbishop of Canterbury. He still had rights, particularly of appointment to clerical livings. After the Commons in late 1641 failed to deprive him of these powers, for much of the following year Laud managed to get the House of Lords to approve many of his nominations. Neither he nor the king took such a hard line on ecclesiastical matters as before. Charles, for instance, allowed the Dean and Chapter of Winchester to lease land for over three lives, while Laud accepted the petition of the parishioners of Horsham, Sussex, that Mr Conniers was 'a man unfit' to be their incumbent.[59] But when the Commons started to recommend ministers of whom he thoroughly disapproved, Laud procrastinated, and thus implemented the Henrician statute which laid down that if the archbishop failed to act the advowson would default to the king.

Matters came to a head in the spring of 1643, and involved Laud's old adversaries from Merton College, Oxford. In February Dr Heath of Merton urged Laud to appoint Edward Corbet, also of Merton, to the rich living of Chartham, Kent. A few days later the archbishop received a letter from the king, written in late January, ordering him to appoint John Reading to the living. At the end of February parliament told Laud to give it to Richard Culmer, a religious fanatic who had once urinated in Canterbury Cathedral to prove his contention that it was not the building itself, but the services celebrated therein, that were sacred. A decade earlier the archbishop had suspended Culmer from his living, although not, as might be expected, for pious pissing, but for refusing to read aloud the *Book of Sports* from his pulpit.[60] To further complicate matters, Edward Hudson claimed that he had been recommended for the post, and asked Laud to give it to him. The archbishop dug in his heels, begging the Upper House not to involve him in this distasteful matter any further, and to allow Nathaniel Brent to act on his behalf, as he had done a few months earlier with the living of St Leonard's, Foster Lane, London.

The case of Ezekiel Johnson proved to be the last straw. On 13 May 1643 he petitioned the Lords that even though they had recommended him for the living of Paulerspury, Northamptonshire, a Mr Ingram had gone to Oxford and got the king to give him a writ under the Great Seal, on the strength of which he proceeded to turn Johnson out of the rectory, sold off his corn, and forbade the parishioners to pay him tithes. Even though it seems that Johnson had been expelled from the rectory a dozen years earlier for simony, the Lords were tired of this divided and chaotic system of clerical appointments, and on 17 May 1643 they passed an ordinance suspending the archbishop's jurisdiction. A month later parliament punished Laud for his recalcitrance by confiscating his property.[61]

For a long time the archbishop, who was personally a frugal man, had been feeling the pinch of his straitened circumstances. In July 1641 he begged the House of Lords that he should be excused paying taxes, or else be assessed at the same rate as the other bishops, since he had no money. Early the next year parliament confiscated weapons worth £300 from his stores, and in the autumn ordered that all incomes due the archbishop be paid to them. Laud felt the effects immediately, having to explain to Reading that in 'these broken times' he had been only able to collect £160 of the £200 due from the rents of the Bray estates which he had promised them to help support apprentices. He would have liked to make up the difference from his own purse, he said, but it was empty.[62] Perhaps he took comfort from the report that parliament was using his rents to help support the king's children: certainly one hopes that he was not aware that the money was in fact going to pay the expenses of the Westminster assembly of Presbyterian divines.[63] On 9 November 1642 Captain Brown's company of soldiers took over Lambeth Palace, apparently without parliament's approval – or so the latter maintained. The Lords rejected Laud's request that his books be moved to a safer place for storage, and did nothing to stop the army from requisitioning his horses. More galling was parliament's appointing as Keeper of Lambeth Palace Alexander Leighton, the minister whom a dozen years before in Star Chamber Laud had voted to be imprisoned during the king's pleasure, fined £10,000, have his ears cut off, and be branded on the cheeks for insulting bishops.[64] Parliament promptly turned Lambeth Palace into a prison for their opponents, and sold off Laud's property to pay for the war (Leighton bought £37. 10s. 9d. worth, including 'an old iron pot' for four shillings, and some used lumber).[65] So the palace's once proud ex-tenant had to petition the Lords that because 'he hath neither lands, leases, nor money' they divert some income from his sequestered estates 'to supply the necessities of life'.[66]

Laud's friends had deserted him. Even Dr Duck refused Laud's nomination of him as Judge of the Prerogative Court of Canterbury to appease the popular clamour for his disgrace:

> Then there was also Doctor Duck.
> The Proverb says, What's worse than ill luck.
> We hope that this Parliament his feathers will pluck
> For being so busy, Doctor Duck.[67]

Even more painful was the loss Laud recorded on 23 September 1641: 'Mr. Adam Torless, my ancient, loving and faithful servant, then my steward, after he had served me full forty-two years, died to my great loss and grief.' Laud wondered how he could go on as his adversities mounted.[68] The following spring the sinew in his right leg snapped with a great crack as he was walking back from the Sunday sermon. At first he thought it was a broken floorboard, but when the pain came on he realised he had hurt himself just above the heel, in the same place as he had in February 1627. Laud spent two months in bed until he was able to walk downstairs with the aid of a servant and a staff to hear a sermon preached by Ralph Josselin. It was not worth the effort. Josselin 'preached with a venom, becoming Bedlam, with treason sufficient to hang him in any other state ... his personal abuse of me was so foul and palpable, that women and boys stood up in the church to see how I could bear it ... I humbly thank God for my patience.'[60] He told Sir Philip Warwick that the worst thing about being in prison was having to worship in the Puritan fashion, which was 'not against me only, but against the truth and majesty of God'.[70]

On 28 December 1641 Thomas Weld, a Puritan minister who had just returned from a ten-year stay in New England, came to see Laud in the Tower. Asked if he remembered him, Laud said he did not, until reminded that he had suspended Weld from his living at Terling, Essex. When Weld accused him of trying 'to bring Popery into the Kingdom', Laud roundly replied that Weld and his Puritan cronies 'by the Ignorance, and ... by their Railing and other boisterous Carriage would soon actually make more Papists by far than I intended, and that I was a better Protestant than he, or any of his followers'.[71] While some visitors came to gloat, others came to prey on him. For instance in February 1642, a mysterious stranger claiming to be a Mr Hunt visited him with what he claimed were further articles of impeachment. Believing he was trying to obtain a bribe in return for having them dropped, Laud threw him out of his cell, but afterwards regretted not having asked the Lieutenant of the Tower to arrest him.[72]

Gradually the conditions of the archbishop's confinement grew worse. In November 1642 parliament limited him to two servants, but after he petitioned the Lords that he was 'destitute of all company and other help' they relented by allowing him an additional cook. The following month they stopped him from walking about the Tower, ordered that he only be allowed to talk to other prisoners in the company of a warder, and that he could no longer send his servants into London to buy food or other necessities. The following May, on the Lords' instructions, Prynne went to the Tower with ten soldiers. As three men covered the door with cocked muskets, he burst into the archbishop's cell. Laud demanded to see his warrant, which Prynne showed, before searching the room and confiscating twenty-two bundles of papers, including Laud's diary and private devotions. So blatantly did Prynne admire a pair of gloves that Laud felt that he had to give them to his tormentor – who promptly claimed that they had been a bribe.[73]

Some visitors were more welcome. Laud was delighted to see Edward Pococke, the Arabic lecturer at Oxford, on his return in 1641 from studying in the Levant. Pococke told him that in Paris he had seen their mutual friend Hugo Grotius, who had urged him to escape: he himself had done so nailed up in a consignment of books.[74] Laud refused. That was what his enemies wanted: they would take it as a confession of guilt. He was too old to run. Where could he go? To France, and confirm the charges that he was a Papist? To the Low Countries, which were full of Anabaptists who hated him as much as he despised them? When an emissary from Elizabeth of Bohemia presented Her Majesty's compliments, Laud seemed most grateful.[75] But Bishop Goodman complained that when he visited the Tower 'I was saluted with a frown, crabbed words, you had not the patience to hear me, as if I were an idiot.' Goodman was further hurt by the fact that his gifts of some cheese and lamprey pies were returned, until someone explained that the archbishop was no longer allowed to receive such presents.[76]

It took Laud some time to come to terms with his imprisonment. In 1641 he felt that he had done nothing wrong in introducing the new prayer book, and that if he had it to do over again he would not change a thing. 'God quiet this storm,' he prayed later that year, 'though . . . I know not why it was rained so high against me.' Events outside the walls of the Tower impinged on him less and less. Although he noted the impeachment of Williams and the other eleven bishops, and the passage of legislation abolishing episcopacy, the outbreak of hostilities did not concern him much. When in March 1643 he learned that someone had proposed in the Commons that he be sent into exile to New England he noted that 'it appeared so foul and horrible a practice, that it was generally rejected'.[77]

Overall Laud surmounted his ever-tightening confinement remarkably well. He was growing older, and yet his health was as good as before, if not better. The issues were clearer, the villains more obvious. His self-pity had something to be sorry about, his sanctimoniousness had real suffering to justify itself, his paranoia had actual and immediate enemies to give it substance, while his faith, which even in good times possessed more than a tinge of martyrdom, now had an appropriate challenge to conquer. 'I cannot but be sensible of the great affliction that lies upon me,' he wrote, 'yet by God's mercy I have two great comforts, my innocence, and my patience.' While in a statesman escapism is usually a dangerous flaw, for a prisoner it can be a healthy protection. So too is reverting to normal tasks. Laud had been an academic and a college president. From his cell in the Tower he reviewed the regulations for the new library at St John's, went over the procedures for the care of the coin collection at the Bodleian, and tried to supervise the charities he had set up at Reading. Until Prynne stole them, he had his papers, and continued to write his diary, while working on a History of his Troubles. He also drafted a long, and massively erudite reply to Lord Say and Sele's attacks, defending the rule of bishops.[78] He read widely: the works of Galen, the ancient Greek physician, were an especial comfort. All these activities helped him to survive from day to day. And at night he could use his dreams to give vent to his worst fears, or to escape his confinement:

> Nov. 2. [1642] Wednesday Night, I dreamed that the Parliament was removed to Oxford; the Church undone; some old courtiers came in to see me, and jeered; I went to St. John's and there I found the roof off from some parts of the College, and the walls cleft, and ready to fall down. God be merciful.

> Mar. 10. [1643] Friday, this night proceeding, I dreamed a warrant was come to free me, and that I spake with Mr Lieutenant, that my warder might keep the keys of my lodging, till I had got some place for myself, and my stuff, since I could not go to Lambeth.

> I waked, and slept again, and had the same dream the second time.

And here he might have stayed, a failed, lonely old man, marooned in the Tower, as a civil war stormed across the land destroying the religious legacy he had hoped to leave. All that remained to him were his writings, a growing awareness of himself, his pedantic scholarship, and an increasing courage and tranquillity. From suffering, borne with a patience he had rarely displayed when faced with success, grew some wisdom, a personal ripeness. Here in the Tower he should have been left to die forgotten. But because his enemies decided to bring him to trial and execution, they gave him a reward far greater than any of his friends could ever have bestowed upon him. Laud had the chance of defending himself with calm dignity, and manly courage, and of winning the martyr's crown, which he wore with more honour and more distinction than the academic's hat or the bishop's mitre that had been his caps before.

XIV

'Never afraid to die, nor ashamed to live'

Westminster was the most important political theatre in the British Isles. In Westminster Palace parliament sat, while over the way in Westminster Hall, the largest room in the realm, met those ordinary courts – Common Pleas, King's Bench, Exchequer and Chancery, who, divided by chest-high partitions, and surrounded with stationers' booths, taverns and coffee houses, dispensed justice in the king's name. And here in extraordinary times justice was done to both kings and their servants. In Westminster Hall Edward II had been forced to abdicate, Richard II had been deposed, and Sir Thomas More had been tried for his life. That arch-villain Guy Fawkes was tried in Westminster Hall, which only a few years before had seen the impeachment of the Earl of Strafford, when, in many ways, the first blood of the English Civil War was drawn. Five years later it was to be the setting for the most dramatic trial of all, that of King Charles himself.

Laud was brought to trial in 1644 not in Westminster Hall, but in the smaller chamber of the House of Lords. The archbishop sat in the middle of the hall, facing the Speaker of the House of Lords, with the peers sitting on either side and to his front. Beside the prisoner, at his table, sat his warders, Black Rod and the Lieutenant of the Tower, as well as his counsel. Behind were the House of Commons, who had voted to indict him for capital crimes, while at the back of the hall were the people, the audience, to be instructed on the enormity of the prelate's offences.

Laud's trial, like all state trials, was a show trial. Its purpose was less to discover the prisoner's guilt or innocence than to reveal the heinousness of his crimes. Such a public morality play would placate the Scots, who wanted justice, or revenge, for their sufferings at the hands of the arch-bishop, and – more pertinently – for the use of their army to help rescue parliament's declining military fortunes. South of the border the trial would justify the religious changes that parliament was introducing into England by demonstrating the corruption of the old regime.[1]

For Laud, of course, it was his future and his past that were being

214

decided. Even if few people at the time took much notice, and history has not given the trial the attention it deserves, for him it was the stage on which he could justify his whole life. Not many men are burdened with such a privilege. At times the archbishop rose to the challenge with a dignity that is even more remarkable considering his age and the fact that he had been in the Tower for over three years. Too often, however, he responded with the pettiness all too characteristic of his earlier, more prosperous days. But the archbishop never forgot what the trial meant for his life, career, and place in history. 'And whatsoever the world thinks of me,' he told the court in his opening statement, 'I humbly thank Christ for it,' adding 'that I have so lived that I am never afraid to die, nor ashamed to live.'[2]

When Laud was first arrested in December 1640 it seemed to most people that he would soon meet the punishment he so richly deserved. Yet he disappeared from public attention with a remarkable speed. While he may have helped start the debate, issues changed so fast that they passed him by as he languished, an increasingly irrelevant figure, in the Tower of London. After the Commons voted the first set of impeachment articles against him in March 1641, John Pym tried to dredge up enough evidence for a conviction. Armed with a list of eighteen questions, the Commons' committee summoned Bishops Juxon and Williams from the Tower to ask them if the archbishop had ever discussed reconciliation with Rome, a felony according to the Jacobean statute. Both bishops denied any knowledge of such overtures. Illness forced Pym to hand over the investigation to his friend Oliver St John, whose committee was unable to prove anything, and so the Commons dropped the case for more pressing matters.[3]

Why then was it revived in 1643? It was not to stop the archbishop from exercising his clerical patronage, for parliament had deprived him of those rights ten months before the trial proper began. Neither was the objective of the trial the destruction of a symbol around which defenders of the Church of England might rally, for by 1643 even the most ardent Royalists had little time for the archbishop, who, in any case, had never been a charismatic figure capable of sending the church militant back into battle.

Of course, putting the archbishop on trial would be an opportunity for revealing to the world the odiousness of his policies, and how he plotted to subvert church and state and deliver them tied hand and foot to Rome. Yet by 1643 it is hard to believe that most Englishmen with minds worth making up had not come to a conclusion about such matters. The most a show trial could achieve was to make the religious innovations that parliament was enacting a little more palatable to some Englishmen. Trying Laud would doubtless please the Scots, who were pushing for these changes.[4] Yet if they demanded the archbishop's head on a parliamentary platter, they were especially coy about their desire to destroy the archbishop.

'Canterbury every week is before the Lords for his trial,' Robert Baillie wrote home in February 1644, 'but we have so much to do, and he is a person now so contemptible, that we take no notice of his process.'[5]

Laud had plenty of far more implacable enemies. No one shouted louder than the crop-eared barrister William Prynne that the archbishop must be punished. But it is difficult to credit that politicians as astute as Oliver St John, Sir Henry Vane the Younger, and William Strode, who took over the leadership of the Commons after Pym's death in December 1643, would have let a dog as mad as Prynne run wild after the archbishop of his own accord. It could be that after they unleashed him, Prynne ignored their commands to come to heel, for as Laud bitterly noted, the barrister was 'never weary of anything so he might do me mischief'.[6] More likely they never bothered to control Prynne, for the archbishop was done to death in a strange atmosphere of indifference and intense hatred that fed on the memory of wrongs done long before. For instance, Sir Henry Vane the Younger had not forgotten how harshly Laud had berated him when as an undergraduate he adopted the Puritan views that soon afterwards made him go to New England.[7] On the other hand political considerations might also have influenced the radical member of parliament, who knew that the archbishop's execution could well scupper a negotiated peace with the king, and would certainly divert people's attentions from the unpopular Solemn League and the Covenant with the Scots.[8]

Laud was tried, attainted, and executed amid the rage of civil war. It was a time when the killing of their fellow countrymen had dulled men's senses and made them indifferent to death; they needed further victims. While most people soon lost interest in the trial, Laud had made more than enough enemies bent on destroying him. All factions in the House of Commons welcomed his end, as did the Scots. The horrors of war had dulled public sensibilities so much that there was no outcry against the beheading of a seventy-one-year-old Archbishop of Canterbury. Had England after the war built a memorial to the victims of the Civil War, it might well have chosen a sombre, secluded site, with long walls of black marble, set below the contours of the land, so that the national folly might be hidden at the same time as it was commemorated. On the walls Laud's name could have been engraved, together with the names of those who had fallen at Edgehill, Naseby, and Marston Moor. And, above them all, might have been carved the epitaph that Wordsworth originally wrote for Laud:[9]

> Judged by Foes determined not to spare.
> An old weak Man for vengeance thrown aside,
> Laud in 'the painful art of dying' tried.

If by the time Laud finally went on trial he was not the unknown archbishop, then in many respects he was the irrelevant one. Parliament admitted as much on 16 May 1643 when they postponed the case indefinitely 'by reason of many great and weighty businesses'. It took the Commons five and a half more months to vote a second set of impeachment articles, which they sent to the Lords on 23 October. These elaborated on the first set of March 1641, emphasising the archbishop's crimes against the fundamental laws of the realm. On receiving them Laud requested that money from his sequestered estates might be allocated to pay for his defence, that he might have John Herne of Lincoln's Inn and Chaloner Chute of the Middle Temple as his counsel, and that he might be allowed access to his papers. This the Lords granted, appointing Matthew Hale, also of Lincoln's Inn, as the third member of the defence.[10]

Although the lawyers lost no time in getting down to business, on 31 October 1643 they had to petition the Lords for an extension to prepare Laud's defence. Immediately they touched on the major weakness of the prosecution's case by asking which of the charges were treasonable, and which were merely misdemeanours. Rather than be drawn, their lordships refused to answer, saying that they left it 'to his counsel to do and advise as his counsel shall think most fitting'. When the archbishop appeared before the Lords at ten in the morning of 13 November to answer the charges he denied his guilt. The case was continued because the prosecution was not ready. So tardy were they that four weeks later the Commons had to order them to meet to prepare the evidence 'with all the convenient speed they can'. Then it was the defence's turn to stall. They requested copies of the evidence because only three of the twenty-three bundles of Laud's papers seized by Prynne had been returned as the Lords had ordered. On 6 January 1644 the defence sought a further extension because many of Laud's witnesses, and two of his lawyers, were out of town on the 8th, the date originally set for the start of the trial. The Lords agreed, rescheduling the opening for ten in the morning of 16 January 1644.[11]

When the Lieutenant of the Tower brought the archbishop to Westminster at the appointed time, he had to wait five hours before the Lords were ready. The seventy-one-year-old prisoner was escorted to the bar of the Upper House and kept kneeling while the prosecution was summoned from the Commons. Sir John Maynard opened by arguing that the archbishop's reluctance to bring the case to trial was proof positive of his guilt. Laud replied that the articles of impeachment were too vague to warrant a clear-cut answer, and anyway he needed more time and legal help, and thus sought a postponement of a week and the services of Richard Gerrard of Gray's Inn. The Lords granted both requests, but refused once again to rule on which of the charges were treasonable. So when Laud returned to the House on 22 January – a day so cold that the Thames was frozen, and he had to come by coach – he entered a rambling plea of 'not guilty'. After having once more to order the prosecutors to stop delaying, the Commons requested the Lords to set another date for the start of the trial, which they did, choosing nine in the morning on 12 March 1644, when, after months of procrastination, it finally got underway.[12]

Leading the prosecution was John Maynard, an Oxford graduate who had been a pupil of William Noy's at the Middle Temple, and a counsel at Strafford's trial. Opinions about him varied. 'His pleadings', wrote Anthony Wood, 'were very strong yet they were fair,' while Jonathan Swift thought him 'a knave or a fool for all his law'. Assisting him was John Wilde, Member of Parliament for Worcester, who tended to let his tongue outrun his discretion. Sam Browne, a Cambridge man, was 'very bitter', thought Wood, 'and very insulting', his attacks being the ones that worried Laud the most. Wood described Robert Nicholas, another MP, as 'extremely virulent and had a foul language'. Roger Hill, the junior counsel, was used to dragoon as many witnesses as possible, no matter how unreliable, so long as they were willing to impugn the archbishop. In recruiting hostile deponents – there were plenty anxious to volunteer – he was much helped by Prynne, whose energies were exceeded only by his thirst for revenge.[13]

Of the four defending attorneys, John Herne, Chaloner Chute, Richard Gerrard and Matthew Hale, the latter was the most distinguished. Educated at Oxford and Lincoln's Inn, where he too had been a pupil of Noy's, Hale was one of those men who are drawn to the law from a sense of mission. He spent much of the 1640s defending unpopular prisoners, such as the Duke of Hamilton and Lord Maguire, giving credence to the observation that 'he would have lost all he had in the world rather than do an injustice'. John Herne, another Lincoln's Inn man, was similarly inclined, having defended Henry Sherfield, and Prynne.

The main burden of the defence, however, fell on Laud, who even before the appointment of counsel had recognised the central legal weakness of the other side's case – whether or not the charges amounted to treason. He did most of the legal research for the defence – at least as far as was possible after the seizure of his papers. During the first twenty days of the trial, after the prosecution spent each morning putting its case, he used the two-hour luncheon adjournment to work out a rejoinder which he presented in the afternoon. The notes taken by John Browne, clerk of the parliament, show that the version the archbishop wrote up each evening for *The History of the Troubles and Tryal . . . of William Laud* was fairly accurate, even though he tended to embellish and improve his statements while doing the opposite to those of the other side.

Laud was brought to the bar of the House of Lords at about three on the afternoon of 12 March 1644. After the prisoner had knelt for a little, Lord Grey of Werke, Speaker *pro tempore*, told him to rise. The clerk read out both sets of impeachment articles, as well as the accused's pleas of 'not guilty'. When Laud asked which of the charges were treasonable, Maynard answered that while the court could not give a specific answer, those relating to the subversion of religion and the fundamental laws and government of the land, plus the ones on the introduction of popery and arbitrary government, together amounted to treason. Working on the old adage 'weak point: shout!', Maynard handed over to Wilde, who launched an intemperate attack: the prisoner's crimes were many and obvious; he was 'the author of all the Illegal and Tyrannical proceedings in the Star Chamber, High Commission Courts, and all the other courts'; he had introduced popery, and pandered to Papists; he had subverted the true religion.

In contrast, the archbishop's reply was temperate and dignified. After an understandably rambling start, he found his pace, declaring that while he was not afraid to die, he was not ashamed of his life, nor would he surrender his integrity. Gathering momentum he went on to argue that the charges against him were of two main sorts, legal and religious, and attempted to make the latter subordinate to the former, if only because he felt they were the least dangerous. Perhaps his counsel advised him to follow this tactic: certainly his conscience prompted him to declare that he had been born and bred a member of the Church of England, and had never conspired to alter the religion established by law, nor supported the Church of Rome. The archbishop ended on a surprisingly maudlin note: 'Whatsoever the World may be pleased to think of me, I have led a very painful Life, and such as I would have been content to change, had I well known how.' As he was being led out of the chamber to be rowed back through the winter gloom to his cell, Hugh Peters, the Puritan minister, asked him if he were not ashamed to make such an apology. Laud seemed 'much offended' by the question, while several others called Peters 'an unmannerly saucy fellow'.[14]

During the next five days of the trial Maynard led the prosecution by focusing on the constitutional charges, such as ship money, non-parliamentary taxes, and the damage they had done to the common law. The canons of 1640 were criticised as being passed contrary to the royal prerogative, as were the *jure divino* claims of bishops. By the fourth day the prosecution was getting desperate, alleging that by pulling down the squatters' shops that had been built beside St Paul's Cathedral the archbishop had somehow subverted the fundamental laws of the realm. When a Mrs Foxley charged that Laud had refused her permission to visit her husband, Thomas, the lecturer of St Martin-in-the-Fields, in prison, he scornfully answered, ' 'Tis no treason.' To the charges made on the fifth day involving the altar at Beckington church, Somerset, the archbishop similarly replied, ' 'Tis no innovation, nor against the Law.' By the sixth day Maynard was reduced to citing trivialities such as the two tuns of sack which he alleged Laud had accepted as a bribe, and which the prisoner answered he had returned.[15]

After an initial burst the prosecution seemed to run out of steam. While the Lords heard the first six days of the case in only a fortnight, it took them over two months to hear the next five. On seven occasions they set a date for the trial and then cancelled it, usually after the prisoner had already been brought from the Tower; having kept him hanging around they would then dismiss him.[16] The House of Lords had more pressing business, for very few peers bothered to attend the trial, while the Commons' prosecution was in disarray by the time that Maynard handed over to Robert Nicholas.

Nicholas and, after he became ill in mid-May, John Wilde emphasised the familiar religious charges, including the 1640 convocation and popery. Sir Henry Mildmay and Thomas Chaloner testified that when they were in Rome they had heard people speak highly about Laud. Burton charged that at his Star Chamber trial Laud had declared that 'he did not hold his Bishopric from the King but from God'. Calling the witness 'my mortal enemy', Laud explained that if he argued that the imperial state could not stand without bishops, and 'If I said no Bishop no King, I had a very good master for it, King James'. In an equally defiant and effective riposte, he defended the Oxford statutes and justified the presence of Papist books in his study because 'we shall never answer their arguments unless we see them'. Before returning the lead to Nicholas, Sergeant Wilde summed up the prosecution's second phase by arguing that 'there was too much popery to those times and the bishops did too much usurp'.[17]

During the next eight days of the trial, held between 6 June and 24 July, the prosecution seemed to lose what little cohesion it had left, getting bogged down in a myriad of religious details. Michael Sparke, the printer, testified that Laud had favoured the publication of popish and Arminian books, while other witnesses complained that he had promoted similarly inclined men, such as Montagu, Manwaring, Neile, Wren and Cosin. The prosecution accused him of elevating the altar over the pulpit, and persuading Prince Charles to go to Madrid to court the Infanta. As they grew ever more desperate, the prosecution tried to show that idolatry was Laud's real crime. After asserting that Laud had favoured Catholicism in his doctoral thesis – Nicholas alleged that Laud was somehow responsible for obtaining the best cells for imprisoned Catholic priests. 'I hope that these men do not mean to make the Archbishop of Canterbury Keeper of Newgate,' the prisoner replied sardonically.[18]

Recognising the futility of the prosecution's tactics, on 29 July Nicholas abruptly reverted to the legal charges. But when he accused Laud of drafting speeches for the king, the archbishop replied, 'I did not know this was against the law.' He answered the allegations concerning non-parliamentary taxes by arguing that 'maintenance for a King in a monarchy are due by the law of God and the nation'.[19] On this note the court adjourned until 11 September, the prosecution's case having finally ground to a halt.

At one level it had been a confused presentation. For instance, the prosecution had attempted to link Laud with Rome through his involvement with the Habernfeld Plot, the protection of Sancta Clara (a supposedly French-born Catholic author), and the offer of a cardinal's hat on his promotion to Canterbury. Individually the charges failed to stick. Laud was able to demonstrate that he had promptly brought the Habernfeld Plot and the bribe of a cardinalate to the government's attention, and that his links with Sancta Clara were tenuous in the extreme. Even if he and Sancta Clara had been plotting with each other – a charge which Laud most emphatically denied – it did not constitute a felony, since the Elizabethan statute only applied to conspiracies with native-born Englishmen. The more than 150 witnesses who testified against the archbishop carried little conviction. Elizabeth Eaton said she had not been allowed to see her husband in prison, Alderman Chambers deposed that he had been fined £3,000 for not paying tunnage and poundage, John Miller asserted that after Laud forced him out of the ministry of the Dutch congregation at Maidstone he had to work as a brewer's clerk, while the Lord Mayor of London brought up the City's quarrel about the licensing of a part-time apple-seller in St Paul's churchyard.[20] Individually none of these acts could possibly be construed as treason, but together, argued the prosecution, they amounted to 'cumulative treasons'. The Commons took this argument, which they had advanced during Strafford's trial, one stage further during Laud's. They expanded the medieval theory – which Laud himself had put forward during Prynne's first trial – that treason included promoting disunity between king and subjects into the notion that 'treason could be against the realm as against the king'. This revolutionary idea, which was not fully developed until the trial of Charles I, owed much to the elastic nature of the basis treason statute of 1352 that permitted parliament to define additional treasons not specified in law, and which Laud apparently felt was sufficient authority for the hanging, drawing and quartering of Thomas Bensted for trying to open the Lambeth Palace gates with a crowbar during the May 1640 attack.[21]

Even Prynne had to admit that Laud's defence was remarkably skilful. It was 'as full, as gallant and as pretty a defence of so bad a case', Prynne wrote, 'as was possible for the wit of man to invent'.[22] The archbishop seemed to have developed a sense of serenity, a degree of wisdom, of self-knowledge, that is the tragic hero's reward. Even though at the height of the trial he was being treated for an abscess on his left leg, he never mentioned the ailment in his diary, which no longer contained copious details about his bodily afflictions.[23] In fact he defended himself at considerable physical cost. For instance, the strain of speaking in the Lords resulted in a 'great pain and soreness in my breast for almost a fortnight after', which sounds very much like a heart problem. It was as if, in the last act, suffering had given him the wisdom to rise above life's mortal concerns.

The defence he raised at his trial was highly pragmatic, consisting of five main strategies. First, he refused to admit any guilt about those achievements of which he was proud, such as the Oxford statutes. Second, whenever possible, he argued that his deeds were perfectly legal, constantly replying, ' 'Tis no innovation, nor against the law.'[24] Third, he frequently shifted the blame on to others, particularly corporate bodies. 'This act, be it good or bad, was the act of the High Commission Court, and not mine,' he replied to the charge that he had abused power by punishing Mr Sherfield for smashing the stained glass windows in Salisbury. 'Whatever Dr. Heylyn did let him answer for himself,' he replied to the allegation that his chaplain had brought *Histriomastix* to the authority's attention at his behest.[25] Fourth, he tried to turn the opposition's tenets back against them by, for instance, quoting Calvin to justify his belief in the real presence at Communion, stained glass windows, *The Book of Sports*, episcopacy, and even his contention that the pope was neither the Antichrist nor the Beast of Babylon.[26] His final argument was the most effective one. Relentlessly the defence tried to get the other side to define which of the charges were treasonable, and when Wilde refused to do so, arguing instead that together all the minor indictments amounted to 'cumulative treasons', they poured scorn on this novel construction. 'I crave your mercy, good Mr. Serjeant,' observed John Herne. 'I never understood before this time that two hundred couple of black rabbits would make a black horse.'[27]

It was this argument more than any other that derailed the prosecution, bringing the trial to a crashing halt. It had been a show trial that had failed to demonstrate what it had been intended to prove. The circulation of a bogus letter from the archbishop to 'my ancient friends and fellow students' (a salutation so full of *bonhomie* that anyone with the slightest knowledge of Laud would realise it was a crude forgery) convinced few people that he was prostrate with remorse at having followed Wolsey's disastrous example.[28] Even less effective was Prynne's edition of Laud's diary, which, far from turning people against the archbishop, won him considerable support. Many Puritans saw a fellow sufferer in the guilt-ridden prelate, while Ralph Josselin, who a couple of years earlier had lambasted Laud in a sermon preached before him in the Tower, noted how sorry he was to read that the archbishop had pulled his left hamstring, having himself suffered from the same injury.[29]

Nonetheless, on walking into the Lords' Chamber to start his defence on 14 September 1644, the archbishop was deeply hurt to see that Prynne had distributed newly bound, blue-covered copies of his diary. Once more he inquired which of the indictments were treasonable; three weeks later the prosecution answered weakly, 'We leave to your Lordships' judgment whether any charge be within the Statute' of 25 Edward III which defined that capital crime. Since by 11 October, the last day of the trial, the Lords' judgment was all too obvious, the Commons ended the trial and started to attaint the accused instead.[30] Few doubted what the result would be. The astrologer William Lilly consulted the stars to see 'What death Canterbury should die and when'.[31]

After his rooms had been searched for incriminating documents yet again without success, a petition that the archbishop be attainted was presented to the Commons on 28 October. Five days later he was brought before the Lower House, and after Sam Browne argued for three hours that Laud's offences together amounted to treason, the prisoner requested a postponement to formulate his reply.[32] He answered at some length on 11 November, but to little avail, for the Lower House passed his attainder with only one dissent. Four days afterwards they sent it to the Upper Chamber, where it stalled. So a fortnight later the Commons sent the Lords a message via William Strode 'that if they were not speedy' then the London mob 'would come down again to demand justice'.[33] After testily replying to this crude threat that they were proceeding as fast as they could, a committee of the Upper House met seven times, having asked for all the relevant documents on the case. On 17 December the Lords as a whole voted that while the archbishop was guilty as charged they did not think the charges treasonable at law.

To resolve the deadlock a committee of both houses met and eventually agreed that Laud's crimes were covered by the medieval statute. So two days later, on 4 January 1645, with only nineteen peers present, the Lords passed the attainder and immediately afterwards abolished the Book of Common Prayer.[34]

Somehow it all seemed in keeping with that bleak desperate winter, when the armies were preparing for the last climactic battle, and few men had any illusions left about the romance of going to war. The professional soldiers had come to the fore, those hard men in plain russet-coats or with red Cavalier sashes, who knew what they fought for and hated those who fought for the other side. It was a cruel winter, a season of vicious deeds. On 23 December Sir Alexander Carew was executed for trying to betray Plymouth to the Roundheads. On 1 January 1645 the Parliamentarians led Sir John Hotham out to be shot in the Tower for treason, and although they reprieved him at the last moment, they executed him two days later.

In such a climate of vindictiveness the pardon that the king had given Laud the previous April carried no weight. Even though Laud had been overjoyed to receive it, if only as a token that the king sometimes still thought of him, he was canny enough to return it to Oxford to have some legal technicalities straightened out. He did not produce it until 7 January 1645, saving it to the very last moment, perhaps because resorting to a pardon implied the admission of guilt.[35] The Commons brushed the pardon aside as not worth the parchment on which it had been inscribed. So bitter was the hatred towards Laud, so cruel had the Civil War become, that it took repeated petitions from the condemned, as well as the intervention of the House of Lords, to persuade the Commons not publicly to hang, castrate, disembowel, and cut the seventy-one-year-old archbishop into quarters. Instead they ordered him to be beheaded on Tower Hill on 10 January 1645, giving him less than forty-eight hours to prepare himself for the end.

In many respects Laud had been ready for death for months. His long incarceration, the execution of Strafford, the loss of friends and faithful servants, as well as the belief that those Royalists who had died in battle had given their lives for the Church of England, were a good preparation for his execution. In January 1644 he wrote his will. 'I die, as I have lived in the true orthodox profession of the Catholic Faith of Christ,' he started, 'in full assurance of the Resurrection of it from the grave at the last day. This resurrection I constantly believe my dear Saviour, Jesus Christ, will make happy unto me, his poor weary servant.' He asked to be buried under the altar at St John's, and made a generous bequest to the college 'where I was bred'. He left legacies ranging from £50 to £200 to his various nephews and nieces, and rings or watches to his chaplains. With small gifts he remembered all the parishes in which he had served as a priest. He gave Bishop Wren and Buckingham's widow Kate £100 apiece, and left the like sum to translate his 'Conference with Fisher' into Latin so that 'the Christian World may see and judge my religion'. 'I most willingly leave this world,' he concluded, 'being very weary at my very heart of the vanities of it, and my own sins many and great, and of the grievous destruction of the Church of Christ almost in all part of Christendom, and particularly in this kingdom.'[36]

It was the last will and testament of a man who knew that his life was over. And yet he fought to remain on the stage of history, defending himself with a tenacity that recalled the ambitions of youth and the determination of middle age. Although he was prepared to die, he used any legal defence to prevent his execution, combining resignation with resistance, attack with passivity. After Prynne published his diary, an agonising hurt to so private a man, the archbishop composed a soothing set of personal devotions in which he used biblical texts to confess his sins, and to ask God for His mercy and for strength.[37] If in them he resorted to banalities, to the familiar language of his youth and the daily services of the church he loved, we should not be surprised – in fox-holes originality is an even rarer commodity than atheism. On learning that the Lords had finally passed the attainder he ended *The History of the Troubles and Tryal . . . of William Laud*, giving the manuscript to a friend for safekeeping.[38] Even in the most horrible of holocausts, men have taken comfort from writing the history of their sufferings in order to make sure they were not forgotten. On 8 January Laud made a long confession of faith to his chaplain, Richard Sterne, and was much cheered when Sterne assured him that he had done nothing contrary to law.[39] Later he took Communion with his lawyer John Herne, who had managed to retrieve his copy of the prayer book that Prynne had confiscated. When Laud asked Herne to accompany him to the scaffold, the lawyer begged to be excused 'of that melancholy scene', offering instead the services of his son, also called John.

On the day before his execution the archbishop thanked parliament for sparing him from the terrible death reserved for common traitors, and requested them to allow money from his sequestered estate to be used for his burial. He spent his last day in contemplation and his last night in sound sleep, 'A most assured sign of a soul prepared', commented Peter Heylyn. On waking he prayed silently, until Isaac Pennington, London's Lord Mayor and Member of Parliament, came with a strong guard just before eleven to take him out to Tower Hill.[40]

Laud had dressed with the care to be expected of a man concerned with outward details. He wore his ordinary hat, faced with taffeta, and a new plain cloth gown, a cassock, a broad clerical girdle, and an old-fashioned suit and doublet. Underneath could be seen the traditional red waistcoat and shirt edged in red, his breeches ending in stockings just above the knee. His face was so ruddy that many who saw him walk to Tower Hill with a firm stride, patiently enduring the taunts of the crowd, thought that he must have painted it with rouge. Climbing the scaffold, he surveyed the sea of hostile faces (the crowd numbered some tens of thousands). The strain was obvious. He had to support himself on the bar at the front of the platform. He took off his hat. He put it on again.

Then he started his final sermon with what was, quite literally, a piece of gallows humour. 'This is an uncomfortable time to preach, yet I shall begin with a text from Scripture, Hebrews 12: 1, "Let us run with patience the race that is set before us." I have now come to the end of my race.' His words were conventional yet moving. He admitted that he was a sinner, and 'yet I am as quiet within as ever I was in my life'. He denied that the king had attempted to introduce popery into England: Charles was as true a Protestant as any man in the land. He professed that he had been born and bred a member of the established church, in which faith 'I come now to die. This is no time to dissemble unto God, least of all in matters of religion.'

Preaching done, all passion spent, Laud turned to private devotion. He prayed for God's strength in this difficult moment, for peace in England, for the king, his heirs and successors, for parliaments 'in their just power', and for the church. Finally he recited the Lord's Prayer. After looking out on both sides and below the scaffold several times, he gave private mementoes to friends, including eighteen ten-shilling coins, and eight crowns to John Herne. Handing a copy of the sermon to Dr Sterne, he told the public shorthand writer to make sure that he had got all his words down correctly.

By now the multitude was getting bored. Some had laughed at his speech. One oaf shouted out for his hat, saying that it would do Laud little good where he was going. So crowded had the scaffold become that the condemned man had to beg the spectators to stand back to give him 'room to die'. He put on a white skull cap and took off his doublet, his cuffs and silk girdle, and his cassock, leaving his white shirt, red waistcoat and black breeches as symbols of his martyrdom. Leaning forward to place his head on the block he noticed through chinks in the floorboards that some spectators had managed to get underneath for a better view. Wryly he asked that they might be moved so 'that his blood should not fall upon the heads of the people'. Sir John Clotworthy (the member of parliament who had proposed castrating all Jesuits) shouted out what were the most comfortable words a dying man could say? 'Cupio dissolve et esse cum Christio,' replied the archbishop, perhaps alluding to the secret guilt that had tortured him through so much of his life. When the appropriately named Clotworthy continued to harass him, Laud turned away to give the headsman some money, saying, 'Here honest fellow, God forgive thee, and I do, and do thy office upon me with mercy.'

After lying down and placing his head on the block, he told God that he was coming as fast as he could, and prayed for England and for peace. One of the executioner's assistants reached down and with a sharp knife cut the waistcoat and shirt, pulling them back to leave his short neck clear for the axe's bite. Asking God to receive his soul, Laud touched the block, the signal to the headsman. The blade came flashing down, severing the old man's head from his care-worn body in one clean sweep. 'The executioner presently took up the head, and showed the face to the people,' an eyewitness recalled. 'I saw it plainly in his hand, it looked still, even as before very fresh. It was somewhat past 12 o'clock when the blow was given.'

XV

Epilogue

On 11 January 1645, the day after the execution, as 'the greatest snow in living memory' melted, Laud's body was buried in the church of All Hallows, Barking by the Tower.[1] The coffin was unmarked – the silver nameplate was added later. The entry in the parish register recorded him as 'William Laude Archbishop of Canterbury beheaded traitor'. The vicar of All Hallows, Laud's nephew Edmund Layfield, could not conduct the service for his uncle the archbishop, since parliament had deprived him of his living and thrown him in gaol. An obscure minister, Thomas Fletcher, officiated, courageously using the outlawed prayer book. After he and the few frightened mourners threw handfuls of dirt into the grave, and the sexton closed it up, little lasting seemed to be left of the archbishop, save for his pet tortoise, a remarkably durable animal that lived for another 108 years, until killed as a result of the carelessness of a gardener at Lambeth Palace.[2]

Reaction to Laud's death was muted; few people were interested. When he told his wife of it, Sir Ralph Verney apologised for mentioning so slight an event by explaining that 'there is no news stirring'.[3] The archbishop's enemies naturally rejoiced. In *The Grand Impostor Unmasked*, Dr Burton called him 'subtle, false, traitorous, cruel . . . Satan's second child'. Nehemiah Wallington delightedly wrote to fellow Puritans in New England that 'his little grace, the Bishop of Canterbury, that great enemy of God, his head was cut off'.[4] John Dod, the divine, described Laud's sermon as 'a pitiful dry thing', while the only pleasure expressed by the parliamentary press at the news that 'The Little Firework of Canterbury was extinguished on Tower Hill' was that at last this proponent of liturgy had actually 'preached to the people'.[5] Papists rejoiced as much as Puritans, and it was reported that in Rome there was widespread pleasure at the death of their 'greatest enemy'.[6] With his customary self-centred tact, Charles told his Catholic wife (who had always hated Laud) that God would certainly punish parliament for the archbishop's murder by looking favourably upon the royal cause, before returning to negotiate in even worse faith than usual at the Treaty of Uxbridge.[7] The wild stories that might be expected during a civil war soon circulated: five weeks after the execution *A Charme for Canterburian Spirits* reported that the archbishop's ghost had appeared in several guises and places in London. In a letter of September 1645 to Bishop Cosin, Richard Stewart tried to sum up the career, character and 'martyrdom (for so it was)' of the prelate they had both known, before having to conclude, 'but whether this, and the many like truths, be fit for the pen of an historian, I must wholly leave to your judgment'.[8]

For a modern historian four themes may be used to sum up Laud's life.

First, Laud was a remarkably insecure man. Day and night he was troubled by some hidden guilty secret, the exact nature of which is much less important than the effect it had on his behaviour. Of humble birth, he exaggerated his father's status, being both ashamed and stridently proud of his origins and how far he had risen in the world. Socially and psychologically uncertain, he appeared far crueller than he really was. The sneers that 'he had been raked out of a dunghill' cut him to the quick.[9] Those, such as Peter Heylyn and Edward Hyde, who knew this essentially shy man intimately, all commented on his kindness: none kept a more orderly household than William of Canterbury. But outside the circle of that household he did not bother to cultivate people, perhaps because, as he explained, he had not the time, and since he knew that his motives were so pure he convinced himself that there was no need to do so. Laud found the social graces painful as well as unnecessary. For this reason he was a poor courtier, whose power dwindled in the late 1630s as the king became more and more dependent on his wife and her Catholic friends. A confirmed bachelor, he felt ill at ease in the world of Charles's court, where the feminine influence of the queen was so strong. To such an insecure man the belief that bishops ruled *jure divino* had an immense appeal: being answerable to God, he need not waste time answering men. This made him seem arrogant, while convincing his already outraged opponents that his claims were as blasphemous to his Maker as they were treasonable to his monarch.

It is ironic that the second theme in Laud's life should have created such an intellectual mare's nest. Laud was an academic, and as such should have been aware of the impact of ideas. But he was a college administrator rather than a scholar, keeping unruly fellows in order rather than gently leading young men to the truth. Perhaps a mild, steady pursuit of the truth was too much to expect from the scholarship boy who had, through ability and energy, hauled himself from counting house to college, and on to Canterbury and the king's council. He was relieved to escape from Oxford to London, the centre of power. He was a middle-aged man in a hurry, with the don's emphasis on principle, obsession with detail, and concern for the rightness of his cause. Believing in little, he became a True Believer in himself. He tried to assuage his frustrations at the inevitable delays, caprices and selfishnesses of government with grandiose ideals such as 'Thorough', and with evil villains such as 'Lady Mora'. During his career, ever since his student days at Oxford, Laud needed a bogeyman, someone to blame for all his ills. Ironically, for many Englishman he himself eventually became a bogeyman such as he had feared throughout his life.

Oxford helped make Laud the bureaucrat. He was an example of what happens in universities when the safe, careful men take over, when leadership passes to those who prefer the little details of bureaucracy to the challenges of scholarship and teaching. Incapable of comprehending the big picture, they focus on the little details. They make up forms, write reports, collate data, until they create a dream world in which reality has little bearing. This does not often matter. Most institutions can usually live from day to day, in the comfort of routine, rather than amidst the throes of intellectual fervour. But when a crisis comes, standing orders break down, mediocrity becomes malignancy, mistakes are compounded, and good but little men become grossly evil. In the march of folly towards the civil war, Laud blazed the way.

The fourth and last theme of Laud's life is his limits as an individual. He had been promoted far beyond his capabilities. James had enough sense to recognise this fact; Charles, whose responsibility for causing the Civil War looms even larger when viewed from a slightly different biographical perspective, did not. Laud had been a reasonably good college president, an unusually active university chancellor, who would, as S. R. Gardiner observed, have made a good 'dean of a cathedral in need of restoration'.[10] But as the archbishop's old friend Sir James Whitelocke noted sadly, this 'just and good man' was 'too full of fire'. He went so far beyond himself that eventually he was extinguished before a hostile crowd on Tower Hill.

For eighteen years the archbishop remained in his grave at All Hallows Barking, not far from the place of his execution. In July 1663, after the Restoration brought back the monarchy and the Church of England, and seemed to validate those things for which Laud had lived and died, his coffin was exhumed and taken to Oxford.

> But now our Learned Laud's to Oxford sent.
> St John's made St William's Monument.

So noted a versifier in the All Hallows parish register, where the epithet 'traitor' was scratched out from beside the archbishop's name. As requested in his will, his remains were brought privately to the university city. At ten at night, after the college gates had been locked, ten fellows of St John's escorted the coffin through the deserted streets to the college chapel. The vice-president made a solemn speech to the vice-chancellor, heads of colleges, and members of St John's, the coffin was lowered into the ground just in front of the altar. William Laud had at last come home.

Abbreviations

All dates are Old Style, with the year starting on 1 January. Unless provided by the text, citations are usually given with the date first, followed by the author, addressee, and then the reference. Manuscripts are cited by the call number. Place of publication is not given if London. To save space notes have been grouped, separated by full stops.

Add. MSS	Additional manuscripts in the British Library.
APC	J. R. Dasent, *Acts of the Privy Council of England*, 32 vols (1890–1907)
Baillie, *Letters*	*The Letters and Journals of Robert Baillie*, ed. D. Laing (Edinburgh, 1841–2)
Birch, *Court*	Thomas Birch, *The Court and Times of Charles I*, ed. R. F. Williams (1848), 2 vols
BL	British Library
Bod.	Bodleian Library
Chamberlain, *Letters*	*The Letters of John Chamberlain*, ed. N. E. McClure (Philadelphia, 1939), 2 vols
Clarendon, *History*	Edward Hyde, Earl of Clarendon, *The History of the Rebellion and Civil Wars in England*, (Oxford, 1888), 6 vols
CSP	*State Papers Collected by Edward, Earl of Clarendon*, ed. R. Scrope and T. Monkhouse, 3 vols (Oxford, 1767–86)
CSPC	*Calendar of State Papers Colonial*
CSPD	*Calendar of State Papers Domestic*
CSPI	*Calendar of State Papers, Ireland*
CSPV	*Calendar of State Papers, Venetian*

CUL	Cambridge University Library
DNB	*Dictionary of National Biography*, ed. L. Stephen and S. Lee (1885–1900), 63 vols
Folger MSS	Manuscripts in Folger Shakespeare Library, Washington, DC
Gardiner, *History*	S. R. Gardiner, *History of England, 1603–42* (1893), 10 vols
Hacket, *Scrinia*	John Hacket, *Scrinia Reserata: A memorial offered to the great deserving of John Williams* (1693), 2 parts
Heylyn, *Laud*	Peter Heylyn, *Cyprianus Anglicus, or the History of the Life and Death of William Laud* (1668)
HMC	Historical Manuscripts Commission
Hunt. MSS	Manuscripts in Huntington Library, California
Lambeth MSS	Manuscripts in the Lambeth Palace Library Record Office, London
Rawl. MSS	Rawlinson manuscripts in the Bodleian Library
Rushworth, *Collections*	John Rushworth, *Historical Collections of Private Passages of State* (1680–1701), 6 vols
SP 14–15	State Papers, James I, in Public Record Office
SP 16	State Papers, Charles I, in Public Record Office
STC	A. W. Pollard and G. R. Redgrave, *A Short Title Catalogue of Books Printed in England, Scotland and Ireland* (1969), followed by citation number
Str. P.	Strafford Papers in Sheffield Public Library
Tanner MSS	Tanner manuscripts in the Bodleian Library
Trevor-Roper, *Laud*	H. R. Trevor-Roper, *Archbishop Laud, 1573–1645* (Oxford, 1940 and 1962)
TRHS	*Transactions of the Royal Historical Society*
Wentworth, *Letters*	*The Earl of Strafford's Letters and Dispatches*, ed. W. Knowler (1739), 2 vols
Works	*The Works of the Most Reverend Father in God, William Laud*, ed. W. Scot and J. Bliss (Oxford, 1847–60), 7 vols

Notes

I 'Where I was bred up'

1 *Reliquae Sacrae Carolina* (The Hague, 1649), 262–3.
2 William G. Palmer, 'Invitation to a beheading: factions in Parliament, the Scots and the execution of Archbishop William Laud in 1649', *Historical Magazine of the Protestant Episcopal Church*, LII, 1 (March 1983), 17–27.
3 For more on this debate see R. S. Basher, *The Making of the Restoration Settlement* (1951), and Ian Green, *The Reestablishment of the Church of England* (1976).
4 Quoted by R. C. Richardson, *The Debate over the English Revolution* (177), 38.
5 T. B. Macaulay, 'Hallam's Constitutional History', *Edinburgh Review*, XCV (September 1828), 134.
6 J. B. Mozley, *Essays Historical and Theological* (1878), II, 227. W. E. Collins, *Lectures on Archbishop Laud* (1895), 124. C. H. Simpkinson, 'Laud's personal religion', in Collins, *supra*. J. Morley, *Life of W. E. Gladstone* (1903), III, 480.
7 For a summary see Trevor-Roper, 'Archbishop Laud', *History*, XXXII (September 1945), 181–90.
8 Christopher Hill, *Economic Problems of the Church* (1971), 341.
9 L. W. Cowlie, 'Liberal Christians in the seventeenth and eighteenth centuries', *The Modern Churchman*, XII (October 1969), 56–70. E. C. Bourne, *The Anglicanism of William Laud* (1947), 110. R. Ashton, *The English Civil War* (1978), 110. Stephen Foster, *Notes from the Caroline Underground* (Hamden, Conn., 1978); J. H. Timmis, *Thine is the Kingdom* (University, Alabama, 1974), 33. T. Eustace, *Statesmen and Politicians of the Stuart Age* (New York, 1985), 88.
10 K. Sharpe, 'Archbishop Laud', *History Today* (August 1983), 26–30.
11 *Works*, VI, 87.
12 Laud repeats this point in his annotations to Prynne's attacks, *Works*, III, 262. I am grateful to Daphne Phillips, County Local Studies Librarian, Berkshire, for the point on Laud senior's office holding.
13 John Bruce, *Original Letters and Other Documents Relating to the Benefactions of William Laud . . . to the County of Berks* (1841), 7.
14 Heylyn, *Laud*, 46.

15 Charles Coates, *History and Antiquities of Reading* (Reading, 1802), 227, 417.
16 Heylyn, *Laud*, 47.
17 *Works*, III, 80.
18 *Ibid.*, 234.
19 W. H. and H. C. Overall, *Analytical Index to the series of records known as the Remembrancia, preserved among the archives of London* (1878), II, 30, Alfred B. Beaven, *The Aldermen of the City of London* (1908–13), II, 41.
20 Charles Carlton, *The Court of Orphans* (Leicester, 1974), 65–81.
21 *Works*, III, 198.
22 W. G. Hoskins, 'English provincial towns in the early sixteenth century', *TRHS*, 5th series, VI (1986), 1–20.
23 N. R. Goose, 'Decay and regeneration in seventeenth century Reading: a study in a changing economy', *Southern History*, VI (1984), 53–73.
24 For more on the debate on the economic conditions of English provincial towns see *The Urban History Year Book* for 1976.
25 A. M. Stone, *English Grammar Schools in the Reign of Queen Elizabeth* (New York, 1908), 128–32. A. J. Fletcher, 'The expansion of education in Berkshire and Oxfordshire, 1500–1700', *British Journal of Educational Studies*, XV, 1 (February 1967), 51–7. Lawrence Stone, 'The educational revolution in England', *Past and Present*, 28 (July 1964), 41–80. Joan Simon, *Education in Tudor England* (1969).
26 *Victoria County History*, Berkshire, II, 245ff. *Works*, III, 473.
27 Rosemary O'Day, *The English Clergy: The Emergence and Consolidation of a Profession* (Leicester, 1979), 258.
28 L. Stone, *op. cit.*, Table 6.
29 HMC, *Fourth Report, St. John's MSS*, Appendix 1, 465.
30 Anthony Wood, *Athenae Oxonienses*, 4 vols (Oxford, 1813–20), IV, 266, 278.
31 *Works*, VII, 171.
32 HMC, *Fourth Report*, Appendix 1, 465. *Works*, III, 131–2. Anthony Wood, *History of the Colleges and Halls of the University of Oxford* (1786), I, 540.
33 Wood, *op. cit.*, III, 121.
34 *Works*, VI, 89.
35 Anthony Wood, *The Life and Times of Anthony Wood* (Oxford, 1891–1900), II, 234.
36 J. K. McConica, 'The social relations of Tudor Oxford', *TRHS* (1977).
37 *Works*, III, 132; IV, 444; VI, 238.
38 Bulstrode Whitelocke, *Memorials of English Affairs* (1682; Oxford, 1853), 75.
39 *Works*, III, 252–4.
40 Mark Curtis, 'The alienated intellectuals of early Stuart England', *Past and Present*, 23 (1973), 25–43. Ian Green, 'Career prospects and clerical conformity', *Past and Present*, 90 (February 1981), 110. A. D. Hewlett, 'The University of Oxford and the Church of England in the time of William Laud', Oxford B.Lit. (1934), 49–50.
41 HMC, *Fourth Report*, Appendix I, 465.
42 Clarendon, *History*, 165.
43 L. Stone, *An Open Elite? England, 1540–1880* (Oxford, 1984).

44 L. Stone, 'The educational revolution in England', *Past and Present*, 28 (July 1964), 41–80.
45 Lambeth MSS, 943, 97.
46 Heylyn, *Laud*, 56–9.
47 SP 14/20/53–4.
48 R. R. Winnett, *Divorce and Remarriage in Anglicanism* (1958), 106–8.
49 *Works*, III, 81. Heylyn, *Laud*, 59.
50 J. Nichols, *The Progresses, Processions and Magnificent Festivals of James the First* (1928), I, 559.
51 B. Warburton, *Memoirs of Prince Rupert and the Cavaliers* (1849), I, 436.
52 Frederick Platt, 'Arminianism', *Encyclopedia of Religion and Ethics* (Edinburgh, 1908), I, 807–16.
53 *Works*, III, 304–5.
54 *Works*, IV, 263.
55 For examples of such definitions see W. Lamont, *Marginal Prynne* (1963), 21, and the dictionaries of British history edited by S. H. Stenberg and I. H. Evans (1970), and J. P. Kenyon (1981).
56 *Works*, VI, 292.
57 *Works*, IV, 267–8.
58 J. M. Atkins, 'Calvinist bishops, church unity, and the rise of Arminianism', *Albion*, 18, 3 (Fall) 1986, 411–27.
59 N. Tyacke, 'Arminianism in England in Religion and Politics, 1604 to 1640', Oxford D.Phil. (1968). Simonds D'Ewes, The *Autobiography*, ed. J. O. Halliwell (1845), III, 65.
60 H. C. Porter, *Reform and Reaction in Tudor Cambridge* (Cambridge, 1958). Tyacke, *op. cit.*
61 Rawl. MSS, A289, 78–80.
62 C. M. Dent, *The Protestant Reformers in Elizabethan Oxford* (Oxford, 1983), 231–4. *Works*, III, 133.
63 *Works*, III, 133.
64 *CSPD, 1603–10*, 644.
65 Heylyn, *Laud*, 59–60.
66 14/5/34, Laud to Mountnorris, Str. P., 6, 71–2.

II 'I made all quiet in the college'

1 *Works*, III, 135.
2 *Ibid.*, 134. Heylyn, *Laud*, 60. Anthony Wood, *Athenae Oxonienses*, 4 vols, (Oxford, 1813–20), II, 5–6.
3 Tanner MSS, 338, 323, 329.
4 *Ibid.*, 347–9.
5 *Ibid.*, 350v.
6 *Ibid.*, 338, 340.
7 *Ibid.*, 346v.
8 *Ibid.*, 338, 351.
9 *Works*, III, 135, 172.
10 Tanner MSS, 338, 338.
11 Heylyn, *Laud*, 60–1.
12 *Works*, VII, 1–2.
13 HMC, *Fourth Report*, Appendix, p. 460.

14 William Kellaway, 'Two letters of William Laud', *Journal of Ecclesiastical History*, V (1954), 704–6.
15 SP 14/75/56–7.
16 Tanner MSS, 338, 378v.
17 W. H. Hutton, *S. John Baptist College* (1898), 95–104. Paul Morgan, 'Donations of manuscripts to St. John's College, Oxford, during the presidency of William Laud, 1611–21', *Studies in the Book Trade* (Oxford Bibliographical Soc., ns XVIII), 71–90.
18 J. F. Fuggles, 'A History of the Library of St. John's College, Oxford', Oxford B.Lit. (1975), 106, 112.
19 W. C. Costin, *William Laud, President of St. John's College and Chancellor of the University of Oxford* (Oxford, 1945), 1–8.
20 Tanner MSS, 338, 381–8. *Works*, VII, 4.
21 *Works*, VI, 88–9.
22 *Works*, VII, 3–4.
23 Heylyn, *Laud*, 68–9. SP 14/80/113 and 124.
24 Quoted by D. H. Willson, *James VI and I* (New York, 1956), 452.
25 SP 14/88/61.
26 Heylyn, *Laud*, 68–70.
27 *Works*, VI, 239.
28 *Works*, III, 135.
29 Patrick Collinson, *The Religion of the Protestants: The Church in English Society, 1559–1625* (Oxford, 1982), 90.
30 Peter Clark, ' "The Ramoth Gilead of the Good", urban change and political radicalism in Gloucester, 1540–1640', in Peter Clark, A. G. R. Smith and N. Tyacke, *The English Commonwealth* (New York, 1977), 167–88.
31 John Phillips, *The Reformation of Images* (Berkeley, 1973), 155.
32 *CSPD, 1611–18*, 435.
33 SP 14/90/82.
34 *Works*, VI, 240–1.
35 *CSPD, 1611–18*, 439. Heylyn, *Laud*, 75.
36 *Works*, III, 135. Chamberlain, *Letters*, II, 82.
37 SP 15/93/161.
38 Brian Taylor, 'William Laud, Dean of Gloucester, 1616–21', *Bristol and Gloucester Archaeological Society Transactions*, LXXVII (1958), 85–95.
39 *Works*, III, 136.
40 *Ibid.*, 80–5.
41 *Ibid.*, 136.
42 *Ibid.* Heylyn, *Laud*, 83. J. A. Robinson, 'Westminster Abbey in the early part of the seventeenth century', *Proceedings of the Royal Institution*, XVII (1904), 519ff.
43 HMC, *Third Report*, 18.
44 *Works*, I, 6–10; III, 136. Chamberlain, *op. cit.*, II, 391.
45 Hacket, *Scrinia*, 64.
46 N. Tyacke, 'Arminianism and English culture', *Britain and the Netherlands*, VI (1981), 97.
47 Rawl. MSS, A441, 89.
48 Clarendon, *History*, I, 418.
49 Hacket, *Scrinia*, 8.
50 For example, see his advice to join the parliamentary campaign to impeach Bacon and abolish monopolies. Hacket, *Scrinia*, I, 50.

51 G. W. Thomas, 'Archbishop John Williams', Oxford D.Phil. (1974), 119.
52 Roger Lockyer, *Buckingham: The Life and Career of George Villiers, First Duke of Buckingham, 1592–1628* (1981), 69.
53 SP 14/88/61.
54 Gardiner, *History*, IV, 139.
55 *Works*, III, 136–7.
56 SP14/122/94.

III 'Pastors, labourers, and watchmen'

1 Heylyn, *Laud*, 8.
2 Patrick Collinson, *The Religion of the Protestants: The Church in English Society, 1559–1625* (Oxford, 1982), 23. H. R. Trevor-Roper, 'King James and his bishops', *History Today*, V (September 1955), 571–81.
3 Felicity Heal, *Prelates and Princes: A Study of the Economic and Social Positions of the Tudor Episcopacy* (Cambridge, 1980), 316–18.
4 *Works*, I, 33–59.
5 Heylyn, *Laud*, 86–8. Rushworth, *Collections*, I, 61.
6 Chamberlain, *Letters*, II, 434. CSPD, *1619–23*, 379.
7 Gardiner, *History*, IV, 298.
8 Rushworth, *Collections*, I, 64–5. *Works*, III, 138.
9 Hacket, *Scrinia*, I, 88.
10 Thomas Mason, *Serving God and Mammon* (Newark, Del., 1985), 32.
11 Charles 1, *Letters*, ed. C. Petrie (1968), 8.
12 Roger Lockyer, *Buckingham* (1981), 22.
13 Arthur Wilson, *The History of Great Britain, being the Life and Reign of King James the First* (1653), 147.
14 Gardiner, *History*, III, 98.
15 CSPV, *1621–3*, 88.
16 Heylyn, *Laud*, 95.
17 *Works*, III, 138–9.
18 *Ibid.*
19 W. H. Hutton, *William Laud* (1895), 20.
20 *Works*, V, 377–95. W. L. Bevan, *Diocesan History of St. David's* (1888), 198–9.
21 Kevin Sharpe, *Sir Robert Cotton* (1979).
22 It took a letter from Laud and five years before Cotton returned the manuscript, and even then he retained part of it, which is now in the British Library: Cott. MSS, nero, C.vii, 80–4. J. F. Fuggles, 'A History of the Library of St. John's College, Oxford', Oxford B.Lit. (1975), 129.
23 Quoted by Hutton, *op. cit.*, 146.
24 Patrick, J. Ryan, *The Ecclesiology of William Laud* (Rome, 1964), xv.
25 31/10/34, *Works*, VII, 95.
26 *Works*, III, 157.
27 *Works*, II, 141.
28 *Ibid.*, 159.
29 W. B. Patterson, 'King James I's call for a Ecumenical Council', *Studies in Church History*, IX (1972), 267–75.
30 *Works*, II, 346.
31 This view saved Prince Philip from having to be baptised into the Anglican

Church before his marriage to Princess Elizabeth. 'In the Church of England we have always been ready to minister to the members of the Orthodox Church,' Archbishop Fisher to King George VI, D. Judd, *Prince Philip* (1979), 124.

32 *Works*, II, 103.
33 *Ibid.*, 143.
34 *Ibid.*, 402.
35 My thanks to Michael Novak for this point.
36 *Works*, II, 71–2.
37 *Ibid.*, 426.
38 *Works*, III, 415.
39 *Works*, II, xv.
40 J. P. Sommerville, 'The royal supremacy and episcopacy "jure divino", 1603–40', *Journal of Ecclesiastical History*, 34, 4 (October 1983), 548–58.
41 John New, *Anglican and Puritan: The Basis for Their Opposition* (1964), 55–6, 147. Collinson, *op. cit.*, 18.
42 Sommerville, *op. cit.*, 550.
43 E. C. Bourne, *The Anglicanism of William Laud* (1947), 96.
44 *Works*, I, 94. James I, *Works* (1616), 529–31.
45 *Works*, I, 85.
46 *Works*, II, 150.
47 *Works*, I, 5–6.
48 *Works*, VI, 449.
49 *Works*, II, 91, 137.
50 *Ibid.*, 233–54.
51 Quoted by David Hoyle, 'A Commons investigation of Arminianism and popery at Cambridge on the eve of the Civil War', *Historical Journal*, 29, 2 (1986), 425.
52 A good summary of the debate over religious labels is to be found in M. G. Findlayson, *Historians, Puritanism and the English Revolution* (Buffalo, NY, 1983).
53 E. Bourchier, *The Diary of Sir Simonds D'Ewes* (Paris, 1974), 185.
54 *Works*, III, 159.
55 *Ibid.*, 147.
56 *Ibid.*, 140.
57 *Ibid.*, 141.
58 *CSPD, 1619–21*, 191. *Works*, III, 144. Robert Ruigh, *The Parliament of 1624: Politics and Foreign Policy* (Cambridge, Mass., 1971), 139.
59 Clarendon, *History*, I, 120.
60 *Works*, III, 143.
61 *Ibid.*, 76.
62 Hacket, *op. cit.*, I, 118 and 144.
63 94/26/249. SP 94/28/40.
64 K. Fincham and P. Lake, 'The ecclesiastical policy of James I', *Journal of British Studies*, 24, 2 (1985), 169–207.
65 *Works*, III, 143. In quoting from Laud's diary I have given the obvious abbreviations in full.
66 *Ibid.*, 144.
67 *Ibid.*, 145–6.
68 Rawl. MSS, 392, 356ff. BL Add. MSS, 6469, 208.
69 *Works*, III, 147.

70 Hacket, *Scrinia*, I, 169.
71 Conrad Russell, *Parliament and English Politics, 1621–29* (1979), 164.
72 *Works*, III, 151. Heylyn, *Laud*, 120.
73 Heylyn, *Laud*, 127.
74 S. R. Gardiner, *Debates in the House of Lords . . . 1624 and 1626* (Camden Society, 1879), 95.
75 *Works*, III, 157.
76 *Works*, VI, 1–5.
77 *Ibid.*, 243–4.
78 CUL MSS, Mn IV, 57, no. 12, 280.
79 Heylyn, *Laud*, 131–2.
80 SP 16/1/31.

IV 'A cloud arising'

1 *Works*, III, 159–60.
2 Anthony Wood, *Athenae Oxonienses*, 4 vols (Oxford, 1813–20), II, 349.
3 *Works*, III, 180.
4 Hacket, *Scrinia*, II, 4–5.
5 Clarendon, *History*, I, 82.
6 I. Morgan, *Prince Charles' Puritan Chaplain* (1957), 154–7, argues that Charles and not Buckingham was behind Laud's rise. 15/4/25, Pesaro to Doge, *CSPV, 1625–6*, 25. 17/4/25, Matthew to Carleton, SP 16/1/67. 23/4/25, Salvetti to Florence, HMC, *Skrine*, 10.
7 *APC, 1625–6*, 13. 9/4/25, Chamberlain to Carleton, Chamberlain, *Letters*, II, 609. 13/4/24, Meddus to Meade, Birch, *Court*, I, 10.
8 SP 16/1/31.
9 *Works*, III, 166–7.
10 7/5/25, Chamberlain to Carleton, Chamberlain, *Letters*, II, 616–17. J. Nicholas (ed.), *The Progresses . . . of James the First* (1828), IV, 1040–9.
11 *Works*, I, 93–117.
12 H. Schwartz, 'Arminianism and the English Parliament, 1624–1629', *Journal of British Studies*, 12 (1973), 41–62. C. Bangs, 'All the best bishops and deaneries: the enigma of Arminian politics', *Church History*, XLII (March 1973), 5–16. Peter White, 'The rise of Arminianism reconsidered', *Past and Present*, 101 (November 1983), 34–54. K. L. McElroy, 'The Life and Work of William Laud with Special Reference to His Social and Political Activities', Oxford D.Phil. (1943), 191–212. N. Tyacke, 'Arminianism in England in Religion and Politics, 1604–40', Oxford D.Phil. (1968), 159ff.
13 Gardiner, *History*, V, 254.
14 Schwartz, *op. cit.*, 41–2. I am most grateful to W. Brown Patterson for letting me read a draft of his paper, ' "The Making up of the Rent of our Reformation": King James and the Reformed Synod of Dort'.
15 K. Fincham and P. Lake, 'The ecclesiastical policies of James I', *Journal of British Studies* 24, 2 (April 1985), 190–9.
16 *Works*, VI, 244–6.
17 *Works*, II, 174.
18 *Works*, III, 171–2.
19 *Ibid.*, 169.
20 *Ibid.*, 172.

21 Hacket, *Scrinia*, II, 27. *CSPV, 1625–6*, 290.
22 *Works*, III, 100.
23 Heylyn, *Laud*, 144–5. *Works*, III, 180–2.
24 *Works*, III, 182. Sir William Sanderson, *A Compleat History of the life and raigne of King Charles* (1658), 25.
25 Tyacke, *op. cit.*, 192–208. McElroy, *op. cit.*, 309ff.
26 Rawl. MSS, D 392, 356ff.
27 *Works*, I, 61–90. Heylyn, *Laud*, 145–6.
28 Chamberlain, *Letters*, II, 625.
29 Conrad Russell, *Parliaments and English Politics, 1621–1629* (1979), 313.
30 Trevor-Roper, *Laud*, 443.
31 *Ibid.*, 444.
32 22/5/26, Meddus to Meade, Birch, *Court*, I, 105. Heylyn, *Laud*, 153.
33 *Works*, III, 189.
34 *Ibid.*, 126–7.
35 BL, Sloane MSS, 1775, 23ff.
36 CUL MSS, Patrick, 22, 7.
37 Sir Simonds D'Ewes, *Autobiography* (1845), I, 388.
38 Trevor-Roper, *Laud*, 445–6.
39 Heylyn, *Laud*, 159.
40 *CSPD, 1625–6*, 570.
41 *Works*, I, 118–47.
42 SP 16/116/11.
43 31/9/26, Laud to Scudamore. Trevor-Roper, *Laud*, 449.
44 *Works*, III, 196. See also Birch, *Court*, I, 155.
45 14/7/26, Laud to Scudamore, Trevor-Roper, *Laud*, 446.
46 M. Stieg, *Laud's Laboratory: The Diocese of Bath and Wells in the Early Seventeenth Century* (1983).
47 P. Hemby, *The Bishops of Bath and Wells* (1963), 220–1.
48 Heylyn, *Laud*, 161–4.
49 John Cosin, *Correspondence*, ed. G. Ornsby (Surtees Soc., 1869), I, xxii, 144–5; VI, 300–3.
50 Heylyn, *Laud*, 161–4.
51 *Works*, III, 116.
52 *Ibid.*, 197.
53 H. L'Estrange, *The Reign of King Charles* (1655), 75.
54 Rushworth, *Collections*, 423.
55 *Works*, III, 204.
56 Rushworth, *Collections*, I, 445.
57 Gardiner, *History*, VI, 207–9.
58 Heylyn, *Laud*, 162.
59 *Works*, III, 198–204.
60 Trevor-Roper, *Laud*, 455.
61 *CSPD, 1627–8*, 235.
62 *Cabala sive scrinia sacra* (1691), 111.
63 *Works*, VII, 8, 12–14.
64 *Ibid.*, 8–11. *CSPD, 1627–8*, 317.
65 CUL MSS, Add. 22, 7 and 23, 37.
66 14/5/28, 27/10/28, 15/12/28, Charles to Pembroke, SP 16/103/89, SP 16/119/34, SP 16/122/43. Heylyn. *Laud*, 194. *Works*, VII, 637–9.
67 *Works*, VII, 12–14. Woodward to Windebank, *CSPD, 1627–8*, 575.

68 *CSPD, 1627–8,* 449–50, 454.
69 16/11/27, ? to Meade, Birch, *Court,* I, 285. *CSPD, 1628–9,* 240.
70 *Works,* I, 149ff.
71 Rushworth, *Collections,* I, 149.
72 10 and 27/3/28, Charles I, *Bibliotheca Regia* (The Hague, 1649), 25–6, 37–9. R. C. Johnson *et al., Commons' Debates in 1628* (New Haven, Conn., 1977), 3, 316. *CSPV, 1626–9,* 66–7.
73 SP 16/94/88–9.
74 SP 16/96/31.
75 SP 16/102/47.
76 M. F. Keeler *et al., Lords' Proceedings, 1628* (New Haven, 1985), 600–2.
77 *Ibid.,* 148.
78 *Ibid.,* 30, 148.
79 Richard Corbet, *Works* (1955), 82.

V 'Nothing but trouble and danger'

1 Laud to Scudamore, 19/7/28, Trevor-Roper, *Laud,* 455.
2 *Works,* VII, 14–15.
3 Heylyn, *Laud,* 174.
4 John Milton, 'On Reformation Touching Church Discipline in England', *Works,* ed. W. T. Hales (New Haven, Conn., 1916), 21.
5 John Cosin, *Correspondence,* ed. G. Ornsby (Surtees Soc., 1869), I, 154.
6 *Works,* V, 399–415.
7 Ogbu Kalu, 'Continuity and change', *Journal of British Studies* (Fall 1978), 28–45.
8 My thanks to my colleague Ray Camp for the information on Essex.
9 P. M. Olander, 'Censorship of the Press during the Personal Rule of Charles I', Oxford B.Lit. (1976), 35. Franklin Williams, 'The Laudian imprimatur', *Library,* 29 (1966), 98–104.
10 Lambeth MSS, codex misc, 942, 139.
11 *Acts of the Privy Council, 1630–31,* lll. F. Larkin, *Stuart Royal Proclamations* (1983), II, no. 37, 59, 82, 106.
12 R. Aston, *The City and the Court* (Cambridge, 1979), 195.
13 BL, Sloane MSS, 2728B, 19.
14 Heylyn, *Laud,* 224.
15 Rushworth, *Collections,* II, 76–7.
16 SO 16/114/231. Birch, *Court,* I, 368–9. John Rous, *Diary,* ed. M. A. E. Green (Camden Soc., 1856), 19. William Powell, *John Pory* (Chapel Hill, NC, 1976), microfiche 126.
17 Sir Henry Wotton, *Short View of the Life and Death of George Villiers, Duke of Buckingham* (1642), 25.
18 26/8/28, Laud to Conway, *Works,* VII, 15–16.
19 6/9/28, Laud to Charles, *Works,* VII, 16–18.
20 28/10/28, *Works,* VI, 255.
21 Trevor-Roper, *Laud,* 456.
22 Heylyn, *Laud,* 187.
23 Anthony Weldon, *The Court of King Charles* (1650), II, 48.
24 27/8/28, Carleton to Elizabeth of Bohemia, SP16/114/10.
25 Rushworth, *Collections,* I, 651.

26 W. Notestein and F. Relf, *Commons Debates for 1629* (Minneapolis, 1921), 58, 100, 122.
27 Rushworth, *Collections*, II, 2.
28 *CSPV, 1628–9*, 589.
29 SP 16/140/55.
30 *Works*, VII, 30–1.
31 *Works*, III, 210. Rushworth, *Collections*, I, 662.
32 *CSPD, 1628–9*, 501, 528, 547.
33 *APC, 1628–9*, 1219–20. *Works*, VI, 22.
34 *CSPV, 1629–32*, 448.
35 *Works*, VII, 19, 23.
36 12/9/30, Laud to Dr Pinke, *Works*, VI, 289.
37 24/1/29, 16/6/29, Laud to Ussher, *Works*, VI, 258, 260–2.
38 SP 16/152/4.
39 Gardiner, *History*, VII, 21–3. SP 16/153/41–3.
40 SP 16/143/100–5. Rushworth, *Collections*, II, 7. BL, Sloane MSS, 1775, 74. *Works*, VII, 23–4, 27–8. *CSPD, 1629–31*, 118.
41 *Works*, VI, 265. Gardiner, *History*, VI, 124–5.
42 *Works*, IV, 303.
43 *Works*, III, 217. Christopher Hill, *Economic Problems of the Church from Archbishop Whitgift to the Long Parliament* (Oxford, 1956), 258–64. Isabel Calder, *The Activities of the Puritan Faction in the Church of England* (1957). Trevor-Roper, *Laud*, 4, 108. G. E. Gorman, 'A London attempt to "tune the pulpit": Peter Heylyn and his sermon against the Feoffees for the purchase of impropriations', *Journal of Religious History*, VIII, 9 (1975), 333–49.
44 Rushworth, *Collections*, II, 32. Paul Seaver, *The Puritan Lectureships: The Politics of Dissent* (Stanford, 1970), 248–9.
45 Rushworth, *Collections*, II, 55–7. H. E. I. Phillips, 'The last years of the Court of Star Chamber, 1630–41', *TRHS*, 4th series, 21 (1939), 120.
46 F. Short, *The City of Salisbury* (1957), 70.
47 *Works*, VI, 17–21. Paul Slack, 'Religious protest and urban authority: the case of Henry Sherfield', *Studies in Church History*, 9 (1972), 295–301.
48 *Works*, VI, 234–7.
49 *Works*, III, 221.
50 Heylyn, *Laud*, 264.
51 Bulstrode Whitelocke says that it was Laud who got Heylyn to first bring *Histriomastix* to his attention formally; See Whitelocke, *Memorials of English Affairs* (1682; Oxford, 1853), 18.
52 S. R. Gardiner, *Select Cases in the Star Chamber and the High Commission* (Camden Soc., 1886), 270–1.
53 *Works*, VI, 234.
54 Gardiner, *Select Cases*, 303.
55 *Ibid.*, 180. For another similar case see p. 244 below.
56 Heylyn, *Laud*, 198.
57 S. Foster, *Notes from the Caroline Underground* (Hamden, Conn., 1978).
58 E. W. Kirby, *William Prynne: A Study in Puritanism* (Cambridge, Mass., 1931), 32.
59 Birch, *Court*, II, 120.
60 *Works*, I, 167.
61 Claire Cross, *Church and People, 1450–1660* (1976), 190.

62 CSPD, *1629–31*, 524. Anthony Weldon, *The Court and Character of King James* (1651), 203.
63 Wentworth, *Letters*, I, 31.
64 S. P. Salt, 'Thomas Wentworth and Parliament, 1620–29'. *Northern History*, XVI (1980), 131–68. P. Zagorin, 'Did Strafford change sides?', *English Historical Review*, CI, 398 (June 1986), 149–63.
65 Str. P., 20, 112v.
66 23/1/36, *Works*, VII, 238.
67 *Works*, VI, 326; VII, 410.
68 *Works*, VII, 233.
69 CSPD, *1633–4*, 72.
70 SP 16/234/1.
71 The statue is at present on a traffic island on the south side of Trafalgar Square: *CSPD, 1633–4*, 43.
72 *Works*, VII, 38–9.
73 23/10/37, Conway to Wentworth, Wentworth, *Letters*, II, 124.
74 *Works*, III, 215–16.
75 *Ibid.*, 211. Heylyn, *Laud*, 198.
76 15/10/30, Laud to Potter, *Works*, VI, 291.
77 7/12/30, Laud to Ussher, *Works*, VI, 266–8.
78 26/1/30, Laud to Carleton, *Works*, VII, 35–6.
79 23/2/30, Laud to Ussher, *Works*, VI, 270.
80 13/6/32, *Works*, VII, 43–4.
81 Clarendon, *History*, I, 119.

VI 'The little man is come up trumps'

1 See for example Kilvert to Lambe, 28/8/33, *CSPD, 1633–4*, 196.
2 Gordon Albion, *Charles I and the Court of Rome* (1935) 148.
3 *Works*, III, 219. C. Giblin, 'Aegidus Chaissy, VFM, and James Ussher, Protestant Bishop of Armagh', *Irish Historical Record* (1956), 394, suggests that Chaissy was behind the offer.
4 CSPD, *1633–4*, 207. *Works*, III, 219.
5 22/8/33, Birch, *Court*, I, 277. *CSPV, 1632–6*, 148.
6 *Works*, III, 219.
7 12/9/33, *Works*, VII, 50–1.
8 9/9/33, *Works*, VI, 310–12.
9 8/9/33, Lambeth MSS, 943, 225.
10 18/9/33, SP 16/246/49.
11 HMC, *De La Warr*, 291.
12 SP 16/278/44. K. L. McElroy, 'The Life and Work of William Laud, with Special Reference to His Social and Political Activities', Oxford D.Phil. (1943), 230.
13 Trevor-Roper, *Laud*, 197–200. SP 16/286/85. Rushworth, *Collections*, II, 272–3. Peter Clark, *English Provincial Society* (1977), 366. *Works*, V, 323; VI, 23–8; VII, 134.
14 Trevor-Roper, *Laud*, 197. W. K. Jordan, *The Development of Religious Toleration in England* (1940), 111, 142.
15 *Laud*, VI, 432. F. Heal, 'The Archbishops of Canterbury and the practice of hospitality', *Journal of Ecclesiastical History*, XXXIII (1982), 544–63.

16 *Laud*, VI, 25. K. L. Sprunger, 'Archbishop Laud's campaign against Puritans at the Hague', *Church History*, 44, (1975), 308–20.
17 *Works*, VI, 12–14.
18 *CSPD, 1631–3*, 575.
19 Heylyn, *Laud*, 230–3, 275. *CSPD, 1634–5*, 225.
20 *Works*, VI, 380–1. Rushworth, *Collections*, II, 249–51.
21 21/6/34, Laud and Juxon to Delft, SP 16/270/3. Trevor-Roper, *Laud*, 248–50.
22 *DNB*.
23 *Works*, VI, 528.
24 *Ibid.*, 141.
25 *CSP Colonial, 1574–1660*, 302–3.
26 McElroy, *op. cit.*, 243–4. Charles F. Adams, *Three Episodes of Massachusetts History* (New York, 1892), I, 271–3. *CSPC, 1574–1660*, 259. Rushworth, *Collections*, 409.
27 7/3/30, *Works*, VI, 280.
28 Heylyn, *Laud*, 208.
29 11/9/30, Laud to Bedell, *Works*, VI, 285.
30 H. Kearney, *Strafford in Ireland, 1633–41: A Study in Absolutism* (Manchester, 1959), 122–3. Christopher Hill, *Economic Problems of the Church* (Oxford, 1956), 23.
31 Str. P., 20, 121.
32 *Ibid.*, 6, 157.
33 *Works*, VI, 418.
34 Hill, *op. cit.*, 355. Str. P., 6, 30.
35 Lambeth MSS, 943, 525.
36 Laud to Wentworth, 14/10/33, *Works*, VI, 322.
37 *Concilia Magnae Britanniae et Hibernae*, IV, 496–516.
38 J. W. Stubbs, *The History of the University of Dublin from 1591 to 1800* (Dublin, 1889), 73–6.
39 8/4/36, *Works*, VII, 247–8.
40 *Works*, VI, 467. For other examples see John Bramhall, *Works* (1842–5), I, lxxix, and T. Carte, *The Life of James Duke of Ormond* (Oxford, 1851), I, 49–51.
41 Kearney, *op. cit.*, 216–33. J. P. Cooper, *Land, Men and Beliefs* (1983), 184.
42 *Works*, VII, 647.
43 For more on this see, for example, M. Edelman, *Politics as Symbolic Action* (New York, 1971).
44 Keith Thomas, *Religion and the Decline of Magic* (Oxford, 1971), 148.
45 ?/6/31, SP 16/195/32.
46 Lambeth MSS, 943, 361–3.
47 SP 16/229/116.
48 *CSPD, 1635*, 234.
49 Charles I, *Bibliotheca Regia* (The Hague, 1649), 280–8.
50 Trinity College, Cambridge, MSS, Cullum, 631. Bod. MSS, Rawl., B, 372, 15. *CSPD, 1633–4*, 477, Lambeth MSS, Laud's Register, 200v. *Works*, VI, 344–5.
51 Clarendon, *History*, I, 372. Draft letter in Dell's hand, SP 16/281/34.
52 M. Stieg, *Laud's Laboratory: The Diocese of Bath and Wells in the Early Seventeenth Century* (1983), 305. *CSPD, 1624–34*, 527.

53 Thomas Mason, *Serving God and Mammon: William Juxon, 1582–1663* (Newark, Del., 1985), 78–81.

54 Sir William Sanderson, *A Compleat History of the life and raigne of King Charles* (1658), 118. Trevor-Roper, *Laud*, 346, 351.

55 Lambeth MSS, 943, 475.

56 Str. P., 6, 63–4.

57 *Works*, VI, 478.

58 J. Phillips, *The Reformation of Images: The Destruction of Art in England, 1535–1660* (Berkeley, 1973), 155. G. W. O. Addleshaw and H. Etchells, *The Architectural Setting of Anglican Worship* (1948), 108–46.

59 H. T. Blethen, 'Bishop Williams, the altar controversy and the royal supremacy', *Welsh Historical Review*, 9 (1978), 142–54.

60 *Works*, VI, 23–8. Heylyn, *Laud*, 294.

61 SP 16/250/12.

62 Stieg, *op. cit.*, 297–306. J. A. Robinson, *Documents of the Laudian Period* (Somerset Record Society, 43, 1929), 185.

63 Lambeth MSS, 943, 500.

64 *Works*, V, 367.

65 J. M. Batten, *John Dury, Advocate of Christian Reunion* (Chicago, 1941), 23–61. Conrad Russell, 'Arguments for religious unity in England, 1530–1650', *Journal of Ecclesiastical History*, XVIII, 2 (October 1967), 201–26.

66 HMC, *Fourth Report*, Appendix 1, 160.

67 HMC, *Braye*, 133. CSPD, *1633–4*, xxvi–xxxviii, 509.

68 *Works*, II, 19.

69 23/4/34, Laud to Anstruther, HMC, *Braye*, 131.

70 H. T. Blethen, 'Bishop John Williams and Dissent, 1611–1637', University of North Carolina at Chapel Hill, PhD (1972), 167.

71 CSPD, *1635*, xxi. CSPD, *1637*, 505. *Works*, VII, 417.

72 A. Fletcher, *A Country Community in Peace and War: Sussex, 1600–1660* (1975), 86.

73 I am most grateful to Christopher Haigh for sharing with me (over a most delightful meal at the Rocks in Sydney), his work on the Laudian church.

74 *Works*, VI, 57.

75 Hill, *op. cit.*, 141.

76 24/8/33, Laud to Coke, HMC, *Cowper*, II, 31.

77 Hill, *op. cit.*, 112, 203.

78 William Harrison, *Description of England*, ed. F. J. Furnivall (1978–81), 23.

79 *Works*, VI, 488–9. Draft in Laud's hand of letter from king, CSPD, *1634–5*, 342.

80 Lambeth MSS, 943, 329 and 333.

81 SP 16/270/6. Lambeth MSS, 943, 341, 354–6. *Concilia Magnae Britanniae et Hibernae*, IV, 494, 556–7. Charles I, *Letters* (1935), 88–90. CSPD, *1637–8*, 18. *Works*, VI, 389–90. F. Heal, 'Archbishop Laud revisited: leases and estate management at Canterbury and Winchester before the Civil War', in R. O'Day and F. Heal, *Princes and Prelates* (Leicester, 1981), 129–51.

82 R. Ashton, *The City and the Court, 1603–43* (Cambridge, 1979), 190–2.

83 Paul Seaver, *The Puritan Lecturerships* (Stanford, 1970), 146. Mason, *op. cit.*, 68ff. Hill, *op. cit.*, 275–9.

84 Hill, *op. cit.*, 205.
85 4/10/35, Laud to Wentworth, *Works*, VII, 173.
86 18/1/37, Laud to Wentworth, *Works*,, VII, 309.
87 16/8/37, Laud to Bramhall, HMC, *Hastings*, IV, 55, 70. HMC, *Wells*, II, 414.
88 *Works*, VII, 24–6, 29–33.
89 17/7/35, Laud to Williams, *Works*, VI, 430–1.
90 Seaver, *op. cit.*, 141.
91 P. Collinson, 'Lecturers by combination: structures and characteristics of church life in seventeenth century England', *Bulletin of the Institute of Historical Research*, XLVIII (1975), 182–213.
92 *Bibliotheca Regia* (The Hague, 1649), 238–40. Rushworth, *Collections*, II, 191–3. L. A. Govett, *The King's Book of Sports* (1890), 117.
93 Clark, *English Provincial Society*, 365.
94 PRO, PC2/44/272.
95 It's a good story, told in several instances: 6/12/34, Gerald to Wentworth, Wentworth, *Letters*, I, 166.
96 Lambeth MSS, 943, 129.
97 *CSPD, 1637–8*, 389.
98 J. M. Potter, 'The Ecclesiastical Courts in the Diocese of London', London M.Phil. (1973), 2, 125, 207–11. G. R. Quaife, *Wanton Wenches and Wayward Wives* (1979). *Works*, I, 80–2.
99 SP 16/277/161. SP 16/361/33 and 39.
100 Laud, *Works*, VI, 490–1.
101 Heylyn, *Laud*, 342. F. Larkin, *Stuart Royal Proclamations* (1983), II, 572–4.
102 Laud, *Works*, VII, 121.
103 E. R. C. Brinkworth, 'The Laudian church in Buckinghamshire', *University of Birmingham Historical Journal*, V, 1 (1955), 31–59, argues that the effects of his 1634 visitation in the county were lasting. It is hard to see how they were.
104 Sears McGee, 'Laud and the outward face of religion', *Leaders of the Reformation* (1984), 318–44.
105 J. T. Cliffe, *The Puritan Gentry* (1984), 81.
106 *CSPD, 1635*, xxx–xlv.
107 Fletcher, *op. cit.*, 85.
108 Laud, *Works*, V, 301–70.
109 HMC, *Hastings*, V, 62.
110 M. D. Slatter, 'A Biographical Study of Sir John Lambe, *c.* 1566–1646', Oxford B.Lit. (1952).
111 Hacket, *Scrinia*, II, 98.
112 24/2/27, Mead to Stuteville, Birch, *Court*, I, 199. For a different opinion of Wren see H. A. Jukes, 'Bishop Matthew Wren and the non-conforming monster in the diocese of Norwich', *Historical Studies* (October 1968), and Peter King, 'Bishop Wren and the suppression of the Norwich lectures', *Historical Journal*, (1968).
113 *CSPD, 1637–8*, 287.
114 R. O'Day, 'The ecclesiastical patronage of the Lord Keeper, 1558–1642', *TRHS*, 5th series (1973), 89–109.
115 P. Collinson, *The Religion of the Protestants* (Oxford, 1984), 90.
116 Hill, *op. cit.*, 341.
117 12/10/37, *Works*, VII, 374–5.

118 Lambeth MSS, 943, 401.
119 Clark, *English Provincial Society*, 361–71.
120 *Works*, VI, 484; VII, 313, 345, 349.
121 C. Cross, 'Dens of loitering lubbers: Protestant protests against cathedral foundations', *Studies in Church History*, IX (1972), 231–7.
122 *Works*, VII, 240.
123 Trevor-Roper, *Laud*, 450–3.

VII 'The Richelieu of England'

1 5/4/35, SP16/286/34.
2 12/1/35, Laud to Wentworth, *Works*, VII, 103.
3 Str. P., 5, 89.
4 *CSPC, 1629*, 32, 637. *CSPV, 1632–6*, 63.
5 15/4/34, *Works*, VII, 71–2.
6 Gardiner, *History*, VI, 355–6. *CSPV, 1632–6*, 220–2.
7 14/5/34, Laud to Wentworth, *Works*, VI, 372–3.
8 Martin Havran, *Caroline Courtier, the Life of Lord Cottington* (1973), 127–33.
9 *Works*, III, 221. *CSPV, 1632–6*, 265.
10 P. E. Kopperman, 'Sir Robert Heath', Illinois PhD (1972), 318–22.
11 *Works*, III, 223.
12 Str. P., 20, 121. HMC, *Hastings*, IV, 65–6.
13 *CSPD, 1634–5*, 601.
14 *CSP*, I, 353–4.
15 F. C. Dietz, *English Public Finance, 1558–1641* (1932), 274–84.
16 K. L. McElroy, 'The Life and Work of William Laud', Oxford D.Phil. (1943), 130–42.
17 12/6/35, Laud to Wentworth, *Works*, VII, 141–5. Patricia Haskell, 'Sir Francis Windebank and the Personal Rule of Charles I', Southampton PhD (1978), 126ff.
18 *CSPV, 1632–6*, 399. Str. P. 15(6) 108, quoted by Martin Havran, *op. cit.*, 130.
19 Clarendon, *History*, I, 132.
20 31/7/35, Laud to Wentworth, *Works*, VII, 155.
21 21/10/35, 2/1/36, Laud to Wentworth, *Works*, VII, 197–200, 217.
22 Wentworth, *Letters*, I, 479.
23 *Ibid.*, 420.
24 *Ibid.*, 522–3.
25 *Works*, III, 226.
26 *CSPV, 1632–6*, 540.
27 *CSPD, 1636–7*, 93.
28 11/2/37 and 5/4/37, Laud to Wentworth, *Works*, VII, 315–18, 336.
29 McElroy, *op. cit.*, 160–6. A. H. Siegler, 'Royal Prerogatives and the Regulation of Industry', Chicago PhD (1980), 285–7.
30 *Works*, VI, 520.
31 *Works*, V, 178–80. *CSPD, 1634–5*, 233. *CSPD, 1635–6*, 399.SP 16/249/36.
32 S. R. Gardiner, *Select Cases in the Star Chamber and the High Commission* (Camden Soc., 1886), 46.

33 W. Hunt, *The Puritan Moment* (Cambridge, Mass., 1983), 198.
34 Clarendon, *Life*, 14–15.
35 Franklin B. Williams, 'The Laudian imprimatur', *Library*, 29 (1960), 98–104. P. M. Olander, 'Changes in the Mechanisms and Procedures in the Control of the London Press, 1625–37', Oxford B.Lit. (1976).
36 *CSPD, 1633–4*, 442.
37 18/1/37, Laud to Wentworth, *Works*, VII, 307.
38 *Works*, V, 500–1.
39 *CSPV, 1632–6*, 110.
40 31/8/33, Laud to Roe, *Works*, VII, 48–9.
41 4/12/31, SP16/204/14.
42 *Works*, VI, 417; VII, 126 and 127.
43 HMC, *Braye*, 132.
44 *Works*, VII, 361.
45 For examples see *Works*, VII, 185, 244–5, 252, 312, 321 and 344.
46 *Works*, VII, 297, 352, 367, 361.
47 *Ibid.*, 594.
48 See for instance 20/10/37, Correr to Doge, *CSPV, 1636–9*, 310.
49 *Works*, III, 225.
50 12/9/36, John Lewkener to Thomas Martyn, Mayor of Dartmouth, HMC, *Third Report*, Appendix, 346.
51 16/11/37, Laud to Wentworth, *Works*, VII, 382.
52 28/2/38, Str. P., VII, 10.
53 1/33, *CSPD, 1633–4*, 444. 19/1/36, BL, Stowe MSS, 743, 116.
54 Bod. MSS, Eng. hist., e. 28, 577.
55 SP16/177/13.
56 *Works*, VI, 292.
57 P. Seaver, *The Puritan Lecturerships* (Stanford, 1970), 190.
58 *CSPD, 1633–4*, 538.
59 *Works*, VI, 107.
60 *Works*, III, 221–2.
61 P. Clark, ' "The Ramoth Gilead of the Good": Urban change and political radicalism in Gloucester, 1540–1640', in P. Clark, A. G. R. Smith and N. Tyacke (eds), *The English Commonwealth* (New York, 1977), 167–88.
62 *Works*, VI, 47.
63 Clarendon, *History*, I, 256.
64 Quoted in M. Butler, 'The English Drama and its Political Setting, 1632–42', Cambridge PhD (1981), 231.
65 Sir William Sanderson, *A Compleat History of the life and raigne of King Charles* (1658), 219.
66 J. Bastwick, *The Vanity and Mischief of the old litany* (1637), 1.
67 Clarendon, *History*, I, 266.
68 5/12/36, Laud to Wentworth, VII, 300. SP 16/354/176. Lambeth MSS, 943, 577. *Works*, VII, 355.
69 Heylyn, *Laud*, 355–60. *Works*, VI, 37–70. *A Brief Relation of certain Special and Most Material Passages and Speeches in the Star Chamber* (1638).
70 N. Wallington, *Historical Notices of the Reign of Charles I, 1603–45*, ed. R. Webb (1869), II, 90–9.
71 24/10/37, *CSPV, 1636–9*, 304. Barry Coward, *The Stuart Age*, 157 n. 48. Paul Seaver, *Wallington's World* (Stanford, 1985), 62.

72 S. Foster, *Notes from the Caroline Underground* (Hamden, Conn., 1978), 71.

73 B. D. Roberts, *Mitre and Musket: John Williams, Lord Keeper, Archbishop of York, 1582–1650* (1938), 139–63.

74 24/2/27, Mead to Stuteville, Birch, *Court*, I, 199.

75 *Works*, VI, 335–8; VII, 314–16.

76 *Works*, VI, 349, 351–2, 360–1. *CSPD, 1633–4*, 471, 522–3.

77 2/9/37, Robert Woodford, HMC, *Ninth Report*, II, 496.

78 Charges made twice in 5/4/37 and 28/6/37, Laud to Wentworth, *Works*, VII, 337, 355. 13/1/37, Williams to Laud, *Works*, VI, 481.

79 SP 16/361/98.

80 Rushworth, *Collections*, II, 438.

81 There is a hint of this in 14/7/37, Laud to Lambe, HMC, *Ninth Report*, I, 209.

82 Clarendon, *History*, I, 468.

83 28/8/37, *Works*, VII, 367–72.

84 *Works*, VI, 75.

85 R. R. Orr, *Reason and Authority: The Thought of William Chillingworth* (Oxford, 1967).

86 *Works*, V, 165–6, 184–5.

87 *Ibid.*, 166–7.

88 *CSPD, 1633–4*, 577. Wentworth, *Letters*, II, 242.

89 19/5/35, Gerrard to Wentworth, Wentworth, *Letters* 242. 23 and 29/8/37, and 1/9/37, *Works*, V, 180–2.

90 *CSP*, I, 153–4.

91 14/5/34 and 12/9/36, *Works*, VI, 372–8; VII, 282–6. For a similar jibe see *Works*, VII, 437.

92 30/11/36, Laud to Wentworth, *Works*, VII, 215.

93 Str. P., 17, 282a.

94 Gardiner, *History*, VIII, 138.

95 *CSPD, 1634–5*, 9.

96 Trevor-Roper, *Laud*, 312.

97 Lambeth MSS, 943, 381–8.

98 *Works*, VI, 447; VII, 81–3.

99 19/5/38, Gerrard to Wentworth, Wentworth, *Letters*, II, 165.

100 *CSPV, 1636–9*, 319.

101 *Works*, III, 229–30. Heylyn, *Laud*, 359.

102 Wentworth, *Letters*, III, 222. Caroline Hibbard, *Charles I and the Popish Plot* (Chapel Hill, NC, 1983).

103 See, for example, the examination of George Sprat, water bearer of London, 15/5/34, in *CSPD, 1634–5*, 22.

104 P. W. Thomas, 'Two cultures? Court and country under Charles I', in C. Russell (ed.), *Origins of the Civil War* (1973), 178.

105 9/8/36, Laud to Elizabeth of Bohemia, *Works*, VII, 269.

106 1/11/37, *Works*, VII, 380.

107 *CSPV, 1632–6*, 515.

108 30/11/35, *Works*, VII, 213.

109 W. M. Lamont, 'Macaulay, the archbishop and the Civil War', *History Today*, XIV (1964), 291–6.

110 Sir John Suckling, *Works* (New York, 1910), I, 110.

VIII 'To be your chancellor'

1 *Works*, V, 298–301.
2 *Works*, VI, 262–3.
3 *CSPD, 1629–31*, 46–7. CUL MSS, lett. 12, A30.
4 Heylyn, *Laud*, 208. *CSPD, 1629–31*, 241. N. Tyacke, 'Arminianism in England in Religion and Politics, 1604–40', Oxford D.Phil. (1968), 125–9.
5 *Works*, V, 16–18.
6 *Ibid.*, 18–20, 24–5, 28, 47–9, 70–3.
7 *Ibid.*, 15.
8 *Ibid.*, 39–40.
9 *Ibid.*, 49.
10 G. W. Thomas, 'Archbishop John Williams', Oxford D.Phil. (1974), 223–4.
11 The letter of expulsion from the king was drafted in the hand of Dr Duck, Laud's chancellor, and amended by Laud and Charles: SP 16/198/64.
12 23/8/31, Minute of Proceedings, SP 16/198/5. 26/8/31, Charles to Oxford University, SP 16/198/63. F. S. Boas, *The Diary of Thomas Crossfield* (1935), 57.
13 *Works*, V, 105, 129.
14 *Ibid.*, 183.
15 Bod., Bankes MSS, 40/1.
16 *Works*, III, 233; V, 272; VI, 521 and 578. BL, Add. MSS, 4162, 14.
17 13/1/34, SP 16/258/59. *Works*, VI, 342–4.
18 *CSPD, 1633–4*, 477.
19 *Works*, V, 161–4, 168–9.
20 *Ibid.*, 116–19, 172–3.
21 *Ibid.*, 170–4, 190.
22 *Ibid.*, 190.
23 *Ibid.*, 235–6.
24 N. Tyacke, 'Science and religion at Oxford before the Civil War', in D. Pennington and Keith Thomas (eds) *Puritans and Revolution* (Oxford, 1978), 73–93.
25 Anthony Wood, *The Life and Times of Anthony Wood* (Oxford, 1891–1900), II, 234.
26 SP 16/257/124. *Works*, V, 178–80. *CSPD, 1634–5*, 431–2.
27 *Works*, VI, 340, 388–9.
28 A. D. Hewlett, 'The University of Oxford and the Church of England in the time of William Laud', Oxford B.Lit. (1934), 75. *Works*, VII, 306, 376.
29 *Works*, III, 224; VII, 191–6. *CSPD, 1633–4*, 302. *CSPD, 1635–6*, 382. A. Oswald, 'The Canterbury Quadrangle at St. John's, Oxford', *Country Life*, 9 November 1929. Trevor-Roper, *Laud*, 286.
30 K. Sharpe, 'Archbishop Laud and the University of Oxford', in David Lloyd-Jones, V. Pearl and B. Worden (eds), *History and Imagination* (Oxford, 1981), 148–64.
31 CUL MSS, MN 1, 52, 6, 157–9.
32 23/5/31, 26/5/32, CUL MSS, Lett. 12, A30 and D16. SP16/246/83.
33 John Cosin, *Correspondence* (Surtees Soc., 1869), I, xxx and 274.
34 King's College, Cambridge, MSS, Provost's letter book, IV, 13. Lambeth MSS, 943 457–8.
35 CUL MSS, Add. 22, 115 and 129.
36 CUL MSS, Add. 23, i, 36, 37a. CUL MSS, CUR, 78/55.

37 C. H. Cooper, *Annals of Cambridge* (Cambridge, 1842–53), III, 278.
   Rushworth, *Collections*, II, 324–33.
38 SP 16/237/18.
39 *Works*, VI, 433; VII, 315. Cooper, *op. cit.*, III, 279–84.
40 *CSPV, 1636–9*, 90.
41 SP 16/327/18.
42 *Works*, V, 145–7.
43 Section of Oxford visit based on *CSPD, 1636–7*, xii–xxvii. *Works*, V,
   148–9. J. Taylor, 'The royal visit to Oxford in 1636: a contemporary
   narrative', *Oxoniensis* (1936), 151–9. F. S. Boas (ed.), *The Diary of Thomas
   Crosfield* (1936) 91–3. W. C. Costin, *History of St. John's College* (1958),
   50ff.
44 Anthony Wood, *Life and Times*, I, 46.
45 Heylyn, *Laud*, 318.
46 *Works*, III, 227.
47 *Works*, VII, 278.

IX 'More vinegar than oil'

1 *Works*, III, 227.
2 T. Fuller, *Church History of Britain* (1658), X, 218–19.
3 A. Leo Oppenheimer, *The Interpretation of Dreams in the Ancient Near
   East* (Philadelphia, 1950).
4 Keith Thomas, *Religion and the Decline of Magic* (1971), 197. Peter Burke,
   'L'Histoire social de rêves', *Annales*, 28, 2 (March–April, 1973), 329–42.
5 Thomas Hill, *The Pleasente Art of the Interpretation of Dreams* (1576).
6 *Works*, III, 198, 234.
7 4/10/35, *Works*, VII, 173.
8 C. Hill, *Economic Problems of the Church* (1956), 22. BL, Lands MSS, 985,
   252.
9 *Works*, VII, 138. Str. P., 6, 321.
10 *Works*, III, 220.
11 *Works*, VII, 264, 270.
12 Lucy Hutchinson, *Memoirs of Colonel Hutchinson* (1848), 88.
13 Heylyn, *Laud*, 542.
14 Thomas Mason, *Serving God and Mammon* (Newark, Del., 1985), 151–3.
15 Heylyn, *Laud*, 362.
16 Clarendon, *Life*, 32–4.
17 267/3/35 and 18/9/37, *Works*, VI, 507; VII, 114.
18 8/10/36, *Works*, VII, 493.
19 C. V. Wedgwood, *The King's Peace* (1971), 103.
20 *Works*, VII, 47.
21 J. Bastwick, *The Litany of J. Bastwick* (1637), 6.
22 Tanner MSS, 102, 165.
23 P. Collinson, *The Religion of the Protestants* (1983), 282.
24 James I, *Works*, (1619), 529.
25 *Works*, III, 255.
26 Lambeth MSS, 323.
27 *Works*, III, 201.

28 The correct title of the book is *A Relation of the conference between W. Lawd and Mr Fisher, the Jesuite* (1638).
29 *Works*, III, 227.
30 *Ibid.*, 172.
31 *Ibid.*, 197.
32 *Ibid.*, 173.
33 *Ibid.*, 170, 172, 198.
34 Laud had a repeat of this dream the following July, *ibid.*, 200, 205.
35 T. Birch, *Court*, I, 44.
36 *Works*, VI, 266–8.
37 *Works*, III, 87–90.
38 *Ibid.*, 173.
39 *Works*, VI, 331.
40 *Works*, III, 167. See also III, 150 and 221; VI, 327 and 331.
41 L. B. Smith, *Treason in Tudor England* (Princeton, NJ, 1986).
42 *Works*, III, 144.
43 *Ibid.*, 199.
44 *Ibid.*, 218. John Hacket, *Scrinia*, II, 85, identifies L. L. as Williams, and L. H. as Holland.
45 *Works*, III, 204.
46 *Ibid.*, 170, 268.
47 Roger Lockyer, *Buckingham: The life and Political Career of George Villiers, First Duke of Buckingham* (1981) 22.
48 *Works*, III, 81–2, 136.
49 *Ibid.*, 133–6.
50 *Ibid.*, 217.
51 *Ibid.*, 222.
52 This could refer to 3 March or 3 May. The only reference I can find that remotely fits is to a quarrel he had with 'E.B.' on 3 May 1625. *Works*, III, 142.
53 Trevor-Roper, *Laud*, 449.
54 Sir Simonds D'Ewes, *Journal* (New Haven, Conn., 1923), 400.
55 10/12/34, Roe to Elizabeth of Bohemia, SP 16/178/32.

X 'Who's the fool now?'

1 Details of the Archie incident from Bod., Bankes MSS, 18/24 and 42/30, and from 20/3/36, Gerrard to Wentworth, Wentworth, *Letters*, II, 154.
2 *CSPV*, 1636–9, 387.
3 D. Stevenson, *The Scots Revolution, 1637–44* (Newton Abbot, 1973), 60–5.
4 Rushworth, *Collections*, II, 731–2.
5 *CSPV*, 1636–9, 387.
6 Sir Walter Raleigh, *The Secret History of the Court of King James I* (1811), II, 401–2, says that Archie asked Laud the question three days later when he met him going into a privy council meeting.
7 Heylyn, *Laud*, 236–7.
8 *Works*, III, 428.
9 *CSPD*, 1633–4, 100.
10 Maurice Lee, *The Road to Revolution: Scotland under Charles I, 1625–37* (Urbana, Ill., 1985), 129.

11 *Works*, III, 429.
12 8/10/33, Charles to Bishop Bellenden, Baillie, *Letters*, 422.
13 Rushworth, *Collections*, II, 205.
14 *Works*, III, 301–2.
15 Baillie, *Letters*, 424–8. G. I. R. McMahon, 'The Scottish Courts of High Commission, 1610–38', *Scottish Church History Society Records*, XV (1966), 193–209.
16 W. H. Hutton, 'Two letters by Archbishop Laud', *English Historical Review*, 45 (1930), 107–9.
17 G. Donaldson, *The Making of the Scottish Prayer Book* (Edinburgh, 1954), 50.
18 SP 16/286/16.
19 Charles I, *Bibliotheca Regia* (The Hague, 1649), 115–21.
20 Hamon L'Estrange, *The Reign of King Charles* (1655), 126.
21 Anthony Weldon, 'Description of Scotland', in J. Nichols (ed.), *The Progresses, Processions and Magnificent Festivals of James the First* (1828), III, 338.
22 *Works*, VI, 370–1, 383–4, 419–20, 443–4. SP16/303/11.
23 Baillie, *Letters*, I, 442.
24 *Works*, III, 317n.
25 19/9/35, *Works*, VI, 434.
26 Baillie, *Letters*, I, 439.
27 *Works*, V, 583–606.
28 Baillie, *Letters*, II, 438–9.
29 *Ibid.*, I, 18.
30 L'Estrange, *op. cit.*, 167.
31 Baillie, *Letters*, I, 40–1. *CSPV, 1636–9*, 350.
32 Hacket, *Scrinia*, 64. Donaldson, *op. cit.*, 39, does not accept this story.
33 E. R. Adair, 'Laud and the Church of England', *Church History*, V (1936), 121–40.
34 10/12/34, *Works*, VII, 98n.
35 C. V. Wedgwood, 'Anglo-Scottish relations, 1603–40', *Transactions of the Royal Historical Society*, 4th series, XXXII (1950), 31–48. T. Mason, *Serving God and Mammon* (Newark, Del., 1985), 125. J. Cooper, *The Scottish Liturgy*, quoted by H. Watt, 'William Laud and Scotland', *Scottish Church History Society Records*, VII (1941), 183.
36 *Works*, VI, 455–8.
37 *Works*, III, 310, 318, 336–42.
38 Gilbert Burnet, *History of My Own Time* (Oxford, 1897), I, 40.
39 Lee, *op. cit.*, 224–36.
40 HMC, *Ninth Report*, Appendix II, 241ff and 258 C. Rogers. *The Earl of Stirling's Register of Royal Letters Relating to Scotland and Novia Scotia from 1615 to 1635* (Edinburgh, 1885), lvii–lviii, 751.
41 Baillie, *Letters*, 1–2.
42 G. Donaldson, *Scotland: James V to James VII* (1965), 311.
43 Burnett, *op. cit.*, I, 40. Sidney Burrell, 'Kirk, Crown and Covenant: A Study of the Scottish Background to the English Civil War', Columbia PhD (1953), 250.
44 Clarendon, *History*, I, 145.
45 7/7/37, Laud to Traquair, *Works*, VI, 493–6.
46 Baillie, *Letters*, I, 453.

47 Earl of Hardwicke, *Miscellaneous State Papers, 1501–1726* (1778), I, 95–7.
48 Sir Archibald Johnstone, *Diary*, ed. G. M. Paul (Scottish History Society, 1911), I, 271.
49 C. V. Wedgwood, *The King's Peace* (1971), 111.
50 20/12/37 and 12/1/38, CSPV, *1636–9*, 358.
51 11/11/37, Laud to Wentworth, *Works*, VI, 511–16. Str. P., 7, 37.
52 4/7/37, *Works*, VI, 491–3.
53 *CSPV, 1636–9*, 259.
54 *Works*, VII, 367–72.
55 11/9/37, Laud to Traquair, *Works*, VI, 504–6.
56 *Works*, VII, 396–405.
57 Charles I, *Bibliotheca Regia* (The Hague, 1649), 142–4.
58 *Ibid.*, 145–7.
59 Johnstone, *Diary*, I, 322.
60 *CSPV, 1636–9*, 379.
61 *DNB*. Heylyn, *Laud*, 349–50.
62 H. L. Rubinstein, *Captain Luckless: James, First Duke of Hamilton, 1606–1649* (Totowa, NJ, 1976).
63 *Works*, VII, 539.
64 Hardwicke, *op. cit.*, II, 107.
65 G. Burnet (ed.), *Memoirs of the Lives and Actions of James and William, Dukes of Hamilton and Castlehead* (Oxford, 1852), 56–65. Rushworth, *Collections*, II, 746–7.
66 *Works*, II, 230.
67 S. R. Gardiner, *The Hamilton Papers* (Camden Soc., 1880), 1–2.
68 14 and 23/5/38, *Works*, VI, 524; VII, 425.

XI 'The beast is wounded'

1 26/11/38, Bod., Add. MSS, C69, 8/2/39. Lambeth MSS, 2686, 37.
2 *Works*, VI, 571.
3 Rushworth, *Collections*, II, 754–5. S. R. Gardiner, *Hamilton Papers* (Camden Soc., 1880), 1–2.
4 27/11/38, Earl of Hardwicke, *Miscellaneous State Papers, 1501–1726* (1778), II, 113–21. 29/11/38, Rushworth, *Collections*, 845–9.
5 *Works*, VI, 547.
6 Baillie, *Letters*, I, 475–6.
7 *Works*, VII, 456.
8 Str. P., VII, 63, 1.
9 HMC, *Hastings*, IV, 77–8.
10 14/5/38, Laud to Wentworth, *Works*, VII, 424–9.
11 *Works*, VI, 530. *CSPD, 1637–8*, 571.
12 Str. P., 7, 113.
13 4/10/38, Laud to Roe, *Works*, VII, 486.
14 *CSPV, 1636–9*, 276, 395, 447.
15 *CSPD, 1637–8*, 591.
16 28/11/38, HMC, *Hamilton*, 54.
17 Laud later became a member of this committee. *CSPV, 1636–9*, 435–6. Lambeth MSS, 943, 689, 3/7/38, Gerrard to Wentworth, Wentworth, *Letters*, II, 181.

18 SP 16/400/65. G. Burnet (ed.), *Memoirs of the Lives and Actions of James and William, Dukes of Hamilton and Castlehead* (Oxford, 1852), 127–8.
19 *Works*, VI, 521–7; VII, 487. Str. P., II, 250.
20 Carola Oman, *Henrietta Maria* (1936) 25. Quentin Bone, *Henrietta Maria* (Urbana, Ill., 1972), 29–30. *CSPV, 1625–6*, 607, 614. HMC, *Skrine*, 27.
21 G. Albion, *Charles I and the Court of Rome* (1935), 229.
22 Caroline Hibbard, *Charles I and the Popish Plot* (Chapel Hill, NC, 1983), 90–4.
23 *Works*, VI, 539.
24 *Works*, VII, 496.
25 See, for instance, 24/11/38, Cottington to Wentworth, Wentworth, *Letters*, II, 246.
26 Hibbard, *op. cit.*, 231.
27 *Works*, V, 215.
28 Thomas Mason, 'The Political and Episcopal Career of William Juxon, 1587–1663', Virginia PhD (1975), 166. Gerrard to Wentworth, Wentworth, *Letters*, II, 180.
29 *Works*, II, xxi.
30 K. Sharpe, 'Crown, parliament and locality: government and communication in early Stuart England', *English Historical Review*, CCCXCIX (April 1986), 321–50.
31 Trinity College, Cambridge, Cullum MSS, 031.2. *Works*, VI, 541.
32 *Works*, III 231.
33 *Works*, VII, 524, 552.
34 HMC, *Hastings*, IV, 81.
35 CUL, Add. MSS, 7339/138.
36 *Works*, VII, 458, 459, 472, 475, 477, 494, 529, 530, 546, 585, 587–8, 594, 599. Michael J. Brown, *Itinerant Ambassador: The Life of Sir Thomas Roe* (Lexington, Ky, 1970), 214–21.
37 *Works*, V, 197–8, 201, 211–12, 213–14, 219–20, 240, 252. BL, Add. MSS, 28, 937, 23.
38 *Works*, III, 230; VII, 478.
39 *Works*, V, 195.
40 *Ibid.*, 195–6.
41 *Ibid.*, 198–9.
42 Gerrard to Wentworth, Wentworth, *Letters*, II, 180.
43 *Works*, V, 206–7.
44 *Ibid.*, 233–4.
45 *Ibid.*, 220–2.
46 I am extremely grateful to Dr Charles Mould, Secretary to the library, for sending me a list of the major benefactors.
47 The advowson could be Handborough, Oxfordshire. *Works*, VII, 434, 582. St John's College Library, MS no. 262.
48 Heylyn, *Laud*, 404–5, may have exaggerated his mentor's generosity: see Charles Coates, *History and Antiquities of Reading* (1802), 234, and John Bruce (ed.), *Original Letters and Other Documents Relating to the Benefactions of William Laud . . . to the County of Berks* (1841), 31.
49 27/2/39, *Works*, VII, 558.
50 *Works*, VI, 579–80. Heylyn, *Laud*, 404–5, may have exaggerated Laud's generosity. Bruce, *op. cit.*, 31. Coates, *op. cit.*, 234.

51 29/1/39, Northumberland to Conway, SP 16/410/80. 24/1/39, Smith to Pennington, SP 16/410/8, supports this conclusion.
52 F. Larkin, *Stuart Royal Proclamations* (1983), II, 662–6.
53 *Works*, VII, 526.
54 Lambeth MSS, 943, 43–5. *Works*, VI, 558–60. Heylyn, *Laud*, 380–1.
55 *STC*, 24575.
56 *STC*, 18196.
57 *Works*, VII, 573. *STC*, 15496.
58 *Works*, VII, 577.
59 *CSPD, 1638–9*, 489, 497, 517, 621. O. Ogle, W. H. Bliss and W. D. MacGray (eds), *Calendar of Clarendon State Papers*, 3 vols (Oxford, 1867–76), I, 175.
60 *Works*, II, 363; V, 221; VII, 558. *CSPD, 1639*, 223. E. G. W. Bill, 'Two unprinted letters of Archbishop Laud', *Bodleian Library Record* VI (1960), 617–20.
61 Sir John Suckling, *Works* (New York, 1910), I, 142.
62 3/6/39, Hunt. MSS, STT 1890. I am grateful to Esther Cope for this reference.
63 SP 16/410/8.
64 SP 16/412/102.
65 SP 16/412/103.
66 *CSPD, 1638–9*, xiii.
67 James Howell, *Epistolea-Ho-Elianae* (1903), I, 344.
68 Quoted by J. D. Ogilvie, 'A bibliography of the Bishops' Wars, 1639–40', *Glasgow Bibliographical Society Records*, XII (1932), 1–12.
69 SP 16/412/102.
70 Bod., Bankes MSS, 18/2.
71 C. H. Firth, 'Ballads of the Bishops' Wars', *Scottish Historical Review*, II, 11 (1906), 260.
72 SP 16/538/140.

XII 'A foul business it is'

1 C. V. Wedgwood, *Poetry and Politics under the Stuarts* (Cambridge, 1960), 56. *Works*, III, 232.
2 *Works*, VII, 548–9.
3 *Ibid.*, 559.
4 *Ibid.*, 574–6.
5 SP 16/409/225–324. *CSPD, 1638–9*, 608.
6 Rushworth, *Collections*, III, 886.
7 *Works*, VII, 648–51.
8 *CSPD, 1639*, ix.
9 *Works*, III, 232.
10 *Works*, VII, 574, 583.
11 For example see 1/11/38, Wentworth to Charles, Wentworth, *Letters*, II, 229.
12 Caroline Hibbard, *Charles I and the Popish Plot* (Chapel Hill, NC, 1963), 134. T. D. Whitaker, *The Life and Original Correspondence of Sir George Radcliffe* (1810), 181–3. 12/12/39, Northumberland to Leicester, A. Collins, *Letters and Memorials of State* (1746), II, 623.
13 Thomas Fuller, *Church History of Britain* (Oxford, 1845), VI, 297–8.

14 *Works*, VII, 505–16.
15 *CSP*, II, 82.
16 Sir William D'Avenant, *Dramatic Works* (1872–4), II, 312–26.
17 Heylyn, *Laud*, 451. *Works*, V, 251.
18 *Works*, III, 234.
19 *Works*, V, 259–64.
20 Hibbard, *op. cit.*, 141.
21 A. Fletcher, *A County Community in Peace and War* (1976), 241.
22 SP 16/450/25.
23 HMC, *Hastings*, IV, 86.
24 Brilliana Harley, *Letters* (Camden Soc., 1854), 111.
25 Heylyn, *Laud*, 407. *Works*, VI, 575.
26 SP 16/441/78.
27 J. K. Gruenfelder, *Influence in Early Stuart Elections, 1604–40* (Columbus, Ohio, 1981), 183–95. HMC, *Eleventh Report*, VII, 186. W. H. Hutton, 'Two letters from Archbishop Laud', *English Historical Review*, 45 (1930), 107–9.
28 SP 16/441/113.
29 SP 16/450/108.
30 *Works*, III, 284.
31 *CSPD, 1640*, 113. SP 16/452/31.
32 Hamon L'Estrange, *The Reign of King Charles* (1655), 183.
33 E. Cope, 'The king's declaration concerning the dissolution of the Short Parliament', *Huntington Library Quarterly*, XL, 4 (1977), 325–31. J. H. Elliott, 'The year of the three ambassadors', in D. Lloyd-Jones (ed.), *History and Imagination* (Oxford, 1981), 165–8.
34 *Works*, III, 233. O. Ogle, W. H. Bliss and W. D. MacGray (eds), *Calendar of Clarendon State Papers*, 3 vols (Oxford, 1867–76), II, 148.
35 Gardiner, *History* IX, 101. Henry Oxinden, *Letters, 1607–42* (1933), 163.
36 Edward Hyde, Earl of Clarendon, *The Life of Edward Hyde, Earl of Clarendon* (Oxford, 1857), I, 38.
37 Quoted by W. Hunt, *The Puritan Moment* (Cambridge, Mass., 1983), 287.
38 Oxinden, *Letters*, 174. Rushworth, *Collections*, III, 1180.
39 Lambeth MSS, 943, 717. Heylyn, *Laud*, 453.
40 *CSPD, 1640*, 88.
41 *Works*, III, 236.
42 HMC, *Coke*, II, 255. Frederick von Raumer, *History of the Sixteenth and Seventeenth Centuries Illustrated by Original Documents* (1838), I, 31.
43 Hunt. MSS, EL, 7834. Rushworth, *Collections*, III, 1173–4.
44 F. Larkin, *Stuart Royal Proclamations* (1983), II, 710–12. SP 16/454/39
45 25/5/40, Laud to Conway, *Works*, VI, 604.
46 *Works*, VII, 603. Lambeth MSS, 1030, 97.
47 Heylyn, *Laud*, 422. E. Cope, 'The Short Parliament of 1640 and Convocation', *Journal of Ecclesiastical History*, XXV (April 1974), 167–84.
48 *Works*, II, 285.
49 Heylyn, *Laud*, 429–31. *CSPD, 1640*, 40. *Works*, III, 284–7.
50 17/5/40, SP 16/453/102.
51 Richard Baxter, *Autobiography* (1931), 21.
52 Lambeth MSS, 943, 57. *Works*, VII, 526. BL, Harleian MSS, 787, 95.
53 *Works*, III, 236.

54 P. Collinson, *The Religion of the Protestants* (Oxford, 1982), 145.
55 *Works*, V, 255, 268. E. F. Percival, *Foundation Statutes of Merton College* (1847), 81–96.
56 *Works*, VII, 608.
57 *Ibid.*, 601–4.
58 SP 16/455/no. 38. *Calendar of Clarendon State Papers*, II, 101.
59 *CSPD, 1640–1*, 161–6.
60 Clarendon, *History*, I, 5.
61 HMC, *Ninth Report*, 498. HMC, *De L'Isle*, IV, 267.
62 *CSPD, 1639–40*, xvi.
63 Fletcher, *op. cit.* J. S. Morrill, *The Revolt of the Provinces* (1976). T. G. Barnes, *Somerset, 1625–42* (1961).
64 *CSPD, 1640*, 580. Von Raumer, *op. cit.*, I, 316. Hunt, *op. cit.*, 256–7.
65 *Lords' Journals*, IV, 107.
66 *Works*, III, 237; VI, 584.
67 Hunt. MSS, EL, 7833.
68 *CSPV, 1640–2*, 44.
69 C. H. Cooper, *Annals of Cambridge* (Cambridge, 1842–53), III, 303. *CSPD, 1640*, 193.
70 J. F. MacLear, 'Popular anti-clericalism in the Puritan revolution', *Journal of the History of Ideas*, XVII, 4 (1956), 443–70. R. O'Day, 'The reformation in the ministry, 1558–1641', in R. O'Day and F. Heal (eds), *Change and Continuity* (1977), 75.
71 Quoted by J. P. Sommerville, 'The royal supremacy and episcopal "*jure divino*" ', *Journal of Ecclesiastical History*, 34, 3 (October 1983), 557.
72 *Works*, VI, 572. N. Tyacke, 'Arminianism in England in Religion and Politics, 1604 to 1640', Oxford D. Phil. (1968), 239.
73 C. H. Firth, 'Ballad history of the reigns of James I and Charles I', *Transactions of the Royal Historical Society*, 3rd series, 5 and 6 (1911–12), 43.
74 Lambeth MSS, 1030, 109.
75 William Abbot, 'The Issue of Episcopacy in the Long Parliament', Oxford D.Phil. (1981), 48ff.
76 John Cosin, *Correspondence* (Surtees Soc., 1869–72) I, 32.
77 Quoted M. E. James, *Family, Lineage and Civil Society* (Oxford, 1974), 118.
78 Abbot, *op. cit.*, 262.
79 Hibbard, *op. cit.*, 160ff. Rushworth, *Collections*, III, 1315.
80 SP16/156/135.
81 Quoted H. L. Rubinstein, *Captain Luckless: James, First Duke of Hamilton, 1606–1649* (Totowa, NJ, 1976), 121.
82 SP 16/461/46.
83 Hibbard, *op. cit.*, 172.
84 *CSPV, 1640–2*, 44.
85 *Works*, III, 237.

XIII 'The sty of all pestilential filth'

1 Heylyn, *Laud*, 458.
2 *CSPD*, 1640–1, 242.
3 5/11/40, Hawkins to Leicester, HMC, *De L'Isle*, IV, 339.
4 *Works*, VI, 586.
5 Sir Simonds D'Ewes, *Journal* (New Haven, Conn. 1942), 8. Rushworth, *Collections*, III, 253.
6 HMC, *Various*, II, 259. D'Ewes, *Journal*, 18.
7 Sermon preached by Cornelius Burgess, quoted by E. W. Kirby, 'Sermons before the Commons, 1640–42', *American Historical Review*, XLIV (1938–9), 532.
8 John Cosin, *Correspondence* (Surtees Soc., 1869), I, xxxi. J. T. Cliffe, *The Puritan Gentry* (1984), 194.
9 Baillie, *Letters*, I, 275–7.
10 Hacket, *Scrinia*, I, 138.
11 D. Stevenson, *The Scots Revolution, 1637–44* (Newton Abbot, 1973), 215ff.
12 Sheila Lambert, 'The opening of the Long Parliament', *Historical Journal*, 27, 2 (1984), 265–9.
13 *Commons Debates*, II, 671. D'Ewes, *Journal*, 328.
14 HMC, *Various*, II, 259.
15 Sir Edward Dering, *A Collections of Speeches* (1642), 642.
16 F. Larkin, *Stuart Royal Proclamations* (1983), II, 734–8.
17 A. Collins, *Letters and Memorials of State* (1746), II, 664.
18 *Works*, VI, 589.
19 *Works*, III, 238, 295.
20 A. Fletcher, *The Outbreak of the English Civil War* (1981), 91ff. Rushworth, *Collections*, V, 93.
21 Baillie, *Letters*, I, 280.
22 D'Ewes, *Journal*, 101–2, 154–8.
23 16/12/40, Sir John Coke to his father, HMC, *Cowper*, II, 268.
24 L. B. Larkin, *Proceedings . . . Kent* (Camden Soc., 1862), 92. D'Ewes, *Journal*, 185–6. Rushworth, *Collections*, IV, 113.
25 Fletcher, *op. cit.*, 2.
26 D'Ewes, *Journal*, 269–70. Clarendon, *History*, 230–2.
27 *Works*, III, 238–9.
28 D'Ewes, *Journal*, 181, 240, 310.
29 *CSPD, 1640–1*, 454.
30 D'Ewes, *Journal*, 429.
31 HMC, *De L'Isle*, IV, 360. Henry Oxinden, *Letters, 1607–42* (1933), 191.
32 Baillie, *Letters*, I, 295.
33 Rushworth, *Collections*, IV, 196–202. D'Ewes, *Journal*, 395–7.
34 *Works*, III, 397.
35 9/3/41, Maurice Wynn to Owen Wynn, J. Ballinger, *Calendar of the Wynn Papers* (1927), 271. *Works*, II, 436–7.
36 Heylyn, *Laud*, 480.
37 *Works*, VI, 590.
38 *Works*, III, 241, 438.
39 *Ibid.*, 442–5. Str. P., 40, 60.
40 Fletcher, *op. cit.*, 69.
41 *CSPD, 1641–3*, 213.

42 J. S. Morrill, 'The religious context of the Civil War', *Transactions of the Royal Historical Society*, 5th series, XXXIV (1984), 155–78, and 'The attack on the church of England in the Long Parliament, 1640–42', in D. Beales and G. Best (eds), *History, Society and the Church* (Cambridge, 1985), 157–69.

43 D'Ewes, *Journal*, 214–15. Baillie makes the same point in *The Canterburians* (1640), 120.

44 Sir John Bramston, *Autobiography* (Camden Soc., 1845), 76.

45 D'Ewes, *Journal*, 169–70.

46 Quoted, J. S. Hart, 'The House of Lords and Reformation of Justice', Cambridge PhD (1984), 225.

47 M. L. Schwartz, 'Lay Anglicanism and the crisis of the English Church in the early seventeenth century', *Albion*, 14, 1 (1982), 1–19.

48 Baillie, *Letters*, III, xliii.

49 *Works*, III, 242, 448; V, 298–9. Heylyn, *Laud*, 484.

50 Quotes, William Abbot, 'The Issue of Episcopacy in the Long Parliament', Oxford D. Phil. (1981), 129.

51 Hacket, *Scrinia*, II, 144.

52 Peter King, 'The episcopate during the Civil Wars, 1642–1649', *English Historical Review*, 83 (1968), 523–37.

53 Clarendon, *History*, I, 271.

54 Hart, *op. cit.*, 3–30.

55 Fletcher, *op. cit.*, 106.

56 Lambert, *op. cit.*

57 10/2/42, *CSVP, 1640–2*, 295.

58 25/5/41, HMC, *Cowper*, II, 284.

59 *CSPD, 1641–3*, 298.

60 *DNB. Works*, IV, 283.

61 Rushworth, *Collections*, V, 330. Heylyn, *Laud*, 498. *Works*, III, 248–9, 451. HMC, *House of Lords, Fifth Report*, 61, 80–6.

62 *Lords Journals*, IV, 311. Heylyn, *Laud*, 498. *Works*, III, 456; VI, 594.

63 *Works*, III, 246. *Lords Journals*, V, 439. Peter King, 'Reasons for the abolition of the Book of Common Prayer in 1645', *Journal of Ecclesiastical History*, XXI, 4 (1970), 327–39.

64 Rushworth, *Collections*, II, 55–7. *Works*, III, 247.

65 BL, Add. MSS, 25, 460, 295 and 310.

66 W. Cobbett, *The Parliamentary History of England* (1806–20), I, 117.

67 Brian Levack, *The Civil Lawyers in England, 1603–42* (1973), 195.

68 *Works*, III, 242, 449.

69 Ralph Josselin, *Diary*, ed. Alan MacFarlane (1976), does not mention the incident. *Works*, III, 244–5, 461–2; IV, 9.

70 Sir Philip Warwick, *Memoirs* (1702), 167.

71 Roger Howell, 'Thomas Weld of Gateshead: the return of a New England Puritan', *Archaeologia Aeliana*, 4th series, XLVIII, 303–32.

72 *Works*, III, 244, 460–1.

73 *Ibid.*, 251.

74 Trevor-Roper, *Laud*, 410.

75 HMC, *Lords, Fourth Report*, Appendix 1, 308.

76 SP 16/491/137.

77 *Works*, III, 250. Heylyn, *Laud*, 499.

78 *Works*, III, 111–27; VI, 149ff and 240ff.

XIV 'Never afraid to die, nor ashamed to live'

1 David Griffiths, 'Treason and Idolatry: The Trial of Archbishop Laud', 26–8. I am extremely grateful to Mr Griffiths for letting me read a copy of this excellent unpublished paper. It stresses the English forces leading to the trial and execution.
2 Rushworth, *Collections*, V, 850.
3 Griffiths, *op. cit.*, 1–3. Sheila Lambert, 'The opening of the Long Parliament', *Historical Journal*, 27, 2 (1984), 265–9.
4 W. G. Palmer, 'Invitation to a beheading: factions in Parliament, the Scots and the execution of Archbishop William Laud in 1645,' *Historical Magazine of the Protestant Episcopal Church*, LII, 1 (March 1983), 17–27.
5 Baillie, *Letters*, II, 139.
6 *Works*, IV, 47.
7 *Lives of Eminent British Statesmen* (1838), V, 7.
8 V. A. Rowe, *Sir Henry Vane the Younger* (1970), 66. V. Pearl, 'Oliver St. John, and the "middle group" in the long Parliament: August 1643–May 1644', *English Historical Review*, LXXXI (1966), 490–519.
9 Wordsworth, *Poetic Works*, 418.
10 Rushworth, *Collections*, V, 320, 817–21. Heylyn, *Laud*, 512–13. *Lords' Journals*, VI, 271. W. Prynne, *Canterburie's Doome* (1645), 42.
11 Rushworth, *Collections*, V, 822–4. Heylyn, *Laud*, 514. Prynne, *Canterburie's Doome*, 43. *Lords' Journals*, VI, 285, 303.
12 Rushworth, *Collections*, V, 825–6. Prynne, *Canterburie's Doome*, 47–8. *Lords' Journals*, VI, 339.
13 *DNB*. Anthony Wood, *Athenae Oxonienses*, 4 vols (Oxford, 1813–20), III, 129–30.
14 Rushworth, *Collections*, V, 828–34. Heylyn, *Laud*, 515. Griffiths, *op. cit.*, 8–10.
15 HMC, *Lords*, XI, 374–98. Paul Seaver, *The Puritan Lecturerships* (Stanford, 1970), 251–4, 362.
16 *Works*, IV, 153, 168.
17 HMC, *Lords*, XI, 408–16.
18 *Ibid.*, 430–7. *Works*, IV, 348.
19 HMC, *Lords*, XI, 453–7.
20 *CSPD*, 1641–3, 518–29, 550.
21 Conrad Russell, 'The theory of treason in the trial of Strafford', *English Historical Review*, LXXX (January 1964), 30–50. A. Hast, 'State treason trials during the Puritan Revolution, 1640–1660', *Historical Journal*, XV (1972), 37–52. S. Rezneck, 'History of the parliamentary declaration of treason', *Law Quarterly Review*, XLVI (January 1930), 82–102.
22 Prynne, *Canterburie's Doome*, 462ff.
23 BL, Sloane MSS, 153, 2026.
24 HMC, *Lords*, XI, 385–92.
25 *Ibid.*, 381.
26 Griffiths, *op. cit.*, 19. Rushworth, *Collections*, II, 274.
27 J. B. Williams, *Memoirs of . . . Sir Matthew Hale* (1835), 22.
28 *Works*, VI, 596.
29 R. Josselin, *Diary* (1976), II, 19.
30 HMC, *Lords*, XI, 457–64.
31 Bod., Ash. MSS, 184, 46.

32 Rushworth, *Collections*, V, 834.
33 29/11/44, Humfrey to Buxton, HMC, *Various*, II, 264.
34 *Lords' Journals*, VII, 102, 128–32.
35 Clarendon, *History*, III, 466–7.
36 J. Bruce, *Original Letters and other Documents Relating to the Benefactions of William Laud* (1841), 61–9.
37 *Works*, III, 87–96.
38 *Ibid.*, 119.
39 *Works*, VII, 660–1.
40 The description of his execution is from Heylyn, *Laud*, 531–42, John Hinde's pamphlet in Tanner MSS, 61, 249, and Simon Foster's account in St John's College Library, MS 260, printed in C. Coates, *History and Antiquities of Reading* (1802), 422ff.

XV Epilogue

1 R. Josselin, *Diary* (1976), II, 31.
2 W. E. Collins, *Lectures on Archbishop Laud* (1895), ix, 287, 320.
3 F. P. Verney, *Memoirs of the Verney Family* (1892), II, 204.
4 Paul Seaver, *Wallington's World* (Stanford, 1985), 101.
5 G. G. M. Smith, 'Extracts from the papers of Thomas Woodcock', *Camden Society Misc.* (1907), XI, 55. Quoted, P. Young (ed.), *Leaders of the Civil Wars* (1977), 113.
6 *Works*, IV, 504.
7 J. O. Halliwell, *Letters of the Kings of England* (1846), II, 361.
8 John Cosin, *Correspondence* (Surtees Soc., 1869), 228–9.
9 Heylyn, *Laud*, 47.
10 S. R. Gardiner, *History*, VII, 245.

Index